D0810323

The United States and NATO

THE
UNITED STATES
AND
NATO

The Formative Years

LAWRENCE S. KAPLAN

THE UNIVERSITY PRESS OF KENTUCKY

Chapter 2 reprinted (with revisions) from Ronald Hoffman and Peter J. Albert, eds., *Diplomacy and Revolution: The Franco-American Alliance of 1778* (Charlottesville: University Press of Virginia), © 1981 by the Rector and Visitors of the University of Virginia. Quoted by permission of the publisher.

Chapter 3 reprinted (with revisions) from *Culture and Diplomacy: The American Experience* by Morrell Heald and Lawrence S. Kaplan, eds., and used with the permission of the publisher, Greenwood Press, Westport, Conn. Copyright © 1977.

Chapter 4 reprinted (with revisions) from *Prologue* 12 (Summer 1980): 73–86. Quoted by permission of the publisher.

Chapter 8 reprinted (with revisions) from Francis H. Heller, ed., *The Korean War: A 25-Year Perspective* (Lawrence: The Regents Press of Kansas), © 1977, The Regents Press of Kansas. Quoted by permission of the publisher.

Chapter 9 reprinted (with revisions) from *Diplomatic History* 6 (Spring 1982): 111–23, © 1982 by Scholarly Resources, Inc. Quoted by permission of the publisher.

Appendix A. reprinted (with revisions) from *International Organization* 8 (Fall 1954): 447–67, © 1954, World Peace Foundation; © 1983, Massachusetts Institute of Technology. Quoted by permission of the publishers.

Library of Congress Cataloging in Publication Data

Kaplan, Lawrence S.
    The United States and NATO.

    Bibliography: p.
    Includes index.
    1. North Atlantic Treaty Organization—History.
2. United States—Foreign relations—1945-
I. Title.
JX1393.N67K37 1984   355'.031'091821   84-5087
ISBN 0-8131-1511-6, cloth; -0159X, paper

To Rudolph A. Winnacker
and to the memory of
Walter Lipgens (1925–1984)

Contents

Preface

This book has been in progress for over thirty years, almost as long as NATO has been in existence. The subject was first a by-product of an official study I had undertaken in 1951 for the Historian of the Office of the Secretary of Defense. This culminated in 1980 in a monograph, *A Community of Interests: NATO and the Military Assistance Program, 1948–1951.*

My earliest research had been on the foreign policy of the early Republic, and the contrast between the isolationism that had yielded a century and a half of political nonentanglement and the deliberate commitment under the Atlantic alliance was and is of continuing fascination to me. Some of this absorption is reflected in chapter 2.

That essay and the concluding chapter contain more personal views than the other, more monographic chapters. Both were originally delivered as addresses, the former in Washington in March 1978 at the first bicentennial program of the U.S. Capitol Historical Society, and the latter in Los Angeles as the presidential address for the Society for Historians of American Foreign Relations in December 1981. I wish to express my appreciation to the Capitol Historical Society and to the University Press of Virginia as well as to *Diplomatic History* and its publisher, Scholarly Resources, Inc., for permission to reprint the substance of these papers.

The main body of this volume is contained in chapers 5 through 7, presenting in some detail the role of the United States in the negotiations for the treaty in 1948 and 1949. This is material hitherto unpublished. Its inspiration was drawn less from my work with the Department of Defense than from my collaboration with Walter Lipgens of the University of the Saarland, the prime mover in an ambitious study of the growth of European political unification from 1945 to 1950. His first volume appeared in 1977 as *Die Anfänge der Europeaischen Einigungspolitik, 1945–1950*, vol. 1, *1945–1947* (Stuttgart, 1977) and in English as *A History of European Integration* (Oxford, 1982). He is currently preparing a second volume which will cover the years 1948 to 1950. I am indebted to him for his knowledgeable commentaries expressed in Kent and in Saarbrücken, and in Florence where I joined his seminar in 1978 at the European University Institute. This work will appear under the auspices of the European Community, and some of the materials in this volume will be integrated into that project.

Chapter 4, on the beginning of the Brussels Pact, was published in the summer 1980 issue of *Prologue*, the journal of the National Archives. Chapters 3 and 8 are intended to serve respectively as background for conclusions to the central chapters. I appreciate the permission of the Greenwood Press to reprint, with only slight changes, an essay from *Culture and Diplomacy: The American Experience*, which I wrote in 1977 with Morrell Heald. Similar permission has been granted by the Harry S. Truman Institute and the Regents Press of Kansas to use the version of the chapter that originally appeared in Francis H. Heller, ed., *The Korean War: A 25-Year Perspective* in 1977. Unlike chapter 3, this essay, as chapter 8, has undergone considerable revision.

Lastly, I should say a word about the bibliographic essays. I had thought initially about simply adding to the essay I had produced for *International Organization* in 1954. But while much of the information remains pertinent, the climate in which it was produced has changed considerably. So has the framework for current discussion of the formative years of NATO. I have therefore produced a second bibliographical essay building on the earlier one and reflecting some of the changes that the passage of a generation has made.

In light of the thirty-year germination of this project, I cannot identify fully or even accurately the many individuals who have provided me guidance on sources or commentary on various aspects of the manuscript. The resources of Washington, D.C., particularly the Modern Military and Diplomatic branches of the National Archives, have been of enormous benefit to my studies. The staffs have been uniformly helpful. I should like to give special thanks to Wilber Mahoney and Edward Reese of the Modern Military division and to Milton O. Gustavson, Chief of the Legislative and Diplomatic branches for their special help. Similarly, in the Department of State Historical Office, William Z. Slany and his colleagues Ronald D. Landa and Charles S. Sampson made particular contributions to my efforts.

Outside Washington the archivists and librarians of the Harry S. Truman and Dwight D. Eisenhower libraries and their respective directors, Benedict K. Zobrist and John C. Wickman, made this visitor feel at home in their libraries on every occasion. Dennis E. Bilger in Independence and Martin Teasley in Abilene were especially supportive. In Ottawa former ambassador Escott Reid and D.P. Cole of the Historical Division of the Department of External Affairs extended their considerable aid to my searches in Canadian archives. In London the staff of the Public Record Office in Kew instructed me in the arcane technological aids of that institution, and consoled me when records were unavailable. Patricia Methven, archivist of the Liddell

Hart Centre of Military Archives, showed me how nominally closed papers may be legitimately used by scholars. Their support is appreciated.

I should like also to acknowledge the American Council of Learned Societies for its grant-in-aid. My appointment as NATO Research Fellow in 1980 was of particular service to my studies not only for the travel funds the program provided but also for the access it permitted me to NATO officials past and present. Fernand Welter, director of the fellowship program, was particularly helpful in his recommendations.

Once again I have been served well by friends who made special contributions to the manuscript. Philip G. Johnson's comments at an early stage of the project changed my direction. Marjorie Evans, as always, improved the manuscript with suggestions as well as with her expert typing. Albert H. Bowman and Alice C. Cole read the entire work with the critical attention they gave to my earlier writings. My thanks to them as well as apologies for not always following their knowledgeable advice. This book is dedicated to the historian who gave me the idea for it, even if this may not be the result he had anticipated.

Lyman L. Lemnitzer Center
for NATO Studies
Kent State University
June 1984

1. Introduction

Is it a truism or an act of faith to assert that creation of the Atlantic alliance in 1949 was the most important event in American history since the Treaty of Paris established independence in 1783? Certainly its treatment by historians suggests rather that this is simply one more grandiose statement to stand alongside Wilson's league or the United Nations, if not the Kellogg Pact and the Carter Doctrine, as a symbol of great expectations shattered or illusion perpetrated. It is the rare historian who would agree with Armin Rappaport and call the signing of the treaty the "American Revolution of 1949."[1]

Unlike the League of Nations after a generation, NATO survives; and, unlike the United Nations, it survives today as a meaningful alliance and organization thirty-five years after its creation. The Atlantic alliance began as a response to a European perception that the world destroyed by the ravages of World War II could not be rebuilt without United States involvement. It was not simply a question of a promissory statement of American concern for the fate of Western Europe or even of a massive economic aid program and a modest military support system, all of which were either in process or in prospect by the end of 1947. What was needed was a sense of confidence in Europe that the pull of a communist system would not undermine whatever aid or promises the United States had been willing to make hitherto. This could be provided by a complete abandonment of the cherished American tradition of nonentanglement with Europe that had begun with the Revolution and was enshrined in mythic American concepts associated with Washington's Farewell Address, Jefferson's First Inaugural Address, and the Monroe Doctrine. As addressed in chapter 2, some elements in the North Atlantic Treaty were traumatic, particularly those which undid the isolationist tradition of 150 years.

The decision of the United States to join Europe in a military alliance, no matter how carefully the treaty was disguised, was an anguished one. In retrospect, however, it appears, as Thomas Paterson suggested, relatively easy. The treaty was one of a succession of actions taken by the Truman administration in which Congress and nation played passive and compliant roles.[2] The Senate votes certainly indicated the administration's success, but they masked the evasions, hesitations, and fears of all kinds that plagued American planners as they embarked on a new adventure. For the military, an alliance could drain an already weak establishment; for Congress, it could arouse the isolationism which had been so virulent in the past; for supporters of the United Nations, it could undercut the growth of a new world order and lead to the very war it was designed to prevent; and for the administration, it could victimize American wealth and resources as Europeans utilized an alliance to bleed the superior power.

Yet there was no apparent alternative open to the policymakers. Soviet power, although weakened by war, was paramount in Europe: aggressive demands for a nonagression pact with Scandinavia, muscle flexing by powerful Communist parties in France and Italy, and a coup d'etat in Czechoslovakia set the tone. All Europe would be subject to communism and a divided Germany would be reunited under Soviet auspices unless the United States reversed a pattern of foreign relations. It was not that Europeans doubted American willingness to come to their aid; it was that they refused to consider another liberation. Another 1914 or 1939 could be avoided only if an advance knowledge of American involvement would deter a potential act of war—so General Omar Bradley, chairman of the Joint Chiefs of Staff, observed on the eve of the treaty's signing.[3]

Once again, then, the New World would redress the balance of the old. The echoes of George Canning's evocation of Spain's America were perceptible. In 1826 he could cite the weakness of Spain in the Indies and Britain's mobilization of the former colonies to claim that "I called the new world into existence to redress the balance of the old."[4] While the circumstances in 1948 were vastly different, particularly since the "new world" for Canning was Britain's for the asking, there was still a kinship in the spirit with which Britain's foreign minister, Ernest Bevin, and France's foreign minister, Georges Bidault, wished to manipulate the New World in behalf of the Old. The New World was now considerably more powerful than the Old, and the European leaders had to work harder and more deviously to achieve their objectives. Nonetheless, the New World's strength could be exploited by the wiser heads of the European partners. Such was some of the reasoning of European statesmen when they framed the Brussels Treaty in 1948, as discussed in chapter 4 below.

But NATO was to be more than just a ploy to enlist the United States in the Western Union. Because of the complexities behind America's decision, the European partners were required to make concessions, both real and imagined, to accommodate American entry. Much of the language in the North Atlantic Treaty was a product of a felt need to harmonize a Western collective security agreement with global outreach by the United Nations. Resistance to an alliance in the United States was anticipated as much or more from American supporters of the UN than from traditional isolationists. A significant part of the opinion-making elite after World War II was convinced that the United Nations was the way to ensure the future of the world and of the U.S. By seeming to turn its back on the UN, no matter how stymied that body was by Soviet-American conflict, an Atlantic security agreement could arouse sufficient resentment to destroy the arrangement. Hostility from the new converts to the UN, more than from the discredited isolationists of the 1930s, accounted for many of the twists and turns followed by the Truman administration in moving from the Truman Doctrine to the North Atlantic Treaty, as shown in chapter 3. The Truman administration appeared to feel compelled at almost every opportunity to link the UN Charter with the North Atlantic Treaty as if the alliance were an organ of the Security Council or of the General Assembly.

The device succeeded in winning acceptance of the Treaty at the expense of the ultimate reduction of the importance of the United Nations in American decisionmaking. The UN remained a part of the foreign policy process through the next decade of United States predominance. But expectations of the UN as a surrogate foreign office disappeared permanently from the American scene. The alliance became an instrument of other concerns.

Perhaps the most important of these concerns was the resolution of the German problem inherited from World War II. It took a number of forms. First, the existence of NATO rationalized a defense of western Germany and served as an umbrella for its evolution into a Western-oriented ally. It was no coincidence that the Bizonia and Trizonia, the monetarized Anglo-American and Anglo-Saxon-French zones of Germany, were the site of a Federal Republic. The abandonment of expectations for a Western-Soviet rapprochement was rendered permanent by the merging of the zones. It was even less a coincidence that the Federal Republic was created a month after the Treaty was signed, or that the West would press for admission of the new republic into other European organizations before the summer of 1949 was over. While it is too much to assert, as some scholars have, that American postwar policy centered on the reconstruction of Germany,[5] it was obvious that an appropriate reconstruction of Europe itself, economically as well as militarily, required the exploitation of German resources and their incorporation into the West. Germany was the unstated major issue in every meeting of the allies and in most of the planning sessions within the United States, even as it was excluded from a membership role in the alliance. This theme appears *sotte voce* throughout chapters 5, 6, and 7.

More obvious because it was always on the surface was the French aspect of the German problem. All Europeans, but the French in particular, had suffered too recently from German bestiality to exorcise the experience from their memory. For the French the threat of communism and of Soviet expansionism always had to be weighed against the German menace. The latter was in fact the substance of the Anglo-French treaty of Dunkirk in 1947 and the nominal object of the Brussels Treaty of 1948. French rehabilitation was a vital element in American association with Europe, all the more so because of the powerful Communist minority which seemed poised to bring down the Fourth Republic. But France throughout this period was a difficult partner, at one and the same time wanting American military support and guarantees against Soviet expansionism, and yet resentful of what its statesmen perceived to be an Anglo-American condominium dedicated to the control of Europe. Moreover, as chapters 7 and 8 will show, the French demanded an active British presence on the Continent as much as an American presence to guarantee against the resurgence of a dangerous Germany.

Important though they were, the French and German issues were hardly the only strains in the ungainly alliance of 1949. It is understandable that nine months of intense negotiations were required before the various pieces could be put together, particularly the U.S.-Western Union sessions in the summer and fall of 1948, as followed in chapter 5. The uneasy association of Norway and Denmark was made all the more difficult by the abstention of Sweden, which had taken the initiative in promoting a Nordic alternative to NATO. While, for Denmark and Norway, memories of German occupation in World War II were more powerful than the allure of neutralism, theirs was a wary decision, accentuated by their distrust of France and hostility to Italy or Algeria within the alliance. Portugal and Iceland, far more than Italy, were meaningful to an "Atlantic" alliance, but the former's fascist government undercut the democratic base underlying the Atlantic pact, while the latter seemed distant from the concerns of the European core.

Although military aid was an important element in the alliance, it held few long-term implications in 1949. The alliance was emergency application, a band-aid to cope with internal national problems. If there was a military component at this moment it lay in the readiness of the United States Strategic Air Command in Omaha, Nebraska, to employ its power on behalf of eleven nations outside the United States. The primary role of military power was to deter the Soviet Union from internal subversion within the member nations and from external aggression against their soil. As the short-term defense plan of 1949 revealed, it was not to create a force prepared to strike eastward, or even to defend a thrust from the east.

While the military component of an alliance ordinarily is the predominant one, this does not seem to have been the case in the creation of NATO. The Benelux countries, prime movers in its earliest stages, as chapter 4 discloses, always held aloft aspirations of a united Europe as a goal of the alliance. In this they were joined by Canada, the most articulate champion of nonmilitary collaboration and, through a speech of Prime Minister Louis St. Laurent in

1947, the first member to propose a security pact within the United Nations free from a Soviet veto. If there was a long-run purpose in the North Atlantic Treaty, it was neither the half-hearted claim of strengthening the UN nor the expectation of creating a powerful military establishment. Rather, it was the hope of breaking down the barriers of national sovereignty that had plagued the West since the advent of the nation state and that were held responsible for most of the disasters of the twentieth century.

For an Atlantic association to succeed, the United States had to be engaged as a deus ex machina to do what Europeans could not do for themselves. While compromises among themselves were necessary, the primary concessions in the negotiations for an alliance were made to break down American resistance to membership. Thus Portugal was important for its vital strategic assets in the Azores. Iceland and Canada were not only part of the northern Atlantic communication links between the continents but also served to show latent American isolationists that NATO was more than an entangling European alliance in disguise. Scandinavia and Italy in 1949 were less significant for northern and southern flanks of a potential defense organization than for the weaknesses that made membership in the alliance a psychological prop to their national morale.

The foregoing rationalizations suggest makeshift elements in the creation of the alliance, political trade-offs which explain membership in the alliance of a nation without a border on the Atlantic and a nation with little claim to a common democratic tradition. The charges are justifiable; diplomacy had to address the realities of the time, and the primary reality for Europeans was the necessity to enlist the United States in an alliance. Economic recovery hung on a sense of political and military security that only American involvement could provide.

The price for the Nordic countries was an abandonment of neutralism and the acceptance of distant Portugal and Italy; for France it was a potentially inferior position within an Anglo-American condominium with implications for a German relationship in the future; for the United Kingdom, a dilution of a "special relationship" with the United States. The United States sacrificed a tradition of nonentanglement, and in doing so sought to protect its new investment in the negotiating process. The allies would have to move toward political and military as well as economic integration, and to accept members the core powers of the Western Union would have preferred to reject.

But the rewards were more compelling than the drawbacks. Not only would a blanket of American protection be spread over Western Europe but a military assistance program would be set in motion, as much for its psychological impact as for whatever changes it was expected to make on the individual military establishments of the allies. Military aid was high on the agendas of both France and Britain, even though it was a source of misgivings on the part of the United States Joint Chiefs of Staff. The very fact that the initial military assistance program was introduced in Congress on the same day that the president signed the instrument of ratification of the North Atlantic Treaty was an earnest of the meaning of Article 3; this is a major theme of chapter 7.

Anti-communism served as a lure for American entanglement in Europe. It was a staple in the ideology of many of the European national pressure groups interested in fostering a federated Europe. The horrors of war had energized such units in every country. Enthusiasts such as Count Richard Coudenhove-Kalergi who had been dismissed as dreamers before the war were heartened by the new interest the European movement aroused among political leaders in France, the United Kingdom, and the smaller countries of the Continent. The time perhaps had arrived to achieve the unity that had almost destroyed everything in World War II, and the United States could be a key, both in encouraging unification by its example and in pressuring for it by its economic and military power.

As presented in chapter 4, the idea of European unity held America's attention and appealed to constituencies ranging from former isolationists to friends of the United Nations. The North Atlantic Treaty could be conceived as a means of realizing these aspirations. For Americans it would take the forms of weapons standardization among allied armies; of economic planning, quickening of the pace of tariff reduction, customs unions, and even industrial or agricultural specialization. In a revealing memorandum on the eve of signing of the pact, Secretary of State Dean Acheson observed that European economic and political cooperation would be a major potential beneficiary of the Atlantic Pact. The failure of the European Recovery Program to promote instruments of unification could be corrected through the American connection.[6]

The result would be a new Atlantic entity beneath which a European community would arise, which in turn would achieve security from both internal subversion and external attack. And a vital by-product of the benefits that would flow from it would be a gradual solution of the German problem— "giving the Germans a goal," as Acheson put it, "to work as partners with other Western countries." Such was the future outlined by President Truman in his opening comments to the alliance's foreign ministers on April 3, 1949. There was, however, a recognition, and perhaps a saving grace as well, in his statement that "none of us are under any illusions that the Atlantic pact itself is more than a symbol of our common determination."[7]

Despite Truman's caveat, there was a euphoria accompanying the signing which would dissipate long before the challenge of the Korean War less than fifteen months later. National sentiments which had blunted the integrative purposes of the Economic Cooperation Act persisted. The empty shell of the proudly named Council of Europe that came into being almost simultaneously with the Atlantic alliance symbolized the difficulties of formally shedding political sovereignty. More forthright was the attitude of Britain, which clearly signaled its refusal to identify itself fully as a continental power, and of France, which, while admitting the importance of a cooperative Germany, had no intention of admitting even the most regenerated Federal Republic into the alliance. The ideal of a military specialization in which each nation would produce only what served the whole rather than what protected its own soil or its arms industry remained verbiage, or if accepted moved at a snail's pace toward its goal.

It was not that political integration or German cooperation or military standardization was not pushed in the first year of the alliance. These were requirements openly or covertly demanded by the United States in exchange for the military assistance the allies had requested. Actions were taken: an integrated defense plan was accepted; military end items reached European ports before the first anniversary of the treaty's signing; and committees from London to Washington to Rome were deliberating seriously on how to create a common military, financial, and industrial base for the greater strength of the new organization.

But flaws, some structural, some circumstantial, informed every plan and inhibited many of them. The most immediate in the latter category was the inability of the allies to come up with any proposal that would resolve military insecurity aside from American atomic power, itself threatened by the newly recognized Soviet atomic challenge. Even with American military production at Europe's disposal, the Soviet Union still would dominate Europe in the short run. Knowledge of this reality gave scope to the traditional anxieties of the allies. Perhaps the most formidable of the circumstantial problems was the inherent imbalance between the superpower on the western side of the Atlantic and the pigmies of the eastern shores. The state of dependence was bound to produce suspicion and resentments on both sides, and they did, in good measure, as evidenced in chapter 7. On the one side the United States was always ready to believe that Europeans wished to throw all the burdens upon the rich American partner. On the other, the European allies could bury their differences over a shared conviction that the United States could not be counted upon in a crisis. Britain's demand for a "special relationship" with the United States, and France's rigidity with respect to limits on German revival reflected these sentiments.

A deeper problem, and yet one that has resonance in the hemispheric differences, was the potential incompatibility between an Atlantic association and a European association. Throughout the deliberations on NATO there ran a skein of thinking about a united states of Europe, and with it a separation of Western Europe from the United States as well as from the Soviet bloc. In one form this was the hope nourished by Senator J. William Fulbright and the American Committee for a Free and United Europe. In this view the American function was to assist with all its strength but to stand apart ultimately from the finished product, as shown in chapter 4. From inside the State Department, George Kennan, chairman of the Policy Planning Staff, wished for a "third force," even including Eastern Europe. Where would the United States stand in this kind of organization? Obviously outside the structure.

While there were obvious attractions for Europeans as well as their American friends in this projection, the limitations were equally obvious and much more persuasive. There was never a genuine prospect of the United States turning over unlimited aid, for example, to a European body, such as the Western Union or the Council of Europe, as France discovered when it proposed a common pool of funds in 1950. American controls in the form of bilateral arrangments or base concessions were examples of the specific forms reciprocity would assume. More significantly, Europe's own demands for American involvement to the point of absorption undercut a European union. This, after all, was the leitmotif of the French and British initiatives in 1948 that led to NATO. No matter how wholeheartedly the United States might support a united states of Europe, such action would not satisfy the needs of the day. So when the ideal of European unification clashed with the principle of American connection, the former would have to defer to the latter. The disparity of power between Europe and America and the conflicting symbols of Europe and the Atlantic would haunt the next generation. They have not been solved, even as they have taken on new forms in recent years.

Many of these issues were deferred by an event which transformed the alliance into an organization, the so-called placing of the "O" in "NATO" in June 1950. The invasion of the Republic of Korea by North Korean forces on June 25, 1950 was a turning point in the history of the alliance, and perhaps in the history of American foreign relations as well. The impact on NATO of an event on the eastern extremity of Eurasia was immediate and dramatic, as presented in chapter 8. It assumed four particular forms, all based on a vital decision that was pushed on the United States: namely, that the war in Asia would not refocus American attention upon the Pacific at the expense of new priorities in Europe. The conclusion reached by the National Security Council, led by the State Department and supported by the Joint Chiefs of Staff, was that the Korean War was a Soviet global test of the West's steadfastness, and that a divided Germany could be the next site of Soviet aggression if steps were not taken to deter it. The result was a reassessment of the Atlantic alliance with a view to providing a defense of Europe that would thwart a Korean-style invasion from eastern Germany.

The first consequence of this understanding was a massive increase in military assistance, followed, after two NATO Council meetings, by a commitment of American troops to European territory in the winter of 1951. The recommendations of NSC-68, which had remained as vague and theoretical as most movements in NATO until June, were well on the way to being fulfilled.

The second major consequence was the restructuring of NATO's organization. Regional planning groups disappeared, production and finance committees were revitalized, and a sophisticated military headquarters borrowed from the Western Union model was created in Paris, led by a distinguished United States general, Dwight D. Eisenhower. Under his leadership a series of command decisions was made that embraced the defense of all of Western Europe. A similar command appeared in maritime form in the Atlantic, each under the Standing Group, all accomplished within six months after the beginning of the Korean War. Political reorganization followed in the course of 1951, as the NATO Council assumed new functions for the second time in two years. Initially it was designed as a coordinating body, a periodic meeting place for foreign ministers. At the New York meeting of the Council in 1950 a Deputies Council was established to provide continuity for the foreign ministers. This in turn yielded to an office of secretary-general and permanent representatives to advise him, which emerged from the Lisbon meetings in February 1952.

A third change was the new geographic shape of NATO. Greece and Turkey entered in 1952, and the Federal Republic of Germany in 1955. The former was the easier to negotiate. Greece and Turkey, original sites of Cold War confrontation, had held associate status since the beginning. The need to offer a southern flank of Europe's defense after the creation of SHAPE overcame objections to their membership, even as it challenged the Atlantic character of the alliance.

Lastly, the German question was revived and acquired an urgency that had been lacking before the Korean War. Against strenuous French objections American pressures brought Germany closer to the alliance and within the frame of the military organization. Through an elaborate device first broached by the French, the Federal Republic would provide troops for the defense of Europe within a supranational community under the auspices of NATO. The alternative might have been the abandonment of Europe by the United States, or a German-American military alliance which would have isolated France and destroyed the Atlantic pact. While French concerns ultimately forced the shelving of the European Defense Community, a climate of accommodation was reached between 1950 and 1954 which permitted all Europeans, including the French, to accept the Federal Republic into NATO through a special relationship. The moribund Western Union was revived in 1954 under the

name Western European Union to serve as the vehicle for German entry into
NATO.

The framers of NATO established a treaty that grandiosely listed twenty
years' life in its text and looked to an Atlantic community of a sort that had
never formally existed in the past. Its minor premise was that such an association of the Old and New Worlds would provide a security that would permit
economic and political reconstruction of Europe and would promote the attri-
tion of national sovereignties. Its major premise was that American military
support would offer security against external as well as internal assaults upon
the member nations. Both these premises stood on ground that was either
untested or infirm; their success would depend on psychological more than
material factors.

Until the Korean War the military situation in Europe seemed to permit
an unhurried pace of organizational growth. If the defense of Europe rested on
American nuclear power, the date of delivery of military equipment was not a
matter of great urgency. If there was no rush to standardize weapons in
conformity with pledges of the treaty or to merge sovereignties in pursuit of
European unification, this too was not an immediate problem. There were
rumbles. American negotiators were annoyed at the reluctance of Europeans
to yield base rights in return for military assistance. Europeans' sensibilities
were ruffled by American insistence on bilateral negotiations and by fitful
demands for a greater German role. But these were minor notes of discord.
Even more muted was the European suspicion of American reliability: was
isolationism really dead? Much of the success of the "peace" movement and
the drive for neutralism in 1950 stemmed less from Soviet manipulation than
from French uneasiness about the alliance. It was not the treaty which pushed
passage of the U.S. military aid program. The Soviet possession of the atomic
bomb, known in August 1949, was a more potent agent of change. On the one
hand it helped Congress make up its mind about military assistance to the
allies; on the other it generated a search for new nuclear weaponry as well as a
new and more frightening reevaluation of the Soviet threat.

The Korean War shook the alliance to the core as it tested many of the
Treaty's premises, particularly the reliability of the American pledge to Eu-
rope and of the specific role of military preparation. It also postponed an
answer to the differences between an Atlantic and a European community.
Both presumably would be advanced by a strong NATO reaction to the
Korean War.

The visible, immediate outcome of the Korean War, as suggested in
chapter 8, was demonstrably positive: the alliance created a new defense
structure in SHAPE and SACLANT; the political machinery was reorganized
through the establishment of a secretary-general; NATO was expanded to
include not just Greece and Turkey in 1952 but, more painfully yet suc-

cessfully, the Federal Republic of Germany in 1955. Less immediately visible was the sense of security produced by these actions, which stimulated both a European economic community later in the decade and a series of national *Wirtschaftswunder* that transformed the economies and societies of the European members. Even more difficult to judge was the proof that the alliance could function as a free association of nations which gradually would erode traditional stigmata of national sovereignty.

Not that the United States was above attempting coercion on a number of levels and at various times. But the smaller members were able to hold their own against the larger and maintain positions through an annual review in which decisions were made through consensus.[8] Inevitably this could mean that decisions would not be made at all or that they would be attenuated at times to the point of nullity. French resistance to the European Defense Community was one such example; the inability or unwillingness of the allies to meet the timetables of the Lisbon Conference plans was another. The long drawn-out resolution of a Mediterranean command was still another case of accommodating the concerns of not only all the nations bordering the sea, including Greece and Turkey, but also the United States and the United Kingdom with their special concerns for command.

Still, Europe's defense was enhanced enormously in the years following the Korean War; there was a defense position from north to south of which the earlier Western Union forces could scarcely have even dreamed. And as it proceeded the bastions of national sovereignty eroded or crumbled. The status-of-forces agreements that followed the stationing of American troops in Europe accorded to the host countries the right to try American citizens charged with crimes against their citizens in their own courts under their own laws. This was a necessary concession mutually accepted, but one that deprived American citizens of their constitutional rights. Similarly, the infrastructure agreements begun with the Western Union and taken over by NATO not only encouraged interdependence of national military forces but broke sovereign jurisdictions by allowing pipelines, aircraft, and a communications system to cross national borders freely in the service of a common defense. The result was the interdependence of national armies, a mixture which seemed to make the internecine European wars of the first half of the twentieth century an anachronism in the second half.

There were prices to pay, some of them too high. Preoccupation with a defense posture accelerated a militarization of NATO that not only elevated the American role but served to denigrate possibilities for detente which the death of Stalin and subsequent changes in the Soviet Union after 1953 might have allowed. And as the military character of NATO increased, symbolized by the power as well as the titles of the American supreme allied commanders, the imbalance between American and European power continued. It bred mutual hostility within the alliance and hindered rather than helped the growth of an independent Western Europe and a united Germany.

Heavy and serious as these costs of NATO were to the West in retrospect, they served their purposes. European independence may have been retarded but the European Community was nourished by the Atlantic connection. Whatever its imperfections a generation later, and whatever lost opportunities there may have been because of NATO, the success of the Treaty of Rome creating the Common Market may be credited in good measure to the stability NATO provided. And the failure to come to terms with the Soviet Union, reflected in the continuing division of Germany, may be more apparent than real. With all the resources and the ingenious explanations offered by the Kremlinologists, there is no means of assuring that a genuine alternative to the Truman or Eisenhower positions existed to bring about a Soviet-American rapprochement of an order that would have terminated the Cold War in the mid-1950s. It may be claimed that the division of Germany itself was as much as either side could have achieved in this period. A NATO-related West Germany was probably a solution more satisfactory to the Soviet Union than any other, including neutralization, outside of its incorporation into an Eastern bloc.[9]

The results a generation later are still impressive. But along with new information about the causes of the Korean War and new insights into the posture of Soviet communism, the underside of NATO's activities is as exposed to inspection today as are the more conveniently arranged bulletins of success put out by the NATO Information Directorate. Did the judgment that a divided Germany demanded the same allied response as a divided Korea have validity before 1950? If it is unlikely that the Soviet Union was poised for a military adventure in Germany in 1950, then was the vast NATO military build-up necessary? Did the militarization of NATO, with its huge American component, prolong the Cold War in Europe unnecessarily? These are questions that have been frequently asked over the past generation and frequently answered in language that converted NATO into an instrument of American imperialism wittingly or otherwise, as chapter 9 indicates.

Even if the post-Korean NATO was a necessity and served the peacekeeping purposes it purported to, it kept alive most of the bothersome problems which were either identified in the early negotiations or anticipated immediately after passage of the Treaty. Mutual resentments over the extensive American presence in NATO remain active a generation later, amid charges of European ingratitude and American insensitivity. Not even the years of experience, of a continued American army in Europe—hostages of a sort to American entanglement—were sufficient to convince Europeans of the reality of the "pledge." The plans for the Multi-Lateral Force of the early

1960s and the missile crisis of the 1980s are all testaments to continued European doubts about the United States' behavior in a crisis.

In another area the questions which were never fully explored, questions about the compatibility of Atlantic and European communities, persist to the present. The idea of a "dumbbell" or "two pillars" of NATO—American and European—all foundered on the continuing inability of Europeans and Americans to accept the implications of a potentially united European "superpower" that would make unnecessary the original American involvement in Europe. On lesser planes the questions of 1949 are still questions of 1984—how to standardize weaponry, how to deal with extra-NATO issues affecting the alliance, and how to make effective decisions through consensus.

Yet all these problems, many of which have been periodically expressed in newspaper articles about disarray or terminal conditions, suggest the continuing relevance of the organization to the national lives of its members. The openly expressed discontents are a sign of vitality rather than decadence. Were the situation otherwise, NATO's conflicts would be seen dimly in the back pages of the papers, relegated to the insignificance and obsolescence of SEATO or CENTO. The latter two disappeared almost without notice in 1977 and 1979, respectively. Instead the role of the organization as a stabilizing element responsible for the "generation of "peace"[10] in Europe is a truth accepted by all the parties, even those, as in France and Greece, that loudly distance themselves from the organization but not from the Treaty. The bipolar world has changed since 1949 but the potential for mutual destruction between East and West has not. Europe and America still have to face a hostile Soviet Union. NATO serves as the single most important instrument of coexistence. And beneath its umbrella the erosion of sovereignty at various levels has proceeded for thirty-five years, despite uneven and unproven results.

The formative years of NATO encompassed the establishment of many of the organs which continue to deal not only with Soviet military power but also with the organization of the Western community. The nature of that community is still in doubt, in some ways as much as it was in 1949. But the need to strive for a more rational organization of international life, whether Atlantic union or European union, is still vital. NATO remains a primary means, as long as no better alternative is in sight.

2. The Treaties of Paris and Washington: Two Entangling Alliances

There is a special source of inspiration for this essay that links the treaties of alliance of 1778 and 1949 with the Capitol Historical Society proceedings of 1978. Senate Caucus Room 318, where the four major contributors to this conference made their presentations, was also the place where Cornell professor Curtis P. Nettels spoke at great length and with much passion on May 17, 1949, on reasons why the Senate Foreign Relations Committee should reject the newly signed North Atlantic Treaty. The pact, according to Nettels, was an entangling alliance that would produce unhappy consequences. By joining the Atlantic alliance the United States would "abandon the historic policies of the Nation and substitute therefore a new policy utterly alien to our traditions. We are asked to forsake the unbroken practice of 149 years—the practice of abstaining from peacetime military alliances. We are asked to reject the wisest counsel of the farewell address—that which warns against habitual favoritism and habitual animosity toward particular nations."[1]

There was nothing elliptical about Nettels's warning. The year 1949 marked the 149th, as he noted, since the United States had formally terminated its one entangling alliance with a European power. The Convention of 1800 ending the Quasi War with France had disengaged the United States from an association that had confirmed the worst American suspicions about the evils of Europe: namely, that a small, innocent, and virtuous people would be betrayed by a large exploitive ally. George Washington had explained in his Farewell Address that "an attachment of a small and weak toward a great and powerful nation dooms the former to be the satellite of the latter."[2] It did not seem to occur to Nettels, when he equated the secret Franco-Spanish intrigue of 1779 with the Anglo-Russian Treaty of 1942 or the Franco-Russian Treaty of 1944, that the "great and powerful nation" in 1949 was the United States. Nothing had changed in his view. If Washington had been alive in 1949, he would have repeated his Farewell Address of 1796.

Nettels touched on an enduring theme in American history, the force of isolationism as a protective shield against the wiles of the Old World. The word alliance conjured up for him and for many others all the damage that political connection with Europe had done to the United States in the past and presumably could do in the future.

The differences between the image and the reality of alliance merit more examination than they usually receive. Does an alliance necessarily entangle? If so, does the entanglement necessarily benefit the large partner at the expense of the small? If the advantages are mutual, can they be weighed? In light of these questions I wish to examine both the Paris treaties of 1778 and the Treaty of Washington of 1949. I propose to link 1778, when anxious Americans went to Paris for help in their war against Great Britain, with 1949, when anxious Europeans assembled in Washington to seek American support for their efforts to contain Communist power.

However tainted the idea of alliance may be to the American mind, it has been a fact of world affairs for millennia and a central fact of the nation-state system since the Renaissance. While idealistic purposes may be proclaimed as the objective of the alliance—as in the support of neutral rights in the treaty of amity and commerce of 1778, or in the encouragement of an Atlantic community in the North Atlantic Treaty—these are usually either minor notes or hypocritical ones to mask immediate and practical bargains. A quid is given for a quo; benefits are measured against drawbacks. And they are often psychological in nature. Deterrence against an enemy attack is frequently identified as the most vital function of the North Atlantic Treaty, with the end product being a more satisfactory sense of security for Western Europe. Such is the general nature of a defensive alliance. The Franco-American alliance, on the other hand, was a classic example of an offensive alliance, designed to increase the power of one side to combat more effectively an opposing side.

In both instances the allying process by the larger ally was intended to redress a faltering balance of power. George Liska has made the point that "alliances are against, and only derivatively for, someone or something."[3] Their intention, as in the case of the North Atlantic Treaty, may be to relieve allies from pressures exerted against them by another power. The United States as the core power was the vital ingredient in this process of deterrence in 1949. Only later, after the outbreak of war in Korea, did deterrence appear to require military organization to continue functioning effectively. The purpose of the alliance with France in 1778, on the other hand, was to coerce Britain into accepting the complete independence of the United States. The French decision for alliance was also a decision for war. The British required, in the French view, a reduction of the pride and power which they had gained from the Seven Years' War, and the American rebellion would be the instrument for Vergennes to achieve this goal.

The costs of alliance have to be measured carefully by stronger and weaker ally alike. The latter naturally worries about the potential neglect of its vital interests as the stronger power pursues larger objectives through the alliance. The former in turn must be concerned about overextending its resources through its commitment as well as sacrificing its freedom of action to a smaller, possibly irresponsible, ally that might take actions binding the larger without fear of consequences.

All these considerations were present in 1778. The Founding Fathers looked carefully at the possibilities inherent in French reactions to the American Revolution. John Adams asked all the right questions in March 1776:

How is the Interest of France and Spain affected by the dispute between B[ritain] and the C[olonies]? Is it the Interest of France [to] stand neuter, to join with B. or to join with the C? Is it not in her Interest, to dismember the B. Empire? Will her Dominions be safe, if B. and A[merica] remain connected? Can she preserve her possessions in the W. I.? She has in the W. I. Martinico, Guadeloupe, and one half of Hispaniola. In Case a Reconciliation should take Place, between B. and A. and a War should break out between B. and France, would not all her Island be taken from her in 6 months?[4]

Similarly, at this time and later, French ministers speculated on the advantages and disadvantages of supporting the colonies. Drains on the treasury, dangerous comfort to republicanism, and loss of opportunity to acquire Austrian Flanders were balanced against considerations of reducing British power and arrogance, restoring lost territories in the New World, and replacing Britain as the beneficiary of American commerce.[5]

What are missing in these rational considerations are the irrational, the illogical, the emotional elements that intrude to push policymakers into actions against their own interests or to raise expectations that can never be fulfilled. In the course of American colonial history there had developed an isolationist attitude toward the Old World that distorted as it informed the American understanding of an alliance with France. American isolationism gave a perspective to the Franco-American connection which led inevitably to the conclusion not only that the large ally manipulated the small but that a large European power would always damage Americans in any entangling relationship.

The United States was heir to an isolationist tradition that found a moral distinction separating Americans from Europeans. Europe represented tyranny, poverty, and superstition, while America was home to freedom, opportunity, and tolerance. Politically this tradition meant a republic as opposed to a monarchy; socially it implied fluid class lines as opposed to the rigidity of a European caste system; religiously it signified the triumph of free expression as opposed to European establishments; and economically it presented a contrast between a land available to all who wanted it and a continent where too little land supported too many people.

Responding to these distinctions at the time of the American Revolution, Hector St. John de Crèvecoeur called the American "this new man."[6] It did not matter that American self-perceptions may not have been warranted by the historical evidence; it mattered that those who made the Revolution shared these perceptions and promulgated them with all their distortions in the Declaration of Independence. That document minimized the British origins of the colonies and maximized the differences between Europeans and Americans, between two different peoples who would separate because one of them had broken the contract that had earlier connected them.

Absurd as this interpretation of the British Empire may have been to Englishmen, it had been nourished by more than a century of experience during which time the colonies managed their own affairs with little British interference. Britain came to be considered a distant patron, a sometimes uncertain ally against the Spanish, French, or Indians, a business partner who took advantage of virtuous Americans, a corrupt feudal superior who not only exploited Americans but implicated them in its alien dynastic interests. The Declaration dissolved an undesirable political connection with that nation and presented the thirteen United States to "a candid world" as a species of a new and better order of humanity.

Analysts such as Felix Gilbert have found in this American sense of superiority a wish to serve the world by creating in its own experiment a way of achieving a better society for all peoples. Such is the message he has read in the Model Treaty of 1776, in which the new nation appeared to seek aid abroad to advance an idealistic foreign policy. The avoidance of political entanglement and the support of free trade in the treaty plan may be seen, then, as a means of breaking down all artificial barriers to peace as well as eliminating the props of war. Gilbert found isolationism to have been in the service of an international idea, and "the logical consequence was that in a reformed world, based on reason, foreign policy and diplomacy would become unnecessary, that the new world would be a world without diplomats."[7]

But the Model Treaty, as James H. Hutson has recently pointed out, essentially "proposed commercial reciprocity rather than commercial freedom."[8] Americans wanted from nonentanglement neither an absolute isolation from the outside world nor an international Utopia, but rather their opportunity to manipulate the resources of the New World desired by the Old, in order to win their independence. Foreign relations from the beginning were designed to help the new nation through a difficult birth. Thomas Paine pointed the way in *Common Sense* when he wrote that "the true interest of America is to steer clear of Europe's contentions, which she never can do while, by her dependence on Britain, she is made the makeweight in the scale of British politics." At the same time, Paine saw that American commerce, if "well attended to, will secure us the peace and friendship of all Europe." Hence, the many disadvantages of being connected to Britain, and "our duty to mankind at large, as well as to ourselves," should lead Americans "to renounce the alliance; because any submission to, or dependence on, Great Britain, tends directly to involve this continent in European wars and quarrels, and set us at variance with nations who would otherwise seek our friendship, and against whom we have neither anger nor complaint. As Europe is our market for trade, we ought to form no partial connection with any part of it."[9]

There has been no better definition of American isolationism than that in *Common Sense*. Paine did not call for a policy that would change the balance-of-power system, as many philosophers of the day had wanted. He urged Americans to exploit Europe's need for American products, an idea that obviously impressed John Adams when he recommended to his colleagues on the committee preparing the Model Treaty "that we should avoid all Alliance, which might embarrass Us in after times and might involve us in future European Wars. That a Treaty of commerce which would opperate [sic] as a Repeal of the British Acts of Navigation as far as respected Us and Admit France into an equal participation of the benefits of our commerce . . . would be an ample Compensation to France for Acknowledging our Independence."[10]

The language of the treaty plan contained the same confident tones. The terms for the most part dealt with the many commercial benefits for the two countries that would come from "a firm, inviolable, and universal peace, and a true and sincere friendship betwen the most serene and mighty prince, Lewis the sixteenth . . . and the U.S."[11] With a show of generosity, Article XII of the model would allow the French to retain their access to American fisheries which they had received in 1763. But the king of France was admonished in Article IX never "under any pretence" to attempt to take any part of Canada or Florida or any other part of North America, since it was understood that the United States would take over all territories on the continent that had been under British rule. While there was no specific instruction to the French to enter the war, it certainly was expected. Should Britain declare war against the French in consequence of French aid to the United States, the Americans graciously promised under Article VIII not to assist the British in this circumstance.[12]

What could justify the arrogance of a small, untried republic, lacking a treasury and an army, in offering such an agreement to France? The answer must lie in Paine's and Adam's premise that America was a prize for which Europe should compete, that Britain's folly in abusing the mainspring of its preeminence as a world power should be invitation enough to win France's full assistance without a significant cost to the United States. They were mistaken. When they discovered that their self-confidence was misplaced, the suspicions about all Europeans deepened. The difficulty the Americans subsequently experienced in persuading the French to join their cause served ultimately to convince them that entanglement was dangerous.

But in the short run the Continental Congress did not have the luxury of choice. Its bargaining power declined with Washington's military fortunes in 1776 and 1777, with a consequent softening of the terms the United States would accept for French aid. The congressional commissioners, Benjamin Franklin, Silas Deane, and Arthur Lee were instructed as they left for their assignment in Paris to forgo demanding from the French the same freedom of commerce that the United States would grant to France, "rather than obstruct the farther progress of the treaty."[13] By the end of 1776 Congress was even prepared to meet almost any objection France or any other potential ally might have, just to win their immediate approval. A note of desperation can be found in the communications from the Committee of Secret Correspondence to their commissioners abroad.[14]

When France continued to hesitate in the face of the projected costs of the war and the uncertainty of American fortunes, the commissioners tried mixing blandishments with threats. The French were reminded that Britain's present superiority rested on its control of the American continent and that if the French cooperated with the Americans the power that had been Britain's would then be France's.[15] Additionally, the British West Indies were held out as a reward for entry into the war.[16] A failure to act could mean the subjugation of Americans, who might be persuaded by the British to join them to help make Britain conqueror of the world.[17]

As time went by the quiet hints became open pleadings, asking France to divert British forces in 1777 before they destroyed the Revolution. If America fell, Deane warned, all Europe would suffer from British arrogance. Lee commented bitterly that "we are left, like Hercules in his cradle, to strangle the serpent that annoys all Europe."[18] Finally, they observed that if France did not seize its opportunity to help itself as well as to help the former colonies, the Americans would have no choice but to reunite with Britain, which would endanger French interests everywhere. "The power of Great Britain and N. America divided can never be so dangerous to her," Richard Henry Lee observed, "as when united, abstracted from the consideration of gratitude that must bind her to the affection of our virtuous young republic for timely and effectual aid afforded them in the day of their distress."[19] With greater subtlety and appreciation for French sensibilities, Benjamin Franklin pursued the same course of cajoling, intimidating, flattering, and promising the potential ally a variety of benefits if it should respond, and warning of dire consequences if it should turn away from the United States.

When the great day arrived and France finally responded with two treaties in February 1778, the initial American reaction was one of enormous relief and gratitude. There was no upbraiding the commissioners for abandoning the Model Treaty of 1776, nor was any regret expressed in Congress for the abandonment of the ideal of nonentanglement. Instead, the hard-pressed Congress was anxious "to present the grateful acknowledgments . . . to his Most Christian Majesty for his truly magnanimous conduct respecting these States in the said generous and disinterested treaties."[20] They spoke for the nation at this moment, and the warm rush of good feeling for France was to be expressed periodically over the next generation.

Yet the reactions of gratitude and relief were superficial and transitory. The reality of 1778 was that the treaty of alliance, if not the treaty of amity and commerce, represented a sharp retreat from the bright promise of 1776. It was clearly an entangling alliance, made at the behest of the superior power. As Article VIII explicitly noted, "Neither of the two Parties shall conclude either Truce or Peace with Great Britain, without the formal consent of the other first obtain'd." In other words, the Americans could make no separate arrangement with Great Britain, could not terminate the war unilaterally, even if their objectives had been won, without the approval of an ally whose terms for ending the conflict might not be in consonance with American interests. This was the essence of entanglement. The relationship was further complicated by Article XI, wherein the United States was required to guarantee "from the present time and forever, against all other powers, to wit, the United States to his Most Christian Majesty, the present Possessions of the Crown of France in America as well as those which it may acquire by the future Treaty of peace."[21] This article bound the United States to the defense of the French West Indies in the event of a future war as well as during the current Anglo-French conflict.

So, rather than confirming American belief in their ability to manipulate European powers, the anxieties suffered by the Congress in Philadelphia and by its commissioners in Paris over French hesitations confirmed their belief in the unreliability of the Old World and narrowed the distinctions between the past evils of their former imperial masters and the potential threats of other European nations. France was perceived to have entered the war grudgingly, for its own advantage, and at the moment of its own choosing. It exacted a price the Americans had no wish to pay, including the exercise of proconsular powers by the French ministers in Philadelphia from 1779 to 1782.[22] The great power had its own ulterior motives and a world scheme that could severely limit the freedom of action of the small power. If France gave its blessing to the principle of freedom of the seas, this was not a blow on behalf of morality or a conversion to a new view of international relations; it was a short-term ploy in a long-term opposition to the maritime strength of England. Once the euphoria resulting from France's action had passed, the United States was left with all its suspicions of Europe intact.

Repugnance for political connections with Europe became a vital part of the American isolationist tradition, a fundamental code that made alliances un-American propositions, even into the twentieth century. For 149 years after the signing of the Convention of Morfontaine, no entangling alliance was made with any European nation. Then in 1949 the Truman administration challenged tradition to sign a treaty with eleven powers, including Britain and France—a treaty intended to last at least twenty years. The signing of an alliance, and of necessity an entangling alliance, was an act of courage.

That America was now the great power and France and Britain the lesser ones made little difference to critics such as Nettels, whose memories were fixed on the conditions as well as on the experience of the eighteenth century. A black American churchman, Bishop William J. Walls of the African Methodist Episcopal Zion Church, reminded senators of the Founding Fathers' trauma over Europe. By entering into the North Atlantic pact, the United States would be entangling itself with the very nations that were suppressing democratic impulses in their African colonies in the twentieth century just as they had done in America in the eighteenth century.[23] Another commentator, Alfred Kohlberg, spokesman for the American China Policy Association in 1949, could approve of the Atlantic pact as a step in the right direction if it was balanced by a Pacific pact. He was troubled, however, by "the breaking of a 152-year [sic] tradition of American foreign policy based on the Farewell Address of President Washington, who advised that we make no permanent alliances with European powers, but should rely on temporary alliances when needed."[24] H. M. Griffith, vice president of the National Economic Council, finally reached the conclusion many other critics of the North Atlantic Treaty were groping toward; namely, that if the United States should abandon its policy of abstaining from permanent alliances, "first commended by George Washington," it will "rescind the Declaration of Independence. American freedom of action will be gone. Surrender of freedom of action may well lead to our death as a Nation."[25]

Their message could not have been plainer. However disturbing the Soviet challenge might be for the moment, Europe had not changed; it was still the Continent that would corrupt virtuous America and ultimately drag it down to the destruction that would surely overtake Europe in the future. The image of American innocence was strong enough to withstand recognition on the part of isolationists that the United States of the twentieth century had been transformed from a small maritime nation into a giant, one of two superpowers which emerged from World War II.

It was this American colossus that Europeans saw. American size and American strength seemed to be the only barriers against the onslaught of communism, whether from Communist parties within the West or from Russian pressures from the East. Only American wealth and generosity could rescue Europeans from the consequences of the physical destruction and psychic dysfunction caused by the war. But their very dependence upon the superpower of the West evoked emotions reminscent of the character and tone of American reservations about their eighteenth-century alliance. Fundamentally, there was a suspicion that the United States, to place the words of Washington in a different context, "has a set of primary interests which to us have none or a very remote relation."[26]

Genuine as the common interest in the containment of communism may have been, the European allies suspected that they would function on a global stage as puppets manipulated by the American partner. Uneasiness over this prospect persists to this day, although its intensity has fluctuated over the thirty-five-year history of the Atlantic alliance. Its essence lay in the assumption that the strongest or predominant ally would dismiss the interests of the lesser members as expendable when its own interests were at stake.

Once the initial panic which had led the European allies to accept the alliance had subsided, strains with regard to their inferior status developed. These could never be fully quieted, and they helped to provide a negative gloss on every unilateral action of the United States. For example, the "hot line" between the White House and the Kremlin, designed to prevent such potential casus belli as the Cuban missile crisis or the Six-Day War in the Middle East, involved communications to which the smaller powers were not privy even if their interests were involved. There was always the residual suspicion that acts were taking place over which they had no control but which would have important implications for their security. Even the idea of a balance of terror that grew out of apparent nuclear parity between the two great adversaries in the 1960s invited charges that America's concern for Europe's safety had been sacrificed to its concern for the protection of its own cities. These charges in turn help to explain why Europeans were disturbed by the periodic discussion in Congress on reduction or removal of American troops from European soil; the argument of savings in defense costs or the promotion of the spirit of disengagement did not suffice.

The conflict between the global scope of United States policy and the continental emphasis of European allies was especially prominent in the Korean War of the 1950s and the Vietnam War of the 1960s and 1970s. In both wars the United States claimed that their firm response proved the credibility of their commitments to all alliances, including NATO. Europeans, however, read a different lesson from American actions: Korea diverted American power and energy that would have been better expended in Europe, while the apparent American obsession with the defense of South Vietnam raised doubts about the wisdom of American leadership in any part of the world.

Aside from the problem that a great power's interests might be irrelevant to its allies, there was the continuing difficulty of maintaining pressure on these nations to develop a defense capability that they preferred to leave in the hands of the United States. The United States in the immediate post-Korean period forced its European allies to risk all the advances that had been made under the economic recovery program in order to prove themselves worthy of American military assistance. The Economic Cooperation Administration (ECA), which had carried out the Marshall Plan objectives between 1948 and 1951, gave way to the Mutual Security Program, in which economic aid was placed under a military rubric. When Senator Theodore A. Green was chairman of a Senate subcommittee investigating the state of European service to the alliance in 1951, he stated baldly that Europe had achieved its recovery under the Marshall program, and so "in the future economic aid is to be primarily for the purpose of assisting friendly countries to strengthen their individual and collective defenses. This is our main purpose in the United States. We find it necessary to give up plans for domestic economic development and to concentrate on building our defense. We expect our allies, within the limit of their capacities, to do no less."[27]

The ominous feature of this statement was the understanding that the United States would determine what was "within the limit of their capacities." Western Europe could envisage severe damage to a still precarious economic recovery as it faced inflation and the shortage of materials. Americans did not seem to appreciate that a strong economy could afford to serve both domestic and military needs in ways weak economies could not manage.

American insensitivity also manifested itself to the NATO allies in the plans to defend Western Europe from a possible Soviet invasion. The projected battlefields would be in Europe, not in North America. Preparations for war meant preparations for fighting on their own soil, and if this meant European acquiescence to future liberation of Europe, the allies would rebel. There was a casualness in the manner in which Americans talked defense lines to be made on the Elbe or the Rhine, or even at the Pyrenees, that frightened Europeans. Discussion in 1950 of a token defense on the Elbe with a major stand to be taken at the Rhine aroused the Dutch as well as the Germans.[28] This accusation of insensitivity against the American ally surfaced repeatedly in the 1950s, most notably after West Germany's entry into the alliance when the NATO war exercise CARTE BLANCHE hypothecated a death toll of 1,700,000 people.[29] Such war games, even after they were revised, did little to alleviate suspicions among the lesser powers that the great power managed the alliance at their expense. The consequence of the frequent ruffling, conscious or unconscious, of national sensibilities was an anti-American mood among many of the allies. It rested on a conviction that the alliance was a trap with all the advantages on the side of the United States.

Of all the allies, France has reacted against American suzerainty with greatest vigor, has expressed the deepest suspicions, and in short has behaved most like the United States of the eighteenth century. No country of Europe felt less secure in 1949 than France or was in greater need of external support. It was no coincidence that Georges Bidault, the French foreign minister in 1948, was one of the founding fathers of the Brussels Treaty, the forerunner of the North Atlantic Treaty. His intention was to lure the United States into the Brussels organization to exploit American power without having to sacrifice any European prerogatives.[30]

The plan did not work as France had hoped. The United States did ultimately join the alliance but only after the successor treaty in 1949 had required, in Article III, assurance of "continuous and effective self-help" as well as "mutual aid."[31] France and the other allies as well worried about the terms of the mutuality. The price of American aid came high; it included base rights in Europe and an American role in internal affairs ranging from the length of military service required of each nation's troops to recommendations of how much of a nation's gross national product should be dedicated to the alliance.

Analogies with the eighteenth century are striking. Just as French ministers in Philadelphia and French generals in the field exercised considerable influence through judicious distribution of blandishment and intimidation, along with appropriate funds, so well-staffed military assistance advisory groups now wielded authority in Paris and other allied capitals. They demanded and received the rights and privileges of ambassadors. The American contingent in France was composed of eighty-eight Americans, while Norway was host to an American mission of sixty men. The French were offended, but the most the Americans would do to appease their pride was to remove the patronizing term "advisory" from the title of the American military aid group in Paris.[32] Only then would the French sign the bilateral agreement legitimizing the American mission.

But the issue which evoked the sharpest Franco-American conflict was the American insistence on a German role in the Atlantic alliance. While communism was a serious problem for the French, the potential revival of German power was an even greater problem for them. Americans could not understand why they and Western European nations should provide the resources and manpower to protect German territory when Germans themselves did nothing to serve the common cause. Congress required that American aid be tied to self-help and mutual aid, and both these elements pointed to a German contribution in the form of soldiers. To many Americans the matter was a simple as that. To Frenchmen, however, memories of German behavior under the Nazis half a decade before made it impossible for them to accept Germans as colleagues in a common effort. Lacking the experience of German occupation, American leaders could not fully comprehend the reasons why Frenchmen and other Europeans might shun German help even when such help would compensate for their own inadequate defense efforts.[33]

In the short run the result was the submission of France to American importunities by appearing to consent in 1951 to a German component in a European army. Here was a clear-cut case of a senior partner forcing a junior partner to accept an unpalatable decision. The alternative could have been American abandonment of Europe, and perhaps European abandonment of France.

The humiliating experience of having to come up with a Pleven Plan (named for the French premier in October 1950) and of having to accept a European Defense Community (EDC) was not forgotten. The French nourished their grievances over the years and expressed them in a variety of forms, including the sabotage of the EDC in 1954, the aborted Suez invasion of 1956, and even formal withdrawal from the military functions of NATO in 1966. When the EDC failed, the United States threatened an anti-French alliance with Germany; when the British and French undertook an attack on Egypt without the knowledge of the American ally, the United States joined forces with the Soviet Union, or so it seemed, to foil the enterprise. As Marbois was reputed to have told Americans when they entered into an engagement with the common enemy behind France's back, great powers *"felt & remembered."*[34] Unlike the French in 1782, the United States also complained in 1954 and 1956.

Throughout this chapter thus far the presentation of Franco-American relations in the course of two alliances has documented the assumption that small powers are victimized in the entanglement with a large power. For Americans during the Revolution this conclusion was especially significant because it reinforced an already pervasive belief that political connections of any sort with any European nation, large or small, were inimical to their interest, even to their survival. Embedded in American consciousness, the isolationist tradition remained virulent even when the United States had grown into the status France or England had earlier enjoyed; and yet many isolationist critics of the Atlantic pact spoke as if neither the United States nor Europe had changed over the course of 150 years. If America was no longer small, in their view it was still innocent and susceptible to the corruption of Europe.

Yet it is a moot point that the great power invariably exploits the small in an alliance. The latter possesses an ability to manipulate a relationship by virtue of its vulnerability. The long-term advantages may well fall to the lesser rather than to the greater partner in the alliance. Machiavelli suggested that when a state gives money to an inferior political entity, "she gives an important sign of weakness."[35] Or, as Charles Burton Marshall translated this dictum, "Once we make another state the beneficiary of our aid, we tend in some degree to invest prestige in it. If the receiving state has marked political weaknesses, our giving of aid tends to plight us to the correction of its weaknesses."[36] The end result may be that the client regime has made its weakness an instrument for coercion of the benefactor.

Economists Mancur Olson and Richard Zeckhauser have noted that larger nations in alliances devote larger percentages of their total income to the common venture than do smaller nations.[37] While the senior partners may be annoyed by this disparity and may prod the inferior allies from time to time about their irresponsibility, they should regard their share of the cost as reasonable and as a natural consequence of the conjunction of large and small nations. According to Olson and Zeckhauser, the greater powers place a higher absolute value on the rewards of alliance and presumably have more money to spare than the lesser ones. The latter, having a smaller stake in the outcome, are potential prey to neutralism and are tempted to make their own deals with the enemy. Moreover, they feel rightly that however great their sacrifice may be, it will have relatively small effect on the global balance. Should the major allies be inclined to withhold their aid, the smaller often believe they will have more to lose than the beneficiary power. Therefore, the disproportionate sacrifice fits the circumstances of the alliance.

The Atlantic alliance provides dramatic illustrations of this thesis. If the term entanglement is meaningful, it should also apply to the way in which Western Europe entrapped the United States on the Continent after World War II on the grounds that the future of America hung on the fate of that region. Article V of the Treaty of Washington did not specifically require the United States to defend Europe in the event of attack, but it was understood on both sides that the language of that article, in which "the Parties agree that an armed attack against one or more of them in Europe or North America shall be considered an attack against them all," served that very purpose.[38] Knowledge that an attack on Paris would be treated as an attack on New York was the source of whatever sense of security the treaty offered Europeans in 1949.

When the Korean War converted the treaty into an active military organization, Europeans demanded and Americans granted them (with some trepidation) a permanent American military force stationed in Europe in order to maintain the credibility of deterrence. This was the product of the New

York and Brussels meetings of the North Atlantic Council in September and December 1950, and it was the occasion for a "Great Debate" in the Congress in 1951 over the president's authority to dispatch troops to Europe.[39] Although the United States asked in turn greater European military contributions and a commitment to a German share in the defense of Europe, it is important to observe that the American part of the bargain was fulfilled more effectively and more quickly than the European. France was able to withstand pressures from all sides as it delayed German entry into a European community because it knew that the United States set a high value upon its membership in the alliance, at least in the 1950s, and that no American retribution would follow from its resistance.

As for American global politics entangling Europeans in matters outside their interest and against their wills, the history of the Korean and Vietnam wars fails to sustain most of the charge. British Prime Minister Clement Attlee did fly to Washington in 1950 to restrain President Truman from employing atomic weapons in Korea and—*sotto voce*—to restrain General MacArthur from managing the war single-handedly.[40] He succeeded in his mission, or at least in part of it. NATO's presence in the war turned out to be minimal. The United Nations force was essentially American, while the allies provided token support. In the case of Vietnam their disapproval was open and articulate at a time when the United States had taken a firm stand that the survival of the free world was at stake in Southeast Asia. Despite an agonizing experience suffered in Vietnam, with Britain and France keeping their distance, the United States launched no reprisals. Indeed, when Senator Mike Mansfield, the majority leader of the Senate, proposed periodically in the late 1960s that the United States troop level be reduced or that troops be removed from Europe, the administration invariably heeded the vigorous objections of the European allies.[41]

The Atlantic alliance was and is important to the United States, as its behavior has demonstrated in almost every crisis of confidence. That it is equally if not more important to the European partners has not been quite so evident. This is, however, a vital fact in the longevity of NATO. It has not been American coercion that explains its survival thirty-five years after its inception. The existence of the North Atlantic Treaty may have been designed to inhibit a threat of Soviet invasion that never really existed. But the demoralization of Europe, its pessimism over its future, and the disruptive activities of strong Communist parties in France and Italy were realities in 1949. The linking of America with Europe may be judged a major factor in the psychological revival of the West which sparked the economic miracles of the next generation.

The allies paid a minimal price for the security American arms brought them. When they were unhappy with particular American positions, as in the case of plans for atomic installations in Denmark or of Spanish entry into the organization, they could reject American proposals with impunity. The greatest of all challenges was France's departure from NATO in 1966 without renouncing the North Atlantic Treaty itself. DeGaulle was able to enjoy such benefits as the Treaty conferred without having to pay penalties presumably demanded by military obligations.

The advantages to the smaller ally were even more apparent in the results of the Treaty of Paris than they were in the Treaty of Washington. Vergennes appears to have been as badly entangled in the thickets of France's Spanish connection as were the Americans. Not only did the French depend on Spain's fleet for the success of their war with Britain; they had counted on a more resolute American cooperation in the waging of the war. If one looks objectively at the course of hostilities after the French alliance of February 1778, one can sympathize with France's unhappiness at the slackening of American efforts, at the obvious American wish to let the French finish the fighting for them.

Whether France betrayed the United States through secret talks with Britain and Spain, as Jay and Adams claimed, is open to question. While the American appetite for western territory was not shared by the ally, the foreign minister believed, even as he agreed to restrict the boundaries of the new nation, that he was fulfilling the terms of the treaty. The United States had never really occupied the trans-Appalachian lands, and the record of American troops in Ohio or Kentucky was not such as to assure American sovereignty over that area on the basis of military conquest. While there was French insensitivity to American needs as well as irritation with American demands for fishery rights, Vergennes never objected to Americans gaining such rights as long as there was no infringement upon France's claims.[42] The French felt that they had fulfilled their promise of winning American independence. If there was waffling and secrecy in the process, they were products less of the great power's malevolence than of its inability to extricate itself from the British war without concessions. British naval strength in the Caribbean and Spanish insistence on an equivalence for Gibraltar allowed the French few alternatives.

Whatever grief and embarrassment the United States suffered from the French alliance between 1783 and 1800 had to be weighed against the restrictions on American freedom of action. The facts were that the United States signed a treaty favoring the ally's enemy, then renounced unilaterally the treaties of 1778 and engaged in a naval war with the ally between 1797 and 1800, all without crippling repercussions from the senior partner. Admittedly, the French recalled their envoy, refused to receive the American minister in Paris, interfered with the election of 1796, and shamelessly tried to bribe and threaten peace commissioners who were sent to repair the relationship. Moreover, they seized American properties and imprisoned American sailors in violation of treaty obligations. But it is likely that relations with France would have been much the same without an alliance. The United States was subjected to British control, economically and even militarily. The hostility of France would have followed from these circumstances in any event.

By the time of Morfontaine the alliance had lost meaning for both parties. The Americans were happy to detach themselves from it formally in 1800, while Bonaparte's primary interest in it was to divert them from his plans for Louisiana and their plans for French indemnities for depredations against American commerce during the Quasi War.[43]

Yet cynicism about the later years of the alliance distorts its early significance. Between 1778 and 1783 the alliance worked for both allies and worked remarkably well for the lesser ally. France achieved what it sought initially from the connection: it pried America loose from the British Empire. It even won a foothold of sorts in the American psyche. No matter how ungrateful or suspicious Americans were, there was a residue of good will and special feelings for France which began at this time and which have occasionally burst forth since. If France's participation was a tragedy for France and a personal failure for Vergennes, it was probably more failure for Vengennes than tragedy for France. The French Revolution comes down in history more as triumph than as tragedy.

On balance the smaller power entangled the larger in an alliance that served American interests far more than it served the French. Whether the same results will apply to the history of NATO remains to be seen.

3. Isolationism, the United Nations, and the Cold War, 1947-1949

The experience of World War II taught Americans that the price the nation had paid for its isolationism in the 1930s was too high. They learned that war might have been avoided had the United States been able to accept the principles of collective security. But even as this knowledge impressed itself upon policymakers, the Roosevelt and Truman administrations recognized the difficulty of uprooting an entrenched idea. Political abstention from the Old World meant American freedom from the evils of spheres of influence, alliances, and balance-of-power struggles. The fate of Woodrow Wilson's attempt to bring the United States into the League of Nations was instructive to the makers of foreign policy during the war and postwar years. If America should break with the traditions of Washington or Monroe, the break would have to be in consonance with the spirit of the past, so that identification with Europe would not be identical with the immoral European system of international relations.

It was for this reason that the United Nations became such an important part of American policy in the 1940s. It would be America's chance to redeem the error of 1919 and to do so on its own terms. That is, the United Nations, under American auspices, would not only make another world war impossible but would guarantee security by means of America's traditional practices, or at least what it liked to consider to be its true approach to international affairs—conciliation, mediation, and use of international law. It was not important that the new league was in fact less powerful than the old on paper. It was important simply that America had embraced the world without embracing the destructive power politics of the past. To President Roosevelt and his advisers, the successful making of a world organization was second in priority only to the winning of the war.

Their plans succeeded magnificently. Senate Republicans as well as Democrats were intimately involved in the deliberations on American membership in the new organization, which was to have its headquarters in New York, and the United States would be one of the "Four Policemen" on the Security Council guaranteeing peace for all nations. While lively suspicions of the allies persisted—of the British as well as the Russians—they were submerged in the expectation that the operations of the United Nations would undermine British and Russian spheres of influence in Asia and Eastern Europe, respectively.

In a way the United Nations was "oversold," as a Senate Foreign Relations subcommittee noted a few years later.[1] Acceptable as it was to all but a small band of isolationists, it produced an excessive sense of self-congratulation among a majority of Americans. They could regard it as a surrogate State Department that would permit them a return to more pressing domestic concerns. The Security Council would minimize the need for an extensive national foreign policy. Under its umbrella, massive demobilization of a wartime economy could take place along lines similar to those following the Civil War and World War I, but with an assurance to the American public that the world leadership of the United States would remain intact. What the administration did not anticipate was the flourishing of a variation on the old isolationism, fed by the hope that the new collective security organization would keep America as free of alliances and power politics as the Monroe Doctrine had done in the last century. When, two years after the end of World War II, the National Opinion Research Council polled the public about a need to rearm unilaterally and to make defense arrangements outside the supervision of the United Nations, 82 percent in 1947 and 72 percent in 1948 responded that the United States should not try to work "outside the United Nations" despite the inability of the organization's machinery to function under the threat of a Soviet veto.[2] Ignoring the United Nations carried the pejorative connotations which the idea of entangling alliances once had; unilateral rearmament and bilateral agreements evoked memories of the nineteenth-century European system of balance of power. This reaction did not signify American conversion to world government; rather, it confirmed the identification of the United Nations with the traditional American revulsion against militarism and alliances.

Initially, statesmen of the distinction of Dean Acheson underestimated the meaning the United Nations had acquired for many Americans. Acheson never had illusions about the practicality of the United Nations Charter. The men in his circle shared this sentiment for the most part, and wrote off the public acclaim for the charter as a romantic by-product of America's changing position in the world. This is not to say that George F. Kennan or Acheson felt that the United Nations was useless; it was simply a very limited instrument of American policy. Belatedly they were compelled to respect the fact that newly educated elites sympathetic to the abandonment of the older isolationism during World War II required appeasement of their devotion to the United Nations before they would follow the seminal changes implicit in the containment policy of the late 1940s.

There is some irony in the administration's predicament during the Cold War. Much of the opposition to its assumption of world leadership under the Truman Doctrine, the Marshall Plan, and the North Atlantic Treaty came from partisans of an organization which the administration itself had touted as the only appropriate expression of international responsibility. But when the conflict between the United States and the Soviet Union could not be resolved within the framework of the Charter of the United Nations, the Charter became an obstacle to the implementation of a new program suggested by the ideas of George Kennan. In order to win American support for a strong independent position against Soviet policies in the postwar world, the Truman policymakers had to cope with the shock Americans would feel if they had to recognize the failure of the United Nations.

It was not the extremists or the ideologues of the left or right who created the most problems for the administration's plan to contain Soviet power. Ultimately the trouble was with those members of the articulate majority in the coalition behind the acceptance of military aid, massive economic assistance, and a military alliance. The great labor organizations and business associations—the American Federation of Labor and the Congress of Industrial Organizations, the Chamber of Commerce and the Committee for Economic Development—as well as most of the major religious denominations supported the American position on the Cold War. At the same time, they repeatedly made known their concerns over the apparent inconsistencies between American policy and the United Nations Charter, between pledges of loyalty to the world organization and actions taking place outside its confines. So disturbing were these considerations that the Truman administration felt itself constrained to append to all of its propositions an assertion of collaboration with the United Nations whether or not the professions of loyalty were appropriate or accurate. To win American allegiance to its policies, the administration had to do more than wave the banner of anticommunism; it had to assure the nation that those policies fitted the image of the world that had replaced the older isolationism—a universal collective security implicit in the existence of the United Nations. The Marshall and Acheson State Department of 1947 to 1949 had a difficult semantic task before it.

However wide the differences in interpretation of the origin of the Cold War may be, most historians would observe that until the end of 1946 the United States offered no coherent rationalization of its foreign policy. The Soviet Union was dealt with piecemeal, with the expectation that a thrust in

Germany or a parry in Iran would restore the working relationship of the war period under the benevolent eye of the United Nations. This expectation ended officially when George Kennan's observations, widely disseminated in 1946 by Secretary of the Navy James V. Forrestal, became the basis for policy. As chargé d'affaires in Moscow and as a scholarly and perceptive student of communism, Kennan had propounded the thesis that only patient but firm containment would manage the dynamic ideology of the Soviet system. Conventional diplomacy was irrelevant to the relationship between the two nations. So was the United Nations. Hostility was inherent in the nature of the two systems of society. Only American leadership, by damming the force of the opposition, would save the world and the United States itself.

The first implication of the Kennan hypothesis was the fact of a divided world that could not be bridged by the United Nations. Such was the sense of the men who made policy in the Truman administration of 1947. Because the nation at large did not share their perceptions of international reality, the economic plight of Great Britain and the military problems of Greece provided dramatic settings for policymakers to force America to come to grips with reality. Britain's inability to afford continuous support of the Greek government against Communist opposition became the occasion for the United States to assume the British burden in the eastern Mediterranean. As Kennan put it, "We had no choice but to accept the challenge and extend the requisite aid."[3]

But it was also the occasion to awaken Americans to a wider peril. There was a choice to be made in the trumpeting of a crusade against communism, "in terms," as Kennan put it, more ruefully this time, "more grandiose and more sweeping than anything that I, at least, had envisaged."[4] In the minds of Acheson, Forrestal, and Robert Patterson, nothing short of a morality drama would jar Americans from the complacency reflected in congressional unwillingness to provide aid for suffering Europe. Acheson warned that Greece, engulfed in civil war, opened the way for Soviet penetration of three continents. "Like apples in a barrel infected by one rotten one, the corruption of Greece would infect Iran and all to the East. It would also carry the infection to Africa through Asia Minor and Egypt, and to Europe through Italy and France."[5]

Thus the British received more than they had bargained for in the Manichean response of President Truman, wherein he observed in his address to Congress that "the free peoples of the world look to us for support in maintaining their freedoms. If we falter in our leadership we may endanger the peace of the world—and shall surely endanger the welfare of our own Nation."[6] The gauntlet was thrown down in the winter of 1947 for Americans as well as Russians to pick up. The risk of failure with Congress was considerable. Republican leadership in the 80th Congress, sensitive to the high cost of foreign policy and the exaggeration of executive power that would follow, was not educated to the Soviet menace. Even under the 79th Congress the British loan barely passed in the summer of 1946. The victorious Republicans of 1947 were looking forward to cutting 50 percent from the military budget. As liberal Republican Henry Cabot Lodge, Jr., expressed it, Congress appeared to him "like a man wielding a meat ax in a dark room" who "might cut off his own head."[7]

Given this mood, senatorial reaction at a White House meeting on February 27, 1947, over the prospect of emergency help to the Greeks and Turks devolved on questions of British chestnuts, wasteful expenses, and the dangers of war. The administration had anticipated objections and countered them skillfully by reminding senators of the cost of appeasement and the enormity of the present threat. Senator Arthur H. Vandenberg of Michigan, chairman of the Senate Foreign Relations Committee, was impressed both by Acheson's eloquence and by the absence of reasonable alternatives. Even isolationists were touched by memories of appeasement and contented themselves with grudging acquiescence in actions they described as politically inspired.

Effective though the administration was in winning over congressional leaders in informal discussions, it failed to confront the problem of the role of the United Nations Charter in American planning. Not that the UN was omitted from the president's message on the Truman Doctrine in March. But the language and tone concerning the United Nations were pessimistic about its future. Truman was blunt: "We have considered how the United Nations might assist in this crisis. But the situation is an urgent one requiring immediate action, and the United Nations and its related organizations are not in a position to extend help of the kind that is required."[8] Whatever hopes policymakers may have had of the United Nations a few years earlier were banished long before the president addressed Congress. The reality of world politics, as seen by the men around the president, was reflected, as Joseph Jones has pointed out, in the complete absence of the United Nations from the agenda for the drafting of the message.[9] No one raised an objection that the proposed aid to Greece and Turkey would bypass the United Nations. Vandenberg wrote on March 5 that "I am frank to say I think Greece would collapse fifty times before the United Nations itself could even hope to handle a situation of this nature."[10] Even the passing—and slighting—references to the United Nations in Truman's text were the work of lesser members of the State Department who prevailed over Acheson's advice. To the undersecretary, time was short, and the Soviet veto should have made the futility of the United Nations obvious to all.[11]

Acheson was correct in his perceptions of the United Nations in this crisis. What he and his colleagues had neglected were the lessons they had helped to inculcate in Americans since the beginning of World War II; namely, that there would be no salvation outside the new collective security organization. The alternatives were a return to the suicidal power politics which had devastated the world in the twentieth century or a return to the isolationism which had stilled America's voice in the past. Neither alternative was now acceptable. The answer for most Americans aware of the larger world was only the United Nations, and yet the same men who had helped create it appeared suddenly ready to scuttle it without warning.

The storm that broke over the United Nations in the wake of the president's message to the Congress took the administration by surprise. The diversity as well as the intensity of comment on the bypassing of the United Nations, the revival of power politics, and the destruction of the Charter embraced more than just extremists. Public opinion polls revealed that, up until the Greek and Turkish crisis, the public had believed that the United States was doing everything it could to make the organization effective. If there had been difficulties, they were all the fault of the Soviet Union. Now the public was less sure of guilt; the dismissal of the United Nations under the Truman Doctrine was disturbing. In the spring of 1947 a majority of 56 percent, compared with 25 percent in opposition, favored a greater role for the United Nations over an American unilateral action in aid to Greece and Turkey.[12]

Understandably, the most vigorous opponents of the administration took up the cry. For many, the United Nations was one among many sticks useful for beating the government. The left of Henry Wallace, representing internationalists who felt American obstructionism had pushed the Russians into active hostility, found in the president's message not only another attack upon the Soviet Union but also a sacrifice of the United Nations to a new "ruthless imperialism."[13] Isolationists on the right, always suspicious of Truman's fiscal policies, feared that the Truman Doctrine would be the opening wedge for a vast program of assistance that would destroy the American economy before it could damage the Russians.

For many congressmen, the United Nations was more than a partisan propaganda issue. While Truman's opponents were concerned with the waste of America's resources, as they claimed, they were also worried about the dangers of military aid leading to alliance and war. Senator Robert A. Taft, leader of the Republicans in the 80th Congress, was genuinely troubled by the military implications of the program and wondered why the United Nations had not been made the vehicle to serve the purpose. Peace was at stake. "If we assume a special position in Greece and Turkey, we can hardly . . . object to the Russians continuing their domination in Poland, Yugoslavia, Rumania, and Bulgaria."[14] Internationalists and isolationists, Republicans and Democrats could stand together on this ground.

Such sentiments forced the administration to reconsider the links between its aid proposals and the United Nations. More important, they moved Senator Vandenberg, chairman of the Senate Foreign Affairs Committee, to action. Vigorous and sincere, Vandenberg was also vain and shallow. As Robert Allen and William Shannon saw him from their peephole view of Washington, he was "a man who can strut sitting down."[15] He was susceptible to the flattery Acheson and Lovett were to apply to him over the next two years of his power. The Michigan senator called the omission of the United Nations a "colossal blunder" that must be rectified. Since the influential columnist Walter Lippmann, who also wanted aid for Greece and Turkey, shared this view, the omission was all the more serious a blunder.[16]

Vandenberg, who had believed a month before that Greece would fall "fifty times" before the United Nations would act, paid obeisance to that organ on April 8, 1948, by addressing it as "our first reliance and our prime concern." The senator then urged Ambassador Warren Austin at the United Nations to notify that body of the "emergency and temporary character" of the program and to assure it that "the United States believes that the United Nations and its related agencies should assume the principal responsibility, within their capabilities, for the long-range tasks of assistance required for the reconstruction of Greece."[17] Carrying this point to Congress, Vandenberg tacked on a preamble to the aid bill, explicitly linking the program to the Charter and explaining that the United States was acting only because the United Nations was not in a position to help. Moreover, Vandenberg, in conjunction with Tom Connally of Texas, his Democratic counterpart on the Foreign Relations Committee, wrote a provision into the bill authorizing the Security Council or the General Assembly to terminate American assistance whenever "action taken or assistance furnished by the United Nations makes the continuance of such assistance unnecessary or undesirable." In this way, the problem of compatibility was solved to the satisfaction of Senator Vandenberg and presumably to that of most of his countrymen.

The men who had framed the Truman Doctrine considered the Vandenberg addendum a charade to appease public opinion. Joseph M. Jones, a staff officer in the State Department, admitted that he and his colleagues had missed the issue, but, given the weakness of the United Nations and the urgency of the problem in the eastern Mediterranean, he was not prepared to admit their mistake.[18] Dean Acheson could never take the issue seriously. In his customary sardonic vein, he looked back years later to the act of "political transubstantiation" by which Vandenberg had embraced the Truman Doctrine with more ardor than before. Acheson observed that Vandenberg, joined by Lippmann, "that ambivalent Jeremiah of the Press," had discovered the dreadful crime of "bypassing the United Nations" and had rectified it by giving the international organization a specific role in the legislative program of the United States. Acheson speculated that the "fortunate" sin of omission had produced the opportunity for the Vandenberg blessing to be laid upon the Truman Doctrine, thus guaranteeing its success with Congress and the country.[19]

In their experience with the Marshall Plan, leading to the establishment of the Economic Cooperation Administration, the Truman policymakers were able to manage the issue with greater sophistication than they displayed in the enunciation of the Truman Doctrine. They were helped by the fact that the assistance asked for was exclusively economic and that theoretically the Soviet Union could be a beneficiary. Title I of the ECA bill proclaimed that "Congress finds that the existing situation in Europe endangers the establishment of the objectives of the United Nations." Beyond this general statement, the administration consciously connected the new bill with other agencies in the United Nations that served economic purposes, such as the Food and Agricultural Organization and the Economic Commission for Europe. This harmony was specifically underscored by spokesmen for such prestigious public-spirited groups as the General Federation of Women's Clubs, the League of Women Voters, and the Ad Hoc Commission for the Marshall Plan. The powerful Committee for Economic Development, a group of liberal businessmen from which the leadership of the ECA would be drawn, identified the program as "an affirmation of our own civilization" and hence obviously as vital to American interests as "participation in the United Nations, in the International Monetary Fund, and the International Trade Organization."[20]

Not that voices against the Marshall Plan on the ground of incompatibility with the United Nations were wholly mute. The Progressive party and the American Labor party of New York offered the same objections to the new program that they had expressed against military aid to Greece and Turkey: namely, it represented an American imperialist challenge to the United Nations and the Soviet Union. In some ways it was even more insidious. British and French assets would be assumed by Wall Street before the new program would go into effect. If the United States was serious in its professions of concern for distraught Europe, it would adopt the seven-point program of Henry Wallace, which would place under full control of the United Nations the aid intended under ECA. So advised Arthur Schutzer, state executive secretary of the American Labor party. Far less stridently, but with more effect, the Society of Friends asked for a European program that "should be carried out in the closest possible cooperation with the United Nations." Clearly, the present plan did not meet this request.[21]

Consistent with their position on the Truman Doctrine, conservative nationalists struck at the Marshall Plan because of its identification with the United Nations. The latter was the menace drawing American resources out of the nation and into an octopus of collectivism. Merwin Hart, president of the National Economic Council, claimed in a radio address on February 23, 1948, that "while we are lulled into imagining the UN is all mouth, a harmless debating society, the Planners are busy attaching tentacles to its body. . . . These tentacles are the agencies of the UN." A few weeks earlier Hart had testified in congressional hearings against the aforementioned preamble which "speaks highly of the attainment of the objectives of the United Nations." This was precisely the trouble with the program.[22]

But the opponents of European economic aid lost some of their natural constituencies. The administration's care to entangle the Marshall Plan with the United Nations from the outset and to claim that it was another species of that organization's ongoing agencies mollified some who had been turned away from the Truman Doctrine. Although the *Christian Century* found duplication with the work of the Economic Commission for Europe, it contented itself with a warning, not a repudiation. Its suspiciousness manifested itself in a Freudian slip of the type when it quoted Acheson as saying that American economic aid would be concentrated "in areas where it will be most effective in strengthening the authority of the United States." In the next issue the editor apologized for the error in printing "United States" instead of "United Nations." The Marshall Plan was a gamble in the eyes of the *Christian Century*. It was also "a great venture in statesmanship."[23] Even the acerbic *Nation*, a vigorous critic of the Truman Doctrine, agreed that the Marshall Plan "offers a new hope," although it assumed at first that the program would be under the aegis of the Economic Commission for Europe. Lippmann's clear distinction between "the Truman line" and "the Marshall line"—one unilateral, the other in harmony with the United Nations—made a difference for many friends of collective security.[24]

If there were lingering doubts about the conjunction of the Marshall Plan with the United Nations, the endorsement of leaders of the American Association for the United Nations should have resolved them. Clark M. Eichelberger, its national director, offered a blessing by association: "The Marshall Plan must not be considered disassociated from the United Nations. Its success means stability for the nations of Europe, and the United Nations must derive its strength from stable members." Although the majority of the Philadelphia branch of the United Nations Council would have preferred that the plan be administered by the United Nations, that organization's letter to the Senate Committee on Foreign Affairs observed that "it is important to point out that there was a very significant minority in favor of having the United States administer aid alone."[25] The majority's objection represented a minor caveat; the American friends of the United Nations put their imprimatur on the Marshall Plan.

This success was a tribute to the new sensitivity of the administration's managers. Acheson had made appropriate gestures, as the report in the *Christian Century* suggested. The tactics of congressional approval were well planned and equally well executed. To soothe the endemic fiscal conservatism of Congress, the European aid program was divided into parts, with only a modest interim bill presented in the fall of 1947 and the remainder in the winter of 1948, after the nation had been educated to the importance of ECA.

Europe had already done its part by organizing itself in the summer of 1947 into a conference, under the chairmanship of Sir Oliver Franks, that promised cooperation and self-help on the one hand, and estrangement from Communist Eastern Europe on the other. The Soviet Union and its allies had never been formally excluded, and some of the Eastern European countries would have remained in the European meeting on the Marshall Plan if the Soviet Union had not summarily removed itself and its dependent friends from consideration. Whether a Communist belief in the plan as a dying gasp of capitalism or as an imperialist trick to dominate Europe moved the Russians is immaterial. The Soviet Union's hostility to ECA and its subsequent involvement in the coup d'etat in Czechoslovakia in February 1948 helped tip the balance in Congress in behalf of the Marshall program. As the *New York Times* claimed on January 18, 1948, "Kremlin, as Usual, Comes to the Rescue of ERP." The Communist menace eased the labors of the Herter Committee, a select committee of House members studying the feasibility of the Marshall proposal.

Even without the Soviet Union's inadvertent collaboration, the efforts at alerting the American public to the importance of European aid had been enormous, and the results were impressive. At the apex was the Committee for the Marshall Plan, with former Secretary of War Henry L. Stimson as national chairman. Robert Patterson was chairman of an executive committee that included Mrs. Wendell L. Willkie, Dean Acheson (then in retirement), labor leaders David Dubinsky and James B. Carey, conservative Republican banker Winthrop Aldrich, and liberal Democratic Senator Herbert H. Lehman of New York.

Given the weight of the foregoing names, the particular economic expectations of the National Association of Manufacturers, the American Federation of Labor, and the American Farm Bureau Association, and the favorable views of groups as diverse as Americans for Democratic Action and the American Legion, the administration had reason for optimism. A Gallup poll released on December 7, 1947, showed that in a four-and-a-half-month period the segment of the public which had not "heard or read" about the plan dropped from 51 to 36 percent. Toward the end of the period, those with no opinion declined from 38 to 27 percent. Favorable opinion rose from 47 to 56 percent, leaving only 17 percent opposed to economic aid to Europe. The results were not merely passage of both aid programs by a substantial majority but the silencing of opposition, particularly from the fiscal conservatives and nationalists more concerned with Asia than with Europe.[26] In other words, the men who had pressed isolationism before the war were unable to move in 1948. A final factor in their immobility was an addendum to ECA that included Chiang Kai-shek's China among the beneficiaries in the final version of the legislation.

As of the winter of 1948 the administration could ignore dissenters on the Cold War. The nation had accepted the commitment to use America's enormous economic resources and potential military power to defend beleaguered peoples from Communist military threats and to rehabilitate a continent sufficiently to immunize it from the blandishments of communism. The Truman administration had succeeded in these objectives without unleashing the forces of isolationism in America. But if isolationism was held at bay, it was partly because the United Nations had been held aloft as the organization whose survival precluded the revival of balance-of-power politics and the alliance system. The efforts in behalf of the defense of Greece and Turkey and the economic revival of France and Great Britain under the Marshall Plan had been presented effectively as within the spirit, and even the letter, of the United Nations Charter.

The pose of compatibility could not survive the next phase of the Cold War, however, the joining of an entangling alliance in NATO. The step was taken reluctantly, but inevitably, given the commitment to the survival of Europe. Piecemeal military assistance and long-term financial support were not enough to secure the desperate nations of Europe. To fulfill the irrevocable political obligations they demanded meant reopening the question of the United Nations Charter. There was no avoidance of a direct conflict between a treaty of military alliance and a charter of collective security. To accept one meant to deny the other. The administration tried to keep the facade. It failed, but by 1949, when the alliance was made, the country had been sufficiently prepared to pay a price it might not have paid in 1947 or 1948.

At any event, the Truman administration policymakers could not enjoy the respite that passage of the Economic Cooperation Act should have given them. Even before it was signed on April 3, 1948, five nations of western Europe, all future beneficiaries of the Marshall Plan, banded together to form the Western Union under the Treaty of Brussels. the ostensible occasion for this military pact was the Communist coup d'etat in Prague in February 1948, which ended the last vestige of western influence in Czechoslovakia. The twin shocks of the deaths of Jan Masaryk and Czech democracy reminded Europeans that economic recovery would be worthless, even if it was possible, without the accompaniment of physical security. Could a nation's economy be rehabilitated if its energies were absorbed in fears of invasion or internal subversion? If not, then cooperation in the military sphere was as vital as it had been in the economic. The Brussels pact, with its emphasis on self-help and interdependence in a common defense, was, as John Spanier noted, "a military counterpart to the OEEC."[27]

An American connection with the Brussels Pact was necessary to advance such progress in security as has been made through the Truman Doctrine and the Marshall Plan. There were few alternatives open. Whatever the merits of the argument that Soviet activity in 1948—from the Czech coup in February to the Berlin blockade in June—was the product of American decisions tying the occupation zones in Germany to the West and successfully launching the Marshall Plan, the Truman administration could see only aggression, not response, in Russian behavior. A military link with the Western Union was a logical extension of policies of the past year.

What was distressing in the challenge of the Brussels Pact was not the question of an American commitment. Rather, it was the clarification of the isolationist problem which had been successfully blurred before. Because the United Nations was to have been the new means of voiding the alliance system, the Charter of the United Nations became the forum for the confrontation. The initial hope of Secretary of State Marshall was association, not membership. When British Foreign Minister Ernest Bevin first broached the subject of a mutual defense treaty with France and the Benelux countries in January 1948, Truman and Marshall offered their general blessing. That the transatlantic connection should be construed as an American signature to an alliance was another matter. Alliance would mean that the United States would lock itself into a fifty-year entanglement in which it would be obliged, according to Article 4, to offer the member attacked in Europe "all military and other aid and assistance in their power." The last time the United States had made an entangling commitment to a European power was in 1778, and this had been terminated with relief in 1800. Would Americans in 1948 agree to an arrangement so blatantly at odds with the world view equated with the United Nations?

A temporary way out of the dilemma emerged from an important meeting at Blair House on April 17, 1948, at which Marshall, Robert A. Lovett, Vandenberg, and John Foster Dulles spoke in private what they felt they could not speak in public: the prospect of a transatlantic pact widening the Western Union and built on the regional pattern of the Rio Pact. They all agreed on its necessity, if it could be accomplished under the aegis of Articles 51 and 53 of the Charter of the United Nations, which concerned the legitimacy, respectively, of collective self-defense and regional activity. They admitted to themselves, however, that the question of compatibility with the Charter made the latter an insecure basis for such an alliance.[28]

In light of their irresolution, understandable on the part of an administration fearful of resurgent isolationism in a hostile Congress and of a president unsure of his nomination in an election year, Vandenberg's resolution for Senate approval of the Western Union appeared as a satisfactory, if temporary, compromise. Senate Resolution 234 of June 11, 1948, announced to the world affirmation of "the association of the United States, by constitutional process, with such regional and other collective arrangements as are based on continuous and effective self-help and mutual aid, and as affect national security." Here was an identification with the European organization in terms reminiscent of the Marshall Plan. More striking was the frame of reference for the United Nations. Of the six paragraphs in the resolution, five spoke of the United Nations and American pursuit of its goals "in accordance with the purposes, principles, and provisions of the Charter." A year later Vandenberg made a point of noting that three of six paragraphs in his Senate resolution were specifically intended to make the Charter more workable.[29] By virtue of the resolution, the United States resolved the dilemma of the Blair House meeting. The resolution announced its "association" with the alliance, not membership, and announced also its full devotion to the United Nations without having to prove it. The Senate vote of 64 to 4 permitted more to be done when the time was right.

Of itself, the Vandenberg resolution was never sufficient to give Europeans the sense of security they required. All parties knew this. While covert conversations proceeded among military staff of the prospective allies, no overt movement toward an alliance was initiated until the election campaign had ended. Alliance became the public issue in the president's triumphant State of the Union message of 1949, when the nation was told of negotiations for "a joint agreement designed to strengthen the security of the North Atlantic area." The five Brussels countries became the twelve members of the North Atlantic Treaty, ranging from Canada and the United States through Iceland to Portugal, Italy, and the Scandinavian countries of Denmark and Norway. Part of the reasoning behind the wider scope of the alliance was the greater protection enlarged membership would bring. A larger part of the reasoning, from the American standpoint, was its use in warding off attacks by isolationists against an alliance with exclusively European powers. President Truman observed in Point Three of his State of the Union message in 1949 that "such an arrangement would take the form of a collective defense arrangement under the terms of the United Nations Charter."[30]

Unlike Senate Resolution 234, the North Atlantic Treaty's attempt to exploit a connection with the United Nations evoked protests. The nature of the treaty made it difficult for even the most eloquent defenders to evade charges of American desertion, not only of the traditions of the nineteenth century but also of the idea of collective security which the nation had embraced during World War II. The treaty put the United States into a military alliance with the very countries Washington's Farewell Address and the Monroe Doctrine had warned against. It was an explicit acceptance of the reality of balance of power as the dominant force in international affairs, no matter how liberally the language of the treaty spoke of Article 51 or hinted at its likeness to Articles 52 and 53 of the Charter. Exposure of the conflict between Treaty and Charter was unavoidable.

Not that the administration put aside its mask of compatibility. Acheson prepared the country for the Atlantic pact in a major radio address on March 18, 1949, in which he made a point of observing that "the pact is carefully and consciously designed to conform in every particular with the Charter of the United Nations."[31] He also, however, recognized the embarrassment such a statement could create for the government. He blamed the press for challenging the claim, suggesting in his memoirs that "they were inclined to bring to the reporting of foreign affairs the same nose for controversial spot news that they had learned to look for in City Hall and police-court beats. This did the country and their readers a disservice."[32] James Reston of the *New York Times* presented a different view. He felt that if the Treaty planners had not emphasized the harmony between Treaty and Charter, opponents of one or the other would have had more difficulty in locating their targets.[33]

For all the secretary's hauteur and sarcasm, he was dealing with issues which were both emotional and newsworthy. The United States, by means of a military alliance, was abandoning a tradition of nonentanglement in the politics of Europe. It was hardly surprising that critics, despite the administration's disclaimers, should recognize this fact and react accordingly. The issue of the Charter was nonsense to Acheson; he may have wanted to soothe the country with it, but he expected leaders to understand and to ignore.

Vandenberg, with a greater capacity for self-delusion, convinced himself that the pact could stay "strictly within the Constitution of the United States and within the Charter of the United Nations."[34] Warren Austin's position as ambassador to the United Nations was more painful and required even more elaborate rationalization. He was equal to the assignment. Committed to the ideals of the Charter, he refused to find any incompatibility between the two instruments. He assured himself that the North Atlantic Treaty had nothing to do with older alliances or with the balance-of-power system. "The old veteran, balance of power," he revealed at the hearings of the Foreign Relations

Committee, "was given a blue discharge when the United Nations was formed."[35] The Treaty, meeting the principles of the Charter, obviously would not permit reenlistment of the old system. What made the Treaty necessary was its legal way, as Vandenberg informed one of his constituents, for "peaceful nations to defend international justice and security scrupulously within the Charter but outside the veto."[36]

All of the above images had been marshalled earlier in the Truman Doctrine and the Marshall Plan debates. Conformity of intention with the charter smoothed ambiguities. But unlike the other measures, the Treaty demanded an explication of its text. It was not enough to sprinkle so many references to the United Nations in the text that the unwary reader might believe that the Security Council had drafted the Treaty. A treaty whose title suggested a regional arrangement and whose language emphasized the common culture of a region invited challenge of its harmony with Articles 53 and 54 of Chapter VIII of the Charter. Article 53 states that "no enforcement action shall be taken under regional arrangements or by regional agencies without the authorization of the Security Council." Article 54 provides that "the Security Council shall at all times be kept fully informed of activities undertaken or in contemplation under regional arrangements or by regional agencies." The North Atlantic Treaty could meet neither requirement. The nation whose abuse of the veto made NATO necessary was a permanent member of the Security Council.

Nevertheless, the vagueness of the charter's definition of regionalism tempted policymakers to exploit a connection. Austin asserted that "in certain of its aspects, the Treaty is also a regional arrangement. . . . The point I am making is that if in the operation of the Treaty the signatories go into the exercise of duties that fall within the chapter [VIII], then the chapter applies."[37] It is worth noting, however, that the administration took no chances; no articles of Chapter VIII appear in the text.

The United Nations Charter, Article 51, on the other hand, with its emphasis on the right of individual or collective defense, was specifically identified in Article 5 of the Treaty. Here was a major rampart of legality around which the defenders of the pact intended to rally. Unlike the articles in Chapter VIII, its implementation required no Security Council authorization. It involved an issue anterior to the establishment of the United Nations, the inherent right of self-defense. Ambassador Austin claimed: "In my mind Article 51 does not grant a power. It merely prohibits anything contained in the Charter cutting across existing power."[38] But whether a nation or group of nations could organize for this purpose before an attack was made remained a major question. It raised other questions as well. If the Treaty really conformed to Article 51, was it a wise provision? Would a careless use of this vital article permit any nation to call another an aggressor and then go on to fight a war as if the United Nations did not exist? Senators Forrest Donnell and Claude Pepper pressed the administration for answers to all these questions. If the administration accepted these risks, they would also have to admit that behind the murky language of the Treaty lurked "the old veteran, balance of power," whom Austin was so determined to bury.

The interest groups which had made themselves heard over the Truman Doctrine and Marshall Plan quickly found the trail opened by congressional critics of the Atlantic pact. Liberals and pacifists who had reluctantly accepted the Marshall Plan now claimed to find in NATO confirmation of the fears first raised in the Greek aid bill. Quaker spokesmen were particularly eloquent in their concerns over the fate of the United Nations. In a widely publicized American Friends Service report, *The United States and the Soviet Union: Some Quaker Proposals for Peace*, a challenge was laid down: "Mere statements of loyalty to the United Nations are not sufficient. But statements of loyalty, followed by actions which contribute to the strengthening of the United Nations, and to an extension of its authority could help initiate a new era in which some of the present inadequacies could be overcome."[39] Specifically offensive, in the words of Reverend A. Stauffer Curry of the Church of the Brethren, was the power of the Atlantic Council "to determine when joint action should be taken by signatory nations against an alleged aggressor." In this event, he claimed, "the Council created by the North Atlantic Treaty would in effect sit in judgment upon the United Nations."[40] Familiar unhappy memories were raised by Reverend J. Paul Cotton of Cleveland, who was convinced that exploitive European powers would "undermine the prestige of the United Nations by the promotion of military alliances, which have always led to war, just as the League of Nations was undermined."[41]

The orthodox Left, particularly the survivors of the Progressive presidential campaign, predictably spoke of doom for the United Nations, of war provoked by this measure. Henry Wallace saw the Treaty not only as a violation of the Charter but of Franklin D. Roosevelt's dream of the world's future. Accusing Acheson of "being less than frank with the American people," he said that "the pact substitutes for the one world of the United Nations the two hostile worlds of a 'divided nation.'" His own solutions would be "agreement by both nations to give up all military bases in other United Nations countries and to halt the export of weapons to other nations."[42]

Conservative critics were more muted than they had been about the Truman Doctrine and Marshall Plan. Outside Congress—and inside, too—the rhetoric of anticommunism and the attractiveness of affirmative action on the part of the administration won adherents. Hamilton Fish, a former congressman from New York distinguished for his isolationism in the 1930s, felt "compelled, because of the rotten mess we made of it in Europe, to urge our joining the North Atlantic Pact as a peace measure in defense of the remaining free nations of Europe against Soviet aggression.''[43] Although snares remained in the Treaty, as in the United Nations, as long as Britain and France were present, many of the older isolationists joined reluctantly with liberal internationalists in accepting what they felt was inevitable. Consequently, testimony against the Treaty from the Right was confined to extremists who found NATO part of a Jewish conspiracy for world conquest or who found it, as Merwin K. Hart's National Economic Council did, a foolish waste of funds. Russia would occupy Europe anyway.[44] In such commentary the United Nations was irrelevant as an issue. The Treaty simply substituted for the Charter another insidious threat to American security.

What is impressive about much of the criticism of the pact in 1949 is not that the vulnerability of the administration's position went undiscovered or unexploited. Rather it was that the constituencies which cared were remarkably small. Pacifists and Progressives on the Left were articulate but predictable. They lacked an audience. Even smaller and more eccentric was the radical Right opposition, which appeared the captive of the lunatic fringes of politics; ten years earlier some of its leaders had been part of the mainstream of public opinion.

A striking measure of Truman's success was the ingathering of former liberal critics who had chafed over the Truman Doctrine or the Marshall Plan but now saw no alternative to the Treaty. Charles M. LaFollette, a member of Americans for Democratic Action, bowed to the administration's logic in light of the Communist peril. Borrowing from the record of Roosevelt, as Wallace had done for other purposes, LaFollette saw the treaty as a new version of quarantining aggressors, begun with Roosevelt's "famous speech of October 5, 1937." The ADA paid its respects to the conformity of the pact "with both the spirit and letter of the United Nations Charter." With more enthusiasm, LaFollette accepted the administration's point that the United Nation's "limitations must be faced" and that the troubles stemming from them must be blamed on the Russians.[45]

Acceptance was not without anguish. Unless the liberals ruled out the possibility of the redemption of Communists, they remained uneasy over Cold War measures. Gilbert Harrison of the liberal American Veterans Committee justified the pact only because it "buys time—time that can be used to renew our efforts to strengthen the United Nations and to work through that organization toward the ultimate security of some form of world government with limited but adequate power to prevent aggression."[46]

The administration's victory was dimmed only by the encouragement it continued to give to liberals and conservatives alike who wished to reshape the United Nations to American purposes. Some wanted revision of the Charter to remove the veto power from the permanent members of the Security Council. Others wanted to expel the Soviet Union from the United Nations and create a smaller, more manageable organization. While reform of the

Charter was not of itself objectionable to the administration, the form it might take could undo the security of Europe and the international commitments of the United States.

The new Atlantic Union Committee was a particularly unwelcome ally of the partisans of the pact. An outgrowth of Clarence Streit's original vision of Anglo-American federation, the Atlantic Union Committee saw in the Treaty a halfway house to a new Atlantic federation along the lines of the American Union. Its leaders had been makers of policy in 1947, former Secretary of War Robert P. Patterson and former Undersecretary of State William L. Clayton. Strongly anticommunist, they believed, in the words of Clayton, that the Treaty was "a step that is necessary in order to convince Soviet Russia that the members of the Atlantic Pact will stand together for the preservation of their independence and integrity."[47] They equated the Atlantic federation with a little United Nations that would fulfill the promise of peace.

The vigor of the committee and the fame of its directors were embarrassing to the administration. The Atlantic Union Committee's chairman, Justin Blackwelder, wanted credit for stimulating a "NATO mood" in 1949. He claimed that "people inside the Department of State have told us we were very helpful in getting the Atlantic Pact ratified. The extreme Right was so busy attacking us that it made the Department's job easier."[48] Be this as it may, pursuit of a transformed United Nations invited new attacks from Right and Left: from the Right because of the intimacy with Western Europe that it promised; from the Left because it would sacrifice the original United Nations.

Yet the administration and its congressional allies were themselves responsible for holding out hopes of reforming the charter. The platform of both Republicans and Democrats in the election of 1948 had referred respectively to the removal "of any veto in the peaceful settlement of international disputes" and to leading "the way toward curtailment of the use of the veto." Senator Taft reminded his colleagues, in his denunciation of the treaty on the floor of the Senate, that the Vandenberg Resolution opened with a recommendation for "a voluntary agreement to remove the veto from all questions involving specific settlements of international disputes, and situations, and from the admission of new members." He pointed out that this clause had been conspicuously ignored.[49] He was correct. The administration had no genuine interest in pursuing the removal of the veto to its logical conclusion. To do so would have resulted in the departure of the Soviet Union from the world organization and a worsening of Cold War tensions. Such a consequence might have ended the life of the United Nations or formally converted it into an American protectorate. Neither alternative was desired.

Senator Taft's battle against the North Atlantic Treaty failed. He could not even win the vote of Senator Guy Gillette of Iowa, who had asked rhetorically if the Treaty "is a step within the framework of the United

Nations Charter or is it independent action which might be subversive of the success of world cooperation?"[50] Gillette suspected the latter to be true but joined 81 other senators in voting in favor of the treaty on July 21, 1949.

The administration won an impressive victory. It had been won by marshalling a wide variety of public opinion willing to suspend reservations for the sake of realizing a common objective of peace and security. Without the association with the United Nations, the respectability of the enterprise would have been in jeopardy. NATO would then have been an alliance outside the law, open to attack from every side. Harmonizing Cold War policies with the United Nations was the path the administration followed doggedly from 1947 to 1949 as it hoped to pluck the fruits of collective security while avoiding the thistles of isolationism.[51]

Deviousness and self-delusion were parts of the process of decisionmaking. But given the pressures from Europe in the late 1940s and also the lack of knowledge of Soviet intention, the administration achieved the stability it sought through a series of tradition-shaking changes in American foreign policy. Whatever one's estimation of the wisdom of the public or congressional mind, both the public and Congress are involved in the making of policy in the American democracy. The administration succeeded in fashioning an executive-legislative consensus, undergirded by the support of the articulate public, that permitted passage and implementation of its program.

The process was cumbersome as well as devious. But a frank and detailed presentation of the military and economic assistance programs or an elaboration of the implications of an alliance would have constituted a full repudiation of the isolationist past and the United Nations present. Rightly or wrongly, Truman's advisors believed that such acts would doom their cause.

4. Toward the Brussels Pact: December 1947-March 1948

If ever the time seemed both right and compelling for an entangling alliance between Europe and America, it was the dark winter of 1948. The failure of the London Conference of Foreign Ministers in December 1947 meant that American support for Western Europe would have to assume political and military as well as economic forms. The impasse over Germany seemed to portend a continuing conflict between the United States and the Soviet Union that might destroy Europe. European and American leaders alike recognized that economic recovery built on the Marshall Plan was not possible without a sense of military security, and that neither was attainable without closer links between Europe and America.

Americans themselves seemed prepared to break their isolationist tradition at this time. World War II had rehabilitated the Wilsonian vision of an earlier generation, culminating in the creation of the United Nations. When Soviet-American conflict threatened to nullify the work of the world organization, the Truman administration did not turn inward in the manner of 1920 but instead discovered the virtues of regional organization. What had been vague and desperate hopes of dedicated dreamers such as Richard Coudenhove-Kalergi were no longer a utopian dream but suddenly a genuine possibility.[1] From both political parties there were heard voices speaking the language of European union. As early as January 1947 John Foster Dulles in a major speech at the Waldorf Astoria Hotel in New York discovered in the difficulties over the economic division of Germany the larger issue of Western Europe's debilitating disunity. The solution for Europe would be a movement toward political federation. This theme was taken up by influential journalists from Dorothy Thompson to Walter Lippmann, and was to crystallize in the resolution of Senators William Fulbright and Elbert Thomas on March 21, 1947, that would have Congress favor "the creation of a United States of Europe within the framework of the United Nations."[2]

The Marshall Plan was the American response to these concerns, an expression of support for European unity. In 1947 the economic issue was paramount. Although Fulbright had spoken of the long tradition of European unity that embraced the Roman and Carolingian empires, he emphasized not the idealized past but the realistic problems of the present. Using the crisis in Greece and Turkey as the occasion for presenting his thesis, Fulbright on April 7 coupled his support for aid under the Truman Doctrine with a caveat that "unless we are able to create a different, a more sensible economic and political order in Europe, there is no hope for a prosperous or peaceful solution to her difficulties." His proposal for a united states of Europe would be a matter of good business sense, a means of America's winning repayment of the enormous investment it had made piecemeal in the recovery of Europe. "There is no simple, all-inclusive answer to this question," Fulbright observed, "but one of the essential conditions to any solution is the reestablishment of industry and commerce within the framework of a stable political system."[3]

With the breakdown of the London Conference, Ernest Bevin and Georges Bidault, foreign ministers of Britain and France, had become fully aware that there could be no economic stability without concurrent political and military security. They had discussed the possibility of a Western European defense pact in June 1947 when they were in Paris to respond to the Marshall Plan overtures.[4] Over the next six months Bidault became convinced not only of the need for a European alliance but also of the need for American involvement with it, and he pressed Bevin to bring up the issue with the Americans.[5]

Bevin agreed. Secretary of State George C. Marshall's Pilgrim Society address in London on December 12 offered an opportunity for the British foreign minister to make this case to the Americans, though the message was elliptical if not opaque. At the dinner the secretary of state commented on "the great surge of American public opinion in support of an effort to alleviate the sufferings and hardships of the people on this side of the Atlantic." He also took note of steady growth in relations between the two countries, which he claimed was a "natural growth in the case of two peoples enjoying a common heritage and having a common outlook on the fundamentals of human society."[6] Regarding this language as an overture, the British foreign minister discussed the idea of a common defense system at a private dinner with Marshall at his flat in Carlton Terrace on December 15, and expanded on the theme over the next two days.[7] The arrangements between Europe and America, Bevin assured his guest, would not be "a formal alliance, but an understanding backed by power, money and resolute action. It would be a sort of spiritual federation of the west."[8]

The United States responded on two levels. The secretary of state agreed with the general idea and even went so far as to authorize Gen. Matthew Ridgway, then in New York representing the Joint Chiefs of Staff at the

United Nations, to meet with his British and French counterparts in January 1948.[9] At the same time, Secretary Marshall wanted no public pronouncements of American interest in joining a European organization, preferring, as he did in the Pilgrims Society speech, to talk more of the material aspects of Western unity and of the beneficial effects that the European Recovery Program would have on the regeneration of Europe. In fact, when Bevin asked if he could share the substance of their conversations with the French, Under Secretary of State Robert A. Lovett concurred, as long as he made "clear to the French that our record shows Secretary Marshall indicated that he had not definitely approved any particular course of action and had hoped to receive specific British proposals before making a final commitment."[10]

On balance the American response was not satisfactory to Bevin. He felt he had to go beyond "the unwritten and informal understandings" he had first sought if he was to win a commitment from the United States. In a memorandum sent to the State Department on January 13 Bevin said clearly that the Marshall Plan was not enough to save Europe: "Essential though it is, progress in the economic field will not in itself suffice to call a halt to the Russian threat. Political and indeed spiritual forces must be mobilised in our defence." He was prepared to "seek to form with the backing of the Americans and the Dominions a Western democratic system comprising Scandinavia, the Low Countries, France, Italy, Greece and possibly Portugal. As soon as circumstances permit we should, of course, wish also to include Spain and Germany without whom no Western system can be complete."[11]

Once assured of Marshall's "wholehearted sympathy in this undertaking,"[12] Bevin delivered a major speech in the House of Commons on January 22 in which he announced: "Our representatives at Brussels, The Hague and Luxembourg were instructed yesterday to propose talks in consultation with their French colleagues. I hope that treaties will thus be signed with our near neighbors, the Benelux countries, making with France an important nucleus in western Europe. We shall also have to go outside the circle of our immediate neighbors. We shall have to consider including the new Italy, whose eventual inclusion is no less important than that of other countries of western 'Europe.' "[13] Bevin had opened a path to a European union in which Britain would play a vital part.

At no point did he mention a specific American role in the new political organization of the West. But the excitement that his speech created in the United States sparked the kinds of emotions which could move the United States to commit itself in a way that Secretary Marshall had refused up to this time. Senator Henry Cabot Lodge, Jr., interjected at a Senate hearing that it was a "historic declaration."[14] A leading spirit in kindling American feelings was the Republican foreign affairs advisor—and advisor also to Secretary

Marshall—John Foster Dulles, who George Kennan believed had returned from Europe in December shaken by what he had seen of the "panicky state of mind of the Europeans" and who then added his persuasive voice to reassure Europe. Testifying in support of the foreign assistance bill just two days before Bevin's speech, Dulles stressed the importance of unity: "There is need of sufficient political unity so that these states will present a solid front to any aggressor. The United Nations is not yet a strong enough reliance. So, there might be a regional pact, under article 51 of the United Nations Charter, like our hemispheric pact made at Rio last year. So long as there is no regional unity for security, each nation will be weak and afraid. Each will turn to us for moral and material support which could come, and properly should come, from a unity of their own making."[15] This was just the language Senator Fulbright had long been waiting to hear, as he urged his colleagues to listen closely to Dulles's "unanswerable arguments that this country should encourage the unity of Europe." He also reminded the Senate that his was among the many voices that had expressed similar sentiments over the past year, and that he had spoken for most of them when he introduced his resolution almost a year before to the Senate, which in turn referred it to the Committee on Foreign Relations "where it rests today."[16] Obviously Fulbright saw in the turn of events of the winter of 1948 a chance to bring the idea of a united states of Europe into fruition. Bevin's speech would accelerate the momentum.

Fulbright was not alone in his perceptions. Herbert Matthews, writing for the *New York Times*, found a striking coincidence in the timing of both Dulles's and Bevin's pronouncements and in the proposals for a Paris-Rome customs union a week before.[17] Reporting from Paris, Anne O'Hare McCormick found "an unconscious urge behind the movement that has become more actual in the last few weeks than in as many decades heretofore."[18] It was as if Bevin's initiative had been the signal that American supporters of European unity had been awaiting for years.

But who were these friends of Europe whom Bevin and Bidault obviously wished to enlist behind the defense of Europe? They represented no single view and indeed frequently represented conflicting views. The very fact that vague terms such as union, unification, unity, or even federation were so interchangeable encouraged for the moment each of the groups behind unity to believe that its own solutions to the problems of America or of Europe or of the world were advanced by the proposal for Western union. The submerging of sovereignty under a larger political unit might be the litmus test of unity, but even here there remained the question of how much or what kind of sovereignty would be yielded. Federation itself might mean anything from a functional act of cooperation, as in a customs union, to the fusing to several national governments into a single central government.

Most articulate Americans seeking unity addressed themselves to the world, to the United Nations, specifically, rather than to Europe. World government meant that war would be abolished and the promise of the Four Freedoms of World War II realized. Americans United for World Government in 1947 claimed twenty thousand members in thirty-one states. It was led by such luminaries as Mrs. J. Borden Harriman, former minister to Norway, and the influential news analyst Raymond Swing. Even more single-minded in their efforts on behalf of international government were the World Federalists. At a congress in Asheville, North Carolina, February 22, 1947, these two groups joined forces with four smaller societies to become the United World Federalists with the immediate goal of convoking a constitutional convention to amend the United States Constitution so as to grant new powers to the United Nations.[19] Faith in the United Nations had been so high in the recent past and the divisions within the UN so frustrating that activists received attention from governmental leaders even when their ideas were rejected.

For the European protagonists of unification, from Churchill to Coudenhove-Kalergi, these views were either irrelevant to their needs in 1948 or a diversion from their purposes. They had reason to be disturbed. American federalists agreed only on the need for change. Some wished for an unofficial route avoiding governmental channels as a more favorable milieu wherein a world constituent assembly could prepare the way for a world constitution; others wanted this task to be done by senior statesmen of the leading nations. Still others regarded themselves as "universalists," insisting on a membership that would include all nations, including the Soviet Union, while the "nuclear" supporters either wanted a regional government to serve as model for others or wished to use the power of the United States to recreate the United Nations into an instrument that excluded the Soviet Union.[20] One-worlders and isolationists alike found uses for world federalism.

But more disturbing to European governments because they appeared more practical than the United World Federalists and because their ideas appeared to be closer to those of European federationists were the enthusiasts centered around journalist Clarence K. Streit and his widely celebrated book *Union Now*. His idea in 1939 initially had been to promote a joining of the Anglo-American democracies at a time when the survival of Great Britain was at stake. After the war it came to embrace fifteen North Atlantic democracies including the self-governing dominions of the British Commonwealth. His union would be modeled on the American federal union of 1787.[21]

Given the troubles in Europe in 1948 and the genuine empathy for European unity on the part of American friends, it is understandable that statesmen of the rank of Supreme Court Justice Owen Roberts and Under Secretary of State for Economic Affairs Will Clayton, an architect of the Marshall Plan, would have been attracted to this position. But Streit's position, which was to become that of the Atlantic Union Committee in 1949, signified American membership in the new Europe, with a resulting distortion of the "United States of Europe."

The implications of the American role drew fire from American isolationists who for their own reasons welcomed European federation. Their support of the Marshall Plan was conditioned upon Europe's willingness to stand up to the Soviet Union, and it seemed that the only sensible way for Europeans to make their stand was through unification. "I favor using the Marshall Plan only as a means of persuading western nations to form a federation or union of democratic nations, and to organize a united defense against Soviet Russia. It is their only chance to survive as free nations. If the Socialist governments of western Europe refuse to cooperate for defensive purposes, then we should stop all shipments under the Marshall Plan except food." Such was the verdict of Congressman Hamilton Fish of New York during the February hearings on the European Recovery Program. Only slightly less strident was the opinion of Ray Sawyer, national legislative director of the American Veterans of World War II, testifying before the House two weeks earlier.[21]

The Marshall Plan must not be a one-way street of charity. It must be the two-way street of trade—trade among the 16 nations concerned, and trade between them and the United States. As a condition for receiving aid from the United States, we should insist that the ultimate goal in western Europe be a United States of western Europe, irrespective of what you may call it, a union similar to the Union of independent American States out of which grew the United States of America. United, Europe can stand on its own feet as a powerful united states of Europe. Divided, Europe can only repeat its own history, a history of wars, wars, and more wars.[22]

For what the Atlantic Unionists believed to be the wrong reasons some isolationists emerged as supporters of a federated Europe. Clarence Streit himself wrote an angry and sarcastic note commenting on former isolationist Senator Burton K. Wheeler's espousal of the cause. Streit claimed that Wheeler and his followers pushed for European union so that the United States "would escape responsibility, while enjoying the satisfaction of either seeing our federal principles adopted by others, or, in the event of failure, confirming the view that the British and Europeans are hopeless."[23]

But potential American involvement disturbed Europeans as well. The Atlantic approach to union inspired familiar fears from Gaullists, but it also evoked expressions of concern from statesmen and political thinkers who did not share the anger and contempt frequently identified with the Gaullists' position on America.[24] Such a serious European federalist as the Dutch scholar and statesman Hendriks Brugmans showed no animosity toward the United States but felt that it was "unlikely that the medium states of Europe are

prepared to enter a federation where one power—America—is predominant."
An Atlantic approach of this sort risked the loss of European identity.
Moreover, he recognized that the American experience did not provide a
useful model for Europeans, with their culturally distinct fatherlands. Any
federal system that would unite Europe would have to be "extremely different
from those of the American type. . . . It would therefore be wholly unrealistic
to put the European 'states' on the same footing as those that formed their
'more perfect union' in North America around 1780."[25] Certainly when Winston Churchill first used the term "United States of Europe" in Zurich in
September 1946, he was thinking of a union of Europeans among themselves,
not of Europeans with Americans.[27]

Richard Coudenhove-Kalergi, the leader of European unification in the
early twentieth century and an experienced analyst of the divisive elements
within all the movements, could not have been unaware of ambiguities in the
support of Americans. Yet they seemed to pale in significance to the events of
the winter of 1948. The perilous state of Europe's economies, the growing
fear of Soviet pressure, and the specific crises over the division of Germany
and the prospective elections in Italy all seemed to herald the moment when
the world would witness what he had been preaching since the 1920s: the
creation of a united Europe. Threatened by Communist expansion, Europe at
last seemed ready to move beyond limited intergovernmental acts of cooperation to a genuine union. The United States, motivated both by its own fears of
communism and by its own tradition of enlightened self-interest, would be the
midwife of the new Europe. Coudenhove-Kalergi believed that he could exploit America's obsession with communism to accelerate its support of his
cause.[27]
    It was in high spirits that Coudenhove-Kalergi returned to the United
States in January as secretary-general of his European Parliamentary Union,
expecting to use the congressional debates over the European Recovery Program as the vehicle to win decisive American assistance for his project. In
light of the accelerating pace of American opinion and action since Dulles had
made his seminal speech a year before and since Fulbright had offered his
Senate resolution, it was not surprising that he could anticipate the successful
conclusion of his labors. In the United States every element had at least
seemed to fall into place—White House, State Department, both houses of
Congress, and public opinion. Having credited himself with inspiring Fulbright's resolution on the united states of Europe, he felt no sense of presump-
tion when he told a reporter in New York that he had come back to America to
"coordinate the union of Europe with the Marshall Plan."[28]
    In Washington Coudenhove-Kalergi informed the government that the
Marshall Plan could save Europe not only by its dollars and other material

assistance but by the moral lift it would have upon European unification. He recalled that his "proposals fell everywhere on fertile ground," and he had "thorough" conversations with President Truman and Secretary of State Marshall, both of whom impressed him as being serious and supportive. He spoke also with the principal figures in the State Department, such as Charles E. Bohlen, counselor of the department, George F. Kennan, director of the Policy Planning Staff, and John D. Hickerson, director of the Office of European Affairs. They were all pleased to hear Coudenhove-Kalergi's account of the rapid progress of the European movement and declared themselves ready to serve it in every possible way. Although he did not take credit for Bevin's address to the House of Commons, he did regard it as a complementary promotion of his own efforts to establish the Brussels Pact and to insure passage of the Foreign Assistance Act. Both those objectives came to pass during his 1948 visit to the United States.[29] When he returned to Europe in April he left behind the American Committee for a Free and United Europe which he had founded on April 18, with Senator Fulbright as president and such luminaries as General William Donovan, former President Hoover, former isolationist Senator Burton K. Wheeler, socialist leader Norman Thomas, and former Office of Strategic Services leader Allen Welsh Dulles as members.[30]

The conjunction of the escalating Communist pressure on the West with the Marshall Plan's success and the establishment of the Brussels Pact helped to convince Coudenhove-Kalergi that his hopes were close to realization. The events that followed in 1948 and 1949 did not dim them immediately, but they should have raised some doubts. Would they lead toward a united states of Europe? The Organization of European Economic Cooperation established by the European beneficiaries of the Marshall Plan reflected not a federal approach to unity but intergovernmental cooperation. As another leader of Europe, Jean Monnet, noted, "I could not help seeing the intrinsic weakness of a system that went no further than mere cooperation between Governments."[31] Nor did the North Atlantic Treaty, which grew out of the Brussels Pact, lead necessarily to European union on any but a traditional level of an alliance's obligations. And even if it should, would American involvement be suffocating if the Atlantic alliance truly became an Atlantic community? Were the leaders of France and Britain converts at last, or were they exploiting the language of European union as a way of appeasing or of entangling Americans? By appearing to move toward a united states of Europe they would be more likely to secure the military and other aid needed to fend off Communist pressures.

It is obvious that Coudenhove-Kalergi chose not to look too deeply into the background of the people he encountered and the actions that took place. He was a willing prisoner of his own dreams and of politicians' words. The fact that the preamble of the "Marshall-Plan-Gesetz" seemed to link the promise of European unity to American economic aid ignored both the vagueness of the "joint organization" recommended by Congress and the fact that a preamble, no matter how stirring, carries in itself no legal significance.[32] For Coudenhove-Kalergi to believe that Truman or Marshall or Bohlen hung on his words, let alone was converted by them, was a species of self-delusion. Although the Austrian nobleman was a recognized voice of a new Europe and a positive influence on legislators such as J. William Fulbright, he was for the men in power in Europe and America just a symbol of a constituency that had to be attended to and perhaps even mobilized. But on their scale of priorities Coudenhove-Kalergi and his movement ranked far behind other more urgent issues.

The response of the State Department to his request for a meeting with the secretary of state in February 1948 was signally revealing of the administration's attitude toward European unity as a political movement. In seeking an audience with Marshall through Charles Bohlen, counselor of the State Department, Coudenhove-Kalergi made the point that if he failed to meet with the secretary of state it could damage his work in Europe because "nobody there would understand why I have not seen the Secretary during my prolonged visit to the United States."[33] Bohlen was not much impressed. As he told John D. Hickerson, director for European affairs, "Coudenhove-Kalergi has been on my neck. I saw him when he was down here. You will note that he wants me to try to get him in to see the secretary. Could you let me have an estimate of his standing in Europe and whether his advocacy of European federation is taken sufficiently seriously abroad to justify recommendation that the secretary see him or is it more of a personal gambit?"[34] Hickerson's answer was that Coudenhove-Kalergi's position as secretary-general of the European Parliamentary Union was important enough, in light of Bevin's speech and the "widespread support in this country for some kind of federation," that his request should be accepted. "If he does not see the Secretary for a *few minutes* it might indicate that we have less interest in sponsoring a European federation than is the case."[35]

Such was the actual setting for meeting between Count Coudenhove-Kalergi and Secretary Marshall, as opposed to the description given in the former's memoirs. Bohlen's recommendation to Marshall's staff contained the caveat: "I don't think it needs to be 15 minutes unless the Secretary got interested."[36] The suggestion of fifteen minutes or less evokes an image of busy officials handling a crank if not a bore to whom they paid attention only because of possibly unhappy repercussions if they failed to go through the motions of civility.

American counterparts of Coudenhove-Kalergi received similar treatment; these enthusiasts for European unity had no more to offer policymakers but frequently were too well placed to ignore either as power brokers or as personal symbols. Thus the journalist Dorothy Thompson's interest in publishing a pan-European weekly magazine in the United States that would promote the idea of European unification in Western European countries came to the attention of the State Department as a gratuitous irritant. No matter how noble its motivation, the plan could be interpreted as another American interference in a purely European problem and would invite resentment abroad among friends as well as enemies. Thompson and Coudenhove-Kalergi were considered amateurs who had goals that were either unrealistic or disturbing to American policy. An unsatisfied Dorothy Thompson received a letter of mild encouragement from the secretary of state but with the proviso that the circulation of the new magazine be limited to American supporters of pan-Europe and that it should not be distributed to Europeans.[37]

There was no doubt that European unity occupied the minds of American planners in the winter of 1948. The exigencies of the moment would have demanded no less even if Bevin's speech had not dramatized it. But a united states of Europe that subsumed traditional sovereignties under a new and higher sovereignty taxed their patience. It seemed utopian. More to the point was a European union in the form of a traditional alliance system that would demand military and political as well as economic obligations from America. The policymakers of the State Department saw the direction toward which Bevin and Bidault were pushing, and understood its legitimacy even as they wished to shy away from political commitments.[38]

Theodore C. Achilles, director for Western European affairs in the State Department in 1947 and 1948, recalled a conversation he had with his superior, John Hickerson, on New Year's eve 1947 at the Metropolitan Club in Washington. The conversation had been preceded by generous libations of fishhouse punch. He remembered Hickerson saying, "I don't care whether entangling alliances have been considered worse than original sin since George Washington's time. We've got to negotiate a military alliance with Western Europe in peacetime and we've got to do it quickly." Achilles said, "Fine, when do we start?" Hickerson said, "I've already started it. Now it is your baby. Get going."[39] Hickerson then elaborated. Marshall had told him of his conversation with Bevin at the breakup of the Council of Foreign Ministers when Bevin gave him almost word for word the statement on European union he was to offer to the Commons on January 22. While Marshall wanted to keep the union strictly "European," it was Hickerson who felt that only an American commitment to fight would give substance to that union, and Clarence Streit's *Union Now* was his and Achilles's inspiration for urging an American military alliance as a means of promoting European unity.[40]

But the pace of American collaboration continued to lag behind the thinking of these State Department officers. When Bevin's plan unfolded as an Anglo-French proposal for a union of Western Europe along the lines of the recently completed Treaty of Dunkirk, Hickerson reacted negatively at first. He seemed to share the reservations of Belgium's Premier Paul-Henri Spaak, who felt that the Dunkirk model was sterile since the purpose of this Anglo-French alliance was merely to contain potential German aggression. But while Hickerson called Bevin's first step "highly dubious" he did recommend that the Rio Pact, an inter-American regional defense arrangement, might be the best solution to Europe's security. It would require American adherence, just as the Treaty of Rio de Janeiro did.[41]

Kennan also expressed reservations about making the Dunkirk pact the basis of the projected European union. Unlike Hickerson, he deemed undesirable the military emphasis implied in the Rio and Dunkirk treaties: "Military union should not be the starting point. It should flow from the political, economic, and spiritual union—not vice versa." An obvious military alliance might frighten away rather than attract potential members such as the Scandinavian countries. "If there is to be 'union,'" he asserted, "it must have some reality in economic and technical and administrative arrangements; and there must be some real federal authority."[42]

Bevin had been aware of the many American caveats long before he made his speech, but he listened less to the disclaimers Americans were making and more to the hints of support and even of eventual membership, later if not earlier—at a "second stage" if not at the first stage, as Lord Inverchapel, the British ambassador to the United States, recognized. The British would have accepted, even preferred, the half-way measure of an Anglo-American defense agreement to precede their discussions with the European powers.[43] But even as Lovett dodged this and other ploys to commit the United States to participation in a European union, the American diplomats all gave credence to Bevin's understanding that none of the forthcoming European security arrangements would be effective without American involvement. For the moment there was an impasse. The British and French were convinced that a Western union would be meaningless without American participation; the Americans responded that until Europe organized itself, as in a Western union, the United States could not consider participation.[44]

Fortunately, Dutch and Belgian discomfort with the first Anglo-French proposals for a Western union relieved Americans of having to make an immediate decision. The Low Countries were even more disturbed about the Dunkirk model than the Americans had been and welcomed Lovett's assertion that the Anglo-French proposal to extend the Dunkirk Treaty to Belgium and the Netherlands had been made without Secretary Marshall's approval.[45] The Belgians and Dutch also disapproved of the bilateral nature of Bevin's and

Bidault's plans, which would have had each member sign separately with
Great Britain and France. They made a counterproposal on February 19,
1948, of a regional organization of Western Europe that would have an
economic as well as political and military character in conformity with the
United Nations Charter and worked out with their collaboration.[46] These
divisions within the future Western union underscored Marshall's caution
about American association with the union. Although the United States "has
hastily welcomed Bevin's initiative. . . . We should not be asked to consider
associating ourselves with such program until picture of what western European Govts themselves are going to do about it is much clearer."[47]

Neither demurrers from the State Department nor conflicting views
among the Western Europeans seemed to dampen the excitement displayed by
American enthusiasts for a united states of Europe in the winter of 1948. A
new Europe was an imperative that made the crisis with the Soviet Union an
opportunity, not a disaster; that gave a meaning to foreign aid it would not
have had otherwise. On February 16 before a national conference of mayors at
the Waldorf Astoria, Bernard Baruch, a powerful if nominally private per-
sonage, expressed "great and high hopes of the Marshall Plan, but I have high
hopes of it only if Europe will help itself. The best thing that Europe can do to
help itself is to have some joint union of defense against aggression in which
we should help them." A week later at another meeting in the Waldorf Astoria
former President Herbert Hoover in the presence of Georges Bidault urged the
sixteen nations of the Marshall Plan to constitute themselves as a regional
federal union with links similar to the Rio Pact. Not only did this veteran
isolationist sound like a member of the Vandenberg wing of his party, but the
language was that of the Truman administration. It was even bolder, as
Hoover was moved to observe that George Washington would have amended
his declaration on entangling alliances in the face of Europe's present needs.[48]

The particular historical precedent fitting the current situation, in the
minds of the American foreign-policy elites, liberal and conservative, was
America under the Articles of Confederation in the 1780s, when the Founding
Fathers introduced the federal constitution as the solution to the troubles of
government. America in the 1940s once again would be the inspiration from
Zion, offering not simply arms and monies but a model for a better society.
The popularity of Carl Van Doren's *The Great Rehearsal*, a recounting of the
making of the United States Constitution, lay in the message it offered to its
readers when it appeared in the fall of 1947. Justice William O. Douglas,
writing in the *New York Herald-Tribune*, wanted the book to be "printed in
every language. For the problems it poses are for the several nations, not for
this country alone." Van Doren himself prompted reviewers to make the
comparison, as he noted that his book "might be, though of course no one of

them ever used the term, a rehearsal for the federal government of the future."[49]

The administration took advantage of this mood by reminding senators, as ambassador to Britain Lewis Douglas did in the hearings on the European Recovery Program, of Hamilton's attempts at Annapolis in 1786 to convert a loose confederation into a genuine federal union, and urging Europeans "to arrive at the sort of economic integration among the respective States which finally resulted in the type of economic federal union that we now have." Without claiming that the Europeans of the 1940s were "on all fours with our historical experience," he nevertheless made a point of noticing that the Europeans were taking stock of their situation much as Americans had done in the 1780s. The current movement of France and Italy, the Benelux, and the Scandinavian countries toward customs unions reminded Douglas of the initial actions of the Founding Fathers in making unity out of diversity.[50]

In the midst of the activity swirling about the prospective union of Europe, the Czech crisis erupted late in February 1948. If a normal united states of Europe did not materialize in its wake, it at least accelerated the establishment of the Western union in Brussels as well as the passage of the Foreign Assistance Act in Washington, and made more imminent the intimate American association with Europe that Bevin and Bidault had been seeking. The sudden ending of a Western-oriented democracy in Prague quickly narrowed the gap between the Anglo-French and Benelux positions over union. The new Communist ministry of Klement Gottwald assumed power February 25, Foreign Minister Jan Masaryk fell to his death March 10, and the Treaty of Brussels was signed March 17. The shock was all the greater because the most notable victim of Communist intimidation, President Eduard Benes, had succumbed to the Nazis ten years earlier.

The American response was quick and sharp. Military measures would have to be associated with whatever links the United States would have with noncommunist Europe. As the news of Benes's bowing to Soviet pressure for a Communist-controlled government reached the United States, James Reston of the *New York Times* perceived that Communist maneuvers in Czechoslovakia had brought the security problem into focus alongside the Marshall Plan. The fate of the Czechs was a warning that Europeans by themselves could not contain internal subversion combined with external threats, and that without an American commitment that went beyond economic aid the rest of Europe, most immediately Italy, would suffer the same experience.[51]

The forthcoming Italian elections in April were particularly alarming because of the imminent prospect of a well-organized Communist party winning enough votes to control the cabinet. While it was too late to help Czechoslovakia, it was not too late for the United States to take drastic steps to help Italian democracy. On the eve of the Brussels Pact the National Security Council recommended a series of proposals with respect to American relations with Italy. Among them would be an active administration role in soliciting influential congressmen to announce their opposition to any economic aid to Italy should the new government include parties hostile to the interests of the United States. The National Security Council also urged a strong letter-writing campaign by Italian-Americans to support anticommunist parties in the forthcoming election. And most pertinent in March was a recommendation to "press for immediate inclusion of Italy in negotiations for Western Union and the announcement thereof to the British and French."[52]

Both Bevin and Bidault seized the moment of crisis to press the United States to make the ultimate commitment to the West: namely, to attach itself to the beleaguered West. Bidault wrote an eloquent and poignant note to Marshall asking the United States to give Europe the means to protect itself. He pleaded for "la collaboration de l'ancien et du nouveau monde, si étroitement solitaires dan leur attachement a la seule civilisation qui vaille. . . ."[53]

Bevin was more specific in his importunities. Dismissing the joint U.S.-U.K.-French statement on Czechoslovakia as unlikely to deter Soviet expansion, he advanced the idea of a private meeting of Western Europe, including Italy, with the United States, preferably in Washington, "for the purpose of exploring what steps all may take collectively, or in groups, to prevent the extension of the area of dictatorship."[54]

Although neither Douglas in London nor Marshall in Washington responded in the manner Bevin had hoped, Hickerson did. Taking the initiative once again in his advice to the secretary of state, he emphasized the importance of showing both the Soviets and the Western Europeans "concrete evidence of American determination to resist further Communist encroachment," or risk the spread of a "certain bandwagon effect" that would serve the Communists in Italy and elsewhere.[55] Indeed, on the very day that Hickerson offered his memorandum, March 8, Norway reported its fears that it might have to face Soviet demands for the kind of treaty that would reduce Norway to the level of Czechoslovakia. To make any negotiations among the Western powers successful, it was essential, asserted Hickerson, that the United States "participate in or support such arrangements" as the Europeans make. Hence, he recommended "the possibility of U.S. participation in a North Atlantic-Mediterranean regional defense arrangement based on Articles 51 and 52 of the United Nations Charter and including initially Great Britain, France, Benelux and Italy," to begin in Washington or in Europe on March 15.[56]

The issue of military alliance was suddenly in the air. As early as March 1 the press interpreted President Truman's noncommittal answer to a question about the United States seeking a military tie as confirming that the matter was at least under study: "Slowly and in the manner of a man who is with-holding something in the back of his mind, Mr. Truman said that he could not comment at this time."[57] Within the administration the staff of the National Security Council was charged with drafting papers that would treat the position of the United States with respect to the new Western union and the problem of providing military assistance to its members. To quell incipient panic among Europeans the administration even considered adding a new section, Title VI, to the Foreign Assistance Act of 1948 that would offer military as well as economic assistance.[58]

The fever reached its highest pitch in the first two weeks of March. In Paris the meeting of the Marshall Plan nations that was to produce the Organization for European Economic Cooperation was to open March 15. In London the three Western allies had been meeting since February on German problems that would lead to a currency consolidation within a Trizonia and ultimately to sovereignty for western Germany. From Berlin on March 5 came a dramatic warning from General Lucius D. Clay, commander-in-chief of United States forces in Europe and military governor of the United States Zone of Germany, that war with the Soviet Union "may come with dramatic suddenness."[59]

Small wonder that the Western Europeans put aside their differences at Brussels to sign the collective defense treaty in that city twelve days later. Nor is it surprising that the adherents of the united states of Europe would "have good hopes," as Coudenhove-Kalergi said "of seeing in 1948 or 1949 the great day when all the bells of free Europe will ring to greet the opening of a new and brighter page of history: the birthday of the United States of Europe"; or that they would exult with Spaak on the occasion of approval of the Treaty of Brussels by the Belgian Parliament: "A new page had been turned in the annals of history. A new chapter was about to begin in the Western world."[60] Such was the mood of fear and hope as the Western Union came into being with America's blessing on March 17, 1948.[61]

While their expectations were not wholly illusionary, the chapters and pages of the immediate future would not be dramatically different from those of the past. Too many meanings could be attached to the idea of a "United States of Europe." For the leaders of France and Britain, European unity was primarily a semantic device to entangle Americans in the defense of Europe; their common cause was still expressed most clearly in a classical military alliance, which would be defective without American involvement. For American leaders European unification was important to win public support of their European program, but they were still wary of the designs of Europeans to force greater commitments from the United States than the nation would tolerate. For the interested American public European unity was a vague community to be created in the American image, an idea that was flattering, yet practical if it would assure efficient use of American assistance without the necessity for American membership.

It was the enthusiasm which European federalists found in such abundance among Americans that led them to the conviction that the hour was at hand for the conversion of Western Europe. What they secured instead was the conversion of America. Weighing the risks of moving into a new treaty without guarantees from the United States, Foreign Minister Bevin, according to Gladwyn Jebb, had few doubts: "It seemed pretty clear that the Americans would, in fact, come in in the long run, and recent events in the Continent have made this all the more likely."[62] The result was not the establishment of an independent united states of Europe, but the North Atlantic Treaty Organization. Within a year the Western Union of five became the Atlantic alliance of twelve.

5. Brussels Pact
to Atlantic Alliance:
March-December 1948

The high hopes which European federationists and their American friends had vested in the Brussels Pact and in the president's reaction to it could not be sustained indefinitely. The way to a unified Europe was to be longer and more circuitous than the events of March seemed to indicate. It was not that Truman was unresponsive to the plight of Europe or to the promise which the Brussels Pact seemed to hold for the future. European leaders of the new Western Union and American policymakers in the State Department and National Security Council diverted American assistance along other channels.

The potential of a united Europe burying its divided past in a new strength and prosperity was very much on the president's mind when he pondered his reply to the signing of the Brussels Treaty. But the immediate dangers from communism absorbed him more than the future benefits of unity. The former were so significant that he made last-minute changes in his plans for a St. Patrick's Day address in New York on March 17. The New York speech was to have been, according to White House Administrative Assistant George Elsey, "a trial balloon for a modified 'get tough' policy; trial balloon for Congress." But after becoming aware of an emergency war plan prepared by the Joint Chiefs of Staff in the wake of the Czech crisis, Truman felt he had to deal more vigorously and more urgently with the problems of Europe. Hence, he determined to make a dramatic address to the Congress underscoring his concern for the Western Union and then fly up to New York for his scheduled speech on domestic affairs.[1]

Secretary of State Marshall would have preferred "a weak message" in "simple businesslike" language that would not exude an air of belligerency.[2] But the president was more attentive to the insistence of advisor Clark Clifford that the tone of the message and the legislation it asked would justify a blunt approach. Truman followed Clifford's advice when he informed the Congress that:

At the very moment I am addressing you, five nations of the European community, in Brussels, are signing a 50-year agreement for economic cooperation and common defense against aggression. . . . Its significance goes far beyond the actual terms of the agreement itself. It is a notable step in the direction of unity in Europe for protection and preservation of its civilization. This development deserves our full support. I am confident that the United States will, by appropriate means, extend to the free nations the support which the situation requires. I am sure that the determination of the free countries of Europe to protect themselves will be matched by an equal determination on our part to help them protect themselves.[3]

The foregoing section of his address to the Congress was reprinted in full in his *Memoirs* to underscore the importance Truman attached to his own role in the defense of Europe.[4] The president went on to observe that "we have reached a point at which the position of the United States should be made unmistakably clear. . . . There are times in world history when it is wiser to act than to hesitate. There is some risk involved in action. There always is. But there is far more risk in failure to act."[5] Forthright as this language was, however, it raised immediate questions about what Truman specifically meant by "action." How far was the United States prepared to move in Europe's behalf in the spring of 1948? How far, indeed, was Europe itself prepared to move toward submerging its separate sovereignties under a common rubric, a united states of Europe, in the common defense?

There were no simple answers to these questions. Given the expectations of European statesmen seeking an American alliance and European federationists seeking explicit American activity on behalf of their movements, disappointment was inevitable.

First of all, American membership in the Western Union was quickly ruled out despite the eagerness expressed in a joint message from Bevin and Bidault immediately after the speech: "We are ready, together, with a Benelux representative, to discuss with you what further steps may be desirable."[6] The Americans, however, were not ready. At the first meeting of the United States-United Kingdom-Canada security conversations six days after the treaty was signed, the United States position was that it "should not now participate as a full member in Western Union but should give it assurance of armed support."[7] Even military assistance as "armed support" was vague, certainly much more so than the economic aid program then underway. Consider the admission by Jean Chauvel, secretary-general of the French Foreign Ministry, that "Une de nos idées, en signant le pacte de Bruxelles, avait été de constituer en Europe, comme il avait été fait put l'aide Marshall, un syndicat des parties prenantes qui put faciliter l'exercice de l'assistance militaire américaine."[8] Although the Truman administration did consider a military annex to the ECA bill, Title VI of the Foreign Assistance Act, it was not introduced for fear of damaging the passage of the Marshall program.[9]

For those who looked toward European unification as the primary objective of the Brussels Pact, there was even less reason for satisfaction. The pact was obviously a military alliance of separate sovereignties, and its language, consisting of such terms as "coordination" and "cooperation," was traditional rather than innovative. It did not promise federation. Jean Monnet was disturbed about this problem in the Organization of European Economic Cooperation (OEEC), which grew out of the Committee of European Economic Cooperation (CEEC) meeting in Paris two days before the treaty was signed. With its mere "cooperation between Governments" the OEEC allowed exemptions from decisions which a member nation found onerous. Monnet believed that the results would be "the opposite of the Community spirit." As he reported in his memoirs, he "could not help seeing the intrinsic weaknesses of a system that went no further than mere co-operation between Governments."[10]

Despite caveats the impetus toward unification of Europe went forward in the spring of 1948. If American leaders were cautious about specifics of their commitment to Western Union it was not just their visceral fears of entrapment or their consciousness of isolationism that slowed their pace. They recognized that a too hasty mix of military and economic aid could damage the fragile new fabric of European-American relations. Their first priority must be the successful passage of the Foreign Assistance Act through the Congress. The Western Union as a crystallization of European cooperation served rather than impeded the bill as long as it remained a symbol of potential unity, and in this sense was as much a spur to accelerating the Marshall program as were the Czech and Berlin crises. The latter so moved Senator Kenneth McKellar of Tennessee that he switched his position on March 8 from opposition to the Marshall Plan to support, claiming that "conditions have arisen which have caused me to reconsider the opinion I then reached on the European recovery program."[11]

But the fact that the ECA's future was still not assured induced Fulbright, the most eloquent proponent of European unity, reluctantly to withdraw his amendment on March 8 linking Marshall aid to the progress of European unification. He never wavered in his conviction that the "unification of Europe is essential to the future peace of the world, and that this country should do everything in its power to promote such a union." For him the prospective Brussels Pact was an opportunity to further this cause. "It will be a great tragedy," he claimed "for Europe and for us if the opportunity is missed because of hesitancy or timidity." But he feared that a formal linkage would incur "almost certain defeat" in the Senate which in turn would be "interpreted as this Nation's disapproval of European unity."[12]

A few weeks later Congressman Hale Boggs made one last attempt on March 29 to demonstrate America's insistence upon European unity as a condition for American support. Instead of the United States encouraging the CEEC to "speedily achieve that economic cooperation in Europe," as presented in the Senate version of the bill, Boggs's amendment would delete "economic" and add "and unity" after "cooperation." Such a change presumably would make the American position clearer with respect to the kind of cooperation Europeans should achieve. But speaking as a member of the House Foreign Affairs Committee, John Vorys opposed these and all other such changes as either "a matter of tweedledee or tweedledum, as I think might be argued for this amendment," or a matter of "thrusting our political point of view upon these nations."[13] In creating the Economic Cooperation Administration, Congress ultimately believed that American interest in European unity was already sufficiently well expressed; more might be fodder for hostile propaganda.

Actually the final version of the act, with its reference to the blessings America enjoyed through the absence of internal trade barriers, was considerably more sensitive to the issue of European unity than the initial draft of December 1947 had been. Ernst H. Van der Beugel, director-general and later minister of state for foreign affairs of the Netherlands, was convinced that "the debate, not only in 1948 but also in subsequent years, constituted a constant reminder for the European countries that large sums of aid required positive cooperative action on their part."[14]

Once the Foreign Assistance Act became law in April 1948, the administration was free to pursue more vigorously the various proposals coming out of Washington and the Western Union capitals for implementing the objectives of the Brussels Pact. To win Congress over would require, as did the ECA, continuing evidence of European willingness to unite their efforts. It would also require the exorcising of old American fears of being entangled in a European military alliance. Even before the actual signing of the Brussels Treaty, Foreign Minister Bevin had approached the State Department and the Canadian Department of External Affairs with a proposal for both an Atlantic and a Mediterranean security system, with the United States linked as closely to them as to the new Western Union.[15] The implications of the president's comments on the signing of the Brussels Treaty were translated into security conversations among representatives of the United States, the United Kingdom, and Canada meeting secretly at the Pentagon from March 22 to April 1. But, as already pointed out, American hesitations quickly developed in the course of the Pentagon conversations.

It became clear in these talks that the United States found the Western Union too narrow to join; a larger "Atlantic" organization would have to be devised to protect other countries in danger of Communist subversion or attack. Greece, Turkey, Italy, and even Spain and Germany came under consideration, even though the last had been the one nation named as a potential enemy of the Western Union earlier in the month. Until the time when a "North Atlantic Defense Agreement" could be framed, the American position appeared to be unilateral in its relations with the European allies.[16]

Obviously the long isolationist tradition of the United States was a factor in inhibiting American membership in the Brussels group, or in any larger European alliance for that matter. Was the public prepared to accept an entangling alliance in defiance of the wisdom of the Founding Fathers? The polls indicated that it would, if the language was carefully written, but the Congress hesitated.[17] The acceptance of the ECA had been a painful effort, and this involved not military aid or a military alliance, but the less sensitive issue of economic aid.

A further brake on American temptations to act came from the attitude of the American military establishment toward its involvement in Europe's defense. The Joint Chiefs of Staff had been giving serious consideration both to the issue of alliance and to the question of military assistance. Their reactions in the beginning were resolutely negative. Military assistance sounded like sanction for a raid upon their own severely strained supplies. They were uncomfortable with the implications of a National Security Council document, NSC-7, a general report on the "Position of the United States with respect to Soviet-directed World Communism," which on March 30 recommended a counteroffensive to "strengthen the will to resist of anti-communist forces throughout the world." First priority in this recommendation would be assigned to Europe, and a strong endorsement would be given to the Western Union, along with formulas to be worked out for "military action by the United States in the event of unprovoked armed attack against the nations in the Western Union or against other selected non-Communist nations." While the JCS endorsed the paper's stand on compulsory military service, they looked askance at the recommendation that machine tools be provided for European arms industries and were distressed by the specific point that military equipment and technical information would be included in the "counteroffensive."[18]

The State Department's reaction was that the paper was much too general and open to too many interpretations, but it was mild compared to the military response. Secretary of Defense James V. Forrestal warned the NSC about the "extreme importance to our national security of keeping our military capabilities abreast of our military commitments."[19] The mention of machine tools triggered a concern that their exportation might interfere with American needs or might be subject to capture by Soviet forces.

Behind the immediate impulse to protect their own stocks, the JCS worried about the general weakness of European forces. They assumed that none of the Western powers individually or collectively could stop the Soviets should they wish to march to the Atlantic or to the Channel in 1948. They feared that an American entanglement at this point in an alliance would place the military in the hopeless position of "biting off more than we could chew," to use Ambassador Lewis Douglas's terms.[20]

As important as the problem of military assistance was to the JCS, it was overshadowed by the implications of NSC-9, presented on April 13, 1948, a document prepared to respond to the Western Union's requests. Although, like the findings of the security conversations, it would leave the United States out of the Western Union for the time being, it opened the way for an even more ambitious undertaking, a "Collective Defense Agreement for the North Atlantic Area."[21] The JCS urgently pressed its case against commitments which were beyond the capacity of the nation to fulfill, "unless preparatory measures were completed first."[22]

It was not the opposition of the military, however, that delayed immediate action on the part of the United States. Rather it was recognition by the State Department that negotiations would first have to be made with a wary Senate, led by Senator Arthur H. Vandenberg, the powerful chairman of the Foreign Relations Committee. Vandenberg too was concerned about the nature of future commitments, whether the Rio model of an alliance would allow the majority an excessive role in decisionmaking, whether the absence of the United Nations would undercut its already damaged prestige in the world. Moreover, the senator wanted more assurance that the Europeans were advancing toward integration before more American assistance was provided.[23]

The result was a major modification of NSC-9 as Deputy Secretary of State Lovett cultivated and attended Vandenberg's reservations. In NSC-9/1, issued on April 23, the administration won its objective of sending invitations to the countries of the North Atlantic area, including Italy, Eire, Scandinavia, Canada, and Portugal, as well as the Western Union. Self-help and mutual aid were to be required of all potential signatories.[24] Part of the price for Senate approval was delay in the proceedings, ostensibly because of the short time remaining before the adjournment of the 80th Congress. A more significant factor in congressional delay was an expectation that a new president, undoubtedly Republican, would be needed to create a new consensus for involvement with Europe. The rest of the price was the embodying of the whole concept of an Atlantic alliance within the context of the United Nations Charter, in which Articles 51 and 53, relating to self-defense and regional arrangements, would provide a United Nations' blessing upon the enterprise. All of these ideas were expressed in the Vandenberg Resolution, reported by the Foreign Relations Committee to the Senate on May 19 and adopted as Senate Resolution 239 on June 11, 1948.[25]

It should be noted that the diversion of the United States from membership in the Western Union was not just the consequence of a Senate *Diktat* or of the advice of John Foster Dulles, Vandenberg's mentor. The issue of the United Nations and the worries over Europe relaxing in its own efforts reflected their pressures, but the significant voices in support of delay emerged from within the administration. The military obviously was one such voice. George F. Kennan, chairman of the Policy Planning Staff of the State Department, and Charles E. Bohlen, counselor, shared their reservations. In advance of the United States-United Kingdom-Canada meetings at the Pentagon, the JCS recommended a unilateral stance for the United States pending conclusion of an alliance.[26] Kennan and Bohlen concurred. Kennan felt that a formal alliance was superfluous since the Soviet Union could not be in any doubt about where the United States would stand if it attacked the countries of the Western Union. The very presence of American troops in territory between Russia and Western Europe was "an adequate guarantee that we will be at war if they are attacked." The main point at the moment, according to Kennan, was that there was little that the United States could do to stop the Soviet advance if it was attempted. Hence the direction for the United States was not alliance but massive aid and realistic staff talks with the Western Union's military leaders. If Vandenberg's resolution gave impetus to coordination, standardization, and ultimately integration of Europe's resources, it would serve America's interests well.[27]

While the leaders of the Western Union were uneasy over the direction the conversations were taking, the steps recommended in April and May by American planners fitted into the hopes of European federationists. The American position of strong support without explicit ties was closer to their aspirations than the Western Union plan of merger of America and Europe in a traditional alliance. But the federationists did not require knowledge of these differences to justify their optimism in the spring of 1948. In the euphoria following the Brussels Pact they believed that Americans and European leaders alike would find integration irresistible. All public signals looked favorable as the date for the congress at The Hague grew closer. In addition to such well-known friends of Europe as Fulbright and Boggs, Governor Thomas E. Dewey, a Republican presidential aspirant, came out boldly in favor of federation. Speaking on the campaign trail in Lincoln, Nebraska, on April 8, he asserted that "what is needed to restore stability in the world is a unified Europe—a strong third power devoted to the cause of peace. What is needed is a United States of Europe."[28] No statesman was blunter about his intentions than this potential president of the United States of America.

Given this spirit, Count Coudenhove-Kalergi's announcement in New York on April 23 of a special committee to support a "Free and United

Europe" appeared to be the next logical step toward completion of their hopes. It was a diverse group, with Robert P. Patterson, former secretary of war, as interested in Clarence Streit's movement toward American union with Britain as he was in Coudenhove's plans for European union. Whatever the potential for internal strife among the various factions, all federationists at The Hague in May agreed on the importance of bringing together all competing organizations. As Coudenhove expressed it, "Actually the Soviet Union is primarily responsible for the rapid progress made in the movement for a United Europe. Russia provided the Western European countries with a common danger which convinced them that their main hope for security lay in the formation of a closely knit federated organization."[29]

There was some irony about the role of the Soviet Union as a catalytic agent for unity. Philip Bonsal, the U.S. counselor to the embassy in The Hague, informed the State Department that the Dutch leader Hendriks Brugmans had observed "somewhat bitterly that twenty-five years of arguing this point had been unable to achieve the result that one speech by Mr. Bevin had produced."[30] The sense of common danger had created the Western Union, and even a skeptic like Brugmans believed that the results would redound to the advantage of European unification.

In some ways the British role was as much a matter of irony as the Soviets' role. Despite the opposition of the Labour Party which effectively prevented the Hague meeting from being a gathering of governments, the British connection with federation was present in abundance. Winston Churchill himself was to be presiding officer at The Hague, and would make the inaugural address at the historic Ridderzaal before 800 or more delegates from Western Europe and observers from Eastern Europe. Churchill was supported by 190 members of Parliament, who signed a motion drawn up by Labour member R.W.G. Mackay offering a British endorsement to political and economic unity under a Council of Ministers and calling for an immediate convocation of a constituent assembly.[31] While Britain's traditional uneasiness with a united Continent manifested itself in the posture of the Attlee government, Churchill and Mackay carried a new and different message to Europeans, much as Bevin had in February.

The United States was presented as a benevolent patron, discreetly in the background and yet available when needed. The *New York Times* observer, Anne O'Hare McCormick, saw it as a positive role.[32] So did Churchill, who noted in his speech before the Congress of Europe that he had been "anxious at first lest the United States of America should view with hostility the idea of a United States of Europe. But I rejoice that the great republic, in its era of world leadership, has risen far above such moods. We must all be thankful as we sit here that the nation called to the summit of the world by its mass, its energies and its power, has not been found lacking in those qualities of greatness and nobility upon which the record of famous states depends. Far from resenting the creation of United Europe, the American people welcomed and ardently sustained the resurrection of what was called the Old World now found in full partnership with the New."[33]

This rhetoric contained standard hyperbole, and might have been ignored if it had been expressed by anyone other than the great wartime leader of Britain. Any time Churchill spoke and any place he might appear would attract American attention, and the gathering in The Hague was no exception. The State Department was well aware of the happenings in the Netherlands in May 1948. But there is no evidence that they specifically identified with the goals of such motley groups, no matter how distinguished their representatives. When Duncan Sandys, chairman of the organizing committee of the Hague congress and Churchill's son-in-law, sought an official American message from Secretary Marshall to the conference "in view of historic part you have played in movement for European unity,"[34] the answer was equivocal. The secretary of state hesitated, and after consulting with Rusk and Hickerson, resolved his doubts by deciding against a message. The American embassy accordingly was to "advise Sandys that the secy welcomed any concrete progress toward greater unity of thought and action between free nations of Western Europe but that he does not consider it appropriate to send message to meeting."[35]

Belgium's premier, Paul-Henri Spaak, had recognized the reasons for American caveats. Visiting Washington in April he was able to canvass the extent of American commitment to the Western Union, and to explain a European position to American policymakers. Spaak made a point of stating his belief that war was not imminent, that the Five Powers "are not at present directly threatened by the Russians, and that a treaty between the United States and Western Union might encourage Russian aggression" against those nations omitted from an alliance. But even though a larger guarantee would be welcomed, "the real need was for maximum military coordination at the earliest possible date."[36] This would be the most credible affirmation of Truman's March 17 statement. At the same time Spaak spoke emphatically to Americans about Europe's concern over defending itself. The establishment of a secretariat and a decision to hold military conversations in April was a serious earnest of the Western Union's intentions.

In underscoring Europe's activities Spaak was sensitive to American interests in European integration and in tune with American sensibilities about self-help. While pressure from European leaders would have to be exerted regularly, it should be carefully orchestrated to the American mood. Such was the essential information that Spaak communicated to Sir George Rendel, British ambassador to Belgium, when the foreign minister returned to Brussels. The Americans, Spaak reported, were favorably disposed toward Western Europe, and "were prepared to go a long way towards committing themselves to backing the Brussels Treaty with a promise of military assistance." He cautioned Rendel, though, that the problems of an election year and the necessity to devise the precise political formula would mean some delays.[37]

Still, the willingness of the United States to send observers to the projected defense discussions in London would be a happy augury of future American relations. It permitted the British to relax over the slow implementation of the American part in the Western Union's plans. They purposely withdrew their earlier pressures for a treaty or aid, knowing that such activity for the moment would only invite a negative response, and knowing also that the seeds sown by the Brussels Treaty would grow in time.[38]

This knowledge was not so clear to the French, who were absent from the "Pentagon talks" of March. They knew nothing of them or of the resolution that came from them. Consequently, French leaders were of a mixed mind about the whole process of American association with Europe. On the one hand, as Bevin reported from his meeting with Bidault on April 16, 1948, the French preferred what they perceived to be the American interest in the Brussels powers making their own military arrangements, "since [Bidault] did not wish the Americans to come in, as it were, from the beginning and tell us what we should do."[39] At the same time the French were most anxious for American military aid at the earliest possible date, and were impatient with delays. During the debate over the Vandenberg Resolution, Armand Berard, minister counselor of the French embassy, was seen sitting "alone in the diplomatic gallery" listening to language that fell considerably short of the alliance which the French wanted in the spring of 1948.[40]

Some of the confusion over the differences between U.S. membership in the Western Union and U.S. military aid to the Western Union arose from the differing signals that Europeans sent to Americans. When Spaak visited Washington, Kennan and Bohlen heard what they had preferred to believe: namely, that the Europeans valued an alliance less than they valued immediate military help. Under Secretary of State Lovett, a critical figure in the making of American policy, seemed to share the views of the two dissidents. Spaak's comments made him hesitate about proceeding with a North Atlantic security pact.[41] The consequence might have been a unilateral declaration of the sort which Bohlen and Kennan had recommended.

Hickerson and Achilles, primary actors in the secret March discussions at the Pentagon that led to the idea of an expanded alliance, ultimately prevailed. They were aided by the arguments that Europe's fears were stimulated more by the absence of a binding American commitment and by memories of American isolationism before the two world wars than by the pressure for new weapons. Canada, a participant in the Pentagon talks, was strongly opposed to a unilateral declaration which, it felt, would undermine its own position of support for Europe. Escott Reid, a Canadian architect of the alliance, claims that "if you scratch almost any American long enough, you will find an isolationist. They suffer, and you can hardly blame them, from a homesickness for isolation."[42]

Fortunately for the planners, the sense of urgency that dominated affairs in the early spring had abated temporarily. The Soviet pressures had peaked in March. The Berlin problems were quiescent for the moment; the Italian Communists had been defeated at the polls in April; the Soviet terms for relations with Finland turned out to be milder than anticipated; and the intensity of Soviet propaganda against the West had slackened. Yet the flurry of negotiations between the United States and Western Europe in this period could not have been unnoticed by the Soviet Union, particularly since Donald Maclean, a Communist secret agent of great influence in the British Foreign Office as First Secretary of the British embassy in Washington, was privy to all the activities of the Western Union. Perhaps the Soviet Union, knowing everything, was relieved at the defensive cast of the Western initiatives. So speculated Escott Reid.[43] The full-scale Berlin blockade in June which broke the lull emerged from the German currency reforms of June 18, not from the projected new associations of the United States with Europe.

As for the question of unilateralism versus multilateralism, the Vandenberg Resolution of June 11 terminated the debate. The adherents of a North Atlantic community in the State Department triumphed, although the perceptions of the moment would identify victory with the Senate. By transferring credit and responsibility for initiating aid to Europe as well as a security pact with Europe during the slack period between April 11 and June 11, Truman and Lovett permitted the Senate to believe that it had been a key element in a changing American foreign policy. As Vandenberg was reputed to ask: "Why should a Democratic President get all the kudos in an election year? Wouldn't the chances of Senate 'consent' to ratification of such a treaty be greatly increased by Senatorial advice to the President to negotiate it?"[44] A powerful constituency was won over to the cause of European unity, to European self-help, and to American identification with these ideas. The Vandenberg Resolution, not the secret Pentagon talks of March or the NSC documents of April, opened the way to the Atlantic alliance of 1949.

This may not have been quite the intention of the Senate or even of Vandenberg himself when the resolution passed by a resounding majority of 64 to 4. Only a few rabid dissidents on the Right such as George W. Malone of Nevada, warned against European wiles and the entanglements that would follow, or mild reservationists on the Left such as Fulbright, who once again sought to raise the issue of European unification. Fulbright would have attached to the second paragraph the phrase "Progressive development of regional and other collective arrangements 'for mutual defense and political unity'" in place of "for individual and collective self-defense."[45] Their advice was disregarded.

What emerged from the Senate was a message in which one could find primarily an effort to refurbish the position of the United Nations; five of the six paragraphs refer specifically to its charter:

Whereas peace with justice and the defense of human rights and fundamental freedoms require international cooperation through more effective use of the United Nations: Therefore be it

Resolved, That the Senate reaffirm the policy of the United States to achieve international peace and security through the United Nations, so that armed force shall not be used except in the common interest, and that the President be advised of the sense of the Senate that this Government, by constitutional process should particularly pursue the following objectives within the United Nations Charter:

(1) Voluntary agreement to remove the veto from all questions involving specific settlements of international disputes and situations, and from the admission of new members.

(2) Progressive development of regional and other collective arrangements for individual and collective self-defense in accordance with the purposes, principles, and provisions of the Charter.

(3) Association by the United States, by constitutional process, with such regional and other collective arrangements as are based on continuous and effective self-help and mutual aid, and as affect its national security.

(4) Contributing to the maintenance of peace by making clear its determination to exercise the right of individual or collective self-defense under article 51 should any armed attack occur affecting its national security.

(5) Maximum efforts to obtain agreements to provide the United Nations with armed forces as provided by the Charter, and to obtain agreements among member nations upon universal regulation and reduction of armaments under adequate and dependable guaranty against violation.

(6) If necessary, after adequate effort toward strengthening the United Nations, review of the Charter at an approximate time by a general conference called under 109 or by the General Assembly.[46]

It is worth noting that only Paragraph 3 dealt with the issue of alliances or with military assistance, and even this was couched in the language of the Charter rather than in the parlance of the Brussels Treaty or the Foreign Assistance Act. While a knowledgeable observer could read into the text an acceptance of an Atlantic alliance, this interpretation would not be obvious to the American public, or even to some of the European leaders. A collective arrangement conforming to the Charter of the UN was not what Bevin or Bidault, or presumably Hickerson or Achilles, had in mind when they worked toward mutual security. To conform with the regionalism of Article 53 of the Charter would directly engage the veto power of the Soviet Union as a member of the Security Council to which the regional association would report.

A more accurate rendition of the Vandenberg Resolution appeared in a second revision of NSC-9. NSC-9/2, submitted a week before the Senate Foreign Relations Committee acted on the Vandenberg Resolution, recommended that after the introduction of the resolution (which had been drafted in the State Department), State would advise the Western Union that the "President is prepared to authorize U.S. participation in the London Five Power military talks with a view to: (a) concerting military plans for use in the event that the U.S.S.R. should resort in the short term future to aggressive action in Germany, Austria or elsewhere in Europe, and (b) drawing up a coordinated military supply plan." Moreover, it made clear that the Defense Department would participate in these conversations, and that following the ERP precedent the Europeans "must first plant their coordinated defense with the means presently available, (2) they must then determine how their collective military potential can be increased by coordinated production and supply, including standardization of equipment." At this point the United States would move to screen estimates of supplementary assistance needed and propose legislation accordingly. An annex to NSC-9/2 contained the Vandenberg Resolution, only slightly altered by Kennan before its final submission.[47] NSC-9/3 of June 28 followed with the guidance that produced the North Atlantic Treaty nine months later: namely, military conversations with Americans present, a clear European acceptance of the ERP model for self-help and coordinated defense planning, and congressional action after the presidential election.[48]

The Vandenberg Resolution cleared most of the obstacles to ultimate acceptance of an American military alliance with Western Europe. On July 1, NSC-14 was adopted.[49] It essentially revived the discarded Title VI of the Foreign Assistance Act that would facilitate the procurement of massive military aid for Europe. Five days later the first session of the Washington Exploratory Talks on "regional collective security" convened.[50] The Joint Chiefs of Staff accepted both commitments with reluctance but also with resignation, hoping that specific military obligations would be avoided "unless preceded by at least the degree of military strengthening that the Joints Chiefs of Staff have recommended" for American forces.[51]

If the conditions for a firm and permanent association with the Western Union had been established by the confluence of Senate Resolution 239 and the Berlin crisis of June 1948, its shape was by no means agreed upon by the parties involved. Did it mean that the United States would be the guarantor and expediter of a united states of Europe along the lines proposed by Eu-

ropean federationists at the Hague meeting of May? The requirements of the
Vandenberg Resolution were susceptible to this interpretation, as Europeans
moved toward "progressive development of regional and other collective
arrangements for individual and collective self-defense." The removal of
political and economic barriers which had divided old rivals in the past would
facilitate the efficient use of American aid and promote effective defense as
well as quicker economic recovery for all Europeans. In this way Senate
Resolution 239 could energize the European impulse for unity much as Senator J. William Fulbright and John Foster Dulles had hoped.

But American membership in an alliance did not equate necessarily with
the Europe envisaged by Fulbright or by Coudenhove-Kalergi. The major
emphasis over the next six months, during which the terms of a treaty were
framed, was on an Atlantic alliance, not a European alliance, an issue underscored by the attention given to the potential membership of Iceland or
Canada in the new collective arrangement. The widening and reorienting of
the Western Union was a vital if unstated precondition for American involvement in light of the old American tradition of abstaining from European
connections. An Atlantic link could make a symbolic difference to isolationist
opponents in an election year.

Looking back over the years Gladwyn Jebb, under secretary at the Foreign Office, later Lord Gladwyn, reflected about lost opportunities for a
genuine supranational European community in 1948. He wondered whether,
had he been at the Hague congress of May, he might not have abandoned the
British aloofness toward the mandate of that meeting. He noted that the fears
aroused in Europe and America after the Prague coup of February and the
Berlin blockade of June produced the Western Union and even the Atlantic
alliance. "But what should have accompanied this great reaction of the Western world was an increasing advance toward real European unity also. In other
words, somebody should have then advanced the theory of the 'two poles' in
the Western world and made it an actual condition of consent of America to
entering any definite alliance."[52]

This was precisely what Fulbright and Dulles and other American federationists had identified as their first priority. They could have gone along as
well with Jebb's retrospective belief that the best road to federation lay at
hand in the "enlarging and strengthening of the Brussels Treaty Organization
by making it into a parliamentary body with an international secretariat."[53]
Such a future would have fitted also into George Kennan's "'dumbell' concept: the conbination, that is, of a unit at the European end based on the
Brussels pact, and another unit at the North American end—Canadian-United
States, this time—the two being separate in identity and membership but
linked by an acknowledgement on the North American side that the security
of the European unit was vital to United States-Canadian security, and by a

readiness on the United States-Canadian part to extend to the European participants whatever was necessary in the way of military supplies, forces, and joint strategic planning."[54]

But both Jebb and Kennan were writing twenty years after the event, full of the wisdom of hindsight. Neither of these projections fitted the needs which American planners felt were paramount at the time. The unity of Europe was indeed their concern but it was a matter of indifference whether or not it took the form of a supranational organization. What mattered was close cooperation and coordination in military and economic areas that would make an effective defense against Communist encroachment. Congressional support for an American contribution accepted and even encouraged the language, not the substance, of federation. In this context the idea of a united states of Europe was simply another means of mobilizing American political support for foreign aid. It was the stuff of which party platforms are made.[55]

The nub of the European problem was its defenselessness in the face of perceived Communist power. This could only be overcome by an American presence in Europe—political, economic, and military. If Europeans or their American friends emphasized excessively the plans for European unification their concerns could divert the course of alliance from its main channels. This was a perception shared for different reasons by British and French leaders as well as American.[56]

The one vitally important aspect of European unity that concerned both the Joint Chiefs of Staff and the State Department in the summer of 1948 was the breaking down of economic and military differences among the allies that would permit the maximal utilization of economic aid and military equipment by the recipients. In July the activity was on two fronts: in London, where the Brussels Pact military conversations were witnessed by Major General Lyman L. Lemnitzer, the American participant on "a non-membership basis"; and in Washington, where exploratory talks centered on military assistance to the Brussels Pact nations and a widening of the Pact's membership to other nations, including the United States.[57]

In London the Western Union had tried to identify the establishment of new bodies—the Permanent Consultative Council and its Military Committee—as an earnest of Europe's response to the mandate of the Vandenberg Resolution.[58] Its concern was filling its needs by American aid, rather than implementing or even seriously formulating plans for pooling European resources, standardizing weapons, or expanding military production. With France leading the pressure for its own rearmament, the idea of a European defense appeared to be a cover for gratifying national needs. The Americans resisted these importunities, asserting that the mandate of NSC 14 could be implemented only after the Europeans had demonstrated faith in a supranational defense plan. The hope was for a military equivalent of the

CEEC, something which the Congress would approve as a rational guide to the distribution of aid. Congress, according to Under Secretary of State Lovett, would not accept a "military lend-lease."[59]

Initially the Western Union through its Military Committee was to map out a strategic concept to which the United States could make a contribution. But even here there were serious problems. Among them was the short-range emergency plan HALFMOON, presented by the JCS in the event of a war with the Soviet Union. It had been approved for planning on May 19, 1948, and under different names remained a guide to U.S. military thinking throughout 1948. It assumed the necessity of evacuating Western forces from most of the Continent and making defensive stands in the Cairo-Suez area and in Great Britain; the heart of Western Europe was deemed indefensible.[60] This was a burden for General Lemnitzer's seven-man team in London, since the Continental members of the Western Union could draw no comfort from plans that would accept their conquest before liberation. The strategy of the Western Union was to fight "as far east in Germany as possible."[61]

To cope with European uneasiness the JCS considered the appointment of an American general, Lucius D. Clay, as commander of all forces in Western Europe. This idea circulated in the summer of 1948 but was not implemented, partly because Clay was too occupied with his duties in Germany, partly because of political complications inherent in the relationship of an American officer commanding European troops.[62]

Ultimately British Field Marshal Bernard Montgomery assumed the position of chairman of the Western Union's Commander-in-Chief Committee, charged with drawing up a short-term plan for the defense of Europe as far east in Germany as possible.[63] But beyond providing a summary of forces available for mobilization in 1949 and manpower increases possible if the necessary equipment could be obtained, nothing much was done. Significantly, there was no progress in pooling inventories and production resources to assure a balanced program. Even the list of deficiencies was incomplete and unsatisfactorily screened.[64]

The JCS gave their imprimatur to the Western Union's military proceedings with considerable misgivings. They were concerned that supplies for the allies would initially come from surplus stocks, which might lead to an unacceptable drain upon the military capability of American forces elsewhere. Above all, they were suspicious of Europe's good faith as well as of its ability to make good use of American material.

Many of these suspicions were not confined to the JCS. Under Secretary of State Lovett, chairing the Washington Exploratory Talks, was as suspicious as any military leader in his dealings with French representatives. The latter wanted arms immediately without accepting the carefully worked out preparations which the United States delegation had required under the Vandenberg mandate. The French claimed that the Western Union's organization of a military committee had been an appropriate response to American requirements. The projected Atlantic pact seemed a diversion from the more pressing problem of direct aid to the Western Union nations. More specifically, immediate aid to France was a first priority of the negotiations, as French Ambassador Henri Bonnet insisted.[65] "The cat then came fully out of the bag," as Lovett saw it, when Bonnet complained that the talks were wasting time on long-range programs "instead of developing a current military program and re-equipping the French army."[66]

Despite the annoyance of their allies French persistence did not abate. Charles E. Bohlen, counselor of the Department of State, speculated that French absence from the secret Anglo-American-Canadian talks of April may have been responsible for the direction their arguments took. They were unaware of the substance of the Pentagon meetings, and hence did not recognize or appreciate the importance of an Atlantic connection to American membership and aid.[67]

Concessions were made. As early as July 14, W. Averell Harriman, U.S. special representative in Europe for the ECA, recommended sending a limited number of P-49s or P-51s to equip a selected unit of the French air force. He was thinking of the psychological value which token shipments could have on French morale, much as the delivery of one million rifles had upon Britain in 1940.[68] After months of patient explanation that long-range assistance was the critical issue and that equipment in the short run for large-scale rearming of French forces did not exist, the United States moved toward a compromise. The president approved a transfer from U.S. stocks in Germany to French forces sufficient to equip three French divisions in Germany. In this case the secretary of state was more convinced of the wisdom of this action than was the secretary of defense.[69]

The British concurred in the American decision, if only to help ameliorate the French cabinet crisis of the early autumn. "France is essential to the Western system," Bevin observed in a memorandum to his cabinet, and "her collapse would involve the collapse of the whole."[70] John Russell of the Western Department of the Foreign Ministry believed that the decision to supply U.S. military equipment to French divisions had an excellent effect on the French. But a colleague could not refrain from wondering if the Americans by violating their own rules of coordinated requests have set a bad precedent: "This U.S. unilateral action may encourage other countries to attempt to beat the pistol."[71]

But emergency aid to any one European country was not the major issue before the allies. More disturbing was the threat to the primacy of the Western Union in the terms the United States was asking of the Brussels Pact partners.

The United States pressed for a quickening of mutual aid and an increase in self-help among the European allies, but at the same time made clear the inadequacy of the Western Union as the frame for the new security arrangements. It was both too "European" for American isolationists to accept and too small to be an appropriate deterrent to Soviet aggression. Hickerson observed that "in one sense the Brussels Pact was not broad enough as to membership and in another sense was too broad as to obligation." The economic and cultural clauses would fit an American association. The United States could not simply become an overseas member of the Western Union.[72]

The other extreme, the establishment of a "two-pillar" relationship, was unsatisfactory to Europeans even though if implemented it might have accelerated momentum toward a genuinely federated Europe, as Jebb had noted in his retrospective view of 1948. George Kennan as director of the Policy Planning Staff was a strong supporter of an Atlantic area security pact with "two anchors: the U.S.-Canada anchor and the Brussels Pact anchor which would constitute the actual members of the pact." Other countries might enter into association with the full members and receive guarantees of protection in return for military facilities on their territories.[73]

Most Brussels Pact members shied away from the Atlantic emphasis in the summer of 1948 because they feared it would not entangle the United States sufficiently in the defense of Europe. John Hickerson also opposed the Kennan idea, but for different reasons; he wanted a widening of the Brussels Pact to include Italy and other OEEC countries.[74] This too was unsatisfactory to the negotiators since it would result in attenuating the quantity of American aid. Moreover, they doubted the defensibility of territory beyond the core area of the five Western Union members. At a meeting in The Hague in July in the midst of the Washington talks, their foreign ministers wished to postpone conclusion of any agreement with the Scandinavian countries, including Iceland and Greenland, despite American preferences. Even Bevin went along with this position, leaving Secretary Marshall mystified by the British foreign minister's "sudden reversal of position."[75]

The American official position differed from both Kennan's and the Western Union's. In essence it embodied the views of Hickerson, who wanted a widening of the Brussels Pact to include Italy and other OEEC countries. Lovett was concerned with a nation, such as a hypothetical "Neuralgia," which was prepared to defend itself if properly assisted. If it felt excluded from a particularly European alliance it could either appeal for bilateral American help or yield to Soviet wishes. Both alternatives were to be avoided. The way to help such a beneficiary was to bring it into the alliance, which would insure coordination of its needs with those of the other allies.[76]

The most the Brussels powers could salvage from this appeared in the image of the alliance proposed by Dutch Foreign Minister Eelco Van Kleffens, that of "a peach, the Brussels Pact would be the hard kernel in the center and a North Atlantic Pact the somewhat less hard mass around it."[77] In this context five stepping-stone countries—Norway because of Spitzbergen, Denmark because of Greenland, Portugal for the Azores, and Iceland and possibly Ireland—had claims on the alliance which the core countries could not deny if they wanted the membership of the United States. As Bohlen expressed it at the August 9 meeting of the Ambassadors Committee, "without the Azores, Iceland and Greenland, help could not be got to Europe in significant quantities at all."[78] Earlier Lovett had even suggested that "Greenland and Iceland were more important than some countries in western Europe to the security of the United States and Canada." Thus the American view was that the enlargement of the alliance was a benefit to the allies as much as to the potential new members.[79] The Western Union's counter argument that new commitments would weaken existing arrangements was undercut by the American perception that "it is clear that they do not want others to share in the United States arms pie."[80]

Reflecting the two months of labor, the Washington Paper of September 9 underscored the American position by emphasizing the danger to the security of American and Western Europe if the facilities of the stepping-stone countries were not available to them. If the latter were not brought into the alliance as full members by the end of 1948 it was not for lack of trying. The Washington Paper agreed to the extension of invitations to selected countries before the conclusion of a pact, to see if they would accept full responsibility for the role assigned to them.[81] On November 26 the Brussels Pact responded by recommending the sounding out of Denmark, Iceland, Norway, Portugal, and possibly Sweden for membership.[82] A month later this was carried out, although Ireland declined the invitation to explore the question while Sweden was finally denied an invitation.[83]

The removal of Sweden from the list was a reminder that there were caveats about membership among the stepping-stone countries. Sweden invited American anger with its movement toward neutrality built around a Nordic pact. The United States regarded this development as not only futile and dangerous in the face of Soviet power, but subversive of the interests of the Atlantic alliances should this new arrangement attract the other Scandinavian nations.[84] In fact, Denmark had its own reservations, wanting to be sure that if it became a full member the area covered under the alliance would not "involve Denmark in event of an attack on Iran or other country not in the delineated area." Portugal for its part tempered its traditional ties with Britain with worry over the exclusion of Spain from the association.[84]

Italy was even more difficult to manage, presenting, as the Washington paper observed, "a particular problem." It was an unlikely choice for an ally because of its geographical separation from the Atlantic ocean and because of the special limitations imposed on Italy's military status by the peace treaty of 1947. But given the importance of its strategic location and the shakiness of its Western orientation the question of Italian membership in the alliance, according to the United States representative, required "a satisfactory solution."[86] Yet even Italy had reservations; it was tempted to use an invitation to revise the Treaty and gain concessions on colonies.[87]

It was a combination of France's embrace of an Italian role in the Western Union and the continuing interest of John Hickerson that counteracted the resistance of the northern members and the Scandinavian potential members. The French recognized a precedent that might be used to include Algeria in the alliance, while Hickerson, remembering the great fear of a Communist victory in the spring elections, convinced Lovett to recognize that the means of solving the Italian problem was through its joining the Brussels pact.[88]

The Italian problem remained unresolved in December. Even more remote was the prospect of any arrangement with Spain and Western Germany even though the Washington Paper "recognized that the ultimate relationship" of those countries must be addressed eventually.[89]

Time-consuming and emotion-ridden as the questions of the scope of the alliance were, these were not the central issue before the diplomats. This was the immediate and future security of Europe. If Europeans could be certain that American power would be inextricably harnessed to their defense, other matters—the extension of membership or the shipment of specific supplies—would dwindle in significance.

The core of the obligation was when and how the United States would come to the aid of an ally under attack. The European objective was immediate and inextricable entanglement, while the United States, fearing both exploitation and isolationism, struggled to make its pledge of support consistent with the requirements of the Federal Constitution. Not until the very end of negotiations was language worked out to satisfy the needs of all parties.

The problem stemmed from the potential models that would inform the treaty's authors. Europeans understandably preferred the deceptively simple language of the Brussels Treaty's Article IV, in which the allies would "afford the party so attacked all the military and other aid and assistance in their power." The response of the State Department Working Group to this idea was negative: "The United States could not constitutionally enter into any Treaty which would provide that the United States would be automatically at war as a result of an event occurring outside its borders or by vote of other countries without its concurrence."[90]

The recent Treaty of Rio de Janeiro offered a more usable example for the

United States to develop. For one thing, it was a model that Congress had already accepted as within the tradition of a modernized Monroe Doctrine. For another, it modified the commitment. While Article 3 did observe that an attack against one should be considered as an attack against all parties, Article 4 provided for "individual determination by each Party, pending agreement upon collective measures, of the immediate measures which it will individually take on fulfillment of the obligation."[91]

Nonetheless, there were drawbacks in the Rio model even from the American perspective. It was just a "take-off point," as Lovett noted.[92] The Rio Pact placed insufficient emphasis upon self-help and cooperation or on the integration of economic and military systems. The Europeans, on the other hand, were discontented with the vagueness of the aid to be supplied and the nature of the commitment undertaken. At the Working Group meetings of the Exploratory Talks, Sir Frederic Hoyer Millar and Armand Bérard recommended that more precise language be devised when considering the implications of an attack on any member of the alliance. They wanted to be sure that the response would indeed be as if the attack had been made against every other member, including the United States.[93]

The French were disturbed that in the absence of exact military obligations the provisions for consultations in the Rio Pact would increase rather than decrease the sense of insecurity in Europe. Bohlen, the United States representative at these meetings, could only answer that whatever arrangement might be made involving the United States must recognize the separation of powers in the American government, as did the Inter-American treaty. Although the Rio strategy differed from that of Brussels, he claimed that the "obligation to afford assistance to a country under aggression is similar." In light of a congressional action that had to precede a state of war, the United States could not accept the Brussels article which bound each member to provide "all military and other aid in its power."[94]

Both sides labored to bridge differences. A State Department paper carefully outlined those Rio provisions which would be mutually acceptable, and Hoyer Millar proposed the incorporation of language from the Brussels Treaty that would not directly confront the United States on constitutional issues. Fastening on Article 3 of the Rio Pact, he suggested elaborating on the method of responding to an attack: "by military, economic and all other means within its power."[95]

The result of the negotiations surfaced in the broad compromise presented in the Washington Paper of September containing a blend of the language of both treaties. The document listed both the United States preference for language close to that of the Rio Treaty, and the European variations on the Brussels Pact, and then proposed a compromise that linked individual national response to "constitutional processes."[96] Still, the Europeans were not satisfied. There remained the implication that each party could still decide for itself whether or not an armed attack had occurred, and, if it had, what should be done about it. It could mean all aid from the United States short of war, and this would undercut the psychological effect which the alliance was intended to create. The concern was so deep that the United States retreated from its earlier positions. In the draft treaty of December 24 the negotiators agreed to "taking forthwith military or such other action, individually and in concert with other Parties, as may be necessary to restore and secure the security of the North Atlantic area."[97] While this was not quite all military action "in their power," it did promise action "forthwith," which would have the same effect.

Throughout this period, from July through December, security talks proceeded in different capitals, sometimes with great intensity. The negotiators produced the Washington Paper in September and the draft treaty in December. Between September 10 and December 10 there was a three-month gap in activity during which the various parties to the proceedings reacted to the Washington Paper. The Brussels Pact powers through their Consultative Council formally gave their blessing to a North Atlantic alliance on October 26. Canada provided its reactions in detail in early December.[98] It was the United States, which had been in such haste in the spring, that slowed the pace in the summer and seemed to dawdle in the fall.

The American delay was not inadvertent. Under Lovett's leadership Europeans were required to appear as initiators of treaty conversations, so that the United States would appear as reactors, reflecting on Europe's needs and interests as they unfolded.[99] The pattern fitted the experience of the Marshall Plan, and so did its intention. If Congress was to be supportive, it must be assured that the beneficiaries not only wished aid but would conform to the spirit of mutual cooperation outlined in the Vandenberg Resolution. American aid must be matched by equivalent European sacrifice. Thus the United States referred to neither the Pentagon paper nor any other working paper which would accelerate the negotiating process. Any reference to the tripartite conversations of the spring would have spoiled the image which the State Department was seeking.

The decision to have full and agreed minutes of the Ambassadors Committee further helped to slow movement. A complete record inevitably would inhibit the free exchange of discussion among representatives who knew that their foreign ministries would be in a position to review and challenge any of their positions. The ambassadors had to look over their shoulders at all times. Rarely, as at an occasional informal meeting in Lovett's home, were no records kept.[100] The working groups had more freedom, since only action summaries were compiled; but this was only for a brief period in December.

As time dragged on it was obvious that a major factor in American dallying lay in the knowledge that no action could be taken until the presidential election had been held in November. Common wisdom was that Truman would be replaced by Thomas E. Dewey of New York. Although the bipartisan support of Senator Vandenberg and the shadow Republican secretary of state Dulles was taken for granted, time would be lost even in the mechanics of shifting from one administration to another, from the Democrats to the Republicans. Inauguration of the new president would not take place until January.

Even after Truman had emerged as the surprise victor, the State Department was still reluctant to move too fast. Congress still knew too little about the details of the Treaty, and needed to be courted carefully until it felt a part of the treaty process. Lovett and his colleagues felt that their European partners were still insensitive to the American isolationist tradition, to the role of the legislative branch in the making of American foreign policy, and to the enduring American fear of being taken advantage of by the Old World. Lovett was especially exercised when Paul-Henri Spaak of Belgium, normally the most understanding of European statesmen, spoke enthusiastically in late November of having the North Atlantic Treaty completed by January 1949. If this was possible it could only be done by brushing aside the peripheral members and making a treaty essentially with the Brussels Pact nations alone. According to the American view, any treaty pushed through prematurely would risk offending potential new allies as well as the United States Senate. If Norway or Italy joined, they should also have an opportunity to make contributions to the final shape of the treaty.[101]

There were other blocks to progress from the American point of view. The promises made by the Western Union military leaders were far short of realization in the fall. Screening the defense plans of the Western Union had been a condition of military aid, and there was little likelihood that the Europeans could fulfill this condition before November 15. The United States would have to accept something less. Reluctantly it accepted an interim solution whereby the Military Committee could provide the U.S. representative by mid-1949 with an outline for defense of Europe to the Rhine in place of an overall plan of defense.[102] Unfortunately the Western Union chiefs of staff could do no more than provide a summary of forces available for mobilization in 1949 if the necessary equipment could be obtained.[103] The JCS did accept General Montgomery's announcements as earnests that would permit the United States to provide aid to the Western Union and the enlarged alliance. Nevertheless the Americans also raised unanswered questions about the seriousness of Europeans' intentions to help themselves.[104]

Criticisms of military plans came from another quarter. Kennan's Policy Planning Staff in November warned against excessive attention to military considerations at the expense of economic recovery: "The danger of political conquest is still greater than military conquest." If there must be military preparations to stiffen European morale, they should be clearly tools to win economic and political security. Preoccupation with a military solution indeed could result in greater insecurity if it would tempt the treaty's planners to extend the commitment indiscriminately: "Either all these alliances become meaningless declarations, after the pattern of the Kellogg Pact, and join the long array of dead-letter pronouncements through which governments have professed their devotion to peace in the past; or this country becomes still further over-extended, politically and militarily." In brief, the Policy Planning Staff did endorse the Atlantic security pact for "its specific short-term value" in assuring the sense of security of Europeans; but then undercut the endorsement with a caveat noting that "the Pact is not the main answer to the Russian effort to achieve domination over Western Europe."[105] Irrespective of congressional mood, the American position on the alliance at the end of 1948 was not fully fixed.

There is of course an element of relativity in ascribing excessive caution or unnecessary delay to any of the partners, including Americans, in completing the alliance. The atmosphere of panic which had prevailed in February at the time of the Czech crisis, or in June at the time of the Berlin crisis, abated in the second six months of the year; the fate of Czechoslovakia was sealed, while the Communist menace to Norway and Italy receded. Although the Berlin blockade continued in force throughout the year, the regularity of the American airlift, combined with its positive effect upon German morale, had removed the need for urgent additional actions. Consequently the magnitude of the sacrifices asked of all the allies had time to sink in to national psyches. That time was necessary for the changes to be assimilated. For Americans the critical question was not whether it would abandon its isolationist past; it was the timing and method of the abandonment that led to hesitations. For Europeans the alliance was more complicated. They could unite on the need to lure America into military, economic, and political involvement with their destiny; they had more difficulty with the concomitant requirement to integrate their armies, their economies, and ultimately their polities.

At the risk of excessive simplification it may be claimed that there were three lines of thinking about European integration among those involved in the European-American alliance.[106] The first and most articulate group were proponents of a new European order who saw in a North Atlantic security pact, despite its military imperatives, an opportunity to shape a supranational Europe. Richard Coudenhove-Kalergi's European Parliamentary Union, Hendriks Brugmans' Europeesche Actie, R.W.G. Mackay's Federal Union

Movement, and Edouard Herriot's French Council for United Europe were in the forefront of this activity. All these groups but Coudenhove's had come together by 1948 as the European Union of Federalists.[107]

A separate course was followed by those who sought fundamental changes but who expected no immediate or cataclysmic tranformation of national sovereignty; they looked for functional changes within the Brussels and Atlantic alliances to come later rather than earlier. Rather than be the prisoners of some grand design, they found in Soviet pressures and American responses targets of opportunity. Movement toward federation could be a happy by-product of the crises of 1948. Winston Churchill was probably the most eloquent spokesman of this group, and Jean Monnet the most practical.[108]

But the dominant force connected with European integration was made up of the politicians in power who were prepared to give at least lip service to the ideal of European unification in order to attract American support. Bevin's initiative of January was inevitably qualified by his fear of Britain being absorbed into the Continent; such a fate would compromise Britain's special relationship with the Commonwealth and with the United States. Despite periodic demonstrations of enthusiasm for a new Europe, Bidault and his successor Robert Schuman were hesitant about French integration into a community that would be dominated in the future by Germans or Americans. Their employment of the language of unity, like that of the British, was to facilitate the political entanglement of America and to partake of its resources.[109]

American views of European unification were almost as diverse as those of Europeans. Senator Fulbright, among the most devout of the well-wishers of European integration, had high hopes throughout this period of using America's advantageous bargaining position to press for the abridgment of sovereignty. The Atlantic alliance was a two-tiered arrangement in his eyes; on one level would be Europeans changing their own institutions, and on another, the United States prodding and encouraging changes. John Foster Dulles was less sanguine than Fulbright about Europe's direction. He wondered if America's weight in the alliance might not dull Europe's interest in integration once its security and prosperity had been assured. Other thoughtful viewers, such as Kennan, recognized these dangers and would limit the extent of the Atlantic alliance while urging the Western Union to envisage a Continent that would unite Eastern with Western Europe in a new association.[110]

The major American policymakers were in fact, if not by design, mirror images of their European counterparts. Lovett and Hickerson, like Bevin and Bidault, regarded the unity of Europe as a ploy to win congressional and public support for a new American policy; the strictures of the Vandenberg Resolution were always in mind. Even when they might acknowledge the advantages of European integration on their own merits, the imperatives of the time seemed to subsume the ideal under the more immediate problems of defending Europe against Communist perils. If an American or an Atlantic emphasis would distort the movement toward an independent unified Europe, they would accept the distortion since the alternative was a defenseless Europe.[111]

The issue was not just theoretical. The question of unification became the subject of serious dispute between Britain and France in the course of 1948. And, despite its inclination, the United States could not avoid entanglement. The trouble began when French Foreign Minister Bidault called for the creation of a European parliament during a meeting at The Hague of the Brussels Pact's Consultative Council in July.[112] Although they understood the gravity of France's domestic turmoil, which underlay Bidault's proposal, the British felt betrayed when the French proceeded a month later to ask the Western Union to prepare a meeting on the subject for November 25, 1948. The British delegation had left The Hague meeting believing that further study would precede its implementation. The action was all the more shocking since France more than any other member had lobbied against enlarging the Western Union. To the British a meeting of a European parliament, no meeting how vague its mandate, could lead to embarrassing commitments.[113]

Almost as disturbing as the proposal itself was the apparent support of the United States for a European assembly. When France specifically asked the Brussels Pact members for a meeting of the five powers to consider its convocation, the State Department released the following statement: "As stated in the Preamble of the Economic Cooperation Act, this Government strongly favors the progressively closer integration of free nations of Western Europe. We believe that the world of today requires the taking of steps which before the war would have seemed beyond the range of practical politics. We favor the taking by the Europeans themselves of any steps which promote the idea of European unity or which promote the study of practical measures and the taking of such measures."[114] Secretary Marshall appended comments to the press release for distribution to American missions in Europe which suggested that American approval was more than a formality: "While avoiding premature endorsement of French or any other specific proposal looking [sic] unification of Europe we intend to encourage publicly and privately the progressively closer integration first of free Europe and eventually as much of Europe as possible. There is danger that unless progress can be made rapidly American efforts to help free Europe get back on its feet will have been wasted. There is also danger that partial recovery will produce complacency and reduce European willingness to take bold measures."[115] These sentiments followed closely the views of the *New York Times*. Over a week before, an editorial had observed that "the new French initiative is a happy augury that

Europe is moving in the right direction, and the United States, in contrast to Russia, which is fighting such a development, can be depended upon to do all it can to pave the way for it."[116]

These official and unofficial reactions by the State Department and by America's leading newspaper confirmed fears which had been raised in Britain earlier over the impact of the Hague Congress of May 1948. In thanking the British delegation to that Congress for transmitting resolutions, Prime Minister Clement Attlee cautioned that the "government must take special care to ensure that in growing towards western Europe, the United Kingdom did not move away from the self-governing countries of the Commonwealth." Bevin stated more bluntly his concern that the European assembly would hinder rather than help unity. "Practical collaboration" that would not infringe on national sovereignty was the way to proceed. As leader of the British deputation to the Hague Congress, Churchill stressed his interest in a European Assembly "as a forum for the ventilation of ideas," not an instrument that would create elaborate machinery whose products would be binding upon the members.[117]

The dangers anticipated in June seemed to be realized in August. The French initiative was all the more serious because the meeting of the European Parliamentary Union in Interlaken on September 4 was expected to intensify pressure on Britain to bend to the wishes of federationists. At Interlaken the voices of Coudenhove-Kalergi, of Italian and Belgian delegations, and of R.W.G. Mackay of the United Kingdom pressed for a European Assembly to be convened by the beginning of 1949.[118] Equally distressing was the visible American presence, personified by William Bullitt in his capacity as vice president of the American Committee for a Free and United Europe. His views appeared to support the earlier State Department communique in behalf of the French plan.[119]

Despite assurances from State that no official endorsement of the French proposal was intended, the British continued to be uneasy.[120] Even as State was privately disavowing the public impression, Under Secretary Lovett "spontaneously declared his conviction" that the European nations must either set up some kind of federation or risk the loss of American funds for the ERP and for military defense.[121] There was an increasingly Anglophobic tone in American press and political views on European unity that was not unrelated to the presidential election campaigns. Republican presidential candidate Dewey made federation a subject of his campaign speeches.[122] The British felt themselves held up to abuse for "lagging behind the French" and "hanging back over European co-operation." Such were the concerns of British officials on both sides of the Atlantic.[123]

Most of their worries were alleviated by the end of the year. Coudenhove-Kalergi was dismissed as a visionary with little power; Fulbright's strictures contained nothing that had not been uttered before; and Bullitt was seen as unreliable and uninfluential. It was a relief to the British that little notice was taken in the United States either of Bullitt or of the Committee for a Free and United Europe.[124]

The end result of the momentum for the establishment of a European Assembly was the illusion of movement combined with the reality of stasis, a position "which will satisfy the demand for a move and at the same time avoid any commitment to the dangerous expedients advocated by the Federalists and their allies." In place of an Assembly, Bevin proposed a Council of Ministers meeting at stated intervals. Membership would be open ultimately to states such as Western Germany. A secretariat would be established to conduct investigations and make reports to the Council. This plan was to be effected by a committee of the Western Union, headed by Edouard Herriot.[125] The outline of its product appeared by January 1949 and culminated in the Council of Europe in May 1949.

The intergovernmental character of this new body represented defeat for the federationists of 1948. Attention would now focus on Atlantic rather than European unity. Given the relative ease with which Britain managed to derail the movement toward federation, it is understandable if British leaders perceived the Franco-Belgian position as essentially soft. Robert Schuman was relieved, in fact, by the British alternative. Bevin was informed that the new French foreign minister "for his part would be only too willing to take my scheme in preference to his own official one if he could persuade his wilder 'Federalist' colleagues that only by such acceptance was any progress ever likely to be made in the direction of closer unity which would include Great Britain."[126]

Bevin's position was not wholly cynical. While it is true that he wanted "to spike the guns"[127] of those Americans who claimed that Britain was not moving fast enough, there is no reason to doubt that the leadership of the Brussels Pact saw a European Assembly as a diversion from their appropriate preoccupation with military security and economic recovery. A genuinely integrated Europe would raise such questions as a single budget for the Western Union's defense which none of the partners was prepared to answer.

The United States, for all its public statements in an election year, essentially accepted the compromise. American interest in the distinction between European unity and European unification was mild; what mattered was a perception that the new bonds which were being made would strengthen the common cause. A case could be made that the progress toward unity not only among Europeans but between Americans and Europeans was impressive in the second half of 1948. What would develop in the long run was of less importance in the short run to the men responsible for the governance of the West.

6. Completing the Treaty: January-April 1949

While military insecurity was a consistent problem for the future allies throughout 1948, the role of their adversary, the Soviet Union, appeared to have altered significantly between 1948 and 1949. The urgencies of 1948 were harder to find a year later. Internal Communist pressures in France and Italy were muted; the parties retained much of their popular strength, but no longer did they pose the threat of a parliamentary path to power in Western Europe. And in Eastern Europe the Tito rebellion had succeeded in detaching Yugoslavia from the Soviet grip with no riposte in sight to repair the damage to a hitherto seamless Communist uniformity.

Nor did the success of Mao Tse-Tung's China elicit any immediate enthusiasm from Stalin. Either the Russians feared that Chinese Communist militancy might touch off an unwanted war in East Asia, unleashing more effective aid from the United States to Chiang Kai-shek's Nationalists, or they feared a challenge to their own supremacy in the event of an unqualified Communist victory in China. It is worth noting that as late as July 1949 the Soviet Union had not yet bestowed formal recognition on the People's Republic, that only with the proclamation of the People's Republic on October 3 did the Soviet Union withdraw its representatives from the Nationalist headquarters in Canton.[1]

Perhaps the reason for Soviet caution lay in its rising skepticism over the putative weakness of the West which such fanatics as Andrei Zhdanov had emphasized since the end of World War II. Zhdanov died in July 1948 and was replaced in Stalin's favors by the more pragmatic Georgi Malenkov and Nikita Khrushchev, who were reputed to be concerned with domestic more than foreign affairs.[2] Or the comparatively mild behavior of the Soviet Union may have been governed, as suggested in the previous chapter, by knowledge that the prospective alliance presented more problems for the West than for the East. The presence of the Communist mole Donald Maclean at the center of negotiations in Washington gives rise reasonably to suspicions that Moscow knew the most intimate details about the inner workings of NATO.[3]

None of the foregoing considerations need be equated with Communist acceptance of a resurgent capitalist West. It is more likely that there was division within Soviet ranks over how to cope with the economic revival of Western Europe under American auspices. Even in the early stages of the Marshall Plan the record showed that overall European production in 1949 exceeded the level of 1938 by 15 percent. Concomitantly, as Averell Harriman announced in May, the level of fear of imminent economic collapse "no longer exists as it existed 18 months ago."[4]

The gradual elimination of the Berlin blockade is probably the most dramatic example of Soviet adjustment to the short-term successes of Western efforts at solidarity. The American supplying of beleaguered West Berlin through the harsh winter months was more than just a temporary prop to German morale, and more than just a convincing demonstration of American dedication to its European commitments. It also showed that West German unification was a reality, at least for the moment. The currency issue which precipitated the blockade was dead. Not that the Soviets admitted defeat as such. But their concession was unmistakable. Acheson observed that Stalin's response to the American journalist Kingsbury Smith's question on possibilities of ending the Berlin crisis was a "cautious signal from Moscow."[5] Stalin made no reference to the trizonal currency reforms. In turn the allies agreed not to implement their plans for a unified West German state pending a new round of negotiations on the German problem at an early meeting of the Council of Foreign Ministers.[6]

Such was the setting for the termination of the blockade. It followed elaborate counter signals from Acheson at his State Department press conference on February 2, and secret discussions at the United Nations between U.S. Ambassador Philip Jessup and Soviet Ambassador Jacob Malik a few days later. Stalin won from the West an agreement to convoke the foreign ministers in Paris on May 23, eleven days after the removal of restrictions on access to Berlin. But while the Paris meeting would touch on every aspect of German relations, the Big Three foreign ministers refused to postpone preparations for a new West German government. They proceeded concurrently with the lifting of the blockade.[7]

Acheson interpreted Soviet conduct with regard to Germany to be a tacit admission that Europe under the Atlantic alliance was prospering, and that Western plans for Germany were maturing so well that the Russians were seeking new tactics to redress their failures.[8] Other American leaders were less happy with the outcome. George Kennan found the results to be a mixed blessing in that they blocked progress toward further negotiations and guaranteed the establishment of a permanent West German government that would divide central Europe rigidly into two hostile halves. The blockade and counterblockade raised the wrong questions and produced the wrong answers.[9]

Even diplomats closest to the scene had reservations. Robert Murphy, political adviser to General Lucius Clay in Germany, believed that the American response to the blockade was disastrous, so much so that he should have resigned rather than participate in it. The airlift was a symbol of weakness which "caused Soviet leaders to downgrade United States determination and capability, and led, I believe, to the subsequent Communist provocation in Korea." The sense of triumph that accompanied the end of the blockade was self-deluding. All it proved was that the United States could "keep alive a great city by the use of air transport alone." The major objective which should have been secured was not: namely, insuring legitimate claims for surface-level access to Berlin. Access in May 1949 was no more secure than it had been a year before.[10] Nor was the result a matter of self-congratulation for U.S. High Commissioner Clay. "My own concept of the Soviet proposal is that it means a complete change in Soviet tactics to win Germany," and if the Soviets would accept the new Bonn constitution, it would be to prevent German integration into the West.[11]

Their new tactics had been in evidence since the beginning of the year. Rather than oppose the changing relations in the western zones aggressively, their propaganda played on the contrast between American belligerency and their own pacific disposition. The campaign centered on an ostentatious Soviet support of the United Nations, particularly its visions of a world without armaments. To neutralize the new American allies the Soviets had to picture the United States as a dangerous intruder in Europe seeking to rearm the Germans in its own pursuit of domination. If the German menace in its new form should be effectively revived the Soviets would have to calm the fearful European emotions which had been evoked by the Berlin blockade and by the Prague coup.[12]

The Soviet modus operandi seemed to reveal offensive and defensive patterns. The former concentrated on the malevolent American intentions with respect to the Atlantic pact. While the language of the Communist press was vitriolic, for the most part the actions were not. Mass strikes, sabotage, or even the threat of immediate military intervention was absent. Not that the Russians abjured intimidation. It was just that a prospect of Soviet armies on the march was confined to the Scandinavian countries, where pressures against their joining NATO were particularly intense.

Norway's entry into NATO was accompanied by heavy-handed Soviet efforts to stop the action. There were shades of the Nazi invitation of 1939 for a nonagression pact when the Russians invited Norway to "enter into a non-agression pact with the Soviet Union and thereby put an end to all doubt." The doubt was more Soviet than Norwegian. The Soviets rejected Foreign Minister Halvard Lange's claim that NATO was a regional alliance and that Norway would promise not to permit military bases on its territory.[13]

Sweden's decision against joining NATO was inspired not by acceptance of Communist professions but out of fear that any alternative course would bring Russian soldiers into Finland. It required courage for Norway's Storting to vote, 118 to 11, on March 31 in favor of participating in negotiations for joining the Atlantic alliance.[14]

The French and British did not escape intimidation either. On the ground that the North Atlantic Treaty violated the Franco-Russian and Anglo-Russian treaties of World War II, the Soviet Union threatened to suspend the accords if those nations went ahead with their plans. The Soviet statement chastised the British and French for abandoning their obligations "not to conclude any alliance and not to take part in any coalition directed against one of the High Contracting Parties." Such was the language of the 1942 and 1944 agreements. The intention was to identify NATO as an aggressive coalition with a specific anticommunist objective, which would undermine the validity of the United Nations.[15]

With all the bombast against Western Europeans the violence was verbal. There were no signals of a possible repetition of the Berlin provocation or anything similar to it. In fact, Soviet protestations took place at the very time secret talks on the blockade were being initiated. The reason probably lay in Soviet expectation that the spring session of the General Assembly, scheduled to convene immediately after the signing of the North Atlantic Treaty, would be a suitable forum for denouncing American militarism and German revanchism. NATO would be presented as part of the grand design for world control by the United States. For this attack to work, Communist behavior by contrast had to be exemplary, at least for the moment.[16]

The United Nations General Assembly convened in New York one day after the Treaty was signed, and was expected to be the occasion for a powerful Soviet assault on the alliance. Much of it had been heralded in Moscow's responses to the prospect of a treaty in January and again in March, which may have taken the edge off the sharpness of Gromyko's commentary. It was not until April 13 that the Soviet ambassador took the floor to denounce the alliance. The performance, perhaps as a consequence, lacked the potency which had been fearfully anticipated in London and Paris.[17]

Certainly the presence of a hostile audience in the General Assembly may have been a factor in the relatively offhand Communist treatment of the alliance. At the very time the Communist powers charged the United States with a monstrous conspiracy to destroy the United Nations Charter, the Soviet Union and its allies were on the dock as enemies of the charter. The silence of Asian and African nations eloquently spoke of their isolation. While the Eastern bloc repeatedly asserted its sympathy for the colonized world, its actions in defending Italian claims to former African colonies, presumably to bolster the sagging fortunes of the Italian Communist party, undercut their professions of friendship. Its minority position on curbing the veto power in the Security Council further eroded its credibility as defender of the Charter. The vote of 43 to 6 approving a subcommittee recommendation for voluntary curbs on use of the veto dramatically identified the Soviet Union, not the United States and its allies, as the enemy of the UN.[18] The majority vote betrayed the resentment built up in response to the thirty vetoes cast by Soviet delegates in less than four years. However the North Atlantic Treaty might deviate from the spirit if not the letter of the Charter, its deviation by contrast appeared modest and pardonable.

Failure to win over the UN may have depressed the Communist world but did not immediately alter its methods.[19] A peaceful face continued to be maintained. Indeed, the British ambassador to Italy made a point of noting that Communist party opposition to NATO was "relatively mild" in its behavior. Only 500 Communist youth gathered in front of the Chamber of Deputies and the Ministry of Foreign Affairs. There were no strikes or mass demonstrations otherwise. Their emphasis was on a "peace front," as the Communist newspaper *Avanti* put it, against the "war" pact of the alliance. The Italian Communist posture was replicated elsewhere.[20]

The explanation continued to be the equation of Communism with peace. Sabotage and incitement to civil strife would be deferred until actual military supplies were delivered at European ports. These activities might not only have failed in their purpose in 1949, but would have damaged connections with the peace movement, which for the moment had better prospects for undermining the alliance than any other tool. A Cultural and Scientific Confederation for World Peace was held at the Waldorf-Astoria in New York on March 25–27, just a week before the Treaty of Washington was signed. While the confederation did not issue specific resolutions condemning NATO, it did so elliptically by reaffirming support for the UN and warning of the dangers of the Cold War. Elsewhere peace conferences were held in Bucharest, Tokyo, Mexico City, and Moscow. But it was in Paris that the most spectacular activities took place, befitting the long French tradition of sympathy for the Soviet Union and an equally long tradition of a French mission to the world. From February through April a signature campaign was undertaken for a collective letter to President Truman to announce that France's decision to join NATO did not represent the will of the people. The message of the World Congress of Parisians for Peace was that the Soviet Union was the protagonist of peace, the United States its enemy.[21]

If Soviet conduct seemed hesitant and its policy frustrated in the winter and spring of 1949, the West had its own share of hesitancies and frustrations in its internal relations as well as in its relations with the East. European federation was at a crossroads as the new year began.

The subsurface conflict between Britain and France which had occasionally emerged into the open in the fall of 1948 was more than a French conviction that the British were dragging their feet on the question of unification. On the governmental level the differences were never very great. More important was the central role of European unification as the symbol of France's revival. Only in an integrated Europe could steps be taken to harness Germany into the new Europe. Britain's cautions and caveats, while perfectly sensible from a practical view of the problems in rearranging sovereign powers, was seen as a blow to France's security. By their reservations the British appeared to be abandoning the French in order to sue for special ties with the United States.

These sentiments were not unknown to British diplomats. They provided an explanation for the hostile press commentary which greeted Britain's request for postponement of a January 6 meeting on European union. Lack of time to study proposals was not convincing.[22] And even when Bevin bowed to French and Benelux pressure to meet later in the month, there was little satisfaction from this concession either in Paris or in Brussels. Britain made it clear that it wanted the delegates to a European council—not assembly—to vote by country, not as individuals.[23] The British ambassador to Paris, Sir Oliver Harvey, observed that the French now believed that "we shall in fact prevent anything being established at all and make the idea of European unity still-born." He reminded the Foreign Office that Frenchmen of all factions had clung, wisely or not, to the idea of unity as a panacea for Europe's and France's troubles. Failure to proceed toward that goal would inhibit movement toward solution of German problems. And if the blame was placed squarely on Britain, as it would undoubtedly be, it would have an effect on British relations with the United States.[24]

At the meeting of the Western Union's consultative Council at the end of January the allies agreed to a compromise once again. An assembly was to be created in which voting would be exercised individually, but a committee of ministers would control its agenda. Out of this emerged a Consultative Assembly of the Council of Europe, which with all the limitations in its functions could be acclaimed at the American Embassy in London as "a significant landmark in the development of European unity."[25] Still, it was difficult to overlook the fact that the "assembly" lacked legislative powers and could not deal with matters of national defense. Only the Committee of Ministers could deal with such matters if all agreed.[26] As Gladwyn Jebb noted, the Europeans won their assembly, but "on the strict understanding that the assembly should indeed be purely consultative and there should be no question of its being directly elected." As a palliative, or so the French felt, Strasbourg was to be the headquarters of the secretariat; the French would have preferred Paris, despite the happy symbolism of a Rhineland site.[27] The council would first meet in the summer of 1949.

In all these deliberations British eyes were directed more to American reaction than to French. Jebb observed that the Americans always seemed to want Britain to move along faster toward European unity than was reasonable. But how far and how fast were never made clear. Hoyer Millar at the British Embassy in Washington commented on Foreign Office concerns about Congress, concluding that the urgency for an Atlantic pact would evaporate if the momentum for European unification proceeded too quickly. While conceding that there were isolationist elements in Congress who hoped that a rapid federation of Europe would lessen the need for U.S. military aid or even for an alliance, he countered that they must be balanced against those who felt that it would be wasteful to give military support to countries which were so divided that aid would not be utilized properly. This particular group in the isolationist camp would write off all European nations as future victims of communism. For a larger segment of public opinion in and out of Congress there was a firm conviction that no alliance would be worthy of American involvement unless the beneficiaries made a genuine effort at all forms of collaboration. In conceding the point, Foreign Office spokesman Ivone Kirkpatrick observed wryly that "there is a very small risk of the unification of Europe proceeding so rapidly in the next few weeks that any solid structure will emerge before the Atlantic Pact is signed."[28]

The British were understandably sensitive to American perceptions of European unity and their role in it. In Senator Fulbright they recognized a long-time advocate of European unity who had sought unsuccessfully to include political unification in the original European Recovery Program. Despite repeated setbacks he had not lost his fervor. When the ECA returned to Congress for renewal in February 1949 he had another opportunity to raise the banner of federation. Fulbright was particularly annoyed at Secretary Acheson's casual remark in his testimony before the Foreign Relations Committee that the projected Council of Europe would be a useful forum for developing economic unity. In response to Fulbright's questions about the delegation of genuine power to the new Council, Acheson blandly asserted that no serious issue of sovereignty was involved. To Fulbright erosion of sovereignty was the heart of the matter and proof of the folly in separating economic integration from political integration. For all its good works the ECA tended to encourage nationalism through national economic reconstruction.[29]

Acheson disagreed strongly with this judgment, and accused the senator of being "quite unfair and wrong" in considering the State Department to be indifferent to the political unification of Europe. The OEEC, he felt, was an integrative body that for the first time could push European nations toward the realization of a European economy. In this context the Council of Europe would be one of many steps "that will bring about conditions which will enable these countries to go beyond the present steps which have been taken toward economic integration. They will enable them to go further, perhaps in the direction of political unity." But Acheson insisted that until economic conditions changed, dramatic political transformations were unrealistic and potentially counterproductive.[30]

That the secretary of state was aware of the important segment of opinion which Fulbright represented was apparent in the reports of British Ambassador Franks from Washington to the British Foreign Office. Acheson needed ammunition, he wrote, to answer critics. Franks recommended that publicity be given to the details then being worked out for the Council of Europe to counteract the negative publicity emanating from Paris about British obstructive tactics at the Consultative Council of the Western Union. The day before the hearings were held, Hoyer Millar informed Jebb that the State Department was pleased to receive the communique on the council issued by the Permanent Commission. It permitted Acheson to make positive references to progress, and presumably obviated complaints which Congress might have raised about lack of British cooperation with other Europeans.[31]

Although the interchange between the secretary of state and the Arkansas senator never focused on Britain specifically, the Foreign Office was correct in assuming that Fulbright saw its behavior as a primary obstacle to European union. His informants reinforced his perceptions. Coudenhove-Kalergi, for example, was convinced that a recommendation to remove his name from the letterhead of the American Committee for a Free and United Europe was part of a British plot against him. He associated the move with the activities of a new British-led group calling itself the "European Movement," which favored a kind of European commonwealth as opposed to his more genuine European federation.[32]

This suspicion of British motives impressed Fulbright. In letters to friends he observed that "from recent developments here and from the discussions that I have heard, it seems that the British are pretty definitely opposed to a political federation in Europe. In view of the great influence of the British in our Department of State, I am afraid the prospects for constructive action are rather remote."[33]

The concern of Franks about Congressional hostility may have been excessive, and not simply because of those dangerous influences on the State Department which Fulbright attributed to the British. Acheson was far closer to the mood of Congress than was the senator from Arkansas when he maintained that the United States should not be in a position of appearing to dictate to the Europeans. He suggested, rather, that "the Europeans must devise these measures themselves, and that our attitude is one of helping them and not trying to direct them and tell them what to do." As chairman of the Foreign Relations Committee, Senator Connally made this point more bluntly when he intervened to claim that in the ECA bill, "which deals only with economics, I would feel disposed to take disciplinary action against anybody in the ECA who exceeded his authority and began to meddle with the political situation in Europe. It is not the purpose of this bill to deal with the politics of Europe, either for a union or against a union or half-way between them."[34] It was obvious then that Connally and Acheson were speaking on a different wavelength from that of Fulbright. The latter's point was missed entirely: namely, that without a political framework, clearly drawn economic aid becomes a species of charity. And should such aid revive the economy, the beneficiary would lose the incentive to change the present destructive structure of international relations.[35]

As a consequence of the majority sentiment, resentment against British tactics was minimal. France was the more frequent object of American unhappiness, partly because of the strong Communist influence in that country and partly because of a suspicion that the French would place Germany, united or divided, higher on their list of enemies than the Soviet Union. The State Department recognized the goodwill and good faith of Foreign Minister Robert Schuman's attempts in 1949 to have a closer association of the "Western German entity" with the new European union. But Americans were susceptible to rumors of French sabotage of any organ of the Council of Europe which might produce a revival of German political life. This was the immediate reaction at General Clay's headquarters to statements by the French consul general in Munich to the effect that France would not accept a central German government into a union; it would consider only representatives of the Laender.[36]

Although there were few in Congress or elsewhere in the United States who would oppose the concept of European federation, there were even fewer who considered the idea a vital issue.[37] It lacked a practical application at the time. So it could be embraced by isolationists who wanted America to be freed from a dependent Europe, or by integrationists who saw in federation the beginnings of an Atlantic or world federation, or by realists who wanted maximum effectiveness from American aid. In most cases professions of friendship for a united Europe were accompanied by an endemic suspicion of Europeans—their motives, their abilities, their innate character. Even such warm friends as Fulbright regularly rested their case for a federal Europe on the ground that its absence made economic aid wasteful, an argument which isolationists could share.[38]

But while Fulbright was worried about continuing economic dependence on the United States, he supported the North Atlantic Treaty without taking into account the dependence upon American military power that would follow from American membership in that association. It was John Foster Dulles, in a moment of illumination not widely shared at the time, who may have expressed this point best in his testimony before the Foreign Relations Committee a few months later. He challenged Fulbright with the proposition that "it is possible that the historian may judge that the Economic Recovery Act and the Atlantic Pact were the two things which prevented a unity in Europe which in the long run may be more valuable than either of them." Fulbright had perceived the point with respect to the ECA, but not to NATO.[39]

Europeans as well as Americans ignored Dulles's caveat. The European negotiatiors of the Atlantic pact had their minds in part on the Council of Europe which was to come into being later in the year. But they knew that its significance as a political entity would be far in the future, if ever. Their immediate preoccupation was with the Western Union as a vehicle for European unification, with its many committees in place, and with a military organization to give it a special visibility. Although American officials preferred to keep the Western Union at arms' length, their negotiating partners were all members of the Brussels Pact who wanted to make sure that they would enjoy preferential treatment within the Atlantic alliance over such newer and presumably more peripheral members as Denmark or Italy. The Western Union was the core of the alliance, an example of Western Europeans working together economically and politically in fulfillment of American prerequisites for support.

By mid-winter of 1949 the Western Union was in full operation, at least on paper. In its first ten months it had established under the Consultative Council an integrated defense organization, including a committee of Defense Ministers, a Chiefs of Staff Committee, and a Supply Board. Under the Military Committee was a Commanders-in-Chief Committee charged with the planning of the defense of Europe. Moreover, the Consultative Council had the help of a Finance and Economic Committee to deal with military deficits, new production programs, and the means of financing them.

But beneath the surface of organizational listings lay some significant troubles. The most visible of them was in the relationship between Field Marshal Bernard Montgomery and his deputy, General Jean de Lattre de Tassigny. Montgomery's personality and his manner of communication helped to exacerbate an inherently sensitive Franco-British issue of which nation would lead. As Montgomery swept through Paris, Brussels, and The Hague in his first official visit in late fall of 1948, he managed to ruffle sensibilities wherever he went and whenever he spoke. Belgians were offended by his military command recommendations, and the French by the nature of his position as he defined it.[40] The general made his own dissatisfactions clear as well; he was unhappy with the headquarters the French had placed at his disposal at Fontainebleau.[41] But the nub of the difficulty was a dispute over his functions as military leader. The French regarded him not as commander-in-chief but, as de Lattre would have it, as chairman of a board of commanders. The French insisted that de Lattre, himself a commander-in-chief, was not to be subordinated to the new Supreme Commander but was to accept Montgomery as chairman and arbitrator, as a primus inter pares.[42]

Although *amour propre* was undoubtedly at stake, de Lattre also spoke for a nation desperately concerned about its military weaknesses. Pride alone would make it difficult for a French general to accept the superiority of a British general; memories of defeat in 1940 made it all the more difficult to place the fate of French defense in foreign hands. Despite assurances of personal goodwill toward Montgomery,[43] de Lattre made clear to Americans the depth of French suspicions of British leadership. Montgomery's military role was identified "merely as a cover for British policy with regard to continental Europe and the defense of the British isles." De Lattre accused Britain of wishing to reorder Europe's military defenses for the protection of Britain alone. Such was the French explanation for Britain's insistence on a northward center of gravity through the addition of Scandinavia to NATO, and a concurrent indifference to the southern flank and to the addition of Italy to NATO.[44]

This was not just the outpourings of a jealous colleague. French statesmen of the rank of Vincent Auriol and Paul Ramadier lent de Lattre a sympathetic ear, to the annoyance of the British. The latter were especially distressed with the undermining of Montgomery's position as chairman of the Commanders-in-Chief Committee for fear of its discouraging Belgium's disposition to reorganize its armed forces along the lines of Montgomery's recommendations.[45] At the same time they were cognizant of French fears of being reduced to the role of "junior partner." The British embassy in Paris advised that French reluctance to place their defense in the hands of a British Supreme Commander did not mean that "they are not sincere in preaching European Union." Some appreciation of their "national susceptibilities" must be manifested.[46]

Jealousies and suspicions existed on both sides, but they were not the heart of the Western Union's problems. That was essentially twofold: 1) the severe military weakness in all of Western Europe, and 2) the unlikelihood that any amount of self-help and cooperation could remedy the weakness. A brave mask was asked of the members so that "the slenderness of the military power of the Brussels Treaty countries" would not be obvious, if only for the sake of morale—European and American.[47] But within inner circles the leaders had to cope with a sharp charge from Spaak at the Consultative Council to the effect that the defense organization was proceeding too slowly, even for cosmetic purposes.[48]

There was only one solution that Western Union leaders could envisage, and this would have to be provided by the United States. It was the expectation of aid from America that both smothered anxieties in the Western Union and smoothed every obstacle in the way of an Atlantic pact. The Western Union saw itself as the pivotal element of the alliance, serving as the conduit for all supplies and equipment and perhaps even manpower flowing across the Atlantic. In a speech to the Council of the Republic a month before the signing of the pact, Schuman alluded with some exaggeration to the powerful American presence that would compensate for the inadequacies of even a pooled Brussels Pact force.[49] Did it really matter whether or not Belgium's occupation forces in Germany were reorganized, or that Britain refused to share its weaponry with France, or that the pace of economic integration within the Union was too sluggish? What counted was the character and amount and dependability of American assistance which alone could make a reality of European military integration.

The extent of European dependence upon an American role for its unification held its own ironies. In January, René Courtain, executive secretary for the Conseil français pour l'Europe unie, considered it important for Europe to unite "as a means of defence against possible American interference."[50] But "interference" in the minds of the Western Union leadership was a small price to pay for the values to be received from American participation in European affairs. Not that the Europeans failed to recognize or to resent the pressures they invited. All the parties knew that there was no progress in the pooling of inventories or even in the listing of deficiencies in production resources. They also recognized that Congress would insist on better performance as a condition for the release of military aid.[51]

Western Union nations had to satisfy not only Congress but an increasing bureaucratic infrastructure which the Truman administration had established to institutionalize connections with the beneficiary powers. The Foreign Assistance Correlation Committee, coordinated by Ernest Gross of the State Department, was established in January 1949 to help the various cabinet officials in State, Defense, and the ECA to assume responsibility for the management of the projected military assistance program. The committee operated on the assumption that Europe must bear an appropriate share of the costs or else Congress would not respond to its needs.

To this end, Paul H. Nitze, deputy to the assistant secretary of state for economic affairs, visited American and Western Union diplomats in London and Paris in January to examine the effect of an extensive American military assistance program on the European economy. He discovered that fear of the impact of increases in military production upon their still fragile economies inhibited budgetary increases from the Western Union countries. U.S. aid in the form of dollars and raw materials was seen to be as vital as military items sent directly.[52] Guided by these perceptions the Joint Chiefs of Staff devised an interim plan in the winter of 1949 involving up to a billion dollars for Europe, mostly for small arms, artillery, and communication supplies needed for maintenance of the equivalent of nine U.S. divisions. This aid was designed to bring into full combat readiness such forces as the Western Union could maintain without affecting the economies of its members.[53]

Generous as these intentions may have been they were greeted with mixed feelings by the Western Union. They wanted at one and the same time full American participation in the Union, including responsibility for Europe's defense, and complete American exclusion from the decisionmaking process. Ideally, then, the United States should accept requirements in materiel and arms determined by the Brussels Pact powers, and then retire from the scene while the Consultative Council decided how monies, weapons, and supplies should be shared and employed. Moreover, the Western Union wanted to be certain that its core role in NATO would not be adulterated by the presence of new members. How to reconcile these contradictory objectives became a major source of agitation among the future allies in the weeks before the completion of the North Atlantic Treaty.

A prerequisite for military aid was European initiation and formulation of a request which would symbolize both the desire and the ability of European nations to help themselves as well as to be helped by the United States. To aid in the coordination of European efforts, U.S. Ambassador to the United Kingdom Lewis W. Douglas was appointed chief of the European Coordinating Committee (ECC) in February.[54] Difficulties arose even before requests were filed, as each member jockeyed to avoid being the first in line. The British hesitated for fear that if Britain should make commitments ahead of its allies, the others would assume that it would bear the brunt of future sacrifices. France dallied, presumably because of forthcoming cantonal elections in March which might expose friends of the alliance to excessive public criticism.[55]

Ultimately, a response to the United States was made at a meeting of the Western Union's Finance and Economic Committee on March 11, at which each member identified its perceived needs. This was not what the Americans had expected, since no plans accompanied the request to show how the aid would be used. Their formal requests did not take into account methods of correcting deficiencies in current programs. In fact, the Western Union submitted its request as a single unit—rather than as individual members on a bilateral basis—which would distribute aid according to the needs of individual countries.[56]

The behavior of the Western Union at this juncture obviously reflected a good deal of resentment, not all of it concealed. Some of it was a reaction to the formal and informal conditions set by Americans. There was an arbitrariness, or so Western Union members felt, about the United States threatening to refuse aid to the Netherlands at the very moment negotiations for a security treaty and a military aid program were underway. American diplomatists felt that U.S. arms to the Netherlands would be used to suppress Indonesian forces. Their stance reflected both the Truman administration's position as truce supervisor in the conflict between the Netherlands and its former Indonesian colony, and the Congress's dislike of colonialism. To the Netherlands' partners in the Western Union, United States behavior appeared to be an unwarranted interference in the internal affairs of an ally and an inappropriate interpretation of United Nations obligations toward the Indonesia problem. The other members of the Western Union then rallied to the Dutch side, partly out of concern that similar punishment might be meted out to them in the future, partly out of umbrage at the tone of moral superiority displayed in American anticolonial sentiments.[57]

A formal quarrel with the United States was over its stress on reciprocity, which raised an image of base facilities and the accompanying implication of inferiority, as if Europe were some sort of nineteenth-century colonial outpost. It also focused on bilateral rather than multilateral negotiations, deviating from the Western Union's wish to be considered the exclusive bargaining agent with the United States. The demand that the United States "should require as a matter of principle, that reciprocal assistance, such as base right, materials, labor, services or other forms, be granted, where necessary," as a Foreign Assistance Correlation Committee (FACC) document of February 7 required, seemed to contradict the State Department's support for European integration as expressed in its recommending such devices as a common pool to finance transfers of equipment and supplies from one member of the alliance to another. The issue was exacerbated when it was accompanied by a statement that "if the lack of cooperation was serious, this would mean no aid at all."[58]

Ambassador Douglas in London did his best to anticipate and head off potential quarrels and to offer balm to wounded sensibilities even when he failed to soften American positions. The United States resolved the crisis with the Netherlands, for example, by backing away from what Europeans regarded as an American assertion of a right to interpret unilaterally its obligations to the United Nations in suspending arms shipments to the Netherlands. "In asserting that right," observed Douglas, "we would be acting on assumption that French, British, Luxembourg, and Belgians will be less zealous than ourselves in carrying out our common and identical UN obligations."[59]

The matter of reciprocity, at least as a bilateral relationship, was less soluble. Douglas warned Acheson: "Although all recognize that we will and should have bilateral arrangements on certain matters with individual countries, if U.S. over-emphasizes attitude . . . we can and will be accused of pursuing same tactics as Kremlin vis-a-vis satellites."[60] But he recognized both Congress's will in these matters and the powerful voice of the military insisting on bases as a vital prerequisite for the defense of the alliance. There could be no retreat from this principle.[61] The consequence initially was an exhibition of passive aggression in which Bevin, of all people, took the lead in denying permission to Douglas and his associates on the ECC to comment informally, or even to see, the Consultative Council's draft of its request to the United States for military aid. The most obvious reason for Bevin's unusual behavior was Douglas's stance on reciprocal aid and Bevin's resentment of it.[62]

In effect the Western Union leaders discharged their resentments with this gesture and then returned to a more moderate position. They knew that the manner and content of their request would be unacceptable to Congress. They understood too that Douglas was as sensitive to their concern as any American could be. So when the FACC predictably objected to the proposition that the United States "participate" as a member in the Western Union rather than "assist" its development, the Europeans reacted calmly. While they did not comply fully with American requirements, they did not rule out some form of bilateral agreement.[63] Despite some qualms in the State Department over potentially hostile reactions in the Pentagon and on Capitol Hill, the ECC views prevailed. The day after the Treaty was signed the requests of the Western Union countries were announced to the public, with the United States response following on April 6. The agreement to postpone conflicts was best expressed in the American statement that "the allocation of this materiel and financial assistance will be effected by common agreement."[64]

This compromise did not mean that the issue of reciprocity between the Brussels Treaty powers and the United States was resolved. It would arise again as an inevitable consequence of Congressional hearings and would remain to complicate American attitudes toward European integration. Still, the Western Union's success in blurring the question for the moment was a test of strength which appeared to pass. The Brussels Pact nations were at the center of negotiations for NATO, and their American bargaining partner on military assistance was the ECC. Although that body was supposed to oversee aid to the other European members of NATO, it was primarily involved with the only effective European organization in place—the Western Union. The result in the spring of 1949 was almost as if the making of the Atlantic alliance was the product of a dialogue between two entities—America and the Western Union.[65]

That NATO consisted of more than an enlarged Brussels Pact was evidenced by the American action on April 4 in arranging for Norway, Denmark, and Italy to present requests for aid on the same day as the Western Union members.[66] These outlying nations did not exhaust the list of potential original signatories. The two most important areas in Europe outside the Western Union were Italy on the southern flank and Scandinavia on the northern. More peripheral and less controversial were the cases of Portugal, Iceland, and Ireland. Each of these countries had been the subject of discussion in the exploratory conversations of 1948, and each had an importance based primarily on strategic location. The Brussels Pact nations had spoken of them as "stepping stone countries" or possible "associate members" and always as of lesser importance than the original five European core nations.[67] The Dutch ambassador to the United States, E.N. Van Kleffens, employed the metaphor of "a peach"—the other nations of the new alliance would be the softer mass surrounding the hard kernel of the WU.[68] There was an air of solipsism about this view, although it was always understandable. The reluctance to bring in other powers on terms of equality reflected a Western Union concern over U.S. military aid which might be likened to a peach pie (to extend the metaphor) whose slices would be reduced in size as more pieces were claimed.[69] It required steady American pressure, informed by a strategic interest in Norway's Spitzbergen or Denmark's Greenland or Portugal's Azores, before the Brussels Pact powers finally agreed to continue the search for new members.[70]

Some of the stepping-stone countries ruled themselves out of contention. Sweden, for example, was interested in American arms aid and would consider a loose and open association of its own projected Nordic Pact with NATO. Yet it never gave serious consideration to its own full participation. Its reasons had less to do with suspicions of or dislike for the West than with fears of its Soviet neighbor.[71]

The ostensible dilemma for the West was how to respond to the Nordic bloc which Sweden proposed as an alternative to Scandinavian membership in NATO. If such a Scandinavian defense treaty ruled out links to other Western associations, it would fit Sweden's traditional neutrality as well as appease the Soviet Union's concerns about NATO at its northern door. Sweden made an effort to assure the United States of its Western orientation, and there had to be some consideration in 1948 of a limited connection of the Scandinavian countries with the new alliance.[72]

Tempting as a Nordic bloc was to Denmark and Norway, the critical matter of military aid was uppermost in their considerations. The three Scandinavian countries could not manage without assistance. Their conditions for accepting Sweden's invitation hinged on American arms being furnished to their regional group, as they outlined it in the so-called Karlstad formula in early January 1949. Norway in particular remembered not only the Nazi invasion of 1940 but also its own alarm a year before over a possible Soviet demand for a treaty on the Finnish model. The condition for joining Sweden was an assurance of American arms even if there was no formal NATO connection. Claiming that such aid would be outside the spirit of the Vandenberg Resolution, and recognizing the negative impact of aid to non-NATO nations upon the members of the alliance, the United States rejected Sweden's propositions.[73] Sweden in turn remained aloof from NATO, while Norway, followed by Denmark, entered the alliance as original signatories at the very end of the negotiating process.

Ireland's response to the United States initiative, made final in the winter of 1949, precluded any association as long as Northern Ireland remained part of the United Kingdom.[74] For a time the British were distressed by the familiar prospect of traditional American Anglophobia being aroused by the intrusion of the Irish question into NATO. They need not have been alarmed. There was no popular uproar in the United States over the British presence in Northern Ireland.[75] Nor did American diplomats take up the cause, despite beliefs expressed in London and Dublin that Ireland's physical location would influence American judgment. In an informal conversation with his British counterpart, Spencer Chapin, the U.S. counselor in Dublin, made the point that the Eire government was indulging in "wishful thinking that the Atlantic Pact powers would be prepared to pull the Partition plums out for them." He was right; the United States had ruled out Ireland, although Chapin felt that the American position should have been made clear at the outset of talks.[76] Essentially the United States fulfilled Bevin's hope that the partition issue would be "beyond their competence" and unrelated to defense needs. When Irish Foreign Minister Sean MacBride reproached Acheson for losing "an opportunity for the United States in some tactful way of assisting in the solution of this problem," the secretary of state replied that such interference would have done more harm than good.[77]

The traditional Anglo-Portuguese connection helped soften some discomfort at the idea of Portugal as a full member of NATO. Opposition, though, was inevitable both because of the dictatorial regime which Salazar headed and because of Portugal's own wish to bring Fascist Spain into the alliance as well. Salazar felt himself bound to Franco through an Iberian pact which he felt might be imcompatible with the obligations of the North Atlantic Treaty.[78]

Unlike the case of Ireland, American pressure came down heavily on the vital need for Portuguese-based facilities, particularly in the Azore Islands.[79] It was not that the absence of democracy did not bother Americans; it was merely that self-deception could finesse the problem of dictatorship. When Senator Henry Cabot Lodge asked in executive session how we could square the "common heritage of freedom" with the Portuguese tradition," Theodore Achilles of the Western European desk in the State Department responded that "although its government is not the same form of democracy as we have it, it

is authoritarian, but it is not totalitarian . . . If it is a dictatorship, it is because the people freely voted for it." Appropriate accompaniments to this
exercise in semantics were the rhetorical questions of Senators Tom Connally
of Texas and Theodore Green of Rhode Island, respectively: "Don't we owe
her a little for Vasco da Gama?" and "Didn't she found Massachusetts?"[80]

The relationship of both Italy and Scandinavia to NATO presented a
greater challenge to the Western Union because their membership could tilt
the focus of power in Europe northward or southward. Since neither could be
excluded, which was the first wish of all Brussels Pact members, a contest
inevitably developed between Britain, an advocate of Norway and Denmark,
and France, the major supporter of Italy among Brussels Pact members. It was
in the beginning an unequal contest, since Italy suffered more disabilities as a
potential member than the Nordic nations. Its geographic location was far
from the Atlantic, the peace terms of 1947 would restrict its military development, and its reliability in light of a strong Communist presence was questionable.

France alone among the European powers raised its voice, changed its
earlier position on Italy, and increased its volume as negotiations for NATO
proceeded. Its position by March was clear: France would agree to the inclusion of Norway only in company with Italy. As the French ambassador in
London informed Bevin, there would be little chance of passage for the North
Atlantic Treaty "if Norway was a member of it and Italy not."[81] The British
view was "that we ourselves are not, repeat not, keen on Italy acceding, but
that if both the Americans and the French wish her to accede, we should have
no objection."[82] This was probably an overstatement since the British har-
bored a residual suspicion that the "real French purpose" in pressing for
Italian membership was to facilitate the inclusion of Algeria within the
boundaries of the alliance.[83]

It was not French insistence alone that won for Italy charter membership
in NATO. The American role was preeminent, and within the State Department the influence of John Hickerson, director of the Office of European
Affairs, was the critical factor. From the beginnings of negotiation he served
as the "grey eminence"[84] behind the senior policymakers, listening to their
reservations about Italy and then either working around their objections or
converting them to his views. Hickerson did have an advantage: beyond his
own intimate knowledge of the details of negotiations he had the weight of the
Joint Chiefs of Staff behind him. They overcame their initial concerns of
overextending commitments in the Mediterranean for the sake of a properly
integrated defense of Europe.[85] This required Italy either in the Western
Union or in NATO. But for Hickerson the key issue was that if Italy were
excluded the Italians would lose heart and probably be ripe for future Communist political victories, if not for direct submission to Soviet demands.[86]

Hickerson actually had as many problems with his superiors as he had with Europeans. Lovett was only marginally convinced, and when he retired, Acheson's skepticism had to be overcome.[87] Hickerson used the interregnum in State during January to commit the United States as firmly as he could to the inclusion of Italy as an original signatory.[88] President Truman, like Acheson, might have accepted a related Mediterranean treaty as an alternative. The Senate Foreign Relations Committee was of a mixed mind; the reflex reactions of Connally and Vandenberg were initially negative on the ground of overextension and of dangerous precedent with respect to Greek or Turkish requests for admission of a nation so distant from the Atlantic Ocean.[89]

Hickerson's persistence ultimately prevailed over all objections, in some measure perhaps because the Italian problem was not central to the passage of the treaty. Reminders of the Communist electoral threat of 1948 and considerations of the defense of the southern flank, along with Acheson's assertion that an invitation to Italy was a "European judgment," sufficed to win grudging acceptance from all the parties.[90] Interestingly enough, Italy had its own objections, not only to having to "defend" Scandinavia, but also to the vulnerability an Italian move into NATO would create for pro-Western politicians. Italy's decision ultimately rested on the possible consequences of exclusion from the revived Europe which in turn could destroy the rising confidence in the economy experienced over the past year.[91] Still, with the exception of Hickerson, all the allies could share with Acheson the feeling that "there had never been a well thought out United States position on the exclusion or inclusion of Italy from the Atlantic Pact." It seemed that U.S. negotiators had "drifted into the position" that the European partners had to take a stand on Italy.[92]

For the Brussels Pact nations the question of Italy's or Norway's entry into the alliance was overshadowed by a conflict with the United States in the winter of 1949 on the extent of its commitment to Europe. America's pledge to go to war on behalf of Europe was the heart of the alliance, as well as the point of departure of all negotiations in 1948. Without a firm pledge the Pact would lose its meaning for Europeans. Trouble began with the changing of the guard in the U.S. State Department and the Senate Foreign Relations Committee. Secretary of State Marshall and Deputy Secretary Lovett stepped down from office. Lovett had been at the center of NATO planning not only as chief spokesman of the State Department but also as chief negotiator with the Foreign Relations Committee. He had cultivated a close but delicate relationship with Senator Vandenberg, the Republican chairman of the committee, wherein Lovett would rarely take a step without clearing it over cocktails at the Wardman Park apartment of the senator. With the defeat of the Republicans in the elections of 1948, the chairmanship went to Tom Connally of Texas, former minority leader on the committee. Neither Dean Acheson, the new secretary of state, nor Connally was hostile to the Western Union or to the projected alliance. But they were outsiders to the negotiations, with very different personalities from those of their predecessors and with less at stake in the outcome of deliberations.

The personality factors were important. Acheson could never develop the kind of relationship with Vandenberg that Lovett had enjoyed. To the imperious secretary the Michigan senator was something of a windbag, and a vain one at that, who "was born to lead a reluctant opposition into support of governmental proposals that he came to believe were in the national interest," but only after he had played "legislative games" which would end with his name on a document, such as the Vandenberg Resolution.[93] Lovett had been far more willing to play those games to win over skeptical or ignorant senators, and had even come to appreciate their friendship as well as their support. Kennan, who differed on almost all other issues with Acheson, was equally annoyed with "the elaborate deference" paid to Vandenberg in the State Department.[94] The senator missed the courting after Lovett left office. He observed that Acheson did make some effort to keep up appearances, and recalled that after the treaty had passed "Dean called up . . . and asked if he could drop in his flat on the way home for a drink—and drop in he did. It was *slightly* reminiscent of the old Lovett days."[95]

Acheson had more difficulty with Connally than with Vandenberg. Connally had been jealous of Vandenberg's influence, and so moved as quickly as he could to establish his control as the new chairman of the Foreign Relations Committee.[96] Whatever misgivings the State Department may have had about deferring to his predecessor, at least he was knowledgeable and reasonably malleable. The Texas Democrat had to start from scratch, and even as he continued steps toward the Treaty in January he remained suspicious of Europeans. Moreover, there was to be no replication in his connections with Acheson of the Vandenberg-Lovett axis. The secretary of state was as contemptuous of Connally's pretensions as he had been of Vandenberg's. In practice this meant that the careful understandings reached in the previous year were in danger of unraveling. At best, relations were in temporary disarray over such issues as the terms of Article 5, the basis of the military alliance.

It did not help matters that Walter Lippmann, America's most influential political analyst, upset over Truman's surprise victory, returned from Europe in January to open his own campaign against NATO. He sounded appalled at the prospect of "zealous cold warriors" determined to "draft" into a western coalition any country not occupied by the Red Army. Lippman was convinced that the Soviet forces could be held in check by the threat of American atomic retaliation, not by a collection of "weak and dubious allies."[97]

Nor did it calm European fears that at this moment the U.S. Joint Chiefs of Staff had planned a defense of Europe that would not range beyond the Rhine. And even then it was assumed that evacuation to French and Italian seaports would be necessary in the short run.[98] There was some, but not sufficient, comfort in the emergency effort of General Eisenhower, who had been brought back temporarily from the presidency of Columbia University to serve as acting chief of staff. Given the apparent indefensibility of the Rhine, he called, on February 25, for "a substantial bridgehead" to be held in Western Europe, or if this was not possible, "a return at the earliest possible moment, to Western Europe, in order to prevent the communication of that area with long term disastrous effects on U.S. national interests."[99] Despite the solicitous tone, this kind of thinking was small comfort to Europeans who would have to be liberated after Soviet occupation. Although European partners were not privy to the details of the JCS plans, they were not unaware of American military thinking. In a major statement to the United Press on the day of Eisenhower's policy memorandum, Premier Queille made gloomy reference to the consequences of occupation: "The next time the U.S. would probably be liberating a corpse and civilization would be dead."[100] Their demand for a credible deterrent made a specific American commitment all the more vital.

In this context Acheson's observation at his February 8 meeting with ambassadors, to the effect that the Senate would find the wording of Article 5 unacceptable, fell as a bombshell among the allies.[101] There had been warnings about the need to recognize the constitutional role of the Congress in a declaration of war and about the power of the isolationist tradition in America. But the Europeans had understood by the end of 1948 that a bipartisan decision had been made, and that all problems had been ironed out in the many exploratory meetings of the Western Union powers, Canada, and the United States.

They were mistaken. Lovett had failed to communicate the language of the draft treaty of December 24 to the Foreign Relations Committee. While the phrase "taking forthwith military or other action, individually or with other parties, as may be necessary to restore and secure the security of the North Atlantic area" was not as categorical as the language of Article IV of the Brussels Pact, it was enough to raise the objection that it would commit the United States automatically to military action and so to war. When both Connally and Vandenberg expressed their discontent with Article 5, Acheson then informed his European partners that the senators feared that the "United States was rushing into some kind of automatic commitment." Nor did he dissociate himself from senatorial reservations. The term "military or other action," he claimed was "an unnecessary embellishment."[102] As Escott Reid pointed out, Acheson's "arrogance of expression" needlessly offended the ambassadors of the future allies.[103] But even if Acheson had been personally more sympathetic, the problem would have remained. The Europeans were afraid that changes of language would reduce, even nullify the value of the treaty. After all, Ambassador Bonnet noted, "the draft text as it stood at present had been arrived at after much thought and negotiation . . . after protracted talks." Given inevitable leaks since December popular expectations in Europe had been raised to a high level; to dash them in February could have a catastrophic effect.[104]

Worse was to follow. A week later these confidential matters became headline news when the Kansas City *Times* revealed that Acheson had concealed from the Europeans the extent of the Foreign Relations Committee's unhappiness with Article 5. The paper reported a secret meeting with Halvard Lange, the Norwegian foreign minister, in which Acheson was supposed to have said that while Congress alone could declare war, there would be a moral commitment to fight.

When Senator Forrest Donnell read this "gossip of an irresponsible reporter," as Acheson called it, on the floor of the Senate, he touched off an isolationist reaction that evoked echoes of the debate over the League of Nations in 1919.[105] Vandenberg and Connally rushed to join "irreconcilables" such as Donnell in disclaiming either moral or legal commitments to go to war for Europe. Connally in his customary overblown rhetoric went on to imply that the Europeans might have trapped the naifs of State. "We cannot . . . be Sir Galahads," he intoned, "and every time we hear a gun fired plunge into war and take sides without knowing what we are doing, and without knowing the issues involved."[106] By his relative silence Vandenberg appeared to acquiesce in his colleague's views both on the floor and in committee.[107]

Nothing could have been more destructive to the purposes of the alliance than this parade of emotions. Any change in the eyes of Europeans could only be a change for the worse. The Foreign Relations Committee's suggestions that "as it deems necessary" could replace "as may be necessary" or that "regarded as a threat to peace" replace "shall be considered an attack against them all" demoralized the ambassadors. How far, asked the Foreign Office, should we "willingly allow Article 5 to be whittled away by American Senators?"[108]

Actually Foreign Minister Bevin was willing to go farther than was necessary to accommodate the Senate. He would have preferred a watered-down treaty in the last analysis to no treaty at all, if only because "even with a feeble version of Article 5 we should presumably secure consultative machinery and above all the establishment of a military committee which would be capable of drawing up plans and of dividing up the available arms among the signatory Powers." The language of Article 5 would not matter in the event of war since "the United States would not be able to avoid being involved in the conflict whatever view the Senate took as to its technical right in regard to the declaration of war."[109]

The uproar on both sides of the Atlantic subsided by the end of the month. Oliver Franks pointed out that the Senate debates had been impromptu affairs, and several speakers just impulsively took to the floor without thought to the implications of what they were saying. In fact, the British envoy to Washington wondered if the crisis might serve treaty negotiations by forcing Acheson to "redouble his efforts to push on with his talks with Senators."[110] Franks was right. The secretary of state quickly moved to repair the damage by calling on President Truman to use his considerable influence. After further discussion with Connally, Acheson won a compromise agreement from the Foreign Relations Committee on the pledge of December 24. There was one change: "such action as it deems necessary, including the use of armed force," would be substituted for "such military or other action . . . as may be necessary." The curse of "deems necessary," as Europeans saw it, was removed by inserting 'forthwith" into the critical clause.[111]

No party was enthusiastic over the changes, but all went along. Even Vandenberg, who thought of himself as the father of the alliance, never lost his uneasiness over the possibility of the Senate's losing its power to declare war. As late as the third week of March, Vandenberg was impelled to qualify his support of a speech on NATO that John Foster Dulles was scheduled to make in Philadelphia because it seemed to make "instant war action by the president automatic and inevitable if there is an armed attack on someone else." He insisted that there would be a great difference in America's reaction to an attack on Pearl Harbor and an attack on Norway. The former would require instant response because "we are the contact," while the latter would require no more than "instant consideration." Dulles did his best to answer that even if the American response was not automatic the results must be the same as if they were![112] In retrospect it seems that Bevin's original point— that any treaty, no matter how flawed, would set up the machinery of entanglement—was the key to the success of the alliance.

Although the tone of the debate was lower, some of the emotions raised by considerations of Article 5 reappeared in the matter of the treaty's compatibility with the UN Charter. The question was present from the beginning of negotiations. It was especially visible toward the conclusion of negotiations because of the close proximity between the anticipated time of signing the treaty and the convening of the spring meeting of the General Assembly. This circumstance, as has been noted, would fit into the Soviets' peace offensive against NATO as they orated on the putative conflict between Treaty and Charter.[113] Reports that leading UN officials agreed with the Soviet diagnosis, if not with its intentions, exacerbated matters. For the most part

Secretary-General Trygve Lie maintained a low profile, contenting himself with the observation that NATO "can be a very useful element in building a United Nations system of collective security." But he balanced this tentative endorsement with a strong warning "that no regional arrangement can ever be a satisfactory substitute for the United Nations." Should the world come to accept "alliances as a substitute for the genuine worldwide collective security," then hope for lasting peace would be in vain.[114]

The treaty's vulnerability to this kind of commentary was all the greater because of the concerns of such advocates of NATO as Senator Vandenberg. He had long identified American interests with the primacy of the United Nations, and in his view a major virtue of the Atlantic alliance was its potential strengthening of the Charter. The Treaty's very existence was a by-product of the United Nations' inability to perform its expected functions in the face of Soviet obstruction. This was the burden of Vandenberg's understanding of Senate Resolution 239, and it remained an important underlying consideration for much of the American constituency of NATO.[115]

Ideally, then, Americans would have preferred that NATO fall under Chapter VIII of the Charter, which would have identified the alliance as a regional association. But Articles 53 and 54, the pertinent models in Chapter VIII, required regional organizations to report their activities to the Security Council, on which the Soviet Union sat. For this reason the framers of the pact looked to Article 51 of the Charter, permitting individual and collective defense, as the means of fitting the Treaty legally into the Charter. But even this article raised a problem. Did it permit prior defense arrangements, as the Treaty planned to, or did it allow activity only after aggression occurred? Though personally impatient with these needless niceties, Acheson recognized the weight of public opinion and came up with a legal distinction between "enforcement action" under Article 54 of Chapter VIII, which would be left to the Security Council, and collective self-defense under Article 51, which permitted individual states to work together to deter aggression.[116]

To the British this smacked less of careful casuistry to appease hostile senators than of a conceptual muddle with misleading implications which could bedevil the alliance in the future. With some annoyance E.M. Rose of the Foreign Office put it accurately: "The Americans evidently want the best of both worlds." They wanted to use those clauses of Chapter VIII which fitted their wishes, and to discard those which did not fit.[117] Europeans were discomfited by the specificity of U.S. international law expert Philip Jessup's claim before an audience of Iowa farmers that the Treaty in no way conflicted with the United Nations Charter. The Western Union lawyers preferred to have NATO assume a conformity to the Charter without descending into potentially embarrassing details.[118]

The decision ultimately was to blur the connection between Treaty and Charter. The latter's name was inserted into four of the fourteen articles, and most notably emphasized in the preamble and in Article 7. But while Article 51 was mentioned, no part of Chapter VIII or regionalism was included in the text.

On other problems requiring solutions before the Treaty could be signed, Canada and France were the centerpieces. Canada sponsored inclusion of an economic and social as well as military community within the text. Although this was a comparatively minor concern compared with the grave military problems confronting the allies, it could have changed the character of the alliance if taken seriously. By modifying the politico-military emphasis it would point toward a broader community of interests in the future. This was precisely what the Canadians, the most passionate advocates of Article 2, sought from the Treaty. Public opinion in Canada demanded something more than just a military alliance, whereas in the United States and Britain there was either indifference or hostility to the intrusion of social issues. But Ambassador Hume Wrong of Canada persisted. "It would cause great political difficulty in Canada," he claimed, "if there were no article of non-military nature. There was need for something which reflected the ideological unity of the North Atlantic powers."[119]

In 1948, Article 2 was at the point of being deleted through an Anglo-French arrangement whereby Britain would support the French position on Algeria if France would abandon its support of Canada. But the French backed off when the Benelux accepted the British position but not the French plan for Algeria. Lovett's intervention helped to keep Article 2 in the December 24 draft text of the Treaty.[120]

New tensions developed over Article 2 when Acheson demanded weakening of the language just as Canadians were lobbying to strengthen it. The new secretary's reasoning was that the Senate might be alienated by its implications and so react unfavorably to the entire text. Although this statement conflicted with Lovett's earlier belief that a broader range of the alliance's interests would make the Treaty more acceptable to the Senate, it did fit Connally's reflection that the "general welfare" clause of the U.S. Constitution had created more litigation than any other provision of that document. It also fitted Acheson's instinctive dislike for what he considered to be vague generalities without practical application.[121]

Eventually Prime Minister Louis St. Laurent's personal approach to President Truman softened American opposition, while the French worked out their annoyance with the British by rallying to the Canadian side and going beyond their position to ask for some mention of "cultural" collaboration among the allies.[122] Article 2 represented a compromise which encouraged "economic collaboration between any and all of them" but offered no details to distract from the political and military purposes of the alliance. Without pleasing any party, Article 2 opened the way for the idea of "community" to develop in the future.

In the short run, Algeria provoked a sharper conflict that seemed to strike at more vital interests of France and the alliance. Had the Algerian departments of France not been included within the scope of the Treaty, France might have rejected membership in 1949.[123] In the long run Algeria was to mean little; the portions of North Africa identified clearly and specifically in Article 6 became irrelevant after Algeria won its independence at the end of the next decade.

But with increasing intensity throughout the period of negotiations Algeria was the focus of French attention. None of the allies were ever satisfied with the inclusion of North African territory in the alliance, but there was little choice as long as France was considered the centerpiece of NATO. The French were adamant. When challenged on the appropriateness of commitments to a territory separated from the mainland by water, they could point to Alaska as a similar case of separated territories.[124] Conceivably if the United States had agreed to the inclusion of Algeria earlier, the French would have given up their advocacy of Italy's membership in NATO. What may have been seen initially as a bargaining chip in 1948, became an *idée fixe* in 1949, as they made it clear that the alliance "must not be exclusively oriented toward the north of Europe."[125]

France did not fare quite as well, however, in another issue on which it had an even greater stake: the formal sharing of power with Anglo-Saxon nations. France feared, as Achilles observed, the continuation of the Combined Chiefs of Staff of World War II which had effectively excluded French participation in decisionmaking.[126] French fears were not unrealistic. In March the British chiefs of staff transmitted a paper to the JCS in which they expressed a strong preference for Anglo-American control over the NATO military structure.[127]

To preclude such an arrangement the French argued for a military committee in Article 9 that would be specifically dominated by a tripartite standing group at the chiefs of staff level. This idea found little favor with the smaller powers and even less with the JCS, who were "strongly opposed to anything resembling a 'Tripartite Chiefs-of-Staff.'" After the treaty was signed there would be no way to avoid just such a standing group but for the moment the issue would be deferred.[128]

The duration of the treaty was also periodically in question throughout the negotiations. The fifty-year model of the Brussels Pact was unsatisfactory to Americans and Canadians. Canadian Foreign Minister Lester Pearson wanted a severely limited period—five years—on the assumption that the military emphasis of the alliance would be temporary, to be succeeded later by a more positive North Atlantic Community "growing within the chrysalis of the

North Atlantic alliance," as Escott Reid put it.[129] Although preferring a fifty-year period to lock the United States into an alliance, the Dutch ambassador would take less, such as twenty years, for the "psychological influence" it would have. Anything less would jeopardize Europeans' sense of security.[130] The compromise did just that. Under Articles 12 and 13 the treaty would be in effect for twenty years, but the curse of a permanent alliance that worried senators would be removed by providing for a review after ten years.

After the difficulties attending Article 5 had been resolved at the end of February, the United States seemed to Europeans to press too hard for immediate action on setting a time and place for the signing of the Treaty. Its importunity was all the more unseemly given its responsibility for delays in the negotiations in the first two months of 1949. Initially the Americans recommended Ottawa while the Canadians countered with Bermuda as a suitable Atlantic symbol. The Azores was suggested as an alternative, to reduce cruise time for European signatories. Washington was not on the preferred list, on the ground that if London or Paris was omitted so should the capital of the United States.[131]

By March the Americans had settled on Washington partly because Acheson would have difficulty leaving the city at this time, partly for the beneficial effect the site would have on American public opinion. While acknowledging that it would be hard to justify a visit to Bermuda simply for signatures, the British were annoyed with the "scant courtesy" with which the Americans greeted their views. But since there was nothing that could be done, "we had better swallow the pill smilingly."[132]

The timing of the ceremony caused even more aggravation than its location. Acheson arbitrarily determined that on March 14 the allies should simultaneously announce the date and publicize the occasion. The secretary of state failed to take into account that the French government could not possibly complete its action on that date since Foreign Minister Schuman was scheduled to be in London at that time. Nor would Bevin's cabinet be able to examine the final text until March 15. Hence, Bevin instructed Franks, with some asperity, to "make it quite plain to Mr. Acheson that I am not (repeat not) prepared to agree to the text being published until I have seen it in its final form." Allied disgruntlement was exacerbated by the belief that the Americans had "jumped the gun" by inviting the formerly peripheral nations to participate in the ceremonies as full equals. The judgment of the Permanent Commission of the Western Union was to permit them to accede to the Treaty afterwards, thereby assuring a superior position in the alliance for the core European powers.[133]

The Americans resisted pressures to postpone the announcement, claiming that the newspapers had already received the March 14 date. Moreover, they pointed out that delays might make April 4 impractical for signing, and if this should happen the General Assembly's session could coincide uncomfortably with the signing ceremony. The ministers finally settled on March 18, despite the fact that it fell on a Friday, when attendance in Parliament would be low.[134]

The signing finally took place on April 4 in the imposing Interdepartmental Auditorium on Constitution Avenue. President Truman and Secretary of State Acheson signed for the United States. The foreign ministers and ambassadors of the eleven nations which had approved the final text on April 2 all signed in careful alphabetical order, aware that an important moment in history was passing. Inevitably there were a few sour notes to mar the occasion. Senator Connally complained that the State Department had failed to give senators appropriate places in the ceremony, a display, he claimed, of "poor taste and bad finesse." There was also a note of incongruity in the musical choices of the Marine Corps band which accompanied the ceremony, as Acheson remembered it, with selections ranging from "I've Got Plenty of Nothin'" to "It Ain't Necessarily So."[135]

For such architects of the Treaty as Theodore Achilles and John Hickerson it was time to head for the nearest bar, in the basement of the old Hotel Willard. Achilles noted that "after fifteen months of effort, worry, and tension, the Treaty was a fact. We could relax, grin at each other, and really enjoy a couple of bourbons." More solemnly in London, Hugh Dalton could record in his diary that "it is a final entanglement of US. (& Canada) in Europe. It is the best we can do—&, of its kind, very good—in this miserable situation."[136]

7. Treaty to Organization: April 1949-January 1950

Once the Treaty came into being the center of gravity in the new alliance shifted from Article 5 to Article 3, with its twin objectives of self-help and mutual assistance. It was not that the question of "the pledge" had disappeared or even been reduced in significance. The entangling nature of NATO was its most significant accomplishment from its inception; indeed, it was the commitment to the defense of Europe that was to fire so much emotion in the United States Senate in the course of the Treaty's ratification. But the promises of Article 5 were essentially passive; Article 3, on the other hand, signified activity; raising the level of military expenditures, integrating national efforts, and providing military aid to one another.

The submission of the formal request of the Brussels Pact powers for military and financial aid from the United States on April 5, one day after the signing of the Treaty, was a clear reflection of the allies' priorities.[1] The timing of the presentation had been the subject of intense debate for weeks between the State Department and the European Coordinating Committee. The latter, representing the U.S. political, military, and economic agencies in Europe under the chairmanship of Ambassador Lewis Douglas in London, prevailed over the doubts of their colleagues in Washington who were more attuned to congressional moods. On the same day, the terms of their request were announced, along with the United States' response that assistance in the form of equipment and some financial aid would be asked of Congress after a detailed statement of specific needs had been made. Denmark, Italy, and Norway added their own requests at this time.[2]

If it was obvious that the major preoccupation of the European allies was military aid from the United States, it was equally obvious that the urgent nature of their importunity risked objections from the American partner, particularly from Congress. The State Department was justified in avoiding publicity in March. It appeared to many senators that Europe was primarily interested in an alliance as an umbrella under which it would drain the United States of its resources. And a close examination of the behavior of the West-

ern Union—its unwillingness to come up with a serious plan to remedy its
military deficiencies, its reluctance to cede bases bilaterally to the American
ally, and its stance against bringing other European nations into the alliance as
equals—would sensitize isolationists to the dangers lurking in NATO.

It was not just isolationists with their visceral dislike of Europe who
created difficulties for the administration in April. Within the State Department itself the authoritative voice of George Kennan, chairman of the Policy
Planning Staff, was troubled by the excessively military character of the
alliance. By emphasizing a military assistance program as the first fruit of
NATO the United States would render too inflexible its own—and
Europe's—initiatives toward the Soviet Union.[3] But having raised the expectations of the Europeans, the United States must gratify them if movement
toward collective planning was to follow. "Our position in trying to negotiate
such arrangements," Kennan observed, "will be very seriously weakened if
we find ourselves unable to promise military assistance to other governments
in question. Our whole position in argument must rest largely on the predominance of our contribution and on what we are being asked to do for the
others. If we have nothing to give, we can hardly expect the others to accede
to our views."[4]

Without sharing the subtleties of Kennan's approach, such leading
supporters of NATO as Vandenberg were as upset as any isolationist over the
mingling of military aid with the guarantees of the treaty. The Michigan
senator had long been uncomfortable with the military face of NATO. For
him deterrence and security derived from the American commitment to Europe, not from the specifics of its implementation. This was a vital distinction
for Vandenberg, who objected as well to any automatic equation of an armed
attack with a presidential declaration of war. He feared for the "nullification"
of congressional powers as well as a dilution of Europe's efforts on its own
behalf. The swift interchange between the State Department and European
foreign ministers coupled with the emergence of 1.8 billion dollars as the
projected immediate cost of foreign aid aroused his supicions. As Acheson
reported of a telephone conversation, Vandenberg "felt that the introduction
of the Military Assistance Bill prior to ratification would present the Treaty in
the wrong light in the country. By this he said that meant that the Treaty
would appear to be a mere prelude to the creation of forces in being in Europe
which could resist Soviet aggression, whereas in his opinion the Treaty would
be enthusiastically accepted by the country if it were presented as dealing with
potentialities and with the determination of the country itself to resist aggression if war should start."[5]

Chairman of the Foreign Relations Committee Connally was also unhappy about introducing a military assistance program before the treaty was
ratified, more for the damage the ensuing debate might create on the Senate

floor than for any intrinsic objection to a place for military assistance in the alliance. Unlike Vandenberg, "he did not rate this difficulty very high," since it was common knowledge that the aid program would follow passage of the Treaty. In any event it would be vital irrespective of the merits of the Treaty itself.[6]

The linkage between the Treaty and the military assistance program had been explosive from the moment it was raised. When the Foreign Relations Committee met in secret session on April 12 it was offended by Assistant Secretary of State Ernest Gross's admission that as a result of European pressure the Department had a program "tucked away in our own files in the executive branch, ready for discussion within the committee whenever the committee wanted to do so." Its members felt gulled by State's secretiveness and worried about popular repercussions.[7] As Senator Lodge noted in executive session the day after the Treaty was signed, "There are an awful lot of people upstairs who liked this treaty, but they do not want to have any more taxes. They do not want to imperil the American economy."[8]

Most of the senatorial grievances surfaced at a meeting on April 21 over the administration's inability to relate two complementary actions—passage of both a treaty and an aid bill—to each other. Criticism ranged from opposition to funds being made available for countries outside NATO to fears that the military assistance program would lead to disruption of the United Nations. At the recommendation of Secretary Acheson the administration agreed to postpone submission of the bill until the treaty had been ratified.[9]

Too much may be made of the administration's ineptitude. Granted that it should have anticipated the troubles that did arise, yet pressures from the European allies gave little choice on the matter of aid. While American attention was on the symbolic departure from isolationism represented in Article 5, Europeans made no secret of the priority of Article 3 once the Treaty was signed. For an alliance to have meaning it must be translated into steps toward security. This required immediate guarantees of aid if the Treaty itself was to be ratified by the respective parliaments. France, the most importunate of the allies on the subject, made it clear through the articulate criticism of Gaullists that French defense efforts would be useless unless supplemented by American arms. "Only half the battle" to remove insecurity would be won, according to U.S. Ambassador to France Jefferson Caffery, when the treaty was passed; the other half would be secured only after American military aid was granted.[10]

To underline this point the French government instructed Ambassador Henri Bonnet to inform Washington that France's ratification of the treaty was accompanied by a statement from the Council of the Republic on July 27 that France must be represented in any defense board that would govern military activities of the alliance, and that the United States must make the supply of arms and equipment to the French army its highest priority. To soften its impact upon Congress the French mollified Acheson to the extent of communicating these instructions informally and addressing them to all signatory governments.[11]

The significance of Western Europe's expectations was reflected in the deliberations of the sixth session of the Consultative Council of the Western Union in Luxembourg in mid-June. It was agreed there that no serious actions could be undertaken by the WU's Financial and Economic Committee until the question of U.S. military aid was settled. Spaak confessed that "the economic and financial problems had in fact been studied in water tight compartments and it was difficult to take final decisions before the United States had said clearly what they were going to do." Bevin provided one comforting note at the meeting, based on his conversations with Acheson: the military assistance bill would be presented immediately after U.S. ratification of the Treaty on July 6.[12]

Although his date was three weeks premature the secretary of state had advised Bevin of exactly what the administration planned to do. The bill was entered the same day the president signed the treaty. What was superficially surprising about both the prognosis and the action was the administration's own surprise at the hostility the bill was again to encounter, as strong in July as it had been in April.

An explanation may be found in the way the issue had been isolated during the spring and early summer hearings and debates on the Treaty itself. Critics focused once again on Article 5 and the consequent entanglement of the United States in the coils of Europe. The public hearings in late April and early May were occasions for outbursts of isolationist sentiments on the part of hostile witnesses that drew fire away from military aid.

It was an occasion for witnesses to assert, as Mrs. Agnes Waters of Washington did, that the virtues of isolation would be destroyed by the North Atlantic pact. "It removes distances that are now in our favor, and brings our front lines right up to Russia. . . . Our ancestors had sense enough to put distance between us and the hellholes of Europe, Asia, and Africa; yet these traitors destroy all that we have won in peace and happiness in 150 years of American progress." Leading the list of "traitors" was Dean Acheson, according to A.O. Tittman of the Voters Alliance for Americans of German Ancestry, who noted that the secretary's father was a British-born clergyman: "It should, therefore, not surprise you if some of us don't like Mr. Acheson's deck of cards. Not that he uses super-numerary aces but because there are too many Jacks in it—Union Jacks."[13]

Language of this sort was grist for inveterate isolationists. Senator's Arthur Watkins of Utah and Forrest Donnell of Missouri harped on the specific obligations that would be undertaken under Article 5: Would an attack on

Norway be considered the same as an attack on New York? If so, would congressional authority be usurped if war must follow?[14] Equivocal answers to these questions confirmed the negative judgment of Senator Robert A. Taft, who claimed to prefer a unilateral extension of the Monroe Doctrine to Europe if necessary rather than have the United States involved in a multilateral alliance.

Taft would have been willing to throw the protective mantle of the Monroe Doctrine over Western Europe as long as the United States would be free to interpret the responsibilities of the doctrine. To underscore the point he joined with Senator Ralph Flanders in introducing a resolution on our extending the Monroe Doctrine to Europe as a substitute for the Treaty.[15]

Other affronts to tradition were exposed as Congress and the public looked at the text of the Treaty. Its twenty years could not be reconciled with even the most liberal construction of "temporary alliances for extraordinary emergencies," as stated in the Farewell Address. To make matters worse Secretary of Defense Louis Johnson, successor to Forrestal since April, was reported to have told a gathering of the Daughters of the American Revolution when he was a private citizen in 1948 that not only were military alliances outside America's traditions but the Brussels Pact was an example of the kind of alliance Americans shunned.[16]

Critics from the Left were even more fully represented than those from the Right. They were supported by Quakers and peace groups who could find nothing in the treaty except provocation to the Soviet Union or a step toward war. In the words of Mrs. Clifford A. Bender, speaking for the Executive Committee of the Women's Division of Christian Service of the Methodist Church, "History indicates that the most that can be achieved by military alliances is a temporary balance of power, while they eventually give rise to increasing insecurity and menacing arms race, ending in war."[17]

While the administration could discount these objections by associating them with Communist attacks, it had more difficulty coping with admirers of the United Nations who worried about the damage NATO might inflict on that institution. The careful placement of the names of the UN and its charter in as many articles of the treaty as possible had been designed to disarm critics. In his radio address of March 18 Acheson had made a point of claiming that the pact was "carefully and consciously designed to conform in every particular with the Charter of the United Nations."[18] This was not an easy juxtaposition to defend, given the impossibility of fitting the Treaty within the confines of Article 53 of the Charter. The administration's spokesman sought instead the illusion of compatibility. Questions inevitably would arise over possible misuse of Article 51, whereby a nation citing self-defense committed aggression against another. Senator Donnell and other opposition senators pressed the administration for proof that the article allowed for the right of defense preparations before attack occurred. The language of the defenders was as murky as the text itself.[19]

Still, the leadership of both parties was satisfied. The Treaty went forward from the committee to the floor. The managers of the pact had succeeded in pushing aside questions relating to military aid. But the issue of presidential authority, expressed in a thoughtful exchange between Vandenberg and Dulles, contained dangers for the military assistance program. When Vandenberg urged Dulles to "put more emphasis on our own freedom to implement our admitted obligation and less emphasis upon the summary power and duty of the president,"[20] his meaning went beyond an American response to an armed attack in Europe. It embraced military aid as well. Once the treaty was passed, the problem of presidential prerogative with respect to the aid program would come into focus.

The Senate passed the Treaty 83 to 13 on July 21, with the opponents led by Taft. Four days later the president not only signed the instrument of ratification but also sent the military assistance bill to Congress. In many ways the storm that had brewed in April over premature submission of aid requests of up to 1.45 billion dollars seemed to have taught the State Department very few lessons. As late as June 24 Acheson contemplated submitting the MAP bill before ratification of the treaty. While Congress had been convinced by July that a bill was necessary to give meaning to the Treaty,[21] it was not prepared to accept a bill that would grant to the president power to extend aid to any country he chose "as he deems appropriate." He could even determine what kind of reimbursements the recipients could make in return for aid, and allow those items into the country duty free.[22]

In the face of a congressional outcry against what Vandenberg called a "warlord bill which would have made the President the top military dictator of all time,"[23] the State Department withdrew the bill abruptly. A new bill curtailing presidential power emerged on August 5 under the more pleasing title of "Mutual Defense Assistance."

Not that the revised bill would still dissent. The administration's arguments that aid in the form of U.S. military equipment was needed immediately to tide over Europe's existing forces until NATO's military planning had been completed met strong resistance in Congress. Why should aid be given, it was asked, before evidence was presented to show that Europeans were indeed moving toward unity and would make efficient use of the aid? As Representative Chester Merrow put it, rather than work out problems of military unity later, "I am wondering why would it not be a good idea as a matter of policy to work out a program that in our opinion would produce military unity and lay this down as a condition precedent to the extension of aid."[24] He felt that otherwise the United States would be repeating mistakes made in the ERP. Congressman Walter Judd was more pointed when he asked

General Bradley: "Do you think that if we give money first before [integration] is achieved, that it will be achieved after the money is given?"[25]

The only response the administration could come up with, beyond the unconvincing symbolic importance afforded by immediate activity, was to identify the work of the Western Union as proof of ongoing integration. According to General Bradley, "The western European countries which are the principal ones involved and to which a majority of this equipment goes, already have an organization set up which has been functioning for about a year and we do think they all have arrived at a point in their plans and their organization, where as far as they are concerned, the conditions you are talking about have been met."[26] Secretary Johnson added that the Western Union "is a working reality, and not a mere paper organization. It has been studied by the Joint Chiefs of Staff, who consider it to be basically sound and in consonance with their strategic thinking."[27]

The trouble with this approach was that the Western Union was too unreliable an instrument to distribute immediate aid to an integrated Europe. Even had the progress attributed to it been justified, the logic behind the administration's argument would still be suspect. An interim plan would not have been needed. But a stopgap aid was vital if only because the Western Union was in too many respects a "paper organization." Certainly its own self-image at this time was far from fulfilling Bradley's or Johnson's description. To the dismay of the U.S. delegate to the Western Union, almost nothing substantive had been accomplished on the military level. As in the previous year the requirements presented for outside aid to meet deficiencies in equipment represented a consolidation of individual national requirements rather than an integrated community need.[28] The Commanders-in-Chief Committee had been unable by June to make any visible progress in determining which forces of the member nations would be available for the common defense, partly because the British government would not discuss the question until U.S. intentions with respect to NATO had been made clear. With understatement the U.S. observer at the Western Union noted that "the effects of this stand are, of course, far reaching."[29] Although early in the spring the secretary-general of the WU had spoken of minimizing publicity on defense efforts for fear of its effect on economic recovery, the fact was that all substantive activity was being suspended until the United States would detail the terms of its military aid program.[30]

If the JCS was unaware of this situation at the end of July, they should have been fully apprised of the state of the Western Union's readiness after a visit to Frankfurt, Paris, and London, among other ports of call, in the first two weeks of August. This disarray should have been no surprise to them; the JCS had been a witness to the impotence of the Military Committee for over a year. Indeed, the failure of that committee to provide Americans with useful information had forced the JCS to take an initiative on their own that resulted in the recommendation for $1.45 billion.[31] What they encountered in Europe made it impossible for the JCS to "be in the forefront in the 'Battle of the Amount,'" against congressional critics. The results were too discouraging. The most that Bradley could report upon his return from Europe was that plans were in a preparatory stage.[32]

The Western Union's potential role as the core of NATO made American officials uneasy in another respect. It implied that the organization would serve as spokesman for all the European NATO partners, an implication that the administration did not wish to emphasize. Yet this was precisely what the Brussels powers wanted from NATO, and it was a major source of their enthusiasm for the alliance. The United States was expected to strengthen the weak military center of NATO and thereby solve many of the problems which had beset the military in Fontainebleau in the fifteen months of operations, including the Montgomery-de Lattre conflict of personalities. From the standpoint of its members, American participation in every aspect of the Western Union, on terms of the latter's choosing, would be the catalytic element in promotion of an effective, integrated defense of the West.

What concerned American planners in this scenario was the excessive dependence Europe would continue to have upon the senior partner. It would fuel suspicions of isolationists that Europeans were only interested in unloading the burden of their defense upon the United States. Within the Defense and State departments the equation of Western Union with Europe increased the risk of alienating NATO countries outside the Western Union who understandably would be concerned if such aid as they might receive from the United States was to be screened by the core nations. So even if the Western Union could have served the role it had reserved for itself—or even the role Bradley had identified—it would not have served to unify NATO. Whatever meaning his phrase "working reality" had for Secretary Johnson, he disallowed the WU's pretensions to become the distributing unit for U.S. military aid when he noted that the WU "is not a sovereign entity which has the means of receiving and employing such equipment."[33]

The assertiveness of the Western Union was understandable; it was a logical by-product of the position the Union had occupied as the European agency which negotiated with Canadians and Americans to fashion the Atlantic alliance. Norway, Denmark, Italy, Portugal and Iceland had been accepted into NATO grudgingly as "peripheral" members recruited to perform specific functions for the alliance.[34] Furthermore, the European Coordinating Committee, under whose aegis the military assistance program would function, was primarily identified with the issues of the Western Union. The hearings on the program focused attention for the first time on the larger alliance. By weakening the central position of the Brussels Pact powers NATO in a sense intruded a disintegrating element into the process of European integration.

The relationships among the European members had raised questions in the ECC at its June meeting in London. The committee even wondered if the United States would act "as senior go-between" relating the needs of the WU and non-WU members of NATO. The decision was to have the United States work toward a close relationship, but the decision was as equivocal as the language employed. By using terms such as "hard core countries" and "peripheral pact" countries the ECC reflected the advantage the Western Union had in dealing both with the United States and with Norway or Italy.[35]

Congressional demands that Europe fuse its efforts were much more direct than the State Department's wishes. The Mutual Defense Assistance Act finally signed by the president on October 6 made this clear by withholding nine-tenths of the one billion dollar aid program for Europe until NATO's Defense Committee had approved an integrated defense concept that would be an earnest of the integration of their efforts.[36] Even with these caveats the bill had difficulty passing through Congress.

Psychologically, knowledge of the Soviet Union's successful testing of an atomic bomb, announced by President Truman on September 23, 1949, was as persuasive as the advice of the JCS and the collective wisdom of the adminstration in assuring passage of the Mutual Defense Assistance Act five weeks later. Acheson was convinced that "once again the Russians had come to the aid of an imperiled non-partisan foreign policy."[37] It may have been, as Senator Connally claimed, the most difficult foreign policy bill since the Lend Lease Act of 1941. And this despite the apparent ease with which the Treaty itself had been accepted. Perhaps the reason lay in the magnitude of its dimensions; unlike the Marshall Plan this was not necessarily a program limited to a few years. Connally suggested with customary hyperbole that the Mutual Defense Assistance Program, as it would be known, was "more generous than any program in History—since Noah extended aid to a distressed and desperate group fleeing from engulfment and ruin."[38]

What was asked of Europeans was not only that they show evidence of integration at all levels but that they provide reciprocity through bilateral agreements concluded between the United States and each ally individually. These projected agreements were written into the act, in Section 402, and they were similar in form and spirit to their counterparts in the ECA act. Bilateral agreements would assure Congress both that there would be some control over the use of aid and that the beneficiary nation would specify what it would grant in turn to NATO in general and to the United States in particular. At stake was 900 million dollars.

Nominally, bilateral agreements were intended to comply with the goal of integration of efforts: they emphasized "mutuality of interest" which required sharing facilities hitherto jealously guarded under the rubric of national sovereignty.[39] Thus the charge of American imperialism or neocolonialism would be neutralized with respect to base rights granted Americans in Europe.

Still, base rights smacked of nineteenth-century extraterritorial privileges even in the guise of an alliance. As long as reciprocal assistance—U.S. aid in exchange for a European base facility—would be supervised by large U.S. military assistance advisory groups (MAAGs) in each nation, the allies tended to lose sight of the integrated principle supposedly inherent in reciprocity. There was something humiliating about the necessity of allies accepting an American mission in their capitals to observe how the aid was being utilized; this should be a function of NATO itself.[40]

The Brussels Pact powers tried to cope with American pressure by a show of unity. At the ninth meeting of the Permanent Commission the French delegation pleaded that negotiations on bilateral agreements be "undertaken on the basis of complete agreement between the five; especially if the latter wished to adhere as long as possible to the principle that American aid should be effected by mutual consent between them." They were willing to accept the fact that they would have to conduct negotiations from their individual capitals rather than in Washington, but hoped that "bilateral" treaties would be concluded only after they had consulted among themselves in advance. In the meantime, they protested directly unsatisfactory elements in the draft agreements, such as the passage in Article I that "stressed rather too much that the substance of the agreement was dependent on the will of Congress, a fact that was not very pleasing from the psychological point of view." It meant, as the Belgian delegate pointed out, that Congress could change the contents of the agreements unilaterally by subsequent legislation.[41]

American insistence upon restricting East-West trade was another grievance. Trade control was easily translated into the appearance of interference in a nation's domestic affairs, and could give new energy to the Communists' anti-American campaign in Europe. More muted was a conviction that their own economies would be more damaged by such measures than those of the Soviet enemy. Although export controls were increasingly an issue in domestic politics, the United States could afford greater flexibility on this issue than on the existence of MAAGs or of the JCS demand for base rights. After considerable dickering about the language which would express the U.S. concerns about the export of war-potential material and equipment, the final version of the bilateral agreements, as signed in Washington on January 27, 1950, carried no mention of export controls. They were expendable.[42]

That the European partners were able to hold their own in negotiations despite their complaints was a tribute to the vigor with which they took their positions, both separately and as members of the Brussels Pact. It was also a reflection of American concern to put the pieces of the alliance into place as quickly as possible. Failure to make agreements would risk the loss of funds authorized by Congress and, more significantly, a setback in the secular struggle with the Communist world. In this circumstance the semantics of the allies' compliance with American laws was as important as its substance.

The semantic component of alliance politics was particularly evident in the use of such elliptical, interchangeable terms as "integration," "unity," and "unification" of Europe. Since Congress repeatedly demanded progress as a prerequisite for assistance without specifying the meaning of progress, confirmation could be summoned from a variety of sources. The Western Union, as shown earlier, was a double-edged weapon, and the administration backed away from it.

The new-born Council of Europe, with its promise of political federation, offered another opportunity for the administration to demonstrate to a reluctant Congress that Europe's intentions were serious and that their efforts should be rewarded with American funds. The council was all the more appropriate a vehicle in that it came into being on May 5, 1949, just a month after the signing of the Treaty. Until then European union as such had never been a matter of high priority for Americans, with the exception of a small circle of enthusiasts who for the most part were outside the administration, either congressmen, such as Fulbright and Boggs, or elder statesmen of the rank of William Bullitt or William Donovan. With its grand vision of a new Europe embracing a wider constituency than either the Western Union or NATO, the Council was never more than a means of stroking an American public that expected Europe to stand up to the Soviet Union by itself in the near future. "The Americans want," as a Foreign Office official once phrased it, "an integrated Europe looking like the United States of America—'God's own country.' "[43]

Not that Acheson actually paid much attention to the council; it was only one of many steps toward integration and one that warranted no special pressures from the United States. It was widely recognized, and accepted with equanimity, that the council lacked real authority, that decisions in the Council of Ministers had to be made by unanimous vote, and that the Constituent Assembly could only "deliberate and recommend."[44] The demands for more powers expressed by the spokesmen for the European movement were disregarded, according to Ambassador Douglas, who had watched the negotiations on the scene. When the secretary-general of the European Movement joined Donovan and the American Committee for a United Europe to press the president or the secretary of state or even the ECA administrator to send a message of American support to an early session of the council, American diplomats abroad recommended against the idea. In addition to possibly interfering with purely European affairs, they felt it would be inadvisable to present the European Movement with an opportunity to exploit the United States for its own ends.[45] In place of a warm note the State Department issued a press release on August 12 expressing the secretary of state's gratification over the Europeans' achievement, but in carefully tepid language: the establishment of the council "demonstrates that measures which until recently were considered beyond the bounds of practical politics have come to be practical and have actually been taken."[46]

At Policy Planning Committee sessions, however, the question of where the United States should stand with respect to a united Europe received more serious consideration. Following a conversation with Gladwyn Jebb, then visiting the British embassy, Kennan received a letter from the British diplomat inviting him to speak in the spring of 1949, in the course of a forthcoming visit to London, about the potential problem of a British contribution to European unification.[47] Jebb's invitation set in motion an idea that had occupied Kennan for some time: namely, the implications of "the formulation of a third world power of approximately equal strength to the United States and the Soviet Union."[48] To provide background and perspective Kennan invited distinguished consultants from academic life as well as from other branches of government to attend a seminar on the subject in the third week of June. The guest list included Averell Harriman, Bedell Smith, Hans Morgenthau, J. Robert Oppenheimer, and Reinhold Neibuhr.[49]

Kennan set the tone of the seminar when he claimed that the unification of Europe was vital to the resurrection of Germany. If France was to participate without excessive fears of German domination, Britain's presence in the new Europe was equally vital.[50] Professor Morgenthau seemed to share Kennan's musing that Britain would have to be pushed into unification, and went beyond his conclusion in asserting that without American pressure the British would not move.[51] The alternatives seemed to be little more than wishful thinking, such as Niebuhr's speculation that the Germans might lose their aggressive qualities much as the French did after Napoleon, or General Smith's wistful references to Sweden's history since the eighteenth century as a model for Germany.[52] Kennan's own hopes were never concealed; he wanted unification of Eastern and Western Europe, including both Germanies, with the United States and Britain outside this configuration—and the Soviet Union reconciled to its own exclusion as well.[53] But this was a chimera and he knew it. If the seminar reached any conclusions they were that there was no escape from a major American role in the future of Western Europe, and that military integration might be a more effective means to achieve European unity than political or even economic efforts.

Although it was not represented at these sessions, there was an organization that would vigorously support most of these conclusions. This was the Atlantic Union Committee, founded by Clarence Streit and led in 1949 by former Supreme Court Justice Owen Roberts, former Undersecretary of War Robert P. Patterson, and former Undersecretary of State Will Clayton. Their names carried greater weight than those of their counterparts in the American Committee for a United Europe, and their more aggressive posture toward the

Soviet Union won more adherents in Congress. For them the Atlantic pact, which they strongly supported, was a first step toward a federal union of Atlantic democracies that would include the United States and Canada. Because it appeared to promise a united Europe, it intrigued Senator Fulbright. Clayton indeed claimed to share Fulbright's idea that the best solution would be a European-only federation, but added that only adherence of the United States to such an organization would supply Europeans with the leadership they would continue to lack.[54] As a consequence of their vigorous propaganda, figures of such prominence as New York senatorial candidates Herbert Lehman and John Foster Dulles expressed their willingness to vote for an Atlantic Union Committee resolution in the Senate which would "invite democracies that sponsored the North Atlantic Treaty to meet in convention to explore how far they can apply among their people the principle of free federal union."[55]

Despite the enthusiasm in the Senate that the idea of the Atlantic Union seemed to generate, the State Department was skeptical. It recommended "approval of the spirit reflected in the resolution and of the goals envisaged," but concluded that there should be no fundamental change in U.S. foreign policy. Ostensibly, potential State Department support foundered on the dangers of increased friction with the Soviet Union which might result from this challenge and on the complications it would have for the Charter of the United Nations. In fact, the policymakers had "other reasons" in mind, as John Hickerson suggested. U.S. membership in an Atlantic federal union would undo the efforts currently being made to force Europeans into self-help and mutual aid.[56] So for different reasons Atlantic Union proposal was no more useful than the Western Union or the Council of Europe to serve as proof to Congress of Europe's fulfillment of its terms for military assistance.

The British for their part were as wary of entrapment by the Atlantic Union Committee as were their American partners. Despite the temptation U.S. involvement must have held, British officials resisted the attempts of Clarence Streit to elicit explicit British endorsement of a federal union. Foreign Minister Bevin's advisers even urged him to avoid a meeting with Streit since "competitors who have variations on this theme may also want an appointment." The Atlantic Union plan was too idiosyncratic; it might lead Britain into a trap that would compromise its position as a world power and as a member of the Commonwealth.[57]

The negative response to Streit was predictable. The British felt they had done all they could on behalf of the Continent when they joined the Council of Europe. Their ties to the sterling bloc and their hopes for a special relationship with the United States precluded their surrendering sovereignty beyond a limited point. As Kennan recognized in his preparations for talks with Jebb in London, there was "a ceiling beyond which union in the continent cannot advance—a very low ceiling."[58] Bevin made the British position clear in his report to the cabinet on the first session of the Council of Europe: "The principal objective of our policy is to reconcile our position . . . . We believe that we can effect this reconciliation but that if we are to do so, we cannot accept obligations in relation to Western Europe which would prevent or restrict the implementation of our responsibilities elsewhere."[59]

Given the importance of British cooperation in a Franco-German rapprochement as well as in the integration of economic and military efforts in Europe, it is hardly surprising that Britain's adamancy attracted unfavorable attention in Washington. Its rigidity galvanized in particular Paul Hoffman, administrator of the ECA, who was concerned over the effect of Britain's position on the economic integration of Europe.[60] It was one thing for the British to express their reservations about the Council of Europe or to dismiss the importunities of the Atlantic Union Committee. But for them to disrupt the economic rehabilitation of Europe by such actions as devaluation of the pound in September 1949, which could set back the progress of the past two years, was quite another. Paul-Henri Spaak, former chairman of the OEEC Council of Ministers and currently president of the Consultative Assembly of the Council of Europe, made the point that devaluation imposed on all of Western Europe the burden of producing one-sixth to one-third more goods in order to earn the same amount of dollars.[61]

Beginning with a major speech to the OEEC Council in Paris on October 31, a speech aimed at pushing Britain into the Continent, Hoffman demanded that the OEEC demonstrate its commitment to economic integration, which in turn could only be accomplished through political integration. Although he had consulted the State Department before issuing his "ultimatum," he disregarded the obvious discomfort of Under Secretary of State James E. Webb, who noted that "the requirements for the so-called unification of Europe were by no means so clear in the minds of State Department policy and economic staffs as they appeared to be in his."[62]

In all Hoffman's considerations Britain appeared to be the major obstacle to the salvation of Europe. Britain's planned national economy clashed with the American vision of free trade within a European bloc; its concern for its prerogatives as leader of the Commonwealth foreclosed its proper role as a leader of Europe. At the same time, British officials inhibited others from assuming leadership, as they stood accused of blocking steps toward a Franco-Italian customs union. While France would welcome recognition as the first nation of Europe, its fear of Germany made necessary a sharing of this authority with Britain.

Although the State Department appeared to be part of the ECA effort to dislodge the British from their stance on Europe, it was far more flexible in its behavior and more willing to accept the situation as the British presented it. Kennan's successor as chairman of the Policy Planning Staff, Paul Nitze, might repeat slogans about European integration, but in essence he and his colleagues shared Kennan's judgment that Britain's reasons for opposition were so compelling that "no framework of association which included the United Kingdom but excluded the United States and Canada would be permitted to advance to a stage resembling real merging sovereignty."[63] Acheson only went through the motions of reproaching Britain. Sir Leslie Rowan of the British embassy in Washington could conclude by the spring of 1950 that the State Department did not consider the ECA to be the "right instrument in securing politico-military union; and secondly, they are equally sure that they should *not* write a blueprint for Europe."[64]

Important as the concept of European integration was for the success of the continental economy, it had other applications as well. Integration of Europe could be the vehicle for the successful solution of the German problem. From the beginning NATO was linked to Germany. The creation of the West German state, made possible through the trizonal arrangements of 1948, culminated in the birth of the Federal Republic in May 1949, one month after the signing of the North Atlantic Treaty. Acheson made clear his own belief in the linkage of the two when he expressed his conviction on April 8 that "the success of these negotiations on German affairs had been greatly facilitated by the conclusion of the North Atlantic Treaty. Without it, I doubt that we could have come to a successful conclusion of the agreements at this time."[65]

There was an obvious attraction about a German contribution to NATO, in terms of both the resources Germans could bring to the alliance and the restraints that an Atlantic community might impose on controls on a rehabilitated Germany. Congress responded favorably. On the crassest level German membership in an Atlantic or European community would force Germans to contribute their fair share of the costs to the common defense effort. As Senator Watkins noted, "We certainly are not going to fight all their battles for them."[66] Dulles expanded on this point in more sophisticated language. Fearing that Germany would be tempted to use its potential power as a bargaining chip between East and West, he urged the integration of the Federal Republic firmly into the Western community to obviate a Rapallo-like rapprochement with the Soviet Union. A "temporary alliance" might be made in the future to induce the Soviets to return lost German territories in Eastern Europe. In executive session Vandenberg offered another reason for bringing Germany into association with NATO: membership would dissolve French fears of Germany. Indeed, he claimed that the Treaty itself had already caused a reversal of French attitudes on the German question. French confidence in dealing with its neighbor was "one of the results of even having written the North Atlantic Pact."[67]

Despite an affirmative statement on the advantages of unity and security that Germany might confer on NATO, the report to the Senate Foreign Relations Committee brought no call for action.[68] The administration's language on the German issue was carefully modulated at the Senate hearings on the Atlantic alliance. Its spokesmen were cautious in every instance. Although Harriman noted that West Germany had been accepted into the OEEC for good economic reasons, there was uncertainty about the solidity of democracy in Germany. Hence only in the future, at "such time as there is concrete evidence that there is a real democratic Germany developing," would steps toward a military collaboration be taken. Former Under Secretary of State Lovett concurred with Harriman's judgment, noting that while Germany was discussed in the negotiations over the treaty, "We found that its circumstances at the present time make it impossible to be considered as a participant." As the most responsible official testifying, Secretary Acheson did his best to beg the question. When asked if the inclusion of western Germany would improve the strategic position of the Atlantic powers, he claimed he was no military expert but said that "quite clearly at the present time a discussion of including western Germany in the pact is not possible."[69]

Official caution did not inhibit public outbursts on the subject by congressional committees or private speculations in the Policy Planning Staff.[70] A congressional committee visiting Bonn in November 1949 openly recommended including West Germany in the Western Union. And at the seminars of June the need both for bringing Germany into the West and for preventing it from dominating Europe generated much of the emotion over a British contribution. It also produced a suggestion from J. Robert Oppenheimer that German affiliation could begin with adherence to the Council of Europe.[71] Such an idea did not escape the attention of the Permanent Commission of the Western Union, which discussed in October possibilities of an associate membership for the Federal Republic if the question of the Saar could be managed to France's satisfaction.[72] But no matter how fully integration might take place in the Council of Europe, it was recognized from the beginning that there were limits to the significance of German membership in anything less than NATO itself.[73]

The German question inevitably returned to the role of Britain as a balance to German power and as a reassurance to France. At a meeting of U.S. ambassadors in Europe in October there was agreement that "it is not realistic to expect that France will take the leadership in bringing about western European integration without UK participation," a view shared by Acheson.[74] Kennan, however, queried the wisdom of insisting too strongly on British participation if the result would end in tearing apart European union. This sentiment harked back to the ideas expressed in the June seminars of the Policy Planning Staff, when Kennan and his associates looked for alternatives to "underwriting a German-dominated Europe" and a U.S. or British-connected Europe which would spoil forever a unification of Germany. "Continental union," as he wrote in his memoirs, should be detached from Britain, the United States, and Canada if there was to be serious prospect of a demilitarized united Europe that would include East and West.[75]

For the moment Kennan found the French problem more serious and perhaps more hopeless than the German. France was obviously paranoid on the subject of an Anglo-Saxon conspiracy to encourage German revanchism. "I don't see that there is anything we can do for the French," Kennan claimed. "If anyone can entertain the proposition that the efforts made in this Government to put through and implement the Marshall Plan, the Atlantic Pact, and the Military Arms Program were some sort of cynical joke and that all these things were done only with a view of sudden abandonment of the continent in precisely September 1949, I am afraid, there is no place here for rational arguments." Moreover, he asked if today, with a partitioned, disarmed Germany facing a France linked by treaty to the United States, the French are immobilized by fear, "Can we really expect that the French will show greater capacity for leadership and initiative in Europe at some future date, when Germany has emerged from many of the present controls and handicaps?"[76]

What Kennan suggested is that the British role might not really be relevant to France's situation. French resistance to integration was just as stubborn as British, and considerably more hysterical. Throughout the fall of 1949 Acheson had to assure the French repeatedly that no secret plan to rearm Germany was in the making.[77] No reassurances really sufficed. From the private Washington talks with British or Canadian representatives to formal Anglo-American arrangements for the devaluation of the pound, the French felt themselves excluded and at a special disadvantage. In December 1949 the French delegation expressed its unhappiness at a meeting of the Permanent Commission of the Western Union upon learning "with some surprise via the press of Anglo-American-Canadian agreement on standardization of armament." If this report was accurate, the French claimed, it would prejudge the work of the Brussels Pact operations.[78]

The most serious confrontation of this period took place in September when Ambassador Bonnet asserted that "an historical policy decision" had been taken whereby the economies of the United States, Canada, and the United Kingdom and Commonwealth would function independently of the United States relationship with Europe. This would not only constitute a breach with the principles of the OEEC, WU, and Council of Europe, but would leave "France alone on the Continent with the Germans."[79] Emotions were intensified by the commentaries of major pundits of the American press. The Alsop brothers supported by Walter Lippman connected this "decision" with Kennan's familiar scheme of two strategic groups coexisting within NATO, even as they recognized the unfairness of the charge.[80] But Bonnet himself did not escape criticism since he seemed to be soft on the issue of a European army. According to President Auriol that idea had seduced Americans, who would then proceed to the creation of a German army.[81]

In light of these conflicts confusion on all sides seemed to prevail in the alliance at the end of 1949. Germany was supposedly encouraged to revive under the umbrella of a united Europe, but there were few signs of unified activity. To reassure the anxious French that Britain was fully identified with the new Europe, the United States supplemented its German policy with continued decartelization plans and the continuation of reserved powers under the Occupation Statute. "Thus we have," as the special assistant to the director of the Bureau of German Affairs claimed, "a sufficient array of words and names and alphabetical agencies to permit any official spokesman to write or speak in such manner as to make it appear that the people of the other nations can safely hover beneath the benevolent wings of a gentle but powerful American Eagle." But he went on to ask if we were naive enough to believe that Europeans were "simple-minded." Why should they be comforted about American military support when Secretary of Defense Johnson had announced sizable reductions of the military establishment? Why should they give up sovereign rights for "political integration" when the United States would make no commitments as to which armed forces would be stationed in Europe, at the same time that it seemed to encourage the formation of a German army? "Why argue that France is our greatest problem in Europe when the French, living with the realities of history, have only words as defense and the evidence of an ever stronger Germany as a growing offense."

This cry of despair was uttered in a memorandum that was not distributed. It was less a diatribe against the untrustworthiness of the former enemy than against the absence of a rational, coherent American policy toward Europe. If integration of Europe truly hung on the arming of Germany, the United States was playing a most dangerous game. Even if Chancellor Adenauer had pledged to free Germany from revanchism and militarism (and the U.S. official did not doubt Adenauer's good faith), "Who then protects a new sovereignty? Not we, who have no military! Not the MAP because we can't assure the other nations of the extent of our participation. The MAP is still in chaos. Must we arm our former enemies and gamble on their choice of allies?"[82]

Rhetorical questions of the foregoing kind implied a bleak prospect for the allies in the wake of passage of the Treaty and the military aid program. Certainly much of the charge appeared credible. The United States did want

German resources put to the use of the West but never made its terms clear to Germans, French, or British. But for all the disarray that appeared so prominent in the day-to-day interaction among the major powers of NATO, a movement toward cohesion in the alliance proceeded concurrently with the friction. The Treaty, after all, had passed the ratifying hurdles of all twelve members, beginning with Canada on May 3 and concluding with Italy on August 24. In the case of the United States the passage broke a tradition against entangling alliances that went back to the beginnings of the republic. A major military assistance program had been initiated, no matter how many caveats Congress attached to its final form. And with all the American suspicions about the Western Union's intentions, its experience provided a framework for the growth of the organization. The Western Union served as a regional planning group, and its subsidiary bodies, such as its Military Committee, offered what products it did have directly to NATO. The WU Military Supply Board, on which the United States had placed an observer, was absorbed into NATO's Military Production and Supply Board, while its Finance and Economic Committee became in effect NATO's Defense Financial and Economic Committee.[83]

The major agent for change in the summer and fall of 1949 was a Working Group of the allies, and its initial results were advertised in three sessions of the North Atlantic Council held between September 1949 and January 1950.[84] To assist in formulating an American position a special U.S. task force was established composed of State and Defense representatives. Before the first meetings of the Working Group in August, the U.S. team recommended the establishment of both a civilian and a military cadre for NATO, a proposal that was ultimately accepted. The civilian cadre would be housed in the council, with a finance committee reporting to it on the economic and financial impact of defense plans and on the ability of the allies to carry them out. The military cadre would consist of a Defense Committee made up of defense ministers at the top, with a Military Committee Steering Group and a military supply board under it. In all its deliberations the voice of the U.S. Joint Chiefs of Staff carried special weight.[85]

The issue of a steering group weighed heavily upon all parties. Many of France's suspicions about the Anglo-American special relationship rested on a British idea for reviving the World War II combined chiefs of staff in the form of a NATO military directorate. Italy was equally anxious to be a member of such a group as a symbol of its importance in the alliance. The JCS carefully detached themselves from the British formula by bringing France into a steering group. At the same time they agreed to maintain a "modus vivendi" for continuing the old close ties with Britain within the NATO framework; the British joint services committee would remain in Washington. The question of representation appeared solved by the time of the first meeting of the

NATO Council, when it was announced that a Military Committee, composed of one military representative from each member nation, would provide policy guidance to the Defense Committee, while a Standing Group of the three major powers would operate continuously in Washington.[86]

Pressures from the Western Union core group to take over the organization on as many levels as possible were more difficult to dissolve. There was nothing new about its aspirations; they had been apparent from the inception of negotiations for an Atlantic treaty in 1948. So when the NATO Council delegates at their first meeting agreed to establish five regional planning groups, it was not surprising that the Western European Regional Planning Group, coextensive with the Western Union area, expected not only to be the dominant element in the organization but wanted, as the Brussels Pact Powers always did, the United States to join it as a full member. And, as in the past, the Americans resisted, in order, as the JCS phrased it, "to stimulate them more readily to greater measures of self-help and mutual aid." Should the United States become a member it would be equally logical to join the Northern European Regional Group and other groups as well. The most that the United States would accept was "participation as appropriate." The result was that the United States became a full member of the North Atlantic Ocean Regional Planning Group and the Canada-United States Regional Planning Group while serving as a "consulting member" for the other three planning groups. The most that the U.S. would accept was "participation as appropriate."[87]

Similarly, the JCS advised the interagency negotiating team to oppose Europe's wish to integrate American military resources into the existing Western Union Supply Board and then to label the enlarged unit the NATO Supply Board. The JCS felt there were too many pitfalls in this idea. First, it would elevate a regional planning group's board, Western Europe's, above all the others, and would sabotage the intention of an overall military board to supervise all the organization's activities. Secondly, the submerging of American resources into a NATO pool would render them exposed to the judgment of Europeans. This was unacceptable, if only because it would tempt the allies to pile all the costs onto the affluent Americans. The chief concern of the JCS, as always in the alliance, was to keep the United States free from European interference with strategic choices.[88]

A potential conflict of interest arose also out of the scope of authority to be granted to the Defense Financial and Economic Committee, which like the Military Production and Supply Board, was formally established at the second session of the North Atlantic Council in Washington on November 18. While Europeans were pleased to accept a finance committee sensitive to the limitations of their fiscal abilities and to the potential impact of rearmament upon their national economies, they would have preferred to postpone the workings of the DFEC until the military organs of the alliance had submitted their supply and production programs. Furthermore, they would rather have located the headquarters of the MPSB in Washington, whereas the Americans wanted it in Europe on the grounds that its primary purposes were to increase and coordinate production in Europe. If headquarters were in Washington the focus of its activities might be shifted to the American contribution rather than the European. The issue was resolved for the moment by having both agencies maintain offices in Washington and London.[89]

Most of the organizational pieces of the alliance were fitted together by the winter of 1950, and accomplished with a minimal amount of tension. Such difficulties as did come to the surface at this time were mostly between the United States and the partners of the Western Union. A compromise permitting Western Union committees to continue their accustomed functions until the new NATO groups replaced them assured the continuing special influence of the Brussels Pact powers.[90]

Wrangling for positions in the organization among the other members was relatively mild. Portugal and the Scandinavian countries, recognizing that they had special roles to play, minimized their involvement in other areas. Portugal was reconciled to the knowledge that its membership in the alliance would not conflict with its Iberian obligations, and so avoided the politics of policymaking.[91]

Italy was the exception. It had long been a source of contention, and its membership had been deferred until the very end of the treaty-making process. The Italian government wanted membership both on the Standing Group and on the regional planning group for Western Europe. It rested its case for the latter on the claim that the defense of Western Europe was based on holding a line running from Trieste through the Rhine valley to the North Sea. The allies rejected Italy's application and the validity of its role. Nor would the United States accept Italian representation on the Standing Group or consider an alternative establishment of a single European planning committee. Acheson's assurance that all three European regional committees would meet frequently in combined sessions, along with a warning that Italy's treaty restrictions would limit its role generally, brought Italy into line at this time.[92]

Still, there was a fallout from Italy's membership in NATO that had been anticipated in arguments against bringing that Mediterranean country into the alliance. Greece and Turkey had difficulty in reconciling themselves to Italy's inclusion and their exclusion. The reasons advanced for leaving them out were applicable to any country outside the North Atlantic area. If Italy—a lesser power in the Mediterranean from Turkey's point of view, and a former

Axis enemy—was acceptable to the allies, then the vital strategic position of Turkey along with its considerable military potential should have been a welcome addition to the organization.[93]

It is worth observing that the negotiations on the construction of NATO machinery progressed rapidly between August and January. It may have represented only a "pre-integration organization," in Acheson's words, "aimed to produce general plans for uncoordinated and separate action in the hope that in the event of trouble a plan and the forces to meet it would exist and would be adopted by a sort of spontaneous combustion." These were the words, however, of an elder statesman writing after the Korean War had given a different perspective to the activities of 1949.[94] A comparison of 1949 with 1948 rather than with 1950 would find that NATO's use of WU models, inadequate though many of them were, provided a degree of integration for Europe that would not have been possible otherwise. The United States pushed Europe to accept an American view of military production and supply, and then to undertake a variety of reviews of their common concerns, from the provision of spare weaponry parts to an adjustment of the location of production facilities.[95]

At the same time, the senior partner made an effort to become attuned to the sensibilities of smaller allies. When the Danish representative at the second meeting of the Defense Committee in Paris on December 1 asked that the strategic concept delete from its text specific reference to atomic bombs defending NATO territory, Belgian, Dutch, and Italian ministers objected that the deletion of specific mention of the bomb would dilute the deterrent effect of the strategic plan. A compromise was reached through the following language: "Insure the ability to carry out strategic bombing promptly by all means possible with all types of weapons, without exception."[96]

A more widespread concern agitating most European members of the alliance was that the proposed strategic plan, despite American assurances to the contrary, still subscribed to the principle that Western Europe was indefensible in the short run. They were suspicious about plans circulating in the JCS to the effect that the immediate objective of U.S. forces in Europe after a Soviet attack would be to abandon the heart of the Continent in favor of outposts in the Iberian peninsula and the United Kingdom. The U.S. spokesman conceded that there was little that could be done immediately, but emphasized that the key to success lay in the threat of making such an attack too costly to undertake. Then, under the umbrella of this deterrent, the West would prepare coordinated plans to defend Europe in the future "as far eastward on the Continent as was possible."[97]

This understanding of American thinking disturbed most of the allies. Even the best prognosis, a strong defensive position on the Rhine, was hardly comforting to the Danes or the Dutch. In each instance, as Najeeb Halaby, director of the Office of Military Affairs in the Department of Defense, observed, the NATO allies were "apt to emphasize the need for plans to defend their territories in toto."[98]

European suspicions of the JCS were for the most part justified. The U.S. military chiefs had never concealed their skepticism about the dangers of American commmitments to NATO. Part of their reactions stemmed from nightmarish projections of the American arsenal stripped by greedy Europeans, part from their visceral assumption that Europe was always ready to leave the major burden of Western defense in American hands. But still another part rested on their knowledge that their present state of military readiness could sustain only the evacuation of American troops, with the passing hope that a line of defense might be drawn in the Pyrenees. Even the possibility of a bridgehead in Spain seemed to be sacrificed to the budget cuts mandated by the president in the summer of 1949.[99] Small wonder that analyst Roger Hilsman could call JCS plans for Europe "little more than assignment to withdrawal routes."[100]

The United States' initial position in its short-range expectation was so unsatisfactory to its European partners that it had to be abandoned in favor of a medium-term defense plan (MTDP), to be completed in phases by 1954. Whether or not it was realistic, it offered reinforcement of the Western Union intentions of a stand at the Rhine. It went beyond the Fontainebleau blueprints in anticipating a major shifting in supply lines and specific allocations of individual member role responsibilities, bolstered by American assistance of all kinds. Ninety ready and reserve divisions and a tactical air force of about 8,000 planes were initially projected.[101] Charade though the medium-term defense plan may have been, it checked the deterioration of morale which had greeted the short-term program.[102]

The favorable impact of the MTDP was almost as important for the U.S. Congress as it was for the European allies. Like the establishment of regional planning groups and the completion of bilateral agreements, it reflected the integrated allied effort which Congress had demanded of NATO as a prerequisite for release of authorized funds for military assistance. More to the point, it was embodied in a strategic plan that was to give meaning to the $900 million scheduled for NATO's use. By January 6, 1950, at the third meeting of the North Atlantic Council the Military Committee produced formally the medium-term defense plan that meshed with the strategic concept. Ultimately it would yield a force in Europe capable of containing a Soviet invasion from the point of attack.[103]

The "strategic concept" was a magical term for American supporters of NATO. It encapsulated the virtues of integration as it underscored the principle of "common action in defense against armed attack through self-help and mutual aid." To achieve these results "each nation will contribute in the most effective form, consistent with its situation, responsibilities and resources, such aid as can reasonably be expected of it." This meant that the United States was primarily responsible for strategic air power while Europeans would provide the bulk of tactical air support in addition to "the hard core of ground forces." And mentioned repeatedly was the theme of standardization in as many areas as the allies could manage.

There were no surprises in the final statement. In fact General Bradley had outlined the basic strategy for collective defense before the House Committee on Foreign Affairs as early as July 28. But the period between July and January gave some time to air the doubts and grievances held on both sides of the Atlantic. The result was neither European integration nor American aid. All parties knew the hollowness of most of the pronouncements made in the name of the alliance. Britain's concern for the survival of its dwindling empire, France's worry over the revival of a powerful Germany, and the United States' compulsion to monitor if not control all parts of its largesse to Europe—all militated against a serious transformation of the European body politic. Moreover, the most genuine aspect of change, the American presence in Europe was, as Dulles and Kennan claimed in their different fashions, subversive to the ideal of a united states of Europe. The United States would not only intrude as an alien entity following its own interests in Europe but would also tempt Europe to remain in a dependent status through its unequal powers.

Nevertheless, the alliance sparked a momentum for the reconstruction of Western Europe, and with it an infrastructure to give it some substance. For all its shortcomings the military development of Europe, first under the Western Union and then under NATO, was more substantial than the political and economic forces for integration. When the Korean War erupted fourteen months after the North Atlantic Treaty was signed, there was machinery in place to help break down traditional sovereignty and to promote interdependence in the military relationships that was not to be found either in the Council of Europe or in the Organization for European Economic Cooperation.

8. The Impact of the Korean War

For President Truman, self-conscious about his role in history, the invasion of South Korea on June 25, 1950, was a landmark that would affect the future of America and the world. He never saw it otherwise. On his flight back to Washington from his brother's Missouri farm that fateful day, he reflected on the meaning of the news from Korea. As he reported in his memoirs, he recalled the 1930s. If the invasion "was allowed to go unchallenged it would mean a third world war."[1] In interviews with Merle Miller years later he repeated those sentiments. "The flight took about three hours, and on the way I thought over the fact that what the Communists, the North Koreans, were doing was nothing new at all . . . . Hitler and Mussolini and the Japanese were doing exactly the same thing in the 1930s. And the League of Nations did let them get away with it. Nobody had stood up to them. And that is what led to the Second World War."[2]

The crisis convinced Truman that a worldwide Communist conspiracy had operated in Korea and would manifest itself elsewhere. This conclusion placed China under Soviet direction, and thus made subsequent isolation of the People's Republic an integral part of American foreign policy. To contain China and ultimately to return Chiang Kai-shek to power, the administration had to reorder its affairs in Southeast Asia. The cautious efforts to disengage the United States from France's struggle in Indochina gave way to gradual but increasing American entanglement in the area. ANZUS, SEATO, and bilateral alliances with Korea, Formosa, and Japan all followed. The American commitment to South Vietnam thus became a heritage of the Korean War.

The heritage in Europe has proved no less clear. The vague commitment of American assistance to Western Europe in the event of attack and the lip service paid to mutual support of the many councils established by the Atlantic alliance became specific guarantees of American involvement as the Treaty was transformed into a military organization capable of defending Europe on the ground against attack from the east. If the Russians could act through the North Koreans or the Communist Chinese, they could also employ East Germans as their surrogates. To deter such a threat, a rejuvenated NATO, under American generals, divided Europe into defensible regions, lobbied successfully for inclusion in the alliance of nations on the flanks of NATO (such as Greece and Turkey), and pressed Europeans and Germans to accept the Federal Republic of Germany as a partner in the war against Communist expansionism.

Firm in its belief that no negotiation with the enemy was possible, the United States, during the years after 1950, undertook relentless combat against a conspiratorial enemy whose power seemed enormous, whose appeal was insidious, and whose control centered in Moscow. There was no room in this evaluation for possibilities of diffusion of power or division of nations within the communist world; nor was there any role for neutrals of the emerging Third World. For at least a decade under the Truman and Eisenhower administrations, and to only a slightly lesser extent under the Kennedy and Johnson administrations of the 1960s, the pattern set by the Korean War endured with few changes. Neither Stalin's death in 1953, nor rebellion on the other side of the Iron Curtain in 1956, nor increasing instability in Soviet-Chinese relations, nor the growing power of the nonaligned countries during the 1960s changed America's outlook on the world fashioned in the Korean War. Stopping the advance of the North Koreans seemed to have been the challenge the nation required to institutionalize the Truman Doctrine, to make credible our professed assumption of world leadership. According to Charles E. Bohlen, "It was the Korean War and not World War II that made us a world military-political power."[3]

The well publicized National Security Council document of April 1950 (NSC-68) seems to have been the catalytic agent in the change. The timing of the paper was just right; it was presented six months after the Soviet Union's successful testing of its first atomic device and two months before the Korean War. While it has been widely discussed and carefully analyzed, it remained officially classified until February 1975 and hence an object of continuing suspicion. Could this document be the key to the meaning of the Korean War and so to the events of the past generation? Circumstantial evidence permitted such conclusions. The Truman administration, worried about the implications of the Soviets' possession of nuclear weapons for the defense of NATO, required information from experts about the price to be paid for security in Europe. NSC-68 provided the answer.

Actually NSC-68 was less formidable than its critics believed. It was essentially a comprehensive, general statement of America's military position as of 1950, with recommendations for improving it.[4] Under the leadership of Paul Nitze, chairman of the Policy Planning Staff of the State Department, the National Security Council examined the extreme steps of a preventive war and of withdrawal of all forces to the Americas. It rejected both. It looked at the current modest effort of military assistance to NATO and to other friendly nations, and found them inadequate. The planners concluded that only rapid expansion of the American military forces would permit the United States to deal with the Soviet Union from a situation of strength. No other situation would impress the Communists. The planners determined that in peacetime 20 percent of the gross national product could be expended without disrupting the economy, and urged the raising of $50 billion immediately, almost four times the budget of fiscal year 1950.[5]

There were differing opinions within State over NSC-68, between Nitze on the one hand and Bohlen and Kennan on the other. Bohlen and Kennan feared that publication of the document would scare the administration and Congress into giving a dangerous priority to nuclear weaponry. Another difference developed between the State and Defense departments. While State spoke of a budgetary increase from $13 billion to $35 or $50 billion, Defense, presumably the major beneficiary of the funds, would settle for a mere $5 billion.[6] It seems to be a nice piece of irony that the Joint Chiefs of Staff emerged as more modest in their appetite than the State Department's policy planners.

The nuances of these internal debates were essentially irrelevant to critics who could make causal connections between a declared need for increased military expenditures and a war crisis two months later which justified those expenditures. Not until June 25 did the administration act on the advice of the National Security Council. The Military Assistance Program continued at its leisurely pace; the North Atlantic Council meeting of May 1950 exuded no sense of urgency in its communique; and when war broke out, a modest Defense Department budget proposed for fiscal year 1951 had not yet been accepted by the Senate. Perhaps the reluctance of Defense spokesmen to talk of increases in the manner of their State Department colleagues was a reflection of Secretary of Defense Louis Johnson's sensitivity to the cost-consciousness of Congress. Was the disregard for NSC-68 a sign that the administration had recognized its inability to realize the document's aims?

If so, the Korean War, by design or by accident, served to put NSC-68 into immediate operation. Acheson himself may have been pointing to this result elliptically when he observed in his memoirs that "events in Korea had broken the inertia of thought on many critical matters." Gaddis Smith found NSC-68 to be "a thoroughly Achesonian exposition"; and Ronald J. Stupak has identified the secretary of state as "instrumental in operationalizing NSC #68, the theoretical foundation of rearming the United States when the Korean conflict erupted."[7] That the war unleashed the ambitions of an aggressive secretary, a veritable "commissar of the Cold War," as Ronald Steel has called him, was obvious also to Joyce and Gabriel Kolko. They noted, in the apparent conflict over funds between the civilian and military representatives, the greater martial ardor of civilians whose "desire . . . to spend money as a tool of foreign economic policy . . . was scarcely comprehensible to the docile military men."[8]

All the elements of a plot were present. Even if no direct connection could be made, critics found that policymakers were able to manipulate the situation once it occurred, to push America into a massive armament program for itself and its allies. To win votes in Congress and the approval of the public, they had to raise the Red Scare at home and abroad. The Korean War was their instrument. Richard J. Barnet asked rhetorically how men who could use words with the precision of Acheson could be so imprecise in speaking of a "red tide."[9]

The facts cannot be denied. The Korean War did alter the direction of American foreign policy in such a way that the recommendations of the NSC paper of April 1950 were approved during the summer of that year. It is the interpretation of those facts that is so difficult. Was the attack on South Korea an act comparable to Pearl Harbor, something to have been anticipated and prepared for? The answer is clearly negative. And, like charges about the responsibility for that disaster, could the policymakers be associated with its planning as well as with the exploitation of its results? General George C. Marshall, a participant in both events, was not the target of suspicions in 1950 as he was in 1941. Dean Acheson, a more likely candidate for such accusations (as the comments above indicate), was never seriously affected by them. The revisionist attack on this aspect of Korea never captured popular or congressional imagination. Rather than interpret American behavior at the outbreak of the war as a product of cold-blooded imperialistic planning, David McLellan and John Reuss suggest persuasively that Truman's foreign policy would be better explained "in terms of leaders faced with desperate and compelling choices, forced to act under circumstances of greatest uncertainty, and acting while straining to avoid plunging the world into a new maelstrom."[10] This approach to the problem is applicable to the United States' reaction to the invasion of the Republic of Korea.

The second revisionist argument over Korea is more compelling, if only because the policymakers have frequently raised it themselves: namely, the validity of the imagery of falling dominoes. The Korean War, they claim, forestalled the disaster that would have resulted from successive losses of peoples and territories to Communist control. The minutes of the president's meeting with congressional leaders two days after the North Korean attack reveal his warning: "If we let Korea down, the Soviets will keep right on going and swallow up one piece of Asia after another. We had to make a stand some time, or else let all of Asia go by the board. If we were to let Asia go, the Near East would collapse and no telling what would happen in Europe." Lloyd Gardner quoted this statement from George Elsey Papers in the Harry

S. Truman Library to demonstrate how aware the administration was of the importance of a stand in Korea.[11] Yet, given Truman's frequent public pronouncements, there seems little need to take an unpublished statement from the archives to confirm what the president proudly proclaimed. No taint of conspiracy clings to it.

There are other uses to which the domino principle may be put. Rather than preventing a chain reaction, as Truman and Eisenhower interpreted it,[12] observers can find the dominoes falling from events set in motion by the Korean War. Indeed, the decisions on Korea could explain all events of the next twenty-five years. Stephen Ambrose found that America's conviction that a Communist conspiracy underlay the actions of the North Koreans meant that all national liberation movements would thereafter be labeled Russian proxies. "This view in turn allowed the Americans to dash into Lebanon at President Eisenhower's orders, to attempt by force, with President Kennedy's approval, to overthrow Castro, to intervene in the Dominican Republic at President Johnson's command and most of all to involve this country in Vietnam."[13]

There are shortcomings in this application of the metaphor. The politician or historian can be hypnotized by the picture of dominoes falling one after another along a straight or even a twisted row. That these dominoes can be transferred to historical events beyond a limited span of time is doubtful. While American foreign policy was deeply influenced by the choice to fight in Korea, it need not follow that the row of dominoes is falling today or that it completed its run in the disengagement from Vietnam in 1973. Are the actions of statesmen of one generation fully binding on those of another? Even if events impose constraints on later policymakers, there comes a time when decisions are made independently of the falling of the first domino. The dominoes Truman had in mind were limited in time and space to a few years in Europe, from 1936 to 1939 or 1941. Policies carried out during the Kennedy, Johnson, or Nixon administrations, or even during the Eisenhower administration, had a life of their own. Determinism as an explanation of policymaking has distinct limits.

This chapter assumes that vibrations from the Korean War may still be felt in the mid-1980s but that the war is neither the dominant influence in the shaping of American foreign policy today nor responsible for the direction foreign policy has taken in this generation. Rather, it was a milestone in the evolution of American diplomatic history, a turning point that led to events more clearly identifiable in the period immediately following the war, during the Truman and first Eisenhower administrations.

It was Europe rather than Asia, however, where the impact of Korea might best be observed. The changes there were more profound and the ultimate consequences probably more important. The mutual defense pacts in Asia had the negative objective of forestalling a replication of the event. Granted that there was hope for a prosperous democratic republic flourishing in South Korea, or for a counterrevolution in China springing out of revival of spirit in Formosa, the purpose was to rectify the mistakes of Korea by inhibiting the Communist world from initiating new tests. If such were attempted, American power would prevail through the alliances established for East Asia. There was a rigidity both in purpose and in results.

While many of the same purposes underlay American policy toward Europe in the wake of the Korean War, the nature of problems there provided the occasion for imaginative changes both within the Western European community and between the United States and its NATO allies. Recognition that a divided Germany, like a divided Korea, created conditions in which East Germany could perform the role of North Korea led not simply to strengthening forces or writing more treaties or consigning more funds, as was the case in Asia, but to a transformation of the Atlantic alliance. The United States found itself shedding the substance as well as the language of isolationism, and the Federal Republic of Germany found a way to become assimilated into a new Europe. The election of Eisenhower in 1952 ratified this new course of American foreign policy.[14]

To effect such vast changes in European-American relations demanded diplomatic skills of the highest order. They required American policymakers to deal with a domestic isolationism that blamed defeat in Asia on Communist influences in the Truman administration. The apparent failure of American policy in China permitted McCarthyites to use the language of anticommunism, which the administration itself had employed to win popular support for controversial projects in the past. Propelled by Senator Joseph R.McCarthy's rhetoric, more genuinely isolationist spokesmen, such as Robert A. Taft and Kenneth Wherry, attacked the administration for wasting funds abroad and for accumulating executive power in Europe at a time when the stake for America was in Asia.

Simultaneously the administration had to face a resurgent neutralism in Europe. The events in Korea disturbed and confused Europeans. On the one hand the NATO partners knew that the forces available to them could not stop a Soviet invasion and that the efforts hitherto expended in NATO were insufficient to deter attack in the immediate future. On the other hand they feared that a rapid military build-up could undo the benefits of the Marshall Plan by upsetting their national economies and provoking the very invasion they wished to deter. The relief most Europeans felt at the vigor of America's response to invasion in Korea was mitigated by a suspicion that traditional American priorities in Asia would divert American attention from Europe. Even if Europe remained America's first commitment, would errors of judgment exhibited in managing China's position on Korea be repeated in Europe? The single-mindedness of America's pressure for a German contribution to Europe's defense raised deep suspicions about the qualities of American leadership at a time when to Europeans the memories of Nazi occupation were still so vivid.

The Truman administration had a formidable task in Europe. The surmounting of most of these obstacles provides a tale that has been neglected so far in the historiography of American foreign relations. There are few heroes or villains in it. The details dwell mostly on mistakes, on misunderstandings among the parties, and particularly on the arrogance implicit in America's insistence upon accepting responsibility. Europe, for its part, was frequently jealous of American power, resentful of pressures, and selfish in its use of benefits gained from the alliance.

The day-to-day reading of relations gives the impression that frenzied activities following the outbreak of the Korean conflict widened the gap between Europe and America. From the perspective of a generation later, this view is misleading. A climate of cooperation was created in a few years' time in which symbols of national sovereignty withered and new institutions of an integrated Europe blossomed. Not all have survived; not all have been in the interest of the United States, or in the interest of its allies, or in the interest of detente with the Soviet Union. But for the short run the changes within NATO from 1950 to 1955 brought a sense of security that manifested itself in the economic expansion and political integration of Europe during the next ten years.

Less than fifteen months before the Korean War it seemed that the signing of the North Atlantic alliance by twelve member nations would resolve America's intentions toward Europe. The signature of the United States on the Treaty of Washington on April 4, 1949, meant that Europe could count on American support should an act of aggression be made against any of the partners. By so notifying a potential aggressor, it was expected that there would be no repetition of the experiences of World Wars I and II, when the aggressor did not know America's position. The pact existed to deter such an event. And it seemed to work.

The Russians called off the Berlin blockade and the Federal Republic of Germany came into being five weeks after the Treaty was signed. A military assistance program of more than $1 billion, most of it scheduled for NATO allies, had been introduced in Congress almost immediately after the treaty was ratified in the summer of 1949. By October the Mutual Defense Assistance bill became law, and during the course of the winter of 1949–50 the United States completed a series of bilateral agreements with NATO beneficiaries under Article 3 of the treaty. Within the first year of NATO's history a web of regional planning groups serving the North Atlantic Council was established under Article 9 of the Treaty. The heart of military planning was in the Standing Group of the Military Committee of NATO, composed of representatives of the United States, the United Kingdom, and France. Guiding this steering committee were two other institutions established in October 1949, the Defense Financial and Economic Committee and the Military Production and Supply Board. Respectively, they would study the financial effect of expanded military efforts on each country and recommend measures to increase available supplies.

Most of these accomplishments were published in the communiques of the North Atlantic Council, but few of them were meaningful, and all the participants in the organization at the time knew their deficiencies. The language of cooperation and mutual support was a spindly bridge between promise and fulfillment that could never have borne the weight of a serious challenge from the Soviet Union. American military aid was slight and exceedingly slow in coming.

Congressional limitations helped to account for the sluggish pace. The Mutual Defense Assistance Act of 1949 prevented the president from initiating assistance until he was able to state that it would fit into the integrated defense plan of the North Atlantic area, and this could not be done until bilateral agreements were completed between the United States and each beneficiary. This process took time. Given the obstacles, the official signing of agreements with the NATO allies on January 27, 1950, deserved more than the simple ceremony it received. The first shipment left American ports in March, accompanied by appropriate fanfare. By April 6, according to the first semiannual report of the MDAP, only $42 million of the $1.3 billion authorized had been obligated.[15] That figure reached $52 million by June.

The activities of the Military Production and Supply Board and the Defense Financial and Economic Committee were as sluggish as the flow of military aid. Little serious evaluation of national capacities for sacrifice was made. Nothing beyond a vague Medium Term Defense Plan, calling for positions to be held at the Rhine, was introduced, and there was little expectation of that plan's being realized. The short-range plan involved only procedures for evacuating occupation troops.[16] The NATO machinery was of little help. Committees met in London, Rome, or Paris without coordinating their activities. The foreign, defense, and finance ministers who headed them were too busy with their normal duties to care about the trappings of NATO.

It may be that the air of illusion surrounding the new organization was the product of calculation, not of accident or incompetence. The defense of Europe perhaps would stem from the American nuclear umbrella spread over the NATO allies. Military planning and military assistance, therefore, were psychic props to complement European recovery and to provide justification to the American public for American protection of Europe. At the hearings on extending the military assistance program into 1950, Secretary Acheson justified assistance on these grounds:

The whole purpose of the Marshall Plan and of the North Atlantic Treaty was to prevent war and to preserve peace and the environment of peace which comes from an unwillingness of a potential aggressor to take a chance. Now, that is being successful. We are getting in Europe the economic, spiritual, moral, social strength which will lead them and in company with us, to create the adequate defense so that it will become less and less and less probable that anyone will want to take a chance of aggression in that area.[17]

This is not to say that the administration did not expect efforts in rearmament, in troop commitment, even in specialization within a collective defense plan to be made by the allies. America's own involvement depended on Europe's participating in the enterprise. But the efforts, all told, were intended to be modest, in keeping with the fiscal conservatism of Congress as well as with European fears that diversion of the economies into military channels would dislocate the economic growth carefully nurtured under the Marshall Plan. The shift from civil to military production could create shortages in critical materials, set off an inflationary spiral, and in general jeopardize rather than enhance European security. Politically, even a hint of a German role in European defense, which would follow from a massive effort, would alienate public opinion among the allies. As it was, Communist workers in France and Britain announced their intention to prevent the unloading of the few military supplies that were to arrive in Europe during the spring of 1950.[18] Not a Soviet invasion, then, but the instability of the European partners was the primary NATO concern prior to the Korean crisis.

Even with the careful handling of the NATO publics, the organization remained fragile. Neutralism was not just a Communist device. On the first anniversary of the signing of the North Atlantic Treaty, a dynamic young French journalist, Jean-Jacques Servan-Schreiber, writing for the influential *Le Monde*, aired a point of view shared by many friends of the alliance.[19] He wondered about its purpose. If it was to instill a sense of security in Europeans by giving them the means to defend themselves, it had not succeeded. Should a war break out, Servan-Schreiber claimed, the combined forces of America and Western Europe could not stop it. And if a genuine effort was made to build an imposing military machinery in Europe, the ensuing destruction of European economies would turn victory over to the Soviet Union in the Cold War. He raised the question of American isolationism and suggested that it should not be discounted as a factor in American behavior. Perhaps a neutral stance and accommodation with Russia should be the alternative. This was not Servan-Schreiber's preference. Indeed, he urged a unification of Europe and the vitalizing of the organs of NATO. He articulated a mood which NATO planners had to take into account.

Beneath the public posture, uneasiness within NATO over Soviet possession of nuclear weapons was growing, even as the original assumptions of the Treaty continued. NSC-68 was a measure of this distress. Recommendations that Europe make the financial sacrifice required to build European armies could trigger neutralist sentiments, identified by Servan-Schreiber, into an open and violent rejection of NATO. These sentiments would invite the wrath of senators already disposed to write off the military assistance programs as a trickle that would become a flood of dollars from the American treasury and end with American entanglement in a foreign war brought about by the accumulation of arms. Small wonder that the paper was kept under wraps.

The administration's dissatisfaction manifested itself in guarded statements about the importance of increased European contributions and in its active support of ways to make NATO more efficient. Acheson admitted to the Foreign Relations Committee a few weeks before the beginning of the Korean War that "we are a long way from having an adequate security force for the North Atlantic Treaty, and I think that all the members have got to face the fact that unless there is a very considerable change in the international climate and actions of certain other powers, we may have to put more, rather than less efforts into the defense field."[20] That all was not well with the variety of NATO committees was the message of the North Atlantic Council's communique from London a month before, which announced appointment of deputies to each member's council representative under a permanent chairman to provide continuity and direction for NATO's mission. Charles M. Spofford was the first chairman of the council.

The disparity between public statements about NATO and private sentiments was sharpest with regard to the sensitive issue of a German contribution. A year before, when the North Atlantic Treaty was being debated before the Foreign Relations Committee, it was understood that the dismantling of German industry would be "complete and absolute" and that any "discussion of including West Germany in the pact is not possible."[21] The language remained much the same more than a year later when Acheson repeated assurances to the House Foreign Affairs Committee, deliberating on an extension of the Mutual Defense Assistance Program, that the demilitarization of Germany continued. "There is no discussion of anything else. That is our policy and we have not raised it or revalued it."[22] Technically the secretary of state was correct. In fact, on every level of government in the United States and among the allies, the place of Germany in the defense of Europe was the subject of intense concern and discussion, although it did not reach the stage of policy.

The Germans had been among the first to press for clarification of their position. If there should be war in Europe, where would it be fought and how? In December 1949 the West German government asked formally what plans were being made for its defense in event of a Soviet attack. It feared that NATO would make only a token effort to halt an invasion at the Elbe and then move back to the Rhine. Given the projection of military plans during the winter of 1950, these questions were to the point. Chancellor Adenauer, lacking the facilities of a foreign office, later confessed to using press interviews to broadcast his alarm.[23] While opposing German rearmament, he insisted that if German troops were to be summoned, they should function within "the framework of the army of a German federation." So the *Cleveland Plain Dealer* reported on December 3, 1949. Here was an offer of German assistance on terms that could destroy the Atlantic alliance.

The insufficiency of the Medium Term Defense Plan, particularly the pessimism over defending the European heartland, alarmed the Dutch and Danes as well as the Germans. Dirk Stikker, foreign minister of the Netherlands, claimed to be shocked by the allied strategy of 1950 which was based on defense of the Rhine-Ijssel line.[24] It implied that the northern provinces of the Netherlands as well as German lands east of the Rhine were expendable. The desperate condition of the twelve divisions at NATO's disposal in Europe also moved military spokesmen to consider a German contribution. Even General Pierre Billotte, France's former representative on the military committee, could not envisage a defense of Europe in March 1950 without German rearmament.[25]

Position papers within the State Department concerning the Council of Foreign Ministers' deliberations on Germany pointed in the same direction. As early as November 1949, one of them urged the secretary to point out that "the German problem must be viewed and dealt with in the total context of general developments. It cannot be isolated. What we do in Germany must not be dictated by considerations of what the Germans demand, or even of our respective national interest, but by a fair appraisal of the indispensable requirements of the Western community of free peoples."[26] While admitting the need to display sensitivity to the feelings of European victims of the Nazi experience, it suggested that Americans could bring "a certain detachment to the treatment of German problems which is difficult for other people to attain." But it is clear that such sensitivity as American diplomatists could muster had to be balanced against the danger of inaction in the face of intolerable Russian behavior by its "puppet German regime in the East."[27]

These State Department documents were classified until 1974. There were signals in all major newspapers in the form of rumors and denials by the NATO allies to alert any observer that, whatever the official line, the status of Germany was changing with the intensification of the Cold War. Pressures for ending the dismantling of plants, for close economic integration of Germany into Western Europe, and for admission of West Germany into the Council of Europe, were staples of the Department of State's behind-the-scenes recommendations. France's response was expressed in the Schuman Plan, the European Coal and Steel Community, which would interlock German and French heavy industry in a supranational structure. This Europeanizing of German power, in which Italy and the Benelux countries were represented, was a means of controlling West Germany, rebuilding Europe, and appeasing America's concern for integration.

Despite the Schuman proposal of May 1950, the meeting of the North Atlantic Council did not face up to what the United States regarded as the most urgent forms of Franco-German collaboration: a sizable, integrated army and the use of German men and materiel. No mention of Germany appeared in the council's communique. The most that was done to prepare the public for change was an announcement by the Big Three foreign ministers in a precouncil session that spoke of the gradual integration of Germany into a "European community."[28] The statement was conspicuously silent on military contributions, despite concern for the growth of paramilitary troops in East Germany, manifested in a joint protest to the Soviet Union by the three other occupying powers a week later. Such was the situation within NATO on the eve of the Korean War.

The effect of that conflict on the organization of NATO was immediate and mixed. Europeans breathed a sigh of relief "almost as palpable as a rush of fresh wind on a sultry day," as Anne O'Hare McCormick of the *New York Times* expressed it.[29] But while the NATO partners observed that the United States did not abandon Korea to the Communists, they feared the consequences of actions in the Far East. Conceivably the dynamics of conducting a war, combined with the tradition of "Asia first," could turn American attention from Europe and leave it more exposed to military danger than before.

Germany understandably became the first focus of Western attention. Adenauer claimed to believe that "Stalin was planning the same procedure for Western Germany as had been used in Korea."[30] The NATO leaders agreed. What had been nervous glances at East German police forces a month before were nightmares of invasion in July. A divided Germany, with the preponderance of military strength on the Communist side, could lead to an even greater disaster for the West in Europe than had occurred in Asia.

The specter of sixty thousand East German paramilitary troopers, backed by twenty-seven Soviet divisions in the eastern zone, facing twelve badly equipped and uncoordinated NATO divisions, galvanized American planners. The unspecified target date of a "progressive build-up of the defense of the North Atlantic area" (to use the language of the council's May communique), along with the assumption that present resources were sufficient "if properly coordinated and applied," yielded to a demand for massive armament immediately throughout the alliance.[31]

There was no question in Congress but that the current military assistance bill was inadequate. The president's request for an additional $4 billion in aid met no serious opposition. Emotions of the moment swept away all previous caveats about the program which had limited military aid. In executive session Senator Henry Cabot Lodge, Jr., spoke of the "mortal peril" of Europe and the need for creating a NATO force of fity divisions.[32] By September the president announced plans to reinforce American troops in Europe. It was obvious that the powerful American war machine, which had been mobilized with such effective results in World War II, was poised to come to the aid of its NATO partners. The United States would keep the promise of the North Atlantic Treaty.

Such gratification as Europeans felt over the stirrings across the Atlantic had to be weighed against the price they would have to pay for America's bounty. Congressional inquiry into the administration's plans left no doubt that the cost would be high. At the hearings on supplemental appropriations, the legislators kept pressing witnesses to tell them exactly what expenditures would be made by the allies for the common defense, how many troops they would raise, how much sovereignty would be relinquished to produce a genuinely integrated European army. Most explicit was their demand that Germany be included in the rearming of Europe; their impatience with evasive answers on the German question was rarely concealed. It seemed illogical to them that any credible plan for the defense of the Continent could be made without a German contribution. It also seemed unfair for Europeans and Americans to provide manpower and equipment to protect German territory without Germany sharing in the common sacrifice.

Given the NATO partners' ambivalence on the German question, it is hardly surprising that Acheson and Johnson had difficulty countering congressional queries. When Senator Wherry asked the secretary of state how effective the rearming of France and other Western European countries would be if Germany remained unarmed, Acheson responded that "a program for western Europe which does not include the productive resources of all the countries of western Europe, which included Germany as well as France, and includes the military power of all western Europe, which includes western Germany as well as France, will not be effective in the long-range political sense. Therefore we must include them both."[33] Senator Homer Ferguson wanted to know specifically if Germany, then, was to be rearmed under

NATO supervision. Acheson had to answer no, Germany was not included in the current NATO defense plans.[34] It was difficult for the secretary of state to admit that there was no immediate intention of bringing Germany into the defense program. It was a little less difficult for the secretary of defense because contradictions in their testimonies seemed less evident to him than to Acheson.[35]

The European allies listened to these debates unhappily. Although both the initial relief at American response to the North Korean invasion and the fear of American neglect of Europe had dissipated, new concerns replaced the old. The sense of imminent disaster receded when the Russians did not take credit for the Korean operation or open a German front. Relaxation rather than intensification of efforts was the mood of the late summer of 1950, particularly in September after General MacArthur reversed the tide of Communist advances in South Korea. In this mood American demands for arming Germany and for diverting their economies into military channels sounded to many Europeans more menacing than potential Soviet aggression.

Of all the European allies, the French were most directly involved and most emotionally upset by the German issue. Their sentiments had to be taken into account and harmonized in some fashion with the American conception of NATO, or the alliance would collapse. There was some evidence of a drift toward the inevitable, even if grudgingly. On July 25, France withdrew its objections to German industries manufacturing war materiel for NATO consumption. A month later the ministry was willing to allow German police to be used as a surrogate military arm in the event of an emergency. Was this an opening toward the acceptance of a reconstructed Germany?

Chancellor Adenauer thought it signaled a lowering of French resistance to change.[36] His optimism was buttressed by Winston Churchill's resolution in August at the assembly of the Council of Europe in favor of "the immediate creation of a unified European Army, under the authority of a European Minister of Defense, subject to proper European democratic control and acting in full cooperation with the United States and Canada."[37] In this setting the allied high commissioners asked Adenauer to offer a German view of European security. In one memorandum dated August 29, the chancellor returned to a pre-Korea problem, proposing a West German police force equal in size to the East German paramilitary groups. He responded to the new circumstances by recommending a reinforcement of allied troops in Europe and a provision for German military units within a European army. A second memorandum expressed expectations that the occupation of Germany would end and equality of status would be offered in return for the German contribution to the common defense.[38] Adenauer commanded more than Churchill's support for his views. Stikker had spoken out a month before, stating his personal belief in the need for German rearmament.[39]

The extent of France's acceptance both of a rapid increase in its own rearmament and of a German share in the new Europe defies quantification. Sentiments of leading opinionmakers appeared favorable. Servan-Schreiber, who had spoiled the first anniversary of NATO with his impious reflections on the state of the alliance, had abandoned whatever interest he may have had in France's standing aloof from the Soviet-American rivalry. He urged a single armed force in Europe with contributors served by a permanent Marshall Plan. Such measures as Premier Pleven had proposed to increase France's arms budget were clearly inadequate, according to Servan-Schreiber, no better than a symbolic gesture—like sending an escort vessel to the Korean conflict in place of divisions.[40] Raymond Aron's language was less picturesque, but his recommendations for France's future were equally explicit. Countering this advice were the voice and influence of the prestigious *Le Monde* and of its editor, Hubert Beuve-Méry. Their search for a course that would spare France the psychic cost of a German army and the economic penalties of a massive armament program revived neutralist tendencies.[41] Beuve-Méry evoked the memories of two world wars to ask if the price of liberation once again might not be too high to pay. Would NATO forces, even after their reconstruction, stand fast at the Elbe or at the Rhine?

It was just this kind of questioning that invited doubts among American and British leaders about France's contribution, even if the German issue could be resolved. Suspicions based on France's large Communist bloc and on French behavior in 1940 were rarely articulated, but they were always just below the surface; and at the hearing on critical issues of NATO, congressmen occasionally aired them. The British journal *Spectator* did raise the question boldly in an article entitled "Would France Fight?" The author comforted himself and readers with reflections on the rational qualities of the French character as well as on the initiative France had demonstrated through the Schuman Plan.[42]

No matter how many reservations the allies may have had about the direction of Franco-German relations, they had no choice except to maximize every positive sign they could find in the Pleven ministry. The Schuman Plan seemed to open the way to other kinds of European cooperation and fitted the American interest in a unified European response. Schuman was personally willing to incorporate German units into a European army.[43] France recognized that American dollars, and even increased American troops in Europe, would be insufficient to assure Europe's defense. Manpower was a vital need, and the thirty-six divisions planned for 1955 were required in 1952. The most France spoke of during this period was equipping fifteen divisions on the condition that American supplies and finances be commensurate with these efforts.

Nothing was plainer in the late summer of 1950 than that the fifth session of the North Atlantic Council in New York would center on the *quid* of an integrated European army with a German component in exchange for the *quo* of continuing American assistance. The consequence for Europe would be a severe strain on national economies and a direct confrontation with the German question. The results of a study made of the Medium Term Defense Plan, made by the Council of Deputies on the strength of new estimates of needs and capabilities, pointed to no other conclusion. The American divisions would not be sent into a vacuum or into an allied military system in which each partner was not matching sacrifices.

Despite an abundance of advance signals, the formal American proposal made by Acheson on September 12, 1950, in preliminary meetings of the Big Three foreign ministers emerged as the "bomb in the Waldorf."[44] The impact of the proposal was explosive. But if it was a bomb, it was more a time bomb than a grenade lobbed into a startled assemblage of diplomats. It had been ticking for weeks and had been inspected from all sides by the concerned parties at the Waldorf. The components of Acheson's proposals were familiar. He asked for ten German units of divisional strength under a unified command—a plan in apparent harmony with ideas coming out of Paris. An arrangement of this sort would bind American and British forces more firmly to those of their continental allies.

If the image of a bomb is applicable, it would be in the rigid linking of an integrated command with German involvement. The message was clear: American troops and American aid were contingent on NATO's accepting a German contribution. This single package, as Dean Acheson has pointed out, was largely the work of his colleagues at the Pentagon.[45] It had its attractions. The new organization of NATO and the special provisions to eliminate an independent German force were intended to allay fears of a full-blown German army. But the French reacted as if an American Cadmus were sowing dragon's teeth along the Rhine. Could a thin NATO frame contain marching Germans?

France's position was adamant. Jules Moch, the minister of defense and an implacable foe of German rearmament, left no room for doubt. Schuman, who had professed to be personally in favor of the American plan, cited Moch and President Vincent Auriol as blocks to France's approval of the plan. Although Moch admitted that Acheson did not seek an autonomous army for the Germans, he objected to the integrated arrangement. It would be along the lines of Marshal Foch's authority during World War I. In effect, then, it would be a national army, as the American Expeditionary Force had been, and this was wholly unacceptable to a body of Frenchmen wider than Moch's Socialist constituency.[46]

Schuman argued the case for France before the North Atlantic Council more diplomatically than Moch had done. He raised objections to immediate German rearmament. They ranged from a denial of the assumption that German rearmament would result in increasing the total resources of NATO, to doubts about the legality of incorporating West German units into a European defense force, and the plan's probable rejection by the German and French public. In a major appeal to his allies, Schuman did not demand that they renounce the issue. "I do not decline to do this. What I cannot do, what my government cannot do, at the present time and under the present circumstances, is to reach a premature decision on this problem. Such a decision might, besides, be fatal if it were to become known."[47]

However gracefully Schuman expressed his government's position, it amounted to a rejection of the American proposal. The stance was not surprising; Acheson had anticipated it even as he admitted the logic of the Pentagon's position. In bowing to Pentagon demands, he followed a course which he later claimed was "largely my own fault."[48]

What was more surprising was the council's endorsement of the Pentagon's position. There were misgivings about the dangers of political extortion from the Germans as the West bid for their help. Bevin warned against NATO putting itself "in a position of approaching the West Germans as a suppliant."[49] At the same time he saw no alternative. According to the Dutch foreign minister, "In spite of the atrocities inflicted by Germany on the Netherlands some 80 percent of the Dutch Parliament would probably accept the proposals made . . . by the United States."[50]

After consulting with Lester Pearson of Canada and Halvard Lange of Norway, Stikker took the lead in pressing for a German share in European defense plans. Although his two colleagues wanted to defer action until the Big Three had been apprised of their sentiments, Stikker had Acheson's blessing in developing his argument around a "forward strategy" for NATO, in which Germany would participate "in the proper way and at the proper time."[51] The communique ending the New York meetings reflected the stalemate created by France, but it also reflected the pressures being placed on France. It endorsed the defense of Europe as far east as possible, and promised to examine "the methods by which Germany could most usefully make its contribution" to that defense.[52]

Despite frustration resulting from France's veto, the council meetings in New York generated changes that pushed NATO along new paths. Self-conscious about its isolation, France looked around for means to appease the allies by giving at least the illusion of an invitation to Germany. Even as the meetings were underway, Jean Monnet, the father of the Schuman Plan, was at work on a design to provide a Franco-German connection in the military sphere, analogous to the Schuman Plan in the economic. Or so Joseph Bech, the foreign minister of Luxembourg, told Acheson.[53]

There was a break in the American position, as well, shortly after the council adjourned. The resignation of Secretary of Defense Johnson, an enemy of Acheson's (whose conduct the latter asserted "had passed beyond the peculiar to the impossible"), permitted new initiatives.[54] George C. Marshall succeeded Johnson as secretary of defense on September 21 and immediately reopened channels between the State and Defense departments. Acheson was able to assert that German participation would follow the creation of the unified command. By establishing the structure, with its prominent American component, the French would have time to become accustomed to a German military presence.[55]

It was in this new context that the French unveiled their Pleven Plan on October 24, 1950. Under it the NATO European partners would pledge a special European force to the supreme command, with its own staff system under a European minister of defense. When this army of potentially one hundred thousand men came into being, German contingents would function at the battalion level. The National Assembly applauded. American applause was more subdued, barely a murmur of appreciation for the initiative the French had taken. Privately American diplomatists were dismayed. They felt the French had floated a plan that was fashioned to antagonize Germans by consigning them to an inferior status, and that would do little for European defense in the immediate future.[56]

The Council of Deputies never approved the Pleven Plan. It is unlikely that the French had meant it to be anything more than a vehicle to delay the painful issue of German rearmament. If so, it worked magnificently. The art of diplomacy in blurring the sharp lines of confrontation was fully practiced over the next four years, as variations on the theme of an integrated army followed, one upon another.

In November 1950 the deputies, looking for some measure of progress to report at the next council meeting in Brussels in December, devised the Spofford Compromise between the American wishes and the French offer. The French scrapped the requirement that German contingents join the force only after the European army had been formed and agreed to accept combat teams at regimental strength in place of battalions. The German soldier in a European uniform would never exceed 20 percent of the total force and would serve side by side with Belgians and Italians, all similarly cloaked in a European command under a European defense minister. The minister, in turn, would receive instructions from a supranational council of ministers responsible to a European parliamentary assembly.[57]

The German response to the variety of proposals concerning their role was uneasy at best. Social Democrats complained both of the encouragement rearmament would give to German militarism and of the perpetuation of the division between East and West Germany it would foster. Adenauer was always more optimistic. To him, the European defense force meant an opportunity to enmesh Germany permanently in the Western community so that it might not be a danger to itself or to others. At the same time, the chancellor insisted that any arrangement demeaning to Germany's status in Europe would make mere cannon fodder of its troops. The Brussels meeting addressed many of these concerns by announcing appointment of a supreme allied command. It would have a German representative, pointing the way to political roles in the future for a rehabilitated Germany.[58]

The North Atlantic Council sessions at Brussels set the stage for a conference in February 1951 to develop the European army, and the European Defense Community was a product of these deliberations. For the next two and one-half years there was a painful process of formulating the terms of the treaty and protocols of British and American relations with the community, as well as revisions, amendments, interpretations, and guarantees, before the treaty was ratified. The EDC's members finally signed it in May 1952; the United States Senate approved the protocols in July 1952; more than two years later, on August 30, 1954, the French National Assembly ended debate on ratification of the EDC and scuttled the community.[59]

It is a tale of failure. Was it also an elaborate French hoax? Acheson's sardonic comments in *Present at the Creation* suggest a measure of American suspiciousness from the start. John Foster Dulles's anger and shock at the French legislature's action in 1954 reflects betrayal and disillusionment. By a vote of 88 to 0 on July 31, 1954, the Senate urged the president to give the Federal Republic full sovereignty unilaterally if France did not ratify the EDC. By their behavior the French had demonstrated no intention of submerging French troops in a European army or of accepting German troops alongside their own.

Yet the experience of France and its neighbors in experimenting with a European defense community left its mark. Europe would not have accepted Germany as a NATO partner in 1951; it was prepared to do so in 1954 after failure of the EDC. How much the educational campaign of the preceding three years helped the success of the imaginative Eden proposals associating Germany with NATO through the Western European Union is impossible to say. One can observe that after the Korean War began, West Germany's status underwent visible change. It was no longer an enemy under allied occupation but a full member of the Council of Europe. The high commissioners became ambassadors as the Federal Republic achieved much of the acceptance abroad that Adenauer had hoped would come from a commitment to Western Europe. EDC may have had only a shadow life for three years, but it helped stimulate a solution to the German problem which Europeans, still traumatized by World War II, might not have found otherwise.

NATO might have collapsed in 1950 had France not made a pretense of responding to the conditions the United States placed on continuing assistance and association with Europe. The Pleven Plan legitimized both the decision to reinforce American troops in Germany and the appointment of an American, General Dwight D. Eisenhower, as the first supreme allied commander.

These actions took place at the very time China's entry into the Korean War was focusing almost all of America's attention on Asia once again. Without the earnest of European cooperation provided by the French plan, a reinvigorated American isolationism might have realized the NATO countries' anxieties about American intentions toward NATO.

As it was, criticism of Secretary Acheson mounted steadily through 1950, beginning with McCarthy's unverified charges of Communist officials in the State Department. Senator Wherry demanded the secretary's resignation on August 7. Five days later, four of the five Republican members of the Senate Foreign Relations Committee, joined by Taft, accused Acheson and the president of having invited the Communist attack on South Korea. As Acheson left for the Brussels meeting in December, a congressional caucus of Republicans of both houses asked Truman to remove the secretary. Citing Lincoln's defense of Seward, the president publicly and pointedly rejected the criticism.[60]

Eisenhower's appointment opened a great debate that became the major test of the alliance in its early years, but the administration stood firm. Congressional restiveness over the Truman-Acheson leadership, combined with the latent power of an isolationist suspicion of Europe and traditional concern with the Far East, could have wrecked the ambitious plan to transform the North Atlantic Treaty into a military machine buttressed by a visible American presence in Europe. No matter how illusory, the reconciliation of France and Germany within a Europe that was integrated economically and militarily was the requisite for an American commitment. The policy succeeded under the most adverse of circumstances—when the war in Asia was going badly and the isolationists' attack was going well. It stood even the climactic moment in April 1951 when a vengeful MacArthur came home to a hero's welcome.

Even before Congress held hearings on the assignment of ground forces to Europe, former President Herbert Hoover raised the standard of a "fortress America." He urged the United States, beyond helping Europe with some material assistance, to let that continent alone. The alternative, he said, would be destruction for the entire West.[61] Earlier in December, former Ambassador Joseph P. Kennedy had contrasted the might behind the Iron Curtain with the fatal deficiencies of the West. He told students at the Law School Forum of the University of Virginia that entanglement with Europe and Asia "is suicidal. It has made us no foul weather friends. It has kept our armament scattered over the globe. It has picked one battlefield and threatens to pick others impossibly removed from our sources of supply. It has not contained Communism. By our methods of opposition it has solidified Communism." The only sensible course was to remove Americans from Korea and from

Europe. If the consequence should be the triumph of communism in Western Europe, it would be a short-lived triumph; eventually Europe would follow the path of Tito in Yugoslavia and break loose from Soviet control. But whatever happened there, America's concerns should be with problems in its own hemisphere.[62]

The "great debate" began auspiciously enough for the administration. Despite the unbuttoned rhetoric of these elder statesmen, Acheson claimed that the debate opened in a deceptively amicable atmosphere when the congressional foreign affairs committees met on December 22 to hear him report the results of the Brussels conference. It went well. He spoke of Eisenhower's new responsibilities, of a new Defense Production Board to advance the industrial capacities of the allies, and of the apparent consensus on Germany's future position in Europe's defense. "Nothing sweetens relations between the Secretary and his guardian committees like a little success."[63]

The affability, however, did not last long. Taft, one of the thirteen senators who had voted against the North Atlantic Treaty, raised his voice in the Senate on January 5, 1951. While he did not call for abandonment of Europe, he argued against both military assistance and the dispatch of troops. Assumption of the new role in NATO, Taft argued, would enmesh America in the toils of Europe and increase presidential power. Commitment of troops in Europe should follow, not precede, development of Europe's ability to defend itself, and the numbers should be a token in keeping with "the general spirit of the Atlantic Pact"; otherwise, we might be inciting the Russians to war. In the meantime, Taft charged, the president had no authority to send troops to Europe without congressional approval.[64] Having unburdened himself of his feelings that excessive presidential power and commitments to Europe were harmful to the national welfare, Taft finally voted for the assignment of troops, since congressional approval would be required for specific numbers at specific times in the future.

Dislike of executive domination obviously had a higher priority in Taft's thinking than worry over American membership in NATO, and much of the same spirit pervaded other isolationist criticism in the Senate. The danger of provoking the Soviets to a militant response diminished if such provocation was undertaken by congressional rather than presidential authority. The Wherry Amendment of January 8, providing that "no ground forces of the United States should be assigned duties in the European area for the purposes of the North Atlantic Treaty pending the formation of a policy with respect thereto by the Congress," was the most dramatic attempt to limit the president's power at this time.[65] General Eisenhower's report on his tour of NATO capitals on January 23 provided the occasion for a joint session of the Senate Foreign Relations and Armed Services committees to examine Wherry's call for hearings on the question. They took up most of the month of February.

Military spokesmen carried the bulk of the administration's case before the committees. While Eisenhower addressed himself to the measures European countries were taking to arm themselves, Secretary of Defense Marshall emphasized that NATO was providing exactly what Congress had demanded: a plan for defense of the North Atlantic area. Whether it would succeed depended on support from the United States. Eisenhower and his staff could be only as effective as the means they had to execute their commission. The abilities of the supreme allied commander were beyond question; the intentions of Congress were the nub of the problem, according to the secretary of defense.[66] When Senator William Knowland asked Marshall why the pledge of assistance made in the treaty was not a sufficient earnest of America's intentions, Marshall replied that it had helped morale before the Korean War. "Now we have to meet the situation where they are under duress, are under a continuous threat and a very terrible threat." More was needed.[67] Mindful of the overwhelming share assumed by the United States in the current war, Knowland suggested that American soldiers be limited to a specific percentage of the total manpower needed. Marshall opposed this approach, commenting that it might hamper military movements. "Korea happened to be right close to Japan, where we already had divisions overseas on the ground. The conditions are quite different from those in Europe."[68]

Acheson reinforced Marshall's argument. He pointed out the diminishing usefulness of retaliatory airpower as a deterrent to Soviet aggression. Although airpower still had value, the United States must use the time now available to build its ground forces and those of its allies. The balanced collective force was a matter of immediate urgency, since it would serve notice that would prevent a repetition of the Korean experience. That invasion had awakened Americans and Europeans to more than just "the possibility of bold, naked aggression by the Soviet Union itself . . . . we have seen recent examples of another form of Communist aggression through a satellite."[69]

Arguments in the Senate seesawed back and forth. The Korean example registered with the senators, who were less inclined to let the issue of executive power go unchallenged. Senator Bourke Hickenlooper dismissed Acheson's attempts to cite court decisions granting presidential authority to make commitments of troops abroad, despite the secretary's appeal to "an unbroken practice from the very first days of the Republic."[70] Hickenlooper noted instead the inconsistency with the promises Acheson had made at the hearings on the North Atlantic Treaty in 1949. When he had asked if Article 3 of that treaty would obligate the United States to provide troops as part of developing the allies' capabilities to resist aggression, Acheson in 1949 had given a clear, absolute "No." The only response the secretary could make in 1951 was that he had not changed his view. Conditions had changed making troops necessary irrespective of the claims of Article 3.[71]

Acheson found some comfort in the Republican ranks, notably support from Senator Lodge and Governor Thomas E. Dewey of New York. The latter cited the time limit of Feburary 2, which Wherry had placed in his resolution, as congressional meddling in the delicate area of executive prerogatives. There was a major distinction, Dewey insisted, between a congressional voice in provision of funds for military aid to the alliance and in sending soldiers to the European theater. The fact that the deadline date had passed over three weeks before the time Dewey was testifying indicated the absurdity of a deliberative body attempting to perform functions of the executive.[72] Wherry's resolution failed. So did Taft's effort to postpone sending troops until the allies had reached an agreement on the nature of their international army.

The upshot of the Senate hearings was a resolution approving Eisenhower's command and accepting the dispatch of four additional American divisions to Europe. The resolution also required that no more than the four divisions be sent "without further Congressional approval, and that the Joint Chiefs of Staff certify that the allies were making appropriate progress in collective defense before soldiers left the United States."

Strings attached to the troop assignment demonstrated that the administration's battle with Congress had not ended. In fact, a case may be made that Congress had won its fight to limit executive prerogatives.[73] Its resolution was in keeping with the spirit of the Bricker Amendment to the Constitution, then threatening to hobble executive agreements with foreign powers.

But what was noteworthy about the outcome of the great debate was not restraints on the president or suspicions about NATO's value or anger at delays in securing German contributions, but that all of these factors weighed so lightly in the final balance. Despite the reverses in Korea, the Senate helped the administration endorse the Atlantic alliance and change the course of NATO. The victory was of Eisenhower's European orientation over MacArthur's Asia-first fixation, as Gaddis Smith has observed. "After the winter outburst of 1950–51 the Truman administration did not again suffer a formidable Congressional attack on its European objectives."[74]

Reorganization of NATO made a visible difference in the West's relations with the Soviet Union during the next few years. The most obvious changes involved nations militarily important to the new operational commands established under the supreme allied command in Paris. Greece and Turkey on the southeastern flank and Germany in the center joined the alliance to fulfill the new functions of NATO. The Balkan issue was easier to handle. Although the North Atlantic Council had rejected Greece's and Turkey's initial applications in September 1950, creation of a headquarters under Eisenhower made possible their membership in the alliance in February 1952.

The happy circumstance of Eisenhower's availability was itself a major factor in the success of military reorganization. The consensus over his choice as Supreme Allied commander was such that no clear source of authority for his selection can be identified. His appointment was, as George Elsey has called it, an "Alphonse and Gaston' matter," in which the North Atlantic Council and President Truman "designated" Eisenhower as supreme commander while the Council simultaneously "appointed" him to the post of Supreme Allied Commander, Europe (SACEUR).[75]

Eisenhower's Supreme Headquarters (SHAPE) dominated the military scene by his towering presence, as well as by the perceived need to concentrate such strength as NATO had on the Iron Curtain line; the Atlantic and Channel commands were inevitably secondary. But there was a special advantage at this time in the framework which the Western Union had provided since 1948. Its headquarters at Fontainebleau under Montgomery was a model for SHAPE; its Military Supply Board was absorbed into NATO's Military Production and Supply Board; and its Finance and Economic Committee became the core of NATO's Financial and Economic Board.[76] Despite its own hopes to serve as the agent for Europe, the Western Union itself in effect disappeared in 1951, existing only in the shadow world of staff committees until its reconstitution as the Western European Union in 1954.[77]

General Eisenhower's tour of European NATO capitals in January 1951 epitomized the enduring problems and potential of the alliance. He found a sense of growing confidence expressed by a willingness to subsume conflicts such as the rivalry between de Lattre and Montgomery within the WU under a larger NATO command structure. He also found continuing evasiveness about the extent of each country's contribution to the common defense, a response based on the financial troubles afflicting most of the members.[78] Still, over the next few years the growth of the organization, stimulated by a civilian structure to parallel the military, permitted more optimism than pessimism for the prospects of defense. The emergence of an office of secretary-general in 1952 provided a coherent leadership that the original NATO Council and its successor, the Council of Deputies, could not supply. Lord Ismay, the first secretary general, could claim that NATO strength, with all its limitations, provided a stability in Europe that had not been possible a few years before.[79]

Aside from basic economic problems the questions of command were not fully solved. British sensitivity over an Atlantic Command, and then over a Mediterranean position, took a greater toll of the time and patience of the American partner than France's difficulties in the early 1950s. The United States was slow to recognize Britain's injured pride at losing the SACLANT role. A substitute Channel command was insufficient compensation for the loss of status. While the United Kingdom in the person of Admiral Lord

Mountbatten received a Mediterranean command based in Malta, this assignment was not made final until the spring of 1953, and then appeared to be a pyrrhic victory for the British as the Mediterranean allies refused to commit their forces to British leadership.[80]

Similarly, American insistence that NATO headquarters be moved from London to Paris in 1952 upon the establishment of an international secretariat encountered a resistance from the British that Americans rarely appreciated. British arguments ranged from risks of undue military influence from SHAPE's presence in Paris to the dangers from French communism. The more fundamental issue was the relative loss of British influence on the United States and NATO after all major offices of the organization had been concentrated in France. There were some compensations. The United States abandoned its pressure to separate the office of secretary-general from the chairmanship of the Permanent Representatives. And the combined functions would be handled by the first secretary-general, Hastings, Lord Ismay. Nonetheless, the British continued to lobby for a London headquarters long after the allies—and the United States Kingdom itself—had agreed on Paris.

But the greatest element of instability in this period was the unsettled issue of the integration of the Federal Republic into NATO's defense system. Germany's participation in the alliance, as noted, was more difficult. In retrospect, it is obvious that despite all the pressures for immediate German rearmament, neither Americans nor Europeans assumed that it could be forthcoming immediately, nor that it was even necessary immediately. Congressional inquiries at the hearings on troop assignments, regarding many facets of American foreign relations, included surprisingly little examination of the Pleven Plan, the Spofford Compromise, or plans for the European army then underway. What NATO leaders wanted out of a solution to the German question was permanent engagement of the United States in the alliance. The European Defense Community was primarily a means to secure that end.

There was periodic awareness in both the Truman and the Eisenhower administration that excessive pressures would damage chances of passage of the EDC, achieved in May 1952, and then of ratification. At the end of the Truman administration U.S. Ambassador to France David Bruce stated in a proposed circular telegram that despite its repeated expressions of support the United States must not appear to make the EDC its own: "We feel that the creation of European organizations or institutions is primarily the task for the Europeans themselves."[81] In the following year Eisenhower's ambassador to France, Douglas Dillon, made the point of noting that the Senate's failure to ratify the NATO status-of-forces agreement will lessen the force of "our arguments for ratification of EDC next fall."[82] While he was not urging a lessening of concern for the EDC, he suggested some understanding for France's reluctance to act in light of America's own conduct.

Yet the impression remained firm that the United States was basing the security of Western Europe upon the presence of the EDC and upon its special contributions. In the summer of 1953 Lord Ismay wondered in a letter to Montgomery whether "we have been gravely at fault in putting all our money on the ratification of the EDC Treaty."[83] At the end of the year Secretary Dulles confessed that a publicized statement on the EDC at a NATO meeting in Paris had been intentionally "a means of breaking into the consciousness of the French assembly."[84] The consequence, of course, was trauma and bitterness when France ultimately turned its back on the community in the summer of 1954.

The recovery from the EDC trauma was remarkably quick, not simply in the American response to the proposals of British Foreign Minister Anthony Eden for an arrangement to bring Germany into NATO, but also in French, particularly Premier Pierre Mendes-France's, acquiescence in them. On the American side, Dulles observed that "we will have saved most of the values inherent in EDC."[85] Since the new Western European Union, unlike the old Western Union, would have British (and Italian) membership, there was an "offset" to the absence of the supranational responsibilities which the EDC would have had. The language was grudging and so was the spirit, but there is no doubt that Dulles recognized the importance of accommodating all the partners, including the French, in order to keep NATO alive. On the French side, the substitution of German membership in NATO for the EDC conduit had the saving grace not only of a British connection but of the guarantee of continued American participation in Europe's defense.

The key to Europe's security in 1949 had been the knowledge that America's atomic monopoly would deter Soviet aggression. The Korean War along with the Soviet possession of the bomb had eroded this security. But as a consequence of the "great debate," an invader would encounter American soldiers and assure American involvement in any European conflict.[86] This was the goal of French and other European partners throughout the formative years of NATO. Granted there was an oppressiveness about America's protection, as impatience expressed itself periodically, more vehemently under Dulles than under Acheson. Even so, Western Europeans at the time considered the benefits of the alliance worth the harassment and preachments they had to accept from American leaders in return.

The enormous publicity attending the military expansion of NATO held some of the elements of charade that were to reappear in discussions on Germany. The goals of military expansion were impressive. To defend the Continent from a major ground attack required some one hundred divisions, according to planners in 1951. Even with six American divisions in Europe, the gap was enormous. Twenty-five Greek and Turkish divisions on the southeast flank of NATO swelled the ranks numerically, but did little for the heartland of Western Europe, where France and Britain presented few troops and Germany none, pending signing and ratification of the European Defense Community. The North Atlantic Council at its meeting in Rome in November 1951 decided to establish a force of forty-three divisions by 1954. Three months later the projected force levels reached their peak when the Council at Lisbon approved plans for fifty divisions in 1952, seventy-five in 1953, and ninety-six by 1954. Twelve of these constituted the German component within the EDC.[87] Acheson was sufficiently carried away by the new sense of purpose in the organization that he told the president, "We have something pretty close to a grand slam."[88]

The contrast between the exuberance of NATO leaders at Lisbon in February 1952 and the state of NATO preparedness in 1952 or 1953 or 1954 has led observers to write off NATO goals as a sham. By the end of 1953 there were no more than fifteen NATO divisions facing the Soviets in Germany. Although Roger Hilsman has argued, and Lord Ismay has confirmed, that this was an impressive improvement over the previous year and that those divisions could obviate a surprise ground attack,[89] this was not the message heard in Europe or America at the time—or later. The failure of NATO to meet its reported plans became identified in the public mind with the collapse of the European Defense Community and the apparent willingness of the Eisenhower administration's planners to sacrifice expensive conventional forces for the promise of a cheaper deterrent, implicit in Dulles's talk of "massive retaliation" throughout 1953 and 1954.

Part of the difficulty stemmed from the relaxation among the European partners as the Korean War receded and as the American presence increased. Reasons for sacrificing men, money, and equipment seemed less compelling than the threat posed to their economies and societies by the NATO program. Rearmament had raised the cost of imported raw materials, already inflated by the Korean War. An increasing imbalance of payments accompanied inflation in domestic prices in most allied countries. According to the report of the Mutual Defense Assistance Program, prices of raw materials needed by European manufacturers rose 35 percent during the fifteen months following the outbreak of the war in Korea, while export prices in Europe rose only 12 percent.[90] American offshore purchases in Europe of products for U.S. forces were a welcome palliative, but insufficient.

The North Atlantic Council had addressed the problem at its Ottawa meeting in September 1951 by appointing a Temporary Council Committee, under Harriman of the United States, Sir Edwin Plowden of the United Kingdom, and Jean Monnet of France—the "three wise men" as they came to be known. The committee produced a plan of rearmament that could reconcile higher military expenditures in each member nation with no reduction of the standard of living in those countries. The method was to pay for new armaments out of more efficient production and, above all, out of future purchases the United States would make abroad.[91]

Sensible as the advice was, its delivery in December was unacceptable to the allies. Nor did it fit American plans; the new mutual security program, which had come into effect for fiscal 1952, subsumed economic assistance under a military rubric, to the disadvantage of European economies. Even a provision in the act allowing up to 10 percent of the total budget to be transferred from one category to another could not prevent the dislocation of European economies.[92] The communique at Lisbon, announcing that "the Council took detailed and comprehensive action based on the recommendations of the Temporary Council Committee," had no more meaning than a reader wished to give it.[93]

Perhaps the excessive expectations derived from the loose figures or from temporary bouts of euphoria indulged in by even the most experienced statesmen help explain the skepticism NATO accomplishments frequently evoked. The semiannual reports of the secretary of defense and of the Mutual Security Program, as well as the communiques of NATO Council meetings and official accounts of the secretaries-general, tended either to overwhelm constituents with vague, optimistic generalizations expressed in clichés of the day or to bury them in statistics. Yet clichés can confirm successes as well as conceal failures; and statistics can test them.

Although the American military assistance which poured into Europe in rapidly increasing volume may not have been enough to release counterpart monies among the beneficiaries or even to create the military machine anticipated, they made an impact. Quantitatively, the record of the translation of military aid into what the French called infrastructure—port installations, air bases, fuel storage facilities, pipelines, and signal communications systems to support NATO armies—is impressive. Only fifteen airfields operated in Western Europe when Eisenhower's SHAPE was established in 1951; eventually there were over one hundred such military air bases ready for use. Three hundred signal communications units were begun from Norway to Turkey (although only half of them were completed). More than 3,500 kilometers of interconnected pipelines were started, designed to provide new methods of handling the enormous consumption of fuel by modern jet aircraft.[94]

Was all of this information designed merely for the edification of legislators, particularly American congressmen? What the data cannot tell is the effect of these building programs on traditional conceptions of national sovereignty. When the reader's numbness wears off, one can look behind the statistics and see a genuine military interdependence in Western Europe growing out of these projects. Seaport facilities in one country include pipelines that cross into a second country's territory to serve air bases on the soil of a third country. There are political implications in the blurring of national boundary lines, as well as military implications for defense of all the countries concerned.

While France's departure from the organization ten years later suggests that the mutual dependence was not complete, progress toward the goal of a European community—politically, economically, and militarily—was evident. By pressing for a unification of Europe to maximize the military and economic assistance the United States granted, American planners won more than was apparent at the time. That they may not have anticipated or approved all the paths taken by a revived Europe over the next two decades does not detract from the American contribution to that revival.

The impact of the Korean War on European-American relations may make that event, rather than the signing of the North Atlantic Treaty in 1949, the watershed of American isolationism. The conflict tested America's determination to turn away from the traditional abstention from European political affairs and from military obligations they might impose. Isolationist challenges erupted periodically during this period over a number of issues; they were all defeated. In the course of debates, great and small, during the first half of the 1950s, the idea of alliance took on meanings which may have been hoped for in 1949 but were never truly expected. The European infrastructure for NATO represented one measure of a new interdependence of the allies; American acceptance of status-of-forces agreements was another.

An optimistic interpretation of NATO changes need not rule out examination and judgment of flaws attributed to the alliance and to American leadership. There is little doubt that Acheson's emphasis on building situations of strength from which to negotiate ruled out any possible talks with the Soviet Union during this period. It precluded an appreciation of Soviet fears and needs and gave an unnecessarily harsh cast to the contest with the Soviet Union. American initiative locked the West into an inflexible stance. At the same time, American pressure forced the rebuilding of Germany, without sufficient empathy for the feelings either of the European allies or of the Germans themselves. By embracing Adenauer, American policy helped to insure a division of Germany for a generation, with a vulnerable Berlin remaining a point of friction between East and West. America's political and military weight in Europe stimulated European anger and resentment, which may have been expressed in sublimated form by the Anglo-French Suez invasion of 1956 and, more candidly, by France's posture during de Gaulle's decade of power.

From another angle of observation, the rearmament of the Western European countries, particularly of Germany, may have been unnecessary—the result of America's misdirected initiative in anticipating a Soviet invasion that was never part of Soviet intentions. What point was there in building a military machine operating from the Arctic to the Caucasus if the Russians had no plans to push toward the Atlantic, or even toward the Mediterranean? This may have induced the Russians to establish a counter-NATO, the Warsaw Pact, after Germany entered NATO. Such was the essence of Kennan's warning about the rearming of Germany in the mid-1950s.[95]

Much of the foregoing evaluation, of course, is based on knowledge the historian today does not possess. He can manage to interpret the results of rigidity in the American position and of the pressures for militarizing NATO. He cannot judge the sources of Soviet conduct to learn if Soviet overtures to the West for settlement of the German question in 1952 were genuine. If they were, were they a product of the success of NATO in forcing the Soviet Union to choose new means to effect their foreign policy? Was that policy built around neutralization of Germany for the sake of Russian security, or would a neutralized Germany lead to the dismantling of Western Europe? These speculations point to the larger question of whether the relative peace in Europe after 1949 was not the product of America's involvement in NATO.

While such questions can end only in uncertainty, other questions are susceptible to answers. The period from the outbreak of the Korean War to the signing of the armistice agreements three years later was a time of constructive diplomacy in Europe. NATO became a working alliance, if not of equals, at least of members among whom an informal consensus, the "NATO method," operated to secure collective decisions.

Some of the results of NATO decisions are easily quantifiable. The records reveal the dollars authorized, appropriated, and expended; airfields and headquarters buildings constructed; nationalities mixed in training exercises under a NATO regional command; and protocols to the original treaties affecting the sovereignty of member states. It is more difficult, but still possible, to conclude, as Raymond Aron has done in his *Imperial Republic*, that "the *European* diplomacy of the Truman Administration from 1947 to 1952 was correct; by this I mean that it offered the best means by which to achieve its aims: the reduction of the risks of war to a minimum, the promotion of the recovery of Europe within a climate of security, and the paving of the way for the reconciliation, cooperation, and even unification of the former enemies."[96] In retrospect it is doubtful that any other approach would have yielded greater security or prosperity to the NATO allies.

I am reluctant to leave this subject without raising again the attractive metaphor of the falling dominoes. In examining the development of NATO in light of the Korean War, the emphasis has been on the short run. Where does the short run end and the long run begin? Where does one row of dominoes end and another begin? Or are events always to be considered part of a seamless continuum? It would be as unreasonable to blame President Johnson's errors in Vietnam on the Korean War's impact on American attitudes toward Indochina as it would be to blame Johnson's dismissal of the miltilateral-force idea in 1964 on the 1950 decision of the North Atlantic Council to establish a unified European command. New situations created new possibilities for statesmen to move in more than one direction. The events of the 1960s and 1970s follow more from new arrangments of dominoes than from the one piece set in motion by the North Korean attack on June 25, 1950. If there was a long-range impact of that event, it was in the aggressive American acceptance of the challenge of leadership, particularly executive leadership, with its potential for abuse in domestic and foreign relations. For Europe, the result over the last thirty-five years has underscored the passing of the old American tradition of isolationism.

9. Western Europe in "The American Century"

In the summer of 1981 Willy Brandt, former chancellor of the Federal Republic of Germany and current chairman of the Social Democratic party, was reported to have complained that the United States was treating Germany "like a colony."[1] This charge is one of many similar statements that have emanated from Germany, the United Kingdom, Greece, and the Netherlands in the 1980s. Older as well as younger opponents of NATO base their aversion to the alliance upon a belief that its purposes serve only American imperial interests at the same time that its official policies threaten Europe's security. Anti-Americanism is the language of NATO's European opponents; it has been since the beginning of the alliance.

How valid have these charges been over the past generation? What are the origins of Europe's suspicions about America's policies and behavior? These are questions I rarely considered in the 1950s and 1960s when the United States was at the zenith of its power in Europe. In those years I spent long periods of time as a lecturer in four European NATO nations and took for granted the permanence of the American imperium and the beneficence of its intentions. Now that this era is apparently over, it seems appropriate to look back and ask not only how it began and why it ended but also what was the significance of America's involvement with Europe. I will draw upon some of my recollections of those years as I suggest answers to these questions.

A useful point of departure is a phrase provided by Henry Luce of *Life* magazine in his long February 1941 article entitled "The American Century." Luce opened with a reminder to Americans that whatever the story behind the facts and however shoddy President Franklin Roosevelt's role in the events may have been, the United States was at war with Germany even if no declaration had been made to that effect. But this conclusion, in Luce's mind, should be no cause for gloom, partly because there was no choice; a German victory over Britain would be intolerable to Americans. More importantly, the war would serve only as a preface to the unleashing of American power, for out of the trials of conflict "there may come clear at last the vision which will guide us to the authentic creation of the 20th Century—our Century."[2]

The magnitude of America's success by the end of the war, in which the United States was the only nation to emerge stronger than it had been in the beginning, seemed to justify Luce's vision. The year 1945 opened "the first great American Century," in which the once-dominant Europeans would have their place, but a lesser one. Given the traditional American hostility to Europe, exacerbated by the perception of betrayal in World War I, it would not have been unreasonable to expect America to exact retribution from Europe for its past sins. Indeed, a notable European crime of the interbella period—the unpaid war debts—would be even less likely to be expiated amid the devastation of World War II. But instead of excoriating Europeans for bringing destruction down upon themselves and entangling innocent Americans once again in their coils, the United States sought redemption and not punishment for Europeans.

For many Americans the new order to be established would follow the precepts of Woodrow Wilson or Wendell Willkie, with an international system that would make war obsolete. The United Nations won such a firm grip on the national imagination that this form of internationalism, rather than familiar isolationism, appeared to be the major stumbling block preventing the Truman administration from moving more quickly to cope with Soviet expansion in the late 1940s through traditional alliances. Others thought that American involvement should take the form of a world federation that would transform the United Nations into a genuine world government, an image envisaged by the United World Federalists. Still others saw an Atlantic federation or union, as projected by Clarence Streit, to be the appropriate path for the American Century. For those not animated by idealism, the linkage of American aid with European self-help and integration had the virtue of assuring more efficient use of assistance.

In almost all these postwar thoughts Europe occupied a central place. No longer a corrupter of American virtue, it was a sharer of the American traditions and a partner, if only a junior partner, in the new order. A restored Europe, among other functions, would be a buffer against the expansion of Soviet communism. Having fallen so low in the war, Europe was ripe for fundamental change. A small but eloquent segment of the American foreign policy elite, led by Senator Fulbright, wanted to use the present malleability of Europeans to shape a genuine united states of Europe, a federated system that would be supported but not controlled by the United States. It was in America's self-interest, Fulbright believed, to promote the revival of a strong, unified Europe, as the Marshall Plan recognized. To achieve these results the United States should use its weight to press Europeans to submerge their nationalist traditions under a new political identity. "It will be a great tragedy," Fulbright claimed during the debate on the language of the Economic Cooperation Administration bill, "for Europe and for us if the opportunity is missed because of hesitancy or timidity."[3]

The Truman administration listened more closely to those who believed that Europe's revival could not be won without linkage with the United States in an intimately connected political, economic, or military community. Involving the United States with Europe implied the inability of Europeans to manage unification by themselves; they required American protection against the pressure of Communist expansionism in Europe. American sympathy for unification was the common thread knitting together all these plans. As Carl Van Doren pointed out in his popular *The Great Rehearsal* in 1947, the world should find a model in the action of the thirteen states of the Confederation coming together to write the federal Constitution.[4] In the American Century, America's historic example as well as its present strength should serve the less fortunate parts of the world. The United States was now the steward of civilization, and Europe, unworthy though it might be, would be a beneficiary of that stewardship.

The foregoing is an interpretation of Luce's statement that seems to fit its author's intentions. But it is not a reading that necessarily follows from the subsequent record of the United States in the American Century. One need not be a revisionist to find in Luce's peroration what Fulbright was later to call "the arrogance of power." There was also an invitation to economic exploitation as he conjured up a "vision of America as the dynamic leader of world trade. . . . Let us rise to its tremendous possibilities. Our thinking of world trade today is on ridiculously small terms."[5] In this context the identification of America with the "Good Samaritan, really believing again that it is more blessed to give than to receive," involved more than psychic returns for the giver.[6]

The Marshall Plan of 1947 seems to me to have been an example of Samaritanism as enlightened self-interest. Vast quantities of goods moved across the ocean from 1948 to 1951 to help revive and reorder Europe without expectation of repayment. In the process not only did American industry expand and prosper but also American companies created new consumer markets abroad whose appetites were to be gratified by the establishment of branches in Europe. Over the next generation American products, from automobiles and electronics to carpet sweepers and toothpaste, dominated the European market. A new colonialism appeared in which multinational businesses with corporate headquarters in New York, Detroit, or Akron, extracted dollars from Europe just as surely as the mercantile system of the seventeenth century drew specie from its colonies to the coffers of the mother country. While the rise in productivity of European economies was a striking testament to the success of the European Recovery Program in the 1950s, much of this success was expressed through the export of American industry to European satellites.

One manifestation of American economic suzerainty impressed me in the fall of 1959 when I first drove from Mechelen to Antwerp, a dreary stretch of highway in any season. I recall the brightening of spirits when a huge bill-board, located on the outskirts of Antwerp, announced in the best tradition of a chamber of commerce that B.F. Goodrich Company welcomed the traveler to that city. While this welcome—written in English—was appreciated by this Ohioan, whose home was only a dozen miles away from the Akron headquarters of the rubber company, someone from out of state might have regarded the billboard with less affection. It could even be considered a callous reminder of the American imperium, potentially more galling than the omnipresent Coca-Cola advertisements, which were at least written in the language of the local consumers.

Inevitably, American efforts to help Europeans improve their economic relationships led to actions that diminished European freedom. Political as well as economic control accompanied the American presence in Europe. It bred resentment. Sir William Strang, permanent under secretary of the British Foreign Office, in the course of the 1949 bilateral negotiations for military aid, complained about "the implicit assumption by too many Americans that there is nothing in the world that dollars cannot buy, that the European Recovery Programme gives the United States agents the right to press for changes in our internal policy, and that when Congress says no matter what, European governments must toe the line."[7] The price of resisting American wishes could be the withholding of military or economic aid. France's Pleven Plan and the consequent European Defense Community, abortive though they were, were acts of desperation as the French sought to give the illusion of submitting to the American demand for a German contribution to NATO in 1950 and 1951.

The visible political symbol of the Pax Americana was NATO itself. David Calleo described the position of supreme allied commander as "the rather elaborate apparatus by which we have chosen to organize the American protectorate in Europe."[8] The logic of the argument is impressive. NATO, with its headquarters in Paris in the 1950s, was dominated by well-known military leaders of the stature of Generals Dwight Eisenhower or Alfred Gruenther, each of whom was endowed with more authority and titles to match than the faceless bureaucrats associated with the secretariat-general or the Council of Deputies. The supreme allied commander, always an American, was an appropriate title for the American proconsul whose reputation and influence outweighed those of European premiers, presidents, and chancellors.

But no matter how much damage American political, military, or economic demands inflicted upon the European allies, they were ultimately less important than the cultural threat represented by American civilization. Coca-Cola and chewing gum were less a tribute to American enterprise than an incremental debasement of European culture. American influence was as insidious as the enemies of *Franglais* claimed it to be.[9] While it may be an exaggeration to assert that France's failure to arrest such depravity explains the return of Charles de Gaulle at the end of the 1950s, for all Europeans anti-Americanism was a vital ingredient in the general's mystique. De Gaulle became a frequent object of derision among Europeans for his various pretensions, but one widely circulated story was invariably told with affection. It concerned his grandiose conception of a Europe extending from the Atlantic to the Urals that would serve as the civilizing balance between the two barbarians of the East and the West. Whether the capital of civilization should be Paris was open to debate among Europeans, but there was no debate about the European Ariel to mediate between the two Calibans. This cultural "third force" was more credible to exploited Europeans than a Gaullist *force de frappe*.

The American Century is now gone, having lasted no more than a generation and succumbing sometime during the Vietnam War.[10] Today that "century" looks as distant as the nineteenth. The dollar has no greater luster than the German mark, Japanese yen, or Swiss franc; confidence in an autarchic America, as strong in pre-World War II America as in the postwar era, has been replaced by a dependence upon foreign energy resources. The military strength that once elevated the United States above all nations not only must cope with Soviet parity but also must reconcile itself to the proliferation of what had been a unique nuclear military capability. Even the awesome multinational corporations are no longer equated with American industry. Indeed, the most visible giants are German and Japanese automobile companies planting their own colonies around the world, including on American soil. Some multinationals, particularly the British, are so subtly managed that they produce surprises even for British observers. At a conference on European-American relations at the University of East Anglia in 1980, a number of Britons noted with satisfaction that British Petroleum was the majority stockholder in Sohio, but none of them recognized that Gimbels not only had to watch the activities of Macy's but also had to observe the instructions of its masters in London, the British-American Tobacco Company.[11] Europe today appears to be as heavily engaged in exploiting the American market as the United States is in the European market.[12]

In the process of change the rebellion against American suzerainty seemed remarkably pacific. It was not that Americans always behaved graciously while their supremacy was being challenged. There was an underlying nastiness in the petulance displayed by Secretary of the Treasury John Connally's unilateral decision to suspend the convertibility of the dollar in August 1971, and there was an irritating condescension in the "Year of Europe" which Secretary of State Henry Kissinger proclaimed for 1973. It should be noted, however, that European provocations were serious. The British in the 1940s resisted American insistence that they become Europeans; the French in the 1950s prevented German participation in European defense for half a decade through their subversion of the EDC; and all the allies in the 1960s vigorously deplored American policy in Southeast Asia and in the 1970s moved toward a rapprochement with the Soviet Union at a pace opposed by the senior partner. Nonetheless, the relative ease with which the European allies were able to turn aside or refuse American importunities throughout this period makes it reasonable to question how exploitive American imperialism was in the heyday of the American Century.

The American objective of building a strong, economically viable Europe free of many of the barriers of the past was realized. If General Electric prospered, so did Phillips of the Netherlands; and if General Motors spread its tentacles throughout Germany, it did not do so at the expense of Volkswagen or Mercedes-Benz. The connection between American aid of all kinds and the *Wirtschaftswunder* of Germany and France deserves asseveration. It was not a coincidence. A strong European competitor challenging America at every turn may not have been what the planners of the 1940s had in mind, but the machinery established to promote the restructuring of Europe—the Organization of European Economic Cooperation and the NATO Council of Deputies—logically produced those results. The point is not that some American planners, in and out of government, had mistakenly assumed an indefinite continuation of a junior partnership while at the same time they were creating conditions of independence and competition. The critical issue is that, despite flashes of bad temper, the United States made no effective arrangements to maintain Europe in that posture. If American economic power prevailed in Europe in the 1940s and 1950s, it was because no other was available; and if it diminished in the 1960s and 1970s, the diminution was a consequence of the success of its initial policies.

Efforts were made from the beginning to avoid the stigma of an imperial relationship. The decision made during the Truman administration and expanded in the Eisenhower administration to accept a series of status-of-forces agreements in NATO was evidence of a strong anti-imperial sentiment in the midst of the American Century. Briefly stated, when the United States agreed to commit four additional divisions to NATO in 1951, the troops on European soil were meant to serve not as occupiers of former enemy lands or as auxiliaries for inferior allied forces. They were to be equal partners in a common cause. To make this intention credible, American troops had to be governed by the laws of the nation in which they were serving when they were off duty. This meant that Americans in Europe charged with crimes by the host country would be subjected to a jurisdiction that could deprive them of rights guaranteed under the Constitution. It required courage by both the Truman and the Eisenhower administration to face down the disapproval of Senator John Bricker and his supporters. The Bricker amendment received a great deal of attention for the changes it might make in the conduct of American foreign relations. But the Bricker reservation, reserving exclusive jurisdiction over American personnel abroad to the United States, might have had an equally devastating effect even if it had been accorded much less attention by the press in the early 1950s. A small band of senators regaled the chamber and committee hearings with prospective terrors in store for unwary American boys abroad, stories from having a hand cut off for stealing a loaf of bread to long prison terms without trial by jury. The fact that mutilation was practiced in Saudi Arabia, a nation distinctly outside NATO, or that European courts were invariably more lenient with American offenders than were courts-martial, did not disturb the orators. They failed, however, to prevent the government from abandoning constitutionally protected rights in order to promote a sense of equality of status within the alliance.[13]

A sense of American dominance hung more heavily over Franco-American relations. France's defection from NATO in 1966 was the culmination of its attempts to free itself from the Anglo-Saxon yoke. But no Brezhnev Doctrine was imposed to force de Gaulle into line. France managed to detach itself from the obligations of the organization while continuing to accept the benefits of the treaty. Based on my observations as a regular visitor to NATO's political headquarters in Brussels over the past few years, the French are present in considerable numbers. They still complain, but their complaints are less against Washington than against their own government for forcing NATO to exchange the City of Light for a provincial outpost in Belguim. While Paris is less than two hundred miles away and the food in Brussels is justly appreciated, one cannot quarrel with the judgment that Belgian cuisine is heavier than French. Such is one of the burdens Frenchmen must bear to support their *force de frappe*.

A much less widely observed challenge to American power by a less likely source arose in 1956 in Iceland. Since World War II that small island of 150,000 people had been important as a link in the defense and communications system of the Atlantic alliance, and consequently became a major base for American aircraft. Inevitably conflict developed between a homogeneous people with limited resources and the intrusive, affluent American military contingent, which affected the economy and the cultural life of the host country. In March 1956 a coalition of Progressive, Social Democratic, and Communist parties passed a resolution in Parliament to have all foreign troops withdrawn, and then in June won an election campaign based on a promise to oust the United States from Iceland. Inasmuch as the Iceland-ers had no army of their own, their audacity in challenging the Americans was courageous. The apparent initial success of their demands was even more remarkable. The imperial power was prepared to bow before the wrath of Iceland. At the end of the year, however, the troops were still in place and the Keflavik base had not been dismantled. The reasons for inaction did not lie in the threat of American retribution or in a plea from the NATO Council. The Icelanders drew back partly as a consequence of the Soviet suppression of the Hungarian revolt and partly because of the implications for the national econ-omy in the departure of the American dollar.[14] If this was American imperial-ism at its most Machiavellian, it was also a notable deviation from the less than subtle postures customarily affected by Secretary of State John Foster Dulles at this time.

That the United States undertook the rehabilitation and reorganization of Europe after World War II—its economy, its defenses, and ultimately its polity—is undeniable. That it did so by pegging the price for its services at such a level that European subordination would follow from its efforts is debatable. Still, temptation accompanies power and may be irresistible. For example, when the United States offered Europe military equipment to build its resistance to communism, it asked for concessions that the beneficiaries were reluctant to grant. Special base rights, agreement to withhold strategic materials from Communist countries, and proof of efficient use of materials granted them were not necessarily unreasonable requirements. But they were galling nonetheless when spelled out in bilateral negotiations at a time when the United States was touting the virtues of integrated activities. They were to be enforced by military missions in each country, some of which, as in the case of Norway, were larger than the entire Norwegian Foreign Office.[15] Such was American behavior in "the different world" of NSC-68, as Walter LaFeber aptly expressed it, in which Europeans would play a subordinate role in the American-shaped Cold War.[16]

Where, then, does one begin to harmonize genuine American efforts to avoid the stigma of imperialism in Europe with equally genuine evidence of exploitive behavior politically, economically, and culturally throughout the American Century? The question of intention is as reasonable a starting place as any, even if evil intentions may not be necessary for imperialism to flourish.[17] At the end of World War II, U.S. domestic pressures were a mix of wishes to disengage from the commitments war had created, to encourage the United Nations to serve as a surrogate State Department, and to assume that the economic advantages implicit in the most powerful economy of the world would permit expansion of that economy without embarrassing ties. Whatever the American responsibility for the behavior, the Soviet stance ultimately determined the nature of America's European role. But in the aftermath of war it was an unsure role, distorted by the Truman administration's initial indecisiveness about its own direction, that affected the final decision. The trouble was less a revived isolationism than the acceptance of the United Nations as the way of the future by most of the foreign policy elites. A military alliance, bilateral or multilateral, it was feared, would undermine the foundations of the new world order.[18]

The most significant efforts to link Europe to an American destiny came not from Americans but from European leaders, particularly French and British. Ernest Bevin's celebrated call for a Western union in the winter of 1948, and the Brussels Pact that followed it, were less steps toward the independence of Europe than both a *cri de coeur* for help from the United States and a device to bring the United States into an alliance. The public message was that Europe would rebuild in all areas with American help; the private signal was that no amount of self-help or cooperation was sufficient. Direct American involvement was the only solution.[19] The European calls for assistance succeeded, even against the better judgment of the State Department. Robert A. Lovett and John D. Hickerson, the American architects of NATO, believed they had no choice.[20] They responded to a crisis of confidence that went to the heart of America's new role in the world. The United States delayed as long as it could and then made an alliance under an Atlantic title to allay European fears. The consequent domination of Europe was not on the U.S. agenda.

In fact, an impressive case may be made for the steadfastness of the American record on behalf of European unification, which resulted in a series of successful actions culminating in the European Economic Community. As Armin Rappaport has recently observed, the creation of the European Coal and Steel Community in 1950 was "the first time a major power fostered unity rather than discord among nations in a part of the world where it had significant interests."[21] Even when the State Department or congressmen drew back from full support it was frequently out of concern lest the United States appear to be interfering excessively in European affairs.[22] But from another angle of observation the requirement of integration was a weapon that forced Europeans to submit to positions on integration against their interests or to give the appearance of doing so, as in France's behavior with respect to the EDC. There was an element of hypocrisy on both sides; Hickerson and Theodore Achilles, for example, admitted that they gave lip service to the idea of European unity only to satisfy American public opinion.[23]

Occasionally there was a direct confrontation that illuminated the issue. In December 1949, at a time when the ECA was publicly chastising Britain for its delinquency in impeding economic integration, Paul H. Nitze, chairman of the Policy Planning Staff of the State Department, tried to impress upon Sir Edmund Hall-Patch, chairman of the Executive Committee of OEEC, the need for greater progress, and observed in passing that political union was as important as economic union to meet the requirements of the ECA. Hall-Patch, losing his composure over Nitze's loose interpretations of the preamble of the ECA Act of 1948, responded that the European Recovery Program "was not an instrument for achieving economic or political union of Europe. It had never been regarded as such and it was pretty late in the day to start looking upon it that way. Moreover, the U.S. government had never made it clear that one of its objectives of policy was the political and economic unification of Europe, let alone what means it proposed toward that end." According to Hall-Patch, Nitze admitted his error.[24]

What emerges from the record is more confusion than hypocrisy. Confusion over both objectives and methods characterized American behavior in the late 1940s. From the wisdom of hindsight it seems incredible that the administration policymakers were unable to anticipate the range of results that might follow from the success of their assistance to a uniting Europe. Among the benefits would be a confident society able to resist blandishments or threats from communism internally or externally. There also would be a common market as free from tariffs as the market of the United States. Together the new European union and America would rise to a new prosperity. But what of the prospect of a different nationalism arising that was not just a revival of older passions but a European nationalism that would produce a competitor and rival of the United States?[25] A monster could be created out of the new Europe. The idea, however, that an independent, united Europe also might be a hostile Europe rarely occurred to Americans until de Gaulle expressed it in a practical French form in the 1960s.[26]

The confusion of the 1940s devolved on immediate contradictions as well. The nub of the problem was the inability or unwillingness of American statesmen to recognize the inconsistency between a projected European federation that was separate from but friendly toward its American model, and a North Atlantic Treaty Organization in which the United States sat on top of every European institution that might grow out of it. Dulles raised a lone voice in 1949 at the hearings on the North Atlantic Treaty when he speculated that "the Economic Recovery Act and the Atlantic Pact were the two things which prevented a unity in Europe which in the long run may be more valuable than either of them."[27] His point, unattended by most of his listeners, was that the ECA had lost an opportunity to recast Europe by not giving more attention to European integration. While Europe might recover its losses and move toward a better economy as a result of U.S. aid, it would make fundamental changes only under duress. The ECA was too timid in its demands on Europe, Dulles claimed, while NATO undercut the movement toward European community by inserting the United States into its midst in the guise of an Atlantic community. The consequences, he feared, would be a continuing dependence upon American power and largess.

Dulles's prognosis was justified up to a point. Nevertheless, the muddled conceptualization of a new Europe in the American Century was mitigated by a traditional assumption that immediate problems were more important than future problems. The crisis of the late 1940s centered on the rescue of Europe from economic disaster, and its defense against impending political disaster caused by the expansion of Soviet-directed communism. To bring American weight to bear on the problem, the language of unification was more important for its present effect upon American public opinion than for the future changes to be made in Europe. What counted at this moment were a military alliance that would restore European confidence and, after Korea, massive military aid to maintain it. In the short run the United States dominated every aspect of the relationship. In the long run, or at least in the span of a generation, the mutual effort has not created a united states of Europe or even a secure Europe; a new generation has new problems, alongside familiar ones in new guises. However incomplete they may be, the unity and even the independence of Europe thirty years later are testimony to the success of the European-American collaboration after World War II. Perhaps the best testimony of all was the brevity of the American Century.

Bibliographic Essays

The first of these essays represents an early effort—one made, in fact, five years after the Treaty was formed—to categorize and assess the significance of the large quantity of literature that NATO inspired in its early years. The second essay looks again at the literature dealing with the first five years of the organization, but from the distance of a generation.

NATO AND ITS COMMENTATORS: THE FIRST FIVE YEARS (1954)

The signing of the North Atlantic Treaty on April 4, 1949, gave rise to a number of books and articles on the North Atlantic Treaty Organization, the volume of which will probably continue for some time. The treaty and the organization that it created represent the clearest challenge to Soviet expansionism since the end of World War II. Through this action twelve nations of North America and western Europe resolved to consider an armed attack against one member an attack against them all, and to create sufficient strength within the alliance to deter potential aggressors. But NATO's continuing interest for commentators stems from reasons other than its value as a weapon against the spread of communism. To some writers NATO appears to be a stimulant that would revive a moribund United Nations; to others it is the beginning of a new kind of alliance unprecedented in history; to still others it is a symbol of America's rejection of isolationism. So vague are some of the treaty's articles and so rapid has been the evolution of the organization that almost any observer could derive whatever meaning he wishes out of NATO's development.

While the multiplicity of connotations associated with NATO has been reflected in the variety of material written on the subject, the majority of articles have been narrative or descriptive in purpose, fragmentary in scope, and journalistic in method. These features are to be expected in the discussion of an organization which has grown so quickly in the few years of its existence that merely sketching its development has been a continuing and taxing job. Little time, consequently, has been left for serious analysis. Even if changes had been less frequent, materials necessary for scholarly research have been withheld by the members of the alliance for reasons of policy as well as of military security.[1] Those writers who have undertaken an analytical

---

1. Available sources of information are official communiques of Council meetings, annual reports of military headquarters, and special publications of the NATO Information Service, such as *NATO Handbook*, 2d ed., (Paris, 1953). In the United States the Senate Foreign Relations Committee and the *Department of State Bulletin* have published pertinent documents and have expressed official views on NATO.

approach to NATO for the most part confine themselves to a special problem, such as NATO's compatibility with the United States Constitution,[2] or quite literally to its periphery—the relations between NATO and Sweden or NATO's relations with the European Defense Community.[3]

Obviously, definitive studies of even a modest scope will have to be postponed until the archives of the participating nations are opened. Nevertheless, the work already done on NATO since 1949 has uncovered a pattern of study that probably will not be changed substantially in the future. Almost without exception the historiography, whether narrative, analytical, or speculative, has fallen into one or more of three major categories connected with the treaty organization. The first and initially most important category concerns the military aspects of NATO, including the political and economic factors which govern military potential in modern warfare. The second contains speculation relating to the development of NATO from a military alliance to some sort of Atlantic community as suggested but not defined by the treaty. The third category covers the problems involved in United States leadership of NATO.

Not until 1952 did any monograph appear which aimed to examine all three categories. A report by a study group of the Royal Institute of International Affairs was published in the fall of 1952, followed six months later by a similar project prepared under the auspices of the Canadian Institute of International Affairs.[4] Both books disclaim the intention of producing a definitive work, and both were sponsored by unofficial and nonpolitical organizations in Great Britain and Canada which nonetheless reflected with considerable accuracy the official attitudes of their respective governments toward the North Atlantic alliance. Similarities extend also to method— group discussion and recommendations, with the author acting primarily as rapporteur[5]—and to conclusions—belief in the efficacy of NATO as a war deterrent and cautious optimism over the future development of an Atlantic community.

The two studies differ widely, however, in style, organization, and scope. The 100-page Canadian report, written by Arthur C. Turner, is clearly written and well conceived, placing equal emphasis on the effect of NATO upon European integration, the Commonwealth, and the United Nations. Among its many virtues are a readable style, careful use of secondary materials, and an incisive analysis of key problems, but the value of the work is somewhat reduced by its deliberate avoidance of both economic problems and military implications. The group felt that an authoritative examination of those areas required more specialized knowledge and greater access to sources than were available to its members.

---

2. Lyman B. Burbank, "NATO and the United States Constitution," *Social Education* 16 (May 1952): 207–9, 221.

3. Harald Wigforss, "Sweden and the Atlantic Pact," *International Organization* 3 (Aug. 1949): 434–43; Clarence C. Walton, "Background for the European Defense Community," *Political Science Quarterly* 68 (Mar. 1953): 42–70; Gerhard Bebr, "European Defence Community and the North Atlantic Alliance," *George Washington Law Review* 22 (June 1954): 637–58.

4. Royal Institute of International Affairs, *Atlantic Alliance: NATO's Role in the Free World* (London and New York, 1952); Canadian Institute of International Affairs, *Bulwark of the West: Implications and Problems of NATO* (Toronto, 1953).

5. Arthur C. Turner's role in the preparation of the Canadian report appears to have been larger than Donald McLachlan's in the British report.

The British report, assembled by Donald H. McLachlan, was more ambitious in its undertaking, examining the work of NATO "as it is actually done," and contrasting "the realities of daily consultation with some of the more ambitious objectives with which the organization has been credited."[6] Within the limits of 150 pages McLachlan discusses how NATO works, the problems it has handled, the lessons it has learned, and the procedures it is evolving. For the most part this study is successful despite the devious path followed by the author. Unlike the clearly organized Canadian report, the British study is clumsily constructed, employing a confusing combination of chronological and topical approaches to the material. Not only is the time sequence occasionally lost but major points are blunted as the report jumps from post-Korean developments in the opening chapter to the tactical problems of Europe before returning to any discussion of the factors that shaped NATO.

For all their shortcomings, these volumes stand in the forefront of NATO bibliography because they cover the larger picture as well as the details. More recent publications, such as Wing-Commander J.D. Warne's study of the NATO defense organization, offer few insights that the British and Canadian reports had not already illuminated.[7] While the latter may not have handled all the problems adequately, between them they have touched upon the many complex issues connected with the North Atlantic Treaty. This essay surveys the problems of NATO, supplementing the views expressed in these two books with the findings of representative monographs. It also examines the type of literature that NATO has inspired in its first five years.

The Military Dimension

Understandably, the category with which most of the articles have dealt is that of the military functions of NATO. The most important and most explicit articles about the North Atlantic Treaty are those which outline means of defense against external aggression, for this military threat had been both the inspiration of the alliance and its most pressing challenge. NATO's response to the challenge in turn has constituted its greatest achievement. While there have been alliances in the past, there is no precedent for the range of political, economic, and military cooperation which NATO has planned since 1949. Conceived in a time of nominal peace and therefore lacking some of the wartime urgency which had solved so many difficulties in past alliances, NATO nevertheless has succeeded in setting up under the aegis of the Council an elaborate military organization designed to operate on a long-term basis. International military headquarters now preside over the defense of Europe and the North Atlantic area, following a pattern established in two world wars.

The allies have also introduced an important innovation in coalition planning. From the beginnings of the North Atlantic Treaty the allies have subscribed to the principle of balanced collective forces, and under the impetus of the Korean invasion have gradually put the principle into practice. The principle involved the assumption by each member of that part of the total effort which it could perform most effectively: troops from France, tactical air force from Britain, and strategic air power from the United States. Similarly, military production has been divided among member nations

6. *Atlantic Alliance*, p. viii.

7. J.D. Warne, *N.A.T.O. and Its Prospect: A Study of the Defense Organization for Western Europe* (New York, 1954).

so that each might specialize in contributing the kind of forces and weapons best suited to its abilities. Departing from its objective tone, the British Study Group was moved to comment that "the work done to find out what each nation can fairly be asked to do for common defense is one of NATO's major achievements; should it prove successful it will be one of the great planning achievements of the century."[8]

Discussion of the military aspects of NATO has been conducted from three principal points of view. One of them reflects the work of the military specialists, experts in their fields, who have commented in their military journals on the development of the organization from the viewpoint of technicians. Writers in technical journals on the role of the Canadian air force, for example, or on the contributions of the Dutch air force to defense of the West generally lack a political orientation.[9] Similarly, the editors of the Irish military review, *An Consantóir*, in analyzing the efforts of the allies to standardize their weapons, display little interest in relating their study to other problems of inter-allied relations or in examining its implications for the concept of sovereignty. After admitting that considerations of economy and national pride hindered standardization, they give most of their attention to strictly military obstacles, such as the differences in the British and American employment of artillery.[10]

Upon occasion, however, technical discussion of a training maneuver clearly echoes the larger struggle between nations and services on matters of politics and strategy as well as tactics. Exercise MAIN BRACE, in which the combined forces of SACEUR and SACLANT conducted joint operations in the eastern Atlantic and the North Sea in September 1952 to test the defenses of northern Europe, was subjected to a kind of criticism that was not specifically concerned with the results of the exercise in terms of efficiency in coordination, training techniques, or other military objectives of the operation. A staff study by the United States magazine *Air Force*, for example, found only one lesson worthy of comment in Exercise MAIN BRACE: namely, the insufficiency of the naval carrier task force as a substitute for NATO air fields in the defense of Scandinavia.[11] The maneuver in this instance served as a pawn in interservice rivalry. On the other hand, British Rear Admiral Horan blamed SACLANT for most of the shortcomings in the conduct of MAIN BRACE; the command of the operation should not have been vested in an American with headquarters in distant Virginia, but in an admiral, presumably British, closer to the scene, as in World War II.[12]

8. Ibid., p. 76.

9. "R.C.A.F. NATO Build-up in Europe Continues," *Air Power* 1 (London, October 1953): 85–87; Hans Kosman, "Dutch Share in Europe's Air Defense," *Aviation Age* 19 (May 1953): 26–27.

10. "Problems of Standardization," *An Cosantóir* 12 (Nov. 1952): 547–49. Many articles of military interest in the military journals of the NATO allies have been translated and digested in the *Military Review* published monthly by the Command and General Staff School of Fort Leavenworth, Kansas.

11. "There Is No Easy Way Out—A Second Look at Mainbrace," *Air Force* 32 (Jan. 1953): 21–23.

12. H.E. Horan, "Exercise Main Brace," *Royal Air Force Quarterly* 5 (Jan. 1953): 33–39.

Experts on military affairs have not confined their labors to military technology; another aspect of this area of NATO bibliography has been presented by journalists aiming at a general rather than a special audience and by military authorities discussing the organization from a broader perspective than that of a military technician. Perhaps the best general picture of NATO's position in postwar Europe that has yet appeared is in Theodore White's *Fire in the Ashes*.[13] In the columns of such papers as the *New York Times*, however, and in such journals as *Foreign Affairs* are to be found piecemeal accounts of the development of the Atlantic alliance, with the volume of writing heaviest immediately after an important Council meeting, after a political crisis in the government of one of the member nations, or after an apparent shift in Soviet policy. Many of those accounts amount to little more than summaries of the best information available, and as such perform a useful service to the public. By piecing together the findings of reporters—the observations of George Fielding Eliot on the formative stage of the organization,[14] the description by John Beavan of the changes effected by the Council meetings at Ottawa and Rome in 1951,[15] and the review by Drew Middleton of the new approaches to military planning in 1953[16]—one may construct a coherent picture of NATO's growth. These accounts have been ably supplemented by firsthand reports of prominent participants in NATO military affairs, such as Colonel Robert J. Wood, former secretary of the SHAPE staff, and Vice Admiral Jerauld Wright, former Deputy United States Representative to the Standing Group of NATO's Military Committee.[17]

Other monographs are more interpretive than factual, reflecting the author's intention to evaluate the effect of a particular change upon the course of NATO's development and the effect of a political or economic event upon NATO's military capabilities. The appointment of General Eisenhower to the newly-established SHAPE in December 1950 was thus the occasion for an acute observer like Theodore White to predict that his task would be insurmountable unless the entire organizational structure was thoroughly modified;[18] while the results of the important Lisbon conference a year later inspired Charles Spofford, former chairman of the now defunct Council of Deputies, to suggest that unless a central economic agency was created the extensive military and political reforms would be wasted.[19] Provocative as these analyses have been, they are basically speculative.

13. Theodore H. White, *Fire in the Ashes: Europe in Mid-Century* (New York, 1953).

14. G.F. Eliot, "Military Organization under the Atlantic Pact," *Foreign Affairs* 27 (July 1949): 24–36.

15. John Beavan, "From Ottawa to Rome," *Twentieth Century* 150 (Nov. 1951): 371–77.

16. Drew Middleton, "NATO Changes Direction," *Foreign Affairs* 31 (Apr. 1953): 427–40.

17. Robert J. Wood, "The First Year of SHAPE," *International Organization* 6:175–91; Jerauld Wright, "The North Atlantic Treaty Organization," *United States Naval Institute Proceedings* 67 (Dec. 1951): 1254–65.

18. Theodore H. White, "The Job Eisenhower Faces: The Tangled Skein of NATO." *Reporter* 4 (Feb. 6, 1951): 12–17.

19. Charles M. Spofford, "NATO's Growing Pains," *Foreign Affairs* 31 (Oct. 1952): 95–106.

A third viewpoint in the category of military writings has been expressed by experts in military science and politico-military affairs who are advocates of special causes which NATO either furthers or impedes. These writers are not interested in particular maneuvers of NATO armies or in the evolution of the military organization, but in the larger question of the utility of NATO as a military instrument. Grand strategy rather than tactics is generally their subject matter, and since the tendency on the part of many of these writers is to view the defensibility of Europe in terms of its effect on the causes they champion, the treatment is frankly subjective and the judgments often Olympian.

In this class are advocates of strategic airpower as the primary weapon against the Communist threat. They harbor deep suspicions about the military mission of NATO. While Major Alexander de Seversky and Brigadier General Bonner Fellers are willing to accept United States commitment to protect the members of NATO from Soviet aggression, they consider the preoccupation with ground forces characterizing NATO military planning to be wasteful and even dangerous. They feel that it fritters away money and energy that should be expended upon airpower.[20]

The wisdom of building up European ground forces has been questioned also by scholars who condemn it as a mistake in American foreign policy planning and as a hindrance in Cold War strategy. Professor Hans J. Morgenthau, for example, fears that NATO's military program is nothing more than an unthinking reaction to the Soviet menace, and suggests that if Europe should recover its strength and prosperity, it would then be an even more likely target for Comunist imperialism because of its wealth or because of its newly-won military capabilities.[21]

European neutralists reach a similar conclusion, but unlike the above-mentioned writers they are not arguing in favor of other and more suitable means of fighting communism. Raymond Aron, a perceptive French journalist, points out that neutralists present only a defeatist argument: that Europe even with American aid can never match Soviet power, that NATO therefore would be no protection in the event of war, and that defense preparations invoke dangers as bad as Communist invasion.[22] From this position it is only a short step to the Communist observation that the real purpose behind the Atlantic Pact is to build bases for an attack on the USSR.[23]

Special causes, however, are not always aligned against NATO's military functions. A champion of the European army, and especially its German contribution, Burkhart Mueller-Hillebrand, admits the inability of the allies to defend Europe solely through national armies, but feels that a European army could perform that mission

20. Alexander P. de Seversky, *Air Power: Key to Survival* (New York, 1950), p. 242; Bonner Fellers, *Wings for Peace* (Chicago, 1953), pp. 94–95.

21. Hans J. Morgenthau, *In Defense of the National Interest: A Critical Examination of American Foreign Policy* (New York, 1951).

22. Raymond Aron, "French Public Opinion and the North Atlantic Treaty," *International Affairs* 28 (Jan. 1952): 1–9.

23. Testimony of Eugene Dennis, General Secretary of the Communist Party, USA, "North Atlantic Treaty," *Hearings*, U.S. Senate, Committee on Foreign Relations, 81 Cong. 1 sess., p. 2:785–90.

successfully.[24] Similarly, Conde de Almina, looking at NATO from the Spanish point of view, doubts the efficacy of any defensive alliance but predicts a glorious future for NATO military forces if they should undertake a crusade against atheistic communism. Such an idological attack, the author claims, would spark revolt wherever NATO troops should strike.[25]

The two articles cited above are based on a belief that their particular approach, if properly pursued, would produce the desired results. These admirers of NATO tend to go beyond a prosaic weighing of NATO assets against the capabilities of potential enemies to find justification for their opinions in the very enormity of the peril, which of itself would inspire the free world with the will and ability to fight successfully if challenged. There is an aura of mystery in explanations of this sort which is found even in the work of such eminently reasonable observers as Drew Middleton and General Kruls of the Netherlands army. Middleton appears to assume that "the will to fight" is more or less the equivalent of the ability.[26] General Kruls is more explicit: "When every European is aware of what he can expect from a Russian victory and of what he can do to help prevent it there will be a unison of devoted effort which will prevent war or, if necessary, bring victory."[27]

The authors of *Atlantic Alliance* and *Bulwark of the West*, frankly partisan in their judgments of NATO's military role, agree that the military progress of the alliance has been its most important contribution to world peace. Turner's report for the Canadian Institute is specially noteworthy for the clarity of its description of the transformation of NATO from a military planning to an operational organization, while the British Study Group is at its best in its analysis of the various tools—the committees and boards—used by the organization to improve its effectiveness. But, despite the objective regard for the historical development of NATO, both books accept the defensibility of Europe, as do Kruls and Middleton, on faith. Had these assumptions been less fixed, the authors might have devoted more space to examining earlier coalitions for the light they could shed on current problems. Inquiry into the reasons for the successes and failures of the Delian and Achaean Leagues of the Greek city states and of the Quadruple Alliance of 1815 might be useful to the study of NATO. Unquestionably the character of the alliance was affected by the equal status accorded each of the allies; the extent to which the leading powers of the alliance could defer to the special needs of individual members without sacrificing the security of all is a central problem of this coalition. William T.R. Fox has discussed political aspects of the problem in two exploratory articles, while Rear Admiral Henry E. Eccles has presented some of the problems of military collaboration among the allies on the basis of his experience

24. Burkhart Mueller-Hillebrand, "Nationale Armee Oder Europaarmee?" *Wehrwissenschaftliche Rundschau* 3 (Apr. 1953): 165–68.

25. Conde de Almina, "El Problema militar de Pacto Atlantico," *Cuadernos de politica Internacional* 4 (Oct.–Dec. 1950): 109–18. This article is listed in the *International Political Science Abstracts* published by UNESCO in Paris, 1 no. 3 (1951).

26. Drew Middleton, *The Defense of Western Europe* (New York, 1952), p. 310.

27. H.J. Kruls, "The Defense of Europe," *Foreign Affairs* 31 (Jan. 1952): 276.

on the staff of the Commander-in-Chief, Allied Forces, Southern Europe; but these represent only a first step in the study of coalition operations.[28]

Although the military development of NATO is still in process, the pace has slowed considerably in comparison with the hectic days following the Communist invasion of Korea. Alterations in Communist tactics, political difficulties within the alliance, or inability of the member nations to sustain the economic burdens imposed by NATO, might change at any time the present source of the alliance. But its responsiveness to changing conditions has been a major source of strength. It is significant that the military organization has moved toward a more efficient command structure and more effective utlitization of manpower and equipment with each change. As long as it maintains its vitality, writings on the military phases of NATO will continue to be voluminous.

The Political Community

Most commentaries on the political role of NATO have assumed, with the authors of *Atlantic Alliance*, that NATO's function is to "create an Atlantic Community for purposes going beyond the defense of Western Europe."[29] But despite the Royal Institute's reference to "expressed purpose," just what kind of community NATO was supposed to develop is not clearly stated in the text of the North Atlantic Treaty. Concerned primarily with the need to defend Europe in 1949, the framers of the Treaty filled the bulk of the text with detailed statements of territories to be defended, provisions of ratification, and measures to be taken in the event of attack, and left only the preamble and Article 2 free for nonmilitary aspects of the alliance. Additionally, the explicit terminology reserved for the military articles of the Treaty presents a striking contrast to the vague expressions of Article 2, in which the members promised to "contribute toward the further development of peaceful and friendly international relations by strengthening their free institutions, by bringing about a better understanding of the principles upon which these institutions are founded, and by promoting conditions of stability and well-being."

Possibly because the nature of the political community envisaged under the Atlantic alliance received so little attention from the authors of the Treaty, the hopes and fears of interpreters were freely indulged without the restraint which clear definitions in the text might have imposed upon their imaginations. Consequently, the blueprints of the Atlantic community that have appeared in the last five years range over the whole ideological spectrum, from world federation to a regional assembly for special problems, sharing only the premise that NATO is more than a military association.

To some partisans of world federation NATO appears as a potential threat to their plans for converting the United Nations into a world government by acting as a devisive force among the noncommunist nations in that organization. These observers, whose opinions were most clearly expressed in one of James P. Warburg's periodic

28. William T.R. Fox and Annette Baker Fox, "Britain and America in the Era of Total Diplomacy," Memorandum No. I (1952), Center of International Studies, Princeton University; William T.R. Fox, "NATO and Coalition Diplomacy," in *Annals of the American Academy of Political and Social Science* 278 (July 1953): 114–19; Henry E. Eccles, "Allied Staffs," *United States Naval Institute Proceedings* 79 (Aug. 1953): 859–69.

29. *Atlantic Alliance*, p. ix.

reviews of American foreign policy, feel that instead of becoming the nucleus of a world community NATO might drive the other members of the United Nations into the Soviet orbit and precipitate the war it sought to forestall.[30] This view is not held by World Federalists alone; Grayson Kirk, writing one month after the signing of the North Atlantic Treaty, feared that its logical consequence would be the bipolarization of the world and the subversion of the United Nations.[31]

Other proponents of federalism, however, welcome NATO as the proper instrument for promoting a federal union of the Atlantic democracies as a base from which a world government capable of enacting and enforcing a world law might be built. If such a measure should result in the disruption of the United Nations, the supporters of the Atlantic union would accept that fate without too many regrets inasmuch as their hopes for the United Nations rest upon the countries represented in the Atlantic alliance. Soviet obstructionism and the inability of many of the members of the United Nations to assimilate the type of government which the Atlantic Union Committee anticipated has long since made the United Nations a questionable instrument for realizing their hopes. NATO, on the other hand, offers new possibilities to the friends of Atlantic union. Owen Roberts urged that the next step after military preparations should be the creation of an actual federation which would control the foreign and defense policies of the constituent states just as the United States conducts those functions for New York and Texas.[32]

But NATO need not serve as a substitute for the United Nations or even as a means of transforming its structure and purposes. According to Frank Tannenbaum, NATO might well act as a temporary instrument in performing special services within and even on behalf of the United Nations. While he recognizes the danger of the free world's confusing NATO with the United Nations and abandoning the latter for the former, he suggests that NATO may do exactly what the framers of the North Atlantic Treaty put into their preamble; namely, implement "the purposes and principles of the Charter of the United Nations" by deterring potential aggressors from disturbing the peace in the North Atlantic area.[33]

A major preoccupation of both critics and framers of the prospective Atlantic community has been its relationship to the United Nations. Behind the assumptions of both proponents and enemies of NATO has been the idea, usually unstated, that the United Nations should have made such an organization as NATO unnecessary, that there should have been no need for both organizations in the postwar world. The difficulty in reconciling NATO with the United Nations lies in the fact that the Charter

30. James P. Warburg, *Faith, Purpose, and Power: A Plea for a Positive Policy* (New York, 1950), pp. 108–13, 128–31. However, Cass Canfield, chairman of the Executive Committee of the United World Federalists, in his testimony before the Senate, accepted NATO as an emergency measure even though he shared Warburg's fears. *North Atlantic Treaty Hearings*, 3:841–87.

31. Grayson Kirk, "Atlantic Pact and International Security," *International Organization* 3 (May 1949):239–51.

32. Owen J. Roberts, "Atlantic Union Now," *Foreign Policy Bulletin* 30 (Apr. 7, 1951): 3–4.

33. Frank Tannenbaum, "The Balance of Power versus the Coordinate State," *Political Science Quarterly* 67 (June 1952): 173–98.

of the United Nations did not take into account the later bipolarization of world power. A concert of the great powers working in harmony, not regional groups struggling to achieve a balance of power, was the collective security system envisaged in 1945. Accordingly, as Hans Kelsen points out, the Charter never provided for regional alliances to assume the burden of keeping the peace, and the efforts to fit the North Atlantic Treaty into the scheme of the United Nations had no clear justification whether the Treaty is regarded as a regional association or as an act of collective self-defense. Further obfuscation has resulted from the absence of any mention in the text of the North Atlantic Treaty of "regional" organizations, which is attributed by Professor Kelsen to the fact that the provisions of the United Nations Charter dealing with regional organizations do not provide for collective defense or enforcement action without authorization of the Security Council. Even Article 51 of the Charter, permitting the exercise of individual or collective self-defense, leaves the possibility that preparations for defense planned under the North Atlantic Treaty might not be able to come into effect until after an attack has been made.[34] Because of faults inherent in the texts of both the United Nations Charter and the North Atlantic Treaty, contradictory interpretations of the meaning of NATO have been inevitable. The only obvious concomitant of Kelsen's analysis is that attempts to relate NATO to the United Nations can do little to define the nature of the Atlantic community in terms of international law.

The authors of British and Canadian volumes treat the problem of the United Nations by assuming that there is no problem. A functional approach to international cooperation automatically removes NATO from any competition or even comparison with the conceptual scheme of the United Nations. Instead of regarding NATO as a potential world government in microcosm, the British and Canadian studies consider NATO a response to special needs, and its development largely a matter of meeting those needs. Only so much sovereignty in military, political, or economic spheres should be surrendered as is necessary to create a viable defense of Europe, but the extent of this sacrifice should never be static. Military cooperation to meet the organization's objective required political and economic cooperation as well, which would increase as the organization evolved. With each change—establishment of a Council of Deputies, integrated military headquarters, a Defense Production Board, or a permanent secretariat—the habit of collaboration would grow steadily, fostering the development of a "NATO method" that would harmonize national and collective points of view.[35]

But neither the British nor the Canadian group, conscious of their commitments to interests outside the Atlantic area, looks beyond a "NATO method" to a NATO goal. While permitting the new organization to handle an increasing number of functions, they admit no infringement upon the independence of each member nation without fully realizing that the gradual relaxation of sovereignty in various areas inevitably

    34. Hans Kelsen, *Recent Trends in the Law of the United Nations: A Supplement to "The United Nations"* (New York, 1951), pp. 920–25.
    35. *Atlantic Alliance*, pp. 124, 127.

affects the "independence" of their governments. Ultimately their approach should lead to some institutional form of Atlantic community, but because of their attitude toward the subject, the authors do not explore the various directions that the growing organization might take.

Because one English observer did look at the possible end-product of western cooperation, the caution of the British and Canadian reports becomes more comprehensible. Professor Lionel Robbins of the University of London suggested in 1950 that the results might not be at all favorable to the national interests of Britain or the United States, for an economic or political community operating within NATO but excluding the United Kingdom might have interests apart from those of its colleagues in the Atlantic alliance. A European customs union within the new federation might seriously affect the welfare of the Anglo-American countries, which have had to stay out of such a union because of their global commitments.[36] Such is one possible conclusion of functional cooperation. Another observer referring to the same continental community that disturbed Robbins welcomed the Schuman Plan as the beginnings of a new and powerful neutral grouping which would abandon NATO and serve as mediator between the United States and the Soviet Union.[37] Two years later, when the Schuman Plan and the European Defense Community plan had been formulated, still another critic found seeds of disunion in the growth of internal institutions that excluded the United States, the United Kingdom, and Scandinavia from their membership. He feared that a new "Holy Roman Empire" dominated by a Roman Catholic western Germany might cut NATO into two antipathetic halves.[38]

While these projections invoke somewhat chimerical dangers, they do not by any means exhaust the variety of configurations offered by the idea of an Atlantic community. After all, the community need not be considered in terms of a problem of sovereignty confined to a limited geographical area, as described above. The community need not be even geographically regional, since the text of the North Atlantic Treaty makes no specific limitations, and the present scope of the organization, extending from the Pacific to the Caucasus, does not lend itself to a narrow interpretation of regionalism. B.K. Sandwell suggested that the Atlantic community could be defined legitimately in terms of a common culture and common interests, and thus permit the inclusion of such countries as Australia, New Zealand, and South Africa.[39] This idea was not wholly academic. Sir Percy Spender, the Australian ambassador to the United States, proclaimed—at the very same time that the Sandwell article appeared—that Australia's future was bound up with that of NATO, "since the protection it

36. Lionel Robbins, "Towards the Atlantic Community," *Lloyds Bank Review*, London, n.s., 17 (July 1950): 1–25.

37. Jacques Gascuel, "Vers une politique européenne," *Politique Etrangère* 15 (Sept. 1950): 437–46.

38. E. Løhen, "Mot en europeisk fastlandsføderasjon" ("Against a Continental Federation"), *Internasjonal Politikk*, Bergen, 10 (1952): 228–32. This article appears in the *International Political Science Abstracts* 3, no. 1 (1953).

39. B.K. Sandwell, "North Atlantic-Community or Treaty," *International Journal*, Toronto, 7 (Summer 1952): 169–72.

affords and will progressively afford extends far beyond the geographical area covered by its member nations."[40] Because of this fact he deplored the lack of existing machinery through which the voice of Australia might be heard in the making of decisions that affect an area wider than the territory of the NATO countries.

The contrast between the worldwide community drawn together by a common tradition and the parochial grouping within NATO illustrates the possible extent of "functional cooperation." One compromise solution, attempting to embrace as many ideas as possible on the reorganization of NATO, envisaged a confederation consisting of three equal and coordinate parts—the United States, the Commonwealth, and a continental union along the lines of the European Defense Community. Although the concept found favor on both sides of the Atlantic,[41] neither the theoretical nor the empirical approach supplies an answer at this time to the question of whether the community will be global in scope or restricted to the Schuman Plan countries, a limited collaboration for specific purposes or a supranational federation, a successor to the United Nations or independent of it. The main trouble seems to lie with the history of the organization rather than with the historians. The member nations of NATO have not made up their minds about the problem, and the writing on the nonmilitary aspects of the alliance reflects their uncertainty. Unlike the commentators on the military functions of NATO, students of the Atlantic community lack materials for their work. The brief and inconclusive life of the Atlantic Community Committee, set up at the Ottawa meeting of the council in September 1951 and absorbed by the council at Lisbon in February 1952, points up their difficulties. There is no question that a community of interest and culture binds the countries of the Atlantic, but, as A.D.P. Heeney, permanent delegate of Canada to the North Atlantic Council, informed an unofficial conference on the Atlantic community: "The Atlantic Community and NATO are neither the same nor co-extensive."[42] Even Walter Lippmann, one of the keenest observers of the Atlantic community, noted in 1952 that functionally NATO is primarily a military community and little more.[43]

The American Role

A third significant area of study is the relationship of the United States to the North Atlantic Treaty Organization. It is important initially because of the distinctive place it occupies in this nation's diplomatic history. Potentially America's membership in the Atlantic alliance has more serious implications for America's economy, political

40. Percy C. Spender, "NATO and Pacific Security," in Norman D. Palmer, ed., "The National Interest—Alone or with Others?" *Annals of the American Academy of Political and Social Science* 282 (July 1952): 115.

41. "Un esprit atlantique est-il possible?" *Révue de Défense Nationale* 9 (May 1953): 544–55; Theodore Geiger and H. Van B. Cleveland, *Making Western Europe Defensible: An Appraisal of the Effectiveness of a United States Policy in Western Europe*, National Planning Association, Pamphlet no. 74 (Washington, Aug. 1951), pp. 60–69.

42. A.D.P. Heeney, "Relation of N.A.T.O. to the Atlantic Community," *Report of the First International Study Conference on the Atlantic Community at Oxford, September 7th to 13th, 1952* (London, 1952), pp. 59–60.

43. Walter Lippmann, *Isolation and Alliances: An American Speaks to the British* (Boston, 1952), pp. 43–44.

structure, and foreign policy than any other action since the establishment of the Republic. For the first time since the Treaty of Morfontaine with France in 1800 the United States has committed itself to a military alliance with a European power. Whereas Morfontaine marked the conclusion of a twenty-two year old treaty with a single nation, the North Atlantic Treaty linked the United States formally with eleven, and later thirteen, nations in an organization which might assume a type of political authority that has hitherto been the exclusive property of the nation-state. The signing of the North Atlantic Treaty may be regarded in the future as a symbol of America's repudiation of its isolationist tradition and of its realization of the responsibilities attached to the role of the leading power in the free world.

Considering the implications of the Treaty, commentators both hostile and friendly noted with some surprise that it was received with so much aplomb in the United States.[44] Despite the vigorous debate in the Foreign Relations Committee and on the floor of the Senate over its constitutionality and the commitments it would entail, the nation as a whole seemed to accept the Treaty and the organization merely as a natural outgrowth of postwar tensions. NATO was just another name to be placed beside the United Nations, the Marshall Plan, and the Truman Doctrine. Although such diverse groups as pacifists, Communist sympathizers, and isolationists raised their voices against the Treaty at great length and with great passion, none of them was able to establish the rapport with the public that Senators Borah and Lodge had been able to do a generation before with the League of Nations.[45] Nevertheless, the popular interest that was aroused by the "Great Debate" two years later suggests that the general reaction in 1949 did not necessarily signify a genuine acceptance of new responsibilities.

Lack of widespread interest in these aspects of the new organization may explain why few attempts have been made to place NATO in a historical perspective. While members of the staff of the Senate Foreign Relations Committee provided a full account of the passage of the Treaty and the creation of its organization framework, the study appears to have been written in a historical vacuum.[46] This characteristic holds true also for the books of Bailey and Samuel and of Cheever and Haviland, both of which describe in detail the passage of the Treaty through the Senate.[47] For the former the Treaty is merely a case study of the legislative process; and for the latter, an illustration of the complexities involved in the doctrine of separation of powers rather than an inquiry into the effects the Treaty might have upon traditional concepts of sovereignty.

44. Marquis Childs, "Washington and the Atlantic Pact," *Yale Review* 38 (June 1949): 577–88; "The North Atlantic Pact: Congress and the Military Commitment," *World Today* 5 (July 1949): 296–304; Kirk, "Atlantic Pact."

45. Kirk, "Atlantic Pact."

46. Richard H. Heindel, Thorsten V. Kalijarvi, and Francis O. Wilcox, "The North Atlantic Treaty in the United States Senate," *American Journal of International Law* 43 (Oct. 1949): 633–66, F.O. Wilcox and T.V. Kalijarvi, "The Organizational Framework of the North Atlantic Treaty," *American Journal of International Law* 44 (Jan. 1950): 155–61.

47. Stephen K. Bailey and Howard D. Samuel, *Congress at Work* (New York, 1953), pp. 383–414; Daniel E. Cheever and H. Field Haviland, Jr., *American Foreign Policy and the Separation of Powers* (Cambridge, Mass., 1952), pp. 132–36.

Studies that have tried specifically to relate NATO to the mainstream of American history have been generally superficial. Lyman Burbank's article on NATO and the Constitution, for example, merely affirms NATO's compatability with the articles of the Constitution dealing with the war- and treaty-making powers.[48] While Halford Hoskins and Marina Salvin did bring pertinent historical facts into their respective essays on the formation of the North Atlantic Treaty, they were using the historical setting primarily as background material.[49] More imaginative is Sir Norman Angell's view of the Treaty as a fulfillment of the principles of the Monroe Doctrine: both documents envisage an Anglo-American concert as a deterrent to invasion. This equation, however, is accomplished at the expense of the unilateral character of the Monroe Doctrine.[50] Despite his oversimplified delineation of the American tradition, Angell is one of the few critics who has regarded the Treaty as something more than one of a series of government measures to adjust to postwar conditions.

At first glance it seems unlikely that the members of the British and Canadian study groups should show more interest in NATO's place in the history of the United States than most American writers. And yet the reasons for the former's interest are not hard to find. The obligations that the United States assumed under the Treaty would determine the future of NATO and possibly also the fate of its twelve members. America's understanding of those obligations was influenced by its historical memories. Therefore, when the British and Canadian studies explore American history, they do so in search of clues to the position that the United States will ultimately adopt.

Three years after the ratification of the treaty, they were still not sure of America's attitude. Arthur Turner in the Canadian report was confused by the United States' ideas about supranational government. With some resentment he noted that "most Americans are much readier to cite the example of the Philadelphia Convention of 1787, for the edification of a divided Europe, than they would be to follow that example."[51] And without a clear statement of America's position on surrendering some of its sovereign functions to a larger community, Britain, according to Donald McLachlan, would be unable to declare its own position. In strong language, McLachlan, writing in the winter of 1950–51, underscored the need for the United States to abandon the bilateral approach in dealing with the Atlantic alliance.[52] A year and a half later, however, he sounded more optimistic when he suggested in the Royal Institute study that the obstacles to American membership in a formal community with supranational powers were less formidable than generally realized, and concluded that the United States Constitution granted the government sufficient authority to advance the NATO concept if public opinion supported it.[53] In this respect he was more optimistic

48. Lyman B. Burbank, "NATO and the United States Constitution," *Social Education* 16 (May 1952): 207–9, 221.

49. Halford L. Hoskins, *The Atlantic Pact* (Washington, 1949); Marina Salvin, "The North Atlantic Pact," *International Conciliation*, no. 451 (Apr. 1949): 373–455.

50. Norman Angell, "The Atlantic Pact in the American Tradition," *Yale Review* 28 (June 1949): 597–608.

51. *Bulwark of the West*, pp. 58–59.

52. Donald H. McLachlan, "Rearmament and European Integration," *Foreign Affairs* 24 (Jan. 1951): 276–87.

53. *Atlantic Alliance*, pp. 106–7.

than some American observers. Hajo Holborn and F.S.C. Northrop, writing in the fall of 1953 and the winter of 1954 respectively, observed that a vacillating American policy continues to be a major obstacle in the path of both Atlantic and European integration.[54]

Although the role of the United States in NATO received a treatment in the British and Canadian reports not accorded to any other member of the organization, the treatment reflects, whether consciously or unconsciously, the national preoccupations of Britain and Canada. The United States appears primarily as a focus for their fears and ambitions, and consequently the only facets of America's relations with NATO that are examined are those which have a bearing on the position of the two allies. An example of this is their crediting Prime Minister St. Laurent and Foreign Secretary Bevin with the successes and even the initial conception of NATO without any reference to the work of President Truman, Senator Vandenberg, or Deputy Secretary of State Lovett—or, for that matter, to the important contributions of European statesmen such as Schuman and Spaak. This tendency is even more noticeable in commentaries written by nationals of smaller nations of the alliance. NATO and the United States are considered in the light of the nation's special concerns.[55]

Actually, in terms of numbers, many of the special problems invoked by the North Atlantic Treaty have been extensively discussed in monographs, but the total effect lacks coherence. There has been no full-scale analysis of NATO-American relations. Judging from the subtitle, Blair Bolles intended to make such an analysis for the Foreign Policy Association, although the text shows it to be more a general discussion of the aims of American foreign policy than a thorough dissection of NATO and the United States' position in the organization.[56]

In some ways two State Department pamphlets, one published in 1949 a month before the signing of the Treaty and the other in 1952, provide the best-rounded picture of the American position in NATO.[57] But these publications had the primary functions of serving as homiletical tracts designed to convince Congress and the public of the merits of the organization, and consequently no attempt was made, unlike the unofficial British and Canadian volumes, to probe beneath the surface of the issues which they present so clearly.

The most perceptive examinations of America's relations with NATO have been made in studies of specialized problems involved in this relationship. Such a specialized area is the United States foreign aid program, which Ernest Bloch interpreted as being one of conflict between the goals of economic recovery and rearmament.[58] This

54. Hajo Holborn, "American Foreign Policy and European Integration," *World Politics* 6 (Oct. 1953): 1–31; F.S.C. Northrop, "United States Foreign Policy and Continental European Union," *Harvard Studies in International Affairs* 4 (Feb. 1954): 7–35.

55. Alfred Skar, "Norway and the Atlantic Pact," *Ny Militar Tidskrift* 22 (Nov. 1949) 290–92; summarized in *Military Review* 30 (Sept. 1950): 78–81.

56. Blair Bolles, *The Armed Road to Peace: An Analysis of NATO*, Headline Series, Foreign Policy Association, 92 (Mar.–Apr. 1951).

57. *The North Atlantic Pact*, Department of State Publication 3462, Mar. 1949; *NATO: Its Development and Significance*, ibid., 4630, Aug. 1952.

58. Ernest R. Bloch, "European Rearmament and United States Foreign Aid," *Review of Economics and Statistics* 32 (Nov. 1950): 339–47.

problem is treated more comprehensively in a study by William Brown and Redvers Opie under the auspices of the Brookings Institution. These authors explored the consequences of a program in which the United States appears more concerned with rearmament than do the recipient nations, whose first interest is the health of their economies.[59] Basic to this discussion is the question of how far the United States should and can go to coerce the allies to accept policies which it, as the chief donor, feels to be in the common weal without destroying the NATO process of mutual planning. The issue is heightened by the contrast between the strictly bilateral arrangements used in the military aid program and the multilateral nature of the organization this aid is to serve.

Though there has been no simple solution to the problem of safeguarding America's investment of resources in NATO while promoting the spirit of cooperation among the members, one answer proposed by critics has been the development of new machinery suitable to the exigencies of multilateral diplomacy. A study group of the Woodrow Wilson Foundation, under the chairmanship of Professor William Yandell Elliott, remarked on the preeminent position of military planning in NATO activities, and noted the difficulties encountered by the Department of State in dealing with NATO bodies. The study group recommended clarification of NATO's place in the conduct of United States foreign policy.[60] In response to the need for improved coordination, the Brookings Institution, at the request of the Bureau of the Budget, in 1951 prepared an analysis of the general problem of organizing the government for the administration of overseas operations. In particular, the report reviews the parts which the individual departments and agencies concerned with foreign affairs should play.[61]

Valuable as these studies are to an understanding of the United States' relations with NATO, they present only partial coverage of the subject. The need for clarity in organizational relationships is obvious, but its consideration does not take the place of studies designed to reveal what diplomatic techniques actually were used in the United States' relations with its NATO allies and what lessons have been gained from their use. No works as comprehensive and probing as the British or Canadian reports have appeared which would assess the influence of public opinion upon the official United States attitude toward NATO, or analyze the opinions of the Department of Defense in the decisionmaking processes, or evaluate the effect of United States military and economic aid upon the efficacy of the alliance, or relate the United States' NATO policy to its overall foreign policy. In short, the task of evaluating the position and the stake in NATO held by the United States remains to be done in the same way that Britain's and Canada's positions were analyzed. Only in the annual volumes of the Brookings Institution and Council of Foreign Relations is there any attempt to tie together the various strands of the U.S. relationship with the Atlantic alliance, and this

59. William Adams Brown, Jr., and Redvers Opie, *American Foreign Assistance* (Washington, 1953).

60. William Yandell Elliott, Chairman of Study Group, *United States Foreign Policy: Its Organization and Control* (New York, 1952), pp. 169–70.

61. *The Administration of Foreign Affairs and Overseas Operations*, report prepared for the Bureau of the Budget, Executive Office of the President, by the Brookings Institution (Washington, D.C., 1951).

service is performed primarily on the narrative level in the Council of Foreign Relations volumes.[62] More analytical have been the efforts of the Academy of Political Science and the American Academy of Political and Social Science, each of which has devoted an issue in its journal to reports on NATO from a variety of points of view.[63] While some of the individual essays make notable contributions, these articles as a group comprise the usual random collection of material with all the shortcomings inevitably associated with symposia.

One reason for the lack of synthesis in writings on this subject is that the United States has not yet articulated a definitive policy toward NATO; for the most part it has handled the various NATO questions piecemeal, disposing of each as it came up without measuring it against the requirements of a general program. It is worth noting that many of the articles and books cited above on United States-NATO relations are concerned essentially with topics other than NATO—the military assistance program or the administration of American foreign policy. Unlike the problems involved in writing about the future of the Atlantic community, most of the writings on this subject are grounded on fact, not speculation; but they concentrate on details, on peripheral areas, or on major problems removed from context rather than on the relations of the United States with an organization which could transform the foreign policy of the past.

It seems clear that the fullest accounts of the North Atlantic Treaty Organization have been in the military sphere. Here the greatest advances have been made, and even when they have not come up to expectations, the course of events can be followed and causal relationships established. Organizational changes, problems of command structure, the division of economic burdens, and the sacrifices in sovereignty made in the interest of collective defense have developed in such a way as to permit extensive, if not informed, commentary. No such pattern is available to chroniclers of the Atlantic community that many observers hoped would develop from the military organization. After five years it is still not certain that NATO is to be more than a defense organization, and this uncertainty is responsible for the type of study that has appeared on the subject. In the third category the materials are ample but much too diffuse for writers to assemble with any feeling of confidence. If the position of the United States in NATO remains enigmatic, it is because the United States government has not projected fully its own conception of the nature and purpose of the North Atlantic Treaty Organization.

An illustration of the bibliographical differences between the three major categories under discussion is the status accorded by each to the sequence of time. For the military side of NATO, time has been the frame on which the historian could record and study its growth. The number of forces available to the allies, the manner in which they were organized, the economic and political adjustments needed for their support

62. Brookings Institution, *Major Problems of United States Foreign Policy*, 1949 and succeeding years (Washington, D.C.); Council on Foreign Relations, *The United States in World Affairs*, 1949 and succeeding years (New York).
63. John A. Krout, ed., "The United States and the Atlantic Community," *Proceedings of the Academy of Political Science* 23 (May 1949); Ernest M. Patterson, ed., "NATO and World Peace," *Annals of The American Academy of Political and Social Science* 288 (July 1953).

present a record which shows considerable change between conditions prevailing in 1949 and those that prevail today.

This sense of the passage of time is not prominent in the writings on the Atlantic community. The works in this area have been essentially treatises in political philosophy rather than in history, the authors having the license to reconstruct for themselves the political community of the Atlantic alliance in the absence of a record of events. Developments such as the formation of a European Coal and Steel Community have been so few and so tentative that a pattern is not yet discernible. It is significant that a scholar examining NATO's relationship with the United Nations might arrive at the same conclusions in 1953 that he found in 1949. Time has little meaning in these speculations.

The study of the significance of the United States to NATO suffers also, though to a lesser degree, from the absence of a clear pattern of development. Writers in 1954 have to contend with the same problems that faced commentators five years earlier with limited help from the events that have occurred in the intervening years. Although specific parts of the problem have received historical treatment, they have generally been unrelated to the whole; many of the authors have been interested in NATO only as political scientists seeking information that NATO might add to the principles of government rather than as historians assaying the place of NATO in the larger schemes of things.

NATO AND ITS COMMENTATORS:
THE FIRST FIVE YEARS REVISITED (1984)

It has been thirty years since I made the not particularly bold prediction that NATO would continue to inspire a large volume of commentary. Evidence from the first five years made it reasonable to anticipate wave after wave of published materials, much of it as ephemeral as that of the early 1950s, for the lifetime of an important organization. But the image of the wave also suggests that the greatest activity takes place at its crest—the contemporary moment. And if one looks closely at the temporal scope of writings on NATO, the majority of them deal with the problems of the day. NATO's history seems to be of interest primarily as it affects current debate in the relations between the United States and the world. As the period 1949–54 dropped from view, political scientists and journalists understandably moved on. Historians have not yet taken up the challenge of providing more than a modest current of publications, let alone of sending up new waves of books and articles.

Ten years ago I attempted to account for the relative silence of historians on NATO by suggesting that at least two inhibiting elements had deterred most potential analysts. One was the absence of primary materials, the vital documents from the chanceries of the principal powers as well as the limited number of personal accounts from policymakers. Another was the perception among scholars generally that the subject was of limited importance, at best a by-product of the Truman Doctrine and a cog in the containment plans of the American foreign policy establishment.[1] To a

1. "After Twenty-five Years: NATO as a Research Field," *AHA Newsletter* 12 (Nov. 1974) pp. 6–7.

degree at least the former problem is being solved with the growing availability of contemporary sources. The latter is another matter. As this essay will show, NATO as a field of historical research has attracted some attention from students on both sides of the Atlantic, and this attention will grow considerably in the next few years.

It is worth speculating as to whether much of the expected increase in the popularity of NATO's origins and early years will be the result of draining dry the records of the early Cold War. There is not much room left for young scholars to make an impact on the historiography of the years 1945 through 1948. For fresh materials they must move on to a later stage of the Cold War, whatever importance they attach to the Atlantic alliance. Even now there is some reason to suspect that the shorter-lived Korean War of 1950 holds more intrinsic importance for American diplomatic historians than the creation of the Atlantic pact of 1949, with its longer-sustained influence on history.

Guides and Archives

Whether or not skepticism is called for, the prospects for NATO scholarship are served by useful guides to the subject. British scholar Colin Gordon provided the first comprehensive listing of NATO titles through 1977.[2] Organized chronologically as well as topically, it is the first place to turn for the range of secondary literature on the subject. It should be supplemented by J. Bryan Collester's annotated guide to information sources on the European communities.[3] The recent studies of the beginnings of NATO by Escott Reid, Lawrence Kaplan, and Timothy Ireland in 1977, 1980, and 1981, respectively, also contain bibliographical notes.[4] One measure of the potential importance of NATO to the historiography of American foreign relations is the prominent place—in fact two places—it occupies in Richard Burns's *Guide*, sponsored by the Society for Historians of American Foreign Relations.[5] Additionally, *Historical Abstracts* and *America: History and Life* should be consulted for the latest publications as well as for items omitted in the foregoing bibliographies. Similarly, the special bibliographical notices published quarterly in *Foreign Affairs*, *International Organization*, and particularly the *Atlantic Community Quarterly* should be consulted. A special and most rewarding work is the collection of papers on the archives of the nations of Western Europe, prepared under the auspices of the European Community by Walter Lipgens.[6] While these volumes are designed primarily for study of European unification they are equally important for students of the Atlantic alliance.

2. Colin Gordon, *The Atlantic Alliance: A Bibliography* (New York, 1978).

3. J. Bryan Collester, *The European Communities: A Guide to Information Sources* (Detroit, 1979).

4. Escott Reid, *Time of Fear and Hope: The Making of the North Atlantic Treaty, 1947–1949* (Toronto, 1977); Lawrence S. Kaplan, *A Community of Interests: NATO and the Military Assistance Program, 1948–1951* (Washington, D.C., 1980); Timothy Ireland, *Creating the Entangling Alliance: The Origins of the North Atlantic Treaty Organization* (Westport, Conn., 1981).

5. Richard D. Burns, ed., *Guide to American Foreign Relations since 1700* (Santa Barbara, 1983).

6. Walter Lipgens, ed., *Sources for the History of European Integration, 1945–1955: Archives of the Countries of the Community* (Leyden, 1980).

European archives are more impressive for what they might offer scholars than for what they actually provide. Most of the member nations of NATO have severe restrictions on access to any material under fifty years old, and where documents for the years 1948 and 1955 may be available, they usually exclude anything touching national security. Exceptions may be the Schuman Papers in Metz and the Monnet Papers in Paris, manuscript collections outside the formal structure of governmental archives. Further exceptions may be found in the United Kingdom, where a twenty-year rule is in operation at the Public Record Office. Unfortunately, for the year 1949 the Western Union and NATO are excluded from access. Partial compensation may be found in consulting such papers as Hugh Dalton's papers at the London School of Economics and Lord Ismay's papers at King's College, London. The latter include documents from Ismay's service as NATO's first secretary-general which are unavailable in Brussels.

It is worth noting that efforts are currently underway at both NATO headquarters in Belgium (the secretary-general's files at Evère and SHAPE's records at Casteau) to declassify papers for the early years of both offices. Encouragement for these actions may be taken from the decision made by the Western European Union in 1981 to open up the records of the Consultative Council and the Permanent Commission of the Brussels Treaty Organization. Microfilm reels are available at the Public Record Office in Kew for the years 1948 through 1950. Officials at the WEU are currently reviewing archives for the early 1950s.

United States manuscript sources are the most abundant and the most varied. The point of departure inevitably is the National Archives, particularly the Department of State diplomatic correspondence in Record Group 59. The valuable *Foreign Relations of the United States* series has fallen far behind publication schedule, with thirty rather than twenty years the informal rule at this time. But access to manuscripts is even farther behind schedule. Problems in declassification have prevented scholars from consulting materials beyond 1949 in the diplomatic archives. The situation is somewhat better in the Modern Military division of the National Archives, where records of the Office of the Secretary of Defense and the Joint Chiefs of Staff (RG 330 and RG 218, respectively), though only selectively declassified and occasionally sanitized, are open to inspection throughout the five years under review. Additionally, the extensive use of the Freedom of Information Act has further made available classified materials, even if there is still no completely authoritative way of locating all that may be consulted. The annual volumes of the Carrollton Press's catalog are helpful in guiding scholars through the classification maze.[7]

Washington, however, is not the only location of manuscript materials. The two presidential libraries of the period, Truman and Eisenhower, contain a wealth of material, some of which is open to researchers in Independence, Missouri, and Abilene, Kansas, when they are not in Washington, D.C. These libraries hold papers of the leading policymakers of the administrations as well as those of the presidents. Additionally, such important figures as George Kennan and John Foster Dulles left materials to their alma mater, in this case Princeton. Elsewhere legislative leaders involved in the formative years of NATO have done the same; J. William Fulbright has

7. *The Classified Documents Quarterly Catalog* (Arlington, 1975).

left his collection with the University of Arkansas in Fayetteville, while Arthur H. Vandenberg's is at the Bentley Historical Library in Ann Arbor, Michigan. The Library of Congress, however, holds the Tom Connally Papers in addition to those of such important diplomats as Philip C. Jessup and Charles E. Bohlen.

In addition to personal public papers, extensive interviews compiled over the years are to be found in such centers as the Truman and Eisenhower libraries and in the Oral History Collection at Columbia University. These are particularly important for middle-level officials, such as John D. Hickerson and Theodore C. Achilles of the State Department and General Lyman L. Lemnitzer and John Ohly of Defense, who were more intimately involved in the shaping of NATO than more senior officers of government.

Published Primary Materials

The published memoirs, reflections, and correspondence of leaders of the fifteen member nations of the alliance are far more accessible. Inevitably, they vary in quality as well as in the quantity of information they supply. A few have special features such as Canadian diplomat Escott Reid's, a book that combines history and memoir with unusual success, and French Defense Minister Jules Moch's which offers a unique insight into the question of German integration into Western Europe.[8] Other European actors who recorded their impressions have made NATO only one of many concerns as statemen. Such is the case of German Chancellor Konrad Adenauer, Dutch Foreign Minister and later Secretary-General Dirk Stikker, French minister Jean Chauvel, and even such central NATO figures as Lord Ismay, the first secretary-general, and Paul-Henri Spaak, the most articulate continental leader of the alliance.[9] Others such as Jean Monnet and Gladwyn Jebb identify NATO in their memoirs but make clear that their major concerns are for a Europe organized somewhat differently than in the Atlantic alliance.[10] Vincent Auriol, president of France, has left a daily diary for the entire period; while Sir Nicholas Henderson in the thick of negotiations for the alliance provided his own personal history.[11] For the entry of Germany into NATO, Eden's memoirs emphasizing his role following the demise of the European Defense Community are a major resource.[12]

Two signficant military figures—British Marshal Montgomery and French General Beaufre, present their views in differing ways—Montgomery through memoirs reflecting his contribution to the Western Union as well as to SHAPE;

8. Reid, *Time of Fear and Hope.* Foreign Minister Lester Pearson's memoirs complement Reid's in *Mike: The Memoirs of the Rt. Hon. Lester B. Pearson,* 2 vols. (Toronto, 1973); Jules Moch, *Histoire de rearmament allemand dupuis 1950* (Paris, 1965).

9. Konrad Adenauer, *Memoirs, 1945–53,* trans. Beate Rub von Oppen (London, 1966); Dirk U. Stikker, *Men of Responsibility: A Memoir* (New York, 1966); Jean Chauvel, *Commentaire* (Paris, 1971); Hastings, Lord Ismay, *Memoirs* (New York, 1960); Paul-Henri Spaak, *The Continuing Battle: Memoirs of a European, 1936–1966,* trans. Henry Fox (Boston, 1971).

10. Jean Monnet, *Memoirs,* trans. Richard Mayne (Garden City, N.Y., 1978); Gladwyn Jebb, *Memoirs of Lord Gladwyn* (London, 1972).

11. Vincent Auriol, *Journal de Septennat, 1947–1954,* 7 vols. (Paris, 1970–74); Nicholas Henderson, *The Birth of NATO* (Boulder, 1983).

12. Anthony Eden, *Full Circle: The Memoirs of Anthony Eden* (Boston, 1960).

Beaufre through an overview of NATO.[13] American memoirs are also abundant for this period. While the Truman and Eisenhower volumes provide mostly generalities, the numerous writings of Secretary of State Acheson, particularly his *Present at the Creation*, are vital to any understanding of the American role in the creation of the alliance.[14] Other figures only slightly less important have contributed their views, some of them, such as Secretary of Defense Forrestal's and Senator Arthur Vandenberg's, edited after their death.[15] Of the two major diplomats involved in NATO, Kennan's memoirs are more revealing than Bohlen's although both are important. General Clay from his perch in Frankfurt provides insights into the position Germany occupied in the formation of NATO, as does his aide Robert Murphy. Walter Bedell Smith performs a similar service from Moscow early in the Cold War.[16] W. Averell Harriman's personal papers are closed but one aspect of his varied services, his views of the Soviet relationship, is available in print.[17] Some diplomats chose to present their roles in the guise of historians, in the manner of Escott Reid: John McCloy and Harlan Cleveland, for examples.[18] Others such as Senator Taft and future Secretary of State Dulles presented theirs as campaign statements, with all the limitations of this genre.[19]

Published primary sources of the foregoing kinds were unavailable thirty years ago, with a few exceptions. Other sources were in the public domain in 1954, including treaty records of the Department of State, the *Department of State Bulletin* and the *NATO Handbook*. Senate hearings on the treaty as well as special reports on NATO problems were open to public inspection. Similarly, major documents were easily available in the British *Documents on International Affairs* series and in the *American Documents on American Foreign Relations* published by the World Peace Foundation

13. Bernard Montgomery, *Memoirs* (Cleveland, 1958); Andre Beaufre, *NATO and Europe*, trans. Joseph Green (New York, 1966).

14. Harry S. Truman, *Memoirs, Years of Trial* (Garden City, N.Y., 1955–56); Dwight D. Eisenhower, *The White House Years*, 2 vols. (Garden City, N.Y., 1967); Dean Acheson, *Present at the Creation: My Years in the State Department* (New York, 1960); idem, *Sketches from Life of Men I Have Known* (New York, 1961).

15. Walter Millis, ed., *The Forrestal Diaries* (New York, 1951); Arthur Vandenberg, Jr., ed., *The Private Papers of Senator Vandenberg* (Boston, 1952). Tom Connally, with Alfred Steinberg, *My Name Is Tom Connally* (New York, 1954) is less satisfactory.

16. George F. Kennan, *Memoirs, 1925–1963*, 2 vols. (Boston, 1967, 1972); Charles E. Bohlen, *Witness to History, 1929–1969* (New York, 1973); Lucius D. Clay, *The Papers of General Lucius D. Clay: Germany, 1945–1949*, 2 vols. (Bloomington, 1974); Robert D. Murphy, *Diplomat among Warriors* (Garden City, N.Y., 1964); Walter Bedell Smith, *My Three Years in Moscow* (Philadelphia, 1950).

17. W. Averell Harriman, *America and Russia in a Changing World: A Half Century of Personal Observation* (Garden City, N.Y., 1971).

18. John J. McCloy, *The Atlantic Alliance: Its Origin and Its Future* (New York, 1969); Harlan Cleveland, *NATO: The Transatlantic Bargain* (New York, 1970).

19. Robert A. Taft, *A Foreign Policy for Americans* (Garden City, N.Y. 1952). See also Henry W. Berger, "Senator Robert A. Taft Dissents from Military Escalation," in Thomas G. Paterson, ed., *Cold War Critics: Alternatives to American Foreign Policy* (Chicago, 1971); John Foster Dulles, *War or Peace* (New York, 1950). For the early years see also Ronald Pruessen, *John Foster Dulles: The Road to Power* (New York, 1982).

through 1952 and then by the Council on Foreign Relations. Major official publications of primary importance to students of the first five years of NATO are the *Foreign Relations of the United States*, which are currently available through 1954, and the executive sessions of the Senate Foreign Relations Committee released in the last decade as part of the Senate Historical Series.

General Works

Over the past generation there have been numerous general studies that have touched on NATO in one capacity or another. In the 1960s more than today they were usually classified as "traditionalist," "realist," and "revisionist," or "consensus" and "New Left"; these disputable but convenient categories reflect the influences of the Vietnam War. While postrevisionism has blurred distinctions since the mid-1970s, not only on the wisdom of that conflict but also on the responsibilities to be assigned for originating and prolonging the Cold War, some shading is still found among authors writing today. NATO is seldom in focus, however, either by writers supportive of American foreign policy in the Truman administration or for those opposed. For Joyce and Gabriel Kolko, NATO is simply a logical instrument of American control of Europe. Walter LaFeber in numerous editions of an able survey of U.S. diplomacy since the Cold War still finds little room for the Atlantic alliance as a major entity of American foreign policy. Even a consensus historian such as Herbert Feis makes space for just one short chapter on the subject.[20]

Biographies of major statesmen of the period have included most of the leaders. Only a few of them have assigned NATO a serious role in their careers. A place to begin any study of the early years of NATO from a biographical perspective is the admirable Secretary of State series begun by Samuel Flagg Bemis two generations ago and continued by Robert H. Ferrell. The editor's sketch of George Marshall slights the secretary's responsibilities for the earliest developments of the Atlantic alliance.[21] Gaddis Smith's *Acheson* and David McClellan's study of his State Department years deal more fully with the alliance.[22] Louis Gerson's volume on Dulles is hampered by limitations imposed by classification of documents.[23]

President's Truman and Eisenhower have been subjects of many biographies, although scholarly treatment of Eisenhower has developed rapidly in the last few years since his rehabilitation as a model leader. Robert Donovan's second volume of his authoritative biography identifies the alliance as one of Truman's major achievements

20. Joyce Kolko and Gabriel Kolko, *The Limits of Power: The World and United States Foreign Policy, 1945–1954* (New York, 1972); Walter LaFeber, *America, Russia and the Cold War, 1945–1966* (4th ed., *1945–1980*) (New York, 1967, 1980); Herbert Feis, *From Trust to Terror: The Onset of the Cold War, 1945–1950* (New York, 1970).

21. Robert H. Ferrell, *George Marshall*, in Ferrell, ed., *The American Secretaries of State and their Diplomacy*, vol. 15 (New York, 1966).

22. Gaddis Smith, *Dean Acheson* in Ferrell, *American Secretaries of State and Their Diplomacy*, vol. 16 (New York, 1972); David S. McClellan, *Dean Acheson: The State Department Years* (New York, 1976).

23. Louis Gerson, *John Foster Dulles*, in Ferrell, *The American Secretaries of State and Their Diplomacy* vol. 17 (New York, 1967). An example of a more critical view is Townshend Hoopes, *The Devil and John Foster Dulles* (Boston, 1973).

as president.[24] Robert Ferrell's deft presentation of Truman's presidency also finds in NATO a climax of the administration's seminal changes in American foreign policy.[25] For revisionist positions, Barton Bernstein edited a volume concentrating on Foreign policy in 1968; Bert Cochran follows a similar path in explaining crises in foreign policy as a means of implementing programs.[26] There is less significant literature on Eisenhower and NATO despite his assignment as the first supreme allied commander. While recent studies, such as Blanche Cook's and Fred Greenstein's, reclaim his foreign policy from Dulles's control, Herbert Parmet in 1972 and Douglas Kinnard in 1977 pointed in the same direction.[27]

Secretaries of defense, congressional leaders, and leading diplomats have received considerable attention from scholars and journalists but not in equal portions. The neglect may be in part the function of the official's fame or notoriety in office, in part the scarcity of sources. The contrast between interest in James Forrestal, best expressed in Arnold Rogow's psychobiography, and the absence of any work on his successor, Louis Johnson, cannot be explained by the paucity of papers at the University of Virginia.[28] A study of Johnson's administration in the Department of Defense's forthcoming volumes on the secretaries of defense may change current impressions. While the Vandenberg Resolution at least has been the subject of an important article underscoring his influence,[29] neither Vandenberg nor Tom Connally nor J. William Fulbright has been the focus of a biography commensurate with his importance. On the other hand, Ronald Steel has presented a prize-winning study of Walter Lippmann, while Henry Wallace on the fringe of foreign policy has received favorable attention from Richard Walton and J. Samuel Walker.[30] Although there is no biography comparable to Steel's *Lippmann* for Kennan, Bohlen, or Harriman, this situation may be different when major studies on each of them are completed in the next few years. Brief essays by Thomas Paterson and C. Ben Wright on Kennan, Larry Bland on Harriman, and T. Michael Ruddy on Bohlen are all worth reading.[31]

24. Robert J. Donovan, *Tumultuous Years: The Presidency of Harry S. Truman, 1949–1953* (New York, 1982).

25. Robert H. Ferrell, *Harry S. Truman and the Modern American Presidency* (Boston, 1983).

26. Barton Bernstein, ed., *Politics and Policies of the Truman Administration* (Chicago, 1970); Bert Cochran, *Harry Truman and the Crisis Presidency* (New York, 1973).

27. Blanche W. Cook, *The Declassified Eisenhower: A Divided Legacy* (Garden City, N.Y., 1982); Fred W. Greenstein, *The Hidden-Hand Presidency: Eisenhower as Leader* (New York, 1982); Herbert S. Parmet, *Eisenhower and the American Crusades* (New York, 1972); Douglas Kinnard, *President Eisenhower and Strategy Management: A Study in Defense Politics* (Lexington, Ky., 1977).

28. Arnold A. Rogow, *James Forrestal: A Study of Personality, Politics, and Policy* (New York, 1963).

29. Daryl U. Hudson, "Vandenberg Reconsidered: Senate Resolution 239 and American Foreign Policy," *Diplomatic History* 1 (Winter 1977): 46–63.

30. Ronald Steel, *Walter Lippmann and the American Century* (Boston, 1980); Richard J. Walton, *Henry Wallace, Harry Truman and the Cold War* (New York, 1976); J. Samuel Walker, *Henry Wallace and American Foreign Policy* (Westport, Conn., 1976).

31. Thomas G. Paterson, "The Search for Meaning: George F. Kennan and American Foreign Policy," in Frank J. Merli and Theodore A. Wilson, eds., *Makers of American Diplomacy* (New York, 1974), pp. 553–88; T. Michael Ruddy, "Charles E. Bohlen: Political

For monographs centering specifically on NATO the closest to an archetype is Robert Osgood's *NATO: An Entangling Alliance*, now over twenty years old and primarily interested in the problems of 1960.[32] Still, it made the origins of the organization the centerpiece of America's management of the Cold War. As in the past, political scientists and journalists continue to make the major contributions to the understanding of NATO in American history, even as their interests in the organization are either in its role as model or in crisis management. Klaus Knorr has written a concise essay for the Foreign Policy Association, *NATO: Past, Present, and Prospect*, with the past receiving less attention than the present and future.[33] Edwin Fedder and particularly William T.R. Fox and Annette Baker Fox have followed the fortunes of NATO in its role as an alliance.[34] One of the few scholarly studies to deal with NATO in its historical perspective—in this case as a largely benign species of American imperialism—is David Calleo's *Atlantic Fantasy*.[35] Appropriately, the journalists' contributions, while often acute, are even more caught up in the present than those of the political scientists. But when the present was 1952, Theodore White, an unusually perspicacious observer in any year, limned a picture of the United States and Europe that remains valuable a generation later.[36] Foreign scholars have contributed to the store of useful general studies of NATO's first generation: Pierre Melandri, Walter Laqueur, and Coral Bell are among the most perceptive of them.[37]

It is also worth examining books intended to identify milestones of a later period, often in apocalyptic terms, for what the authors have to say about the beginnings of NATO. Such is the case with the well-written and plausible essays of Richard Barnett and Marcus Raskin, and particularly those of Ronald Steel.[38] Their titles sound a note of doom as they predict the early demise of NATO. But even if their predictions have not yet materialized, the information they gather and the insights they bring to the formation of NATO remain valuable to the student of that period.

Special Studies: NATO and Its Origins

Since the beginnings of NATO go back to the transformation of American foreign policy through the policy of containment, the Truman Doctrine, the Marshall Plan, and

---

Realist," in Jules Davids., ed., *Perspectives in American Diplomacy* (New York, 1976), pp. 279–87; Ben Wright, "George F. Kennan: The Concept of Containment," in ibid., pp. 321–34; Larry I. Bland, "W. Averell Harriman: The Liberal Cold Warrior," in ibid., pp. 299–320.

32. Robert E. Osgood, *NATO: The Entangling Alliance* (Chicago, 1962).

33. Klaus Knorr, *NATO: Past, Present, and Prospect*, Foreign Policy Association, (New York, 1969).

34. Edwin H. Fedder, *NATO: The Dynamic of Alliance in the Postwar World* (New York, 1973); William T.R. Fox and Annette B. Fox, *NATO and the Range of American Choice* (New York, 1967).

35. David Calleo, *The Atlantic Fantasy: The United States, NATO, and Europe* (Baltimore, 1970).

36. Theodore H. White, *Fire in the Ashes: Europe in Mid-Century* (New York, 1953).

37. Pierre Melandri, *L'Alliance atlantique* (Paris, 1979); Walter Laqueur, *The Rebirth of Europe* (New York, 1970); Coral Bell, *Negotiations from Strength: A Study in the Politics of Power* (New York, 1966).

38. Richard J. Barnett and Marcus G. Raskin, *After NATO and the Search for a New Policy in Europe* (New York, 1966); Ronald Steel, *The End of the Alliance: America and the Future of Europe* (New York, 1964).

the conceptualization of containment merit attention. Unlike the Treaty itself, the literature is extensive. Containment in particular has attracted scholarly debate, not least over the question of paternity. David McClellan and Bruce Kuniholm find it a derivative of the Middle Eastern crises of 1945–46, while Richard Powers and Robert Messer emphasize Kennan's traditional role.[39] More contentious has been the question of what Kennan's idea of containment actually was. John Gaddis supports Kennan's own disclaimer about the "X" article, and confirms the flexibility which Kennan himself has claimed about his views. Charles Gati and C. Ben Wright provide different angles of observation, while Eduard Mark not only differs from Gaddis but has continued his differences not only in *Foreign Affairs* but also in the pages of *SHAFR Newsletter*.[40] For the student of NATO and U.S. foreign policy in postwar America there is a point of diminishing returns in such debates, and I suspect that the point was reached some time ago with regard to the authorship if not the exact definition of containment.

The Truman Doctrine as a cornerstone of American policy will probably be recast in each generation; the Nixon Doctrine of 1970 recalled the Truman Doctrine in its claim that it represented the first major change since 1947. For Henry Ryan in the *American Scholar*, the Truman Doctrine was a Manichean expression of American good versus Communist evil, a familiar American visceral reaction to the outside world.[41] Richard Freeland writing in the wake of the Vietnam War found that its rigid anticommunist rhetoric was a deliberate political instrument to mobilize public support behind a new American policy toward Europe. It exaggerated the Soviet menace for domestic reasons. Samuel Kernell disagrees not about the inflammatory rhetoric but about the extent of anticommunist sentiment the Doctrine generated.[42] Kuniholm, on the other hand, finds the Doctrine a pragmatic reaction to the reality of East-West struggle in Greece, Turkey, and Iran before 1947. Thomas Paterson also relates the Truman Doctrine to the Middle East, particularly to the importance of petroleum

39. David S. McClellan, "Who Fathered Containment? A Discussion," *International Studies Quarterly* 17 (June 1973): 205–26; Bruce Kuniholm, *The Origins of the Cold War in the Near East: Great Power Conflict and Diplomacy in Iran, Turkey, and Greece* (Princeton, 1980); Richard J. Powers, "Who Fathered Containment?" *International Studies Quarterly* 15 (Dec. 1971): 526–43; Robert L. Messer, "Paths Not Taken: The United States Department of State and Alternatives to Containment, 1945–1946," *Diplomatic History* 1 (Fall 1977): 297–319.

40. John Lewis Gaddis, "Containment: A Reassessment," *Foreign Affairs* 55 (Oct. 1977): 873–87; Charles Gati, "'X' plus 25: What Containment Meant," *Foreign Policy* 7 (Summer 1972): 22–40; C. Ben Wright, "Mr. 'X' and Containment," *Slavic Review* 35 (Mar. 1976): 1–36; Eduard M. Mark, "The Question of Containment: A Reply to John Lewis Gaddis," *Foreign Affairs* 56 (Jan. 1978): 430–31; John Lewis Gaddis, "Kennan and Containment: A Reply," *SHAFR Newsletter* 9 (June 1978): 26–27; Eduard Mark, "Kennan and Containment: A Surrejoinder," ibid., 9 (Sept. 1978): 28–30.

41. Henry B. Ryan, Jr., "The American Intellectual Tradition Reflected in the Truman Doctrine," *American Scholar* 42 (Spring 1973): 294–307.

42. Richard M. Freeland, *The Truman Doctrine and the Origins of McCarthyism: Foreign Policy, Domestic Politics, and Internal Security, 1946–1948* (New York, 1972); Samuel Kernell, "The Truman Doctine Speech: A Case Study of the Dynamics of Presidential Opinion Leadership," *Social Science History* 1 (Fall 1976): 20–44.

resources to the American economy.[43] John Gaddis's perceptive article in *Foreign Affairs* emphasizes the continuity with precedents; global containment, in his view, did not become national policy until the Korean War.[44]

The Marshall Plan occupies for the most part a less controversial and more benign place among scholars, even though revisionists have had no difficulty seeing it as an obvious example of America's economic control over Europe. Harry Price wrote a semiofficial history a generation ago that still informs most interpretations of the Plan. Michael Hogan observes the important role which the ideal of European integration held in the formulation of the Marshall Plan. Theodore Wilson presents a succinct and favorable interpretation of the four-year history of the Plan in a pamphlet for the Foreign Policy Association from a perspective of thirty years.[45] Hadley Arkes examines it for the lessons it provides in bureaucratic planning and execution. Harold Hitchens dissects the congressional debate over the Marshall Plan to locate its success in the workings of pressure groups orchestrated by the administration. He notes, as does Robert Divine, its role in the election of Harry Truman in 1948.[46] James Kem represented, in Mary Atwell's article, the failed opposition in the Senate. Scott Jackson provides a thorough examination of each step in the formulation of the Plan.[47] The most controversial study to date is John Gimbel's thesis that Germany lay at the heart of the Marshall Plan. By massive support for European recovery Germany could be incorporated into the West with minimal hostility from France.[48]

The Berlin blockade, which quickened the pace of the U.S. involvement in 1948, has been given its due. Philip Jessup, the diplomat most intimately involved, has given two useful accounts of the problem and the events. Jean Edward Smith observes Berlin's role over a generation's time, with special attention to the crisis of 1948–49, while W. Phillips Davison centers his study entirely on the blockade. Davison's judgment is that while the issue heightened Cold War tensions, it was a decided victory for the West. Avi Schlaim has provided the most recent interpretation of the Berlin blockade.[49]

43. Kuniholm, *Origins of the Cold War*; Thomas G. Paterson, *Soviet-American Confrontation: Postwar Reconstruction and the Origins of the Cold War* (Baltimore, 1973).

44. John Lewis Gaddis, "Was the Truman Doctrine a Real Turning Point?" *Foreign Affairs* 12 (Jan. 1974): 386–402. See also his *Strategies of Containment: A Critical Appraisal of Postwar United States National Security Policy* (New York, 1982).

45. Harry B. Price, *The Marshall Plan and Its Meaning* (Ithaca, 1955); Michael J. Hogan, "The Search for a 'Creative Peace': the United States, European Unity, and the Origins of the Marshall Plan," *Diplomatic History* 6 (Summer 1982): 267–86; Theodore A. Wilson, *The Marshall Plan, 1947–1951*, Foreign Policy Association, Headline Series, no. 236 (New York, 1977).

46. Hadley Arkes, *Bureaucracy, the Marshall Plan, and the National Interest* (Princeton, 1973); Harold L. Hitchens, "Influences on the Congressional Decision to Pass the Marshall Plan," *Western Political Quarterly* 21 (March 1968): 51–68; Robert A. Divine, "The Cold War and the Election of 1948," *Journal of American History* 59 (June 1972): 90–110.

47. Mary W. Atwell, "A Conservative Response to the Cold War: Senator James P. Kem and Foreign Aid," *Capitol Studies* 4 (Fall 1976): 53–56; Scott Jackson, "Prologue to the Marshall Plan: The Origins of the American Commitment for a European Recovery Program," *Journal of American History* 55 (Nov. 1979): 1043–68.

48. John Gimbel, *The Origins of the Marshall Plan* (Stanford, 1976).

49. Philip C. Jessup, "The Berlin Blockade and the Use of the United Nations," *Foreign*

In contrast to the writings on the period before 1949, books and articles examining the formation of the Atlantic alliance and its early trials are limited in number and most of them have appeared only in the last few years. Alan Henrikson has written a spirited and persuasive account of NATO's early years, examining as well rationalizations for its scope and duration. Timothy Ireland covers the same ground in book form with special emphasis upon the alliance as a means of solving the German problem.[50] While neither monograph uses manuscript sources they grant a significance to the alliance that has eluded most scholars up to this time. Others look at the creation of the alliance from particular angles of observation. Cees Wiebes and Bert Zeeman point out that the secret Pentagon talks of March 1948 among British, Canadian, and American representatives marked the effective conception of the North Atlantic Treaty. Parley Newman's doctoral dissertation studies the formation of the Treaty with an emphasis on its organizational aspects. Lawrence Kaplan focuses on the symbiotic relationship between NATO and the first military assistance programs. Louis Halle, a member of the original Policy Planning Staff, presents his findings from his official perspective. Armin Rappaport's essay on the "revolution" in American diplomatic history is one of very few to discuss the impact of the Treaty on the isolationist tradition.[51] An East German view exposing the "myth" of the "Soviet Danger" as the major ingredient in the founding of NATO appeared in 1976.[52] All but one of the above monographs were published thirty years after the signing of the Treaty, and they comprise most of the scholarship on the subject.

The impact of the Korean War understandably has yielded no more numerous monographs than have the origins of the Treaty. The outstanding exceptions are the two works of Robert Jordan that explore the beginnings of the International staff and the operations of the secretary-general, whose office was established in 1952. They supplement Lord Ismay's own official survey of NATO's first five years.[53]

David Kepley claims that the "Great Debate" of 1951 over troop assignment to

---

Affairs 50 (Jan. 1971): 163–71; idem, "Park Avenue Diplomacy: Ending the Berlin Blockade," *Political Science Quarterly* 87 (July 1972): 377–400; Jean Edward Smith, *The Defense of Berlin* (Baltimore, 1963); W. Phillips Davison, *The Berlin Blockade: A Study in Cold War Politics* (Princeton, 1958); Avi Schlaim, *The United States and the Berlin Blockade, 1948–1949: A Study in Crisis Decision-making* (Berkeley, 1983).

50. Alan K. Henrikson, "The Creation of the North Atlantic Alliance, 1948–1952," *Naval War College Review* 32 (May–June 1980): 4–39; Timothy Ireland, *Creating the Atlantic Alliance* (see note 4, above).

51. Cees Wiebes and Bert Zeeman, "The Pentagon Negotiations, March 1948: The Launching of the North Atlantic Treaty," *International Affairs* 59 (Summer 1983): 351–63; Parley W. Newman, "The Origins of the North Atlantic Treaty: A Study in Organization and Politics" (Ph.D. diss., Columbia Univ. 1977); Kaplan, *Community of Interests* (see note 4, above); Louis J. Halle, "Origins of the Alliance," *Annales d'Etudes Internationales* 12 (1979): 9–18; Armin Rappaport, "The American Revolution of 1949," *NATO Letter* 12 (Feb. 1964): 3–8.

52. Gerhard Keiderling; "Der Mythos von der 'sowjetischen Gefahr' und die Gründung der NATO," *Zeitschrift dur Geschichtswissenschaft* 24 (Oct. 1976): 1093–99.

53. Robert S. Jordan, *The NATO International Staff / Secretariat, 1952–1957* (Oxford, 1967); idem, *Political Leadership in NATO: A Study in Multinational Diplomacy* (Boulder, 1979); Hastings, Lord Ismay, *NATO: The First Five Years, 1949–1954* (Paris, 1955).

Europe reaffirmed the adminstration's European policy.[54] Changes in military structure after Korea may be found in Andrew Goodpaster's sketch of the first few years of SHAPE.[55] There is a good beginning in George Stambuk's study of American military forces abroad as a springboard for examination of the status-of-forces agreements that converted armies of occupation into allied forces.[56] The European Defense Community, beginning with the Pleven Plan in 1950 and ending in defeat in 1954, is the subject of Edward Fursdon's well-written historical survey. Raymond Poidevin marshals evidence of increasing French concerns over the EDC from 1951 to 1953 and finds reasons for its failure a year later in both national and international events of those years. The way in which the EDC fell may be found in Daniel Lerner's and Raymond Aron's *France Defeats EDC*.[57]

Ever since Warner Schilling, Paul Hammond, and Glenn Snyder published a volume linking strategy and politics to defense budgets, the then classified National Security Council document no. 68 has intrigued historians, particularly because of its close temporal proximity to the Korean War.[58] It seemed to hold the key in 1950 to the future which the Truman administration intended for NATO. Its declassification in 1975 reopened debate on its significance. The issue was taken up in *International Security* in 1979, first by Samuel Wells, who finds in the document a culmination of decades of American anxiety over the Soviet threat, and then by John Gaddis, who sees it as an example of means incommensurate with desire in foreign policy. Paul Nitze, a major author of the document, insists that it was a product of the times, without expectation of any immediate action or changes on the part of the Soviet Union. Joseph Siracusa claims that the major positions established in 1950 were adopted two years before in the wake of the Berlin blockade crisis.[59]

The broad question of nuclear weapons as an instrument of policy which NCS-68 addressed is considered in Bernhard Bechhoefer's survey of postwar negotiations for arms control and in George Quester's examination of the first twenty-five years of nuclear diplomacy. Joseph Lieberman distributes responsibility equally in his view of "The Scorpion and the Tarantula," while Gregg Herken is more critical of the United States for its missed opportunities. The second volume of the official study of the

54. David R. Kepley, "The Senate and the Great Debate of 1951," *Prologue* 14 (Winter 1982): 213–26.

55. Andrew T. Goodpaster, "The Development of SHAPE, 1950–1953," *International Organization* 9 (May 1955): 257–62.

56. George Stambuk, *American Military Force Abroad: Their Impact on the Western State System* (Columbus, 1963).

57. Edward Fursdon, *The European Defence Community: A History* (New York, 1979); Raymond Poidevin, "La France devant le problème de la CED; Incidences nationales et internationales (été 1951 à été 1953)," *Revue d'histoire de la deuxième guerre mondiale et des conflits contemporains* 23 (Jan. 1983): 36–57. Daniel Lerner and Raymond Aron, eds., *France Defeats EDC* (New York, 1957).

58. Warner A. Schilling, Paul Y. Hammond, and Glenn Y. Snyder, *Strategy, Politics, and Defense Budgets* (New York, 1962).

59. Samuel F. Wells, Jr., "Sounding the Tocsin: NSC 68 and the Soviet Threat," *International Security* 4 (Fall 1979): 116–58; John Lewis Gaddis and Paul Nitze, "NSC 68 and the Soviet Threat Reconsidered," *International Security* 4 (Spring 1980): 164–76; Joseph M. Siracusa, "NSC 68: A Reappraisal," *Naval War College Review* 33 (Nov.–Dec. 1980): 4–14.

Atomic Energy Commission explains U.S. nuclear policy in the late 1940s and early 1950s.[60]

The important area of political-military cooperation in NATO—the development of new modes or the refinement of old—has been an ongoing subject of interest, but the satisfactory analyses—the studies of Francis Beer, Morton Kaplan, or Alistair Buchan, for example—give little attention to the beginning of the alliance. Exceptions are James King's, Robert E. Osgood's, and Carol Baumann's monographs, as well as the few that touch on the important area of economic ties.[61] Ronald Ritchie devotes a book-length study to the subject, while Lincoln Gordon, an insider both as economist and as government official, presents a clear picture of the economic aspects of coalition diplomacy in the early years.[62] Gavin Kennedy's useful book on burden sharing in NATO concerns a later generation primarily, but it considers the Olson-Zeckhauser thesis carefully before rejecting it.[63] That is, larger nations in the alliance contribute disproportionately to the common costs because their stakes are larger, a thesis that has application to the formation of NATO.

The NATO Allies and Associates

It is probably not surprising that there is a much larger body of literature encompassing the special factors explaining the connection between individual member nations and NATO. Among the most interesting and useful are essays solicited by *NATO Review* from leading figures who were personally involved in their nation's joining the alliance. The series began in 1979 with an article by Alexander Rendel, formerly of the *Times* of London, and proceeded from the United Kingdom to Iceland through the April 1983 issue of the journal. Others will follow.[64] Inevitably, the message is positive. But such biases notwithstanding, these are not essays in public relations. In many cases they rest on newly released information.

60. Bernard G. Bechhoefer, *Postwar Negotiations for Arms Control* (Washington, D.C., 1961); G.H. Quester, *Nuclear Diplomacy: The First Twenty-Five Years* (New York, 1970); Joseph I. Lieberman, *The Scorpian and the Tarantula: The Struggle to Control Atomic Weapons, 1945–49* (Boston, 1970); Gregg Herken, *The Winning Weapon: The Atomic Bomb in the Cold War, 1945–1950* (New York, 1980); Richard G. Hewlett and Francis Duncan, *Atomic Shield, 1947–1952* (College Park, Md., 1969).

61. James E. King, "NATO: Genesis, Progress, Problems," in Gordon B. Turner and Richard D. Challener," eds., *National Security in the Nuclear Age* (New York, 1960); Robert E. Osgood, "NATO: Problems of Security and Collaboration," *American Political Science* 54 (Mar. 1960): 106–29; Carol E. Baumann, *Political Cooperation in NATO* (Madison, Wis., 1960).

62. Ronald S. Ritchie, *NATO: the Economics of the Alliance* (Toronto, 1956); Lincoln Gordon, "Economic Aspects of Coalition Diplomacy—the NATO Experience," *International Organization* 10 (Nov. 1956): 520–43.

63. Gavin Kennedy, *Burden Sharing in NATO* (New York, 1979); Mancur Olson and Richard Zeckhauser, "An Economic Theory of Alliances," *Review of Economics and Statistics* 48 (Aug. 1966): 266–74.

64. Alexander Rendel, "The Alliance's Anxious Birth," *NATO Review* 27 (June 1979): 15–20; Theodore Achilles, "U.S. Role in Negotiations that Led to Atlantic Alliance," ibid., 27 (Aug. 1979): 11–14, and (Oct. 1979): 16–19; Sven Hennigsen, "Denmark and the Road to NATO," ibid., 27 (Dec. 1979): 18–21, and 28 (Feb. 1980): 14–16; Alexander Rendel, "Un-

Klaus Knorr, editing one of the few major works on the United States and NATO a generation ago, included useful essays on Great Britain and Germany in a book that developed from a Princeton conference on problems of NATO strategy.[65] The "special relationship" between the United States and the United Kingdom has attracted considerable attention. The subject ranges beyond NATO but the alliance has always been an important instrument. The element of "uneasiness" appears in the work of Leon Epstein and Alexander Campbell, and encompasses the problems of a Socialist government's difficult adjustment to a lesser role in world affairs, as well as the question of America's isolationist tradition. Harry Allen brings a more irenic note to his impressive studies of the Anglo-American world, with emphasis on the continuing benefits of the "special relationship" on both sides of the Atlantic.[66]

For France the "uncertain" appears in the title of Marvin Zahniser's survey. While this book does not center on NATO, it places France in the alliance as intelligibly as any scholar has done over the years. While both Edgar Furniss in 1960 and Michael Harrison in 1981 focus on France and NATO in a later period, both find seeds of France's defection from the organization, potential in Furniss's case, in the early experience with American leadership.[67]

Germany for many interpreters was a key to NATO's future, just as France was to NATO's creation. Books have appeared with regularity on German-American or German-NATO relations, from Laurence Martin on the rearmament of Germany in 1963, to James Richardson on the interaction in 1966, Roger Morgan in 1974, and Catherine Kelleher in 1975. Only Martin's essay and the more thorough examination

certainty Continues as Atlantic Treaty Nears Completion," ibid., 28 (Apr. 1980): 15–19; Claude Delmas, "France and the Creation of the Atlantic Alliance," ibid., 28 (Aug. 1980): 21–25; Albano Nogueira, "The Making of the Alliance: A Portuguese Perspective," ibid., 28 (Oct. 1980): 8–13; Escott Reid, "The Miraculous Birth of the North Atlantic Alliance," ibid., 28 (Dec. 1980): 12–17; Olav Riste, "The Genesis of North Atlantic Defense Co-operation: Norway's Atlantic Policy, 1940–1945," ibid., 29 (April 1981): 22–28; Grethe Vaernø, "Norway and the Atlantic Alliance, 1948–1949," ibid., 29 (June 1981): 16–20; Egidio Orgona, "Italy's Entry into the Atlantic Alliance: The Role of the Italian Embassy in Washington, 1948–49," ibid., 29 (Aug. 1981): 19–22, and (Oct. 1981): 29–32; Robert Rothschild, "Belgium and the Longest Lasting Alliance," ibid., 30 (Feb. 1982): 18–22; S.I.P. Van Campen, "How and Why the Netherlands Joined the Atlantic Alliance," ibid., 30 (Aug. 1982): 8–12,and (Sept. 1982): 20–25; Nicolas Hommel, "Luxembourg: From Neutrality to the Atlantic Alliance," ibid., 30 (Dec. 1982): 29–33; Olifur Egilsson, "An Unarmed Nation Joins a Defence Alliance: Iceland as a Founder Member of NATO," ibid., 31 (Apr.1983): 24–31.

65. Denis Healey, "Britain and NATO," and Gordon A. Craig, "Germany and NATO: The Rearmament Debate, 1950–1958," in Klaus Knorr, ed., *NATO and American Security* (Princeton, 1959).

66. Leon Epstein, *Britain: Uneasy Ally* (Chicago, 1954); A.E. Campbell, "The United States and Great Britain: Uneasy Allies," In John Braeman, et al., *Twentieth Century American Foreign Policy* (Columbus, 1971); Harry C. Allen, *Great Britain and the United States: A History of Anglo-American Relations, 1783–1952* (Hamden, Conn., 1969).

67. Marvin R. Zahniser, *Uncertain Friendship: American-French Relations through the Cold War* (New York, 1975); Edgar S. Furniss, *France: Troubled Ally: DeGaulle's Heritage and Prospects* (New York, 1960); Michael M. Harrison, *The Reluctant Ally: France and Atlantic Security* (Baltimore, 1981).

of the same subject by Robert McGeehan in 1971 deal primarily with the problem of a
German contribution to NATO in the early 1950s.[68] There is no comparable monograph on Germany's accession to NATO in 1954–55. Italy has received less academic
consideration, even though its own unusual position in 1949 as a former enemy power
and a country without an Atlantic presence has made it a subject of controversy among
the founding fathers of NATO. Primo Vannicelli's monograph emphasizes the European community as much as NATO, while E. Timothy Smith's dissertation focuses
directly on the accession of Italy to the alliance.[69]

Of the smaller nations the Scandinavian members have been the subject of more
monographs than their Benelux counterparts, primarily because of their closer geographical connections to Eastern Europe and to the Soviet Union and partly because of
the competition of a potential Nordic bloc for their allegiance. The conflicting sentiments between historic neutrality and postwar insecurity are found in Joe Wilkinson's
article on Denmark and in Nikolaj Petersen's on Denmark and Norway. Geir Lundestad presents the problem of a divided Scandinavia, with Norway and Denmark desert-
ing Sweden to join NATO for economic as well as military and political reasons.[70]

Dutch relations with NATO are inextricably connected with Dutch sensibilities
over Indonesia, as Alfred van Staden makes clear in his study of American-Dutch
political relations after 1945.[71] For a broader picture of the Low Countries, Nikolaj
Petersen considers both the Low Countries and the Scandinavian members in his study
of alliance policies of the smaller NATO countries, and concludes that smaller nations
offer fewer problems to the alliance than do the larger members. Nils Ørvik disagrees,
suggesting that the advantages of membership are no better for the small ally than
neutrality would be.[72] While Belgium has not been a major subject, an able group of

68. Laurence W. Martin, "The American Decision to Rearm Germany," in Harold Stein,
ed., *American Civil-Military Decisions: A Book of Case Studies* (University, Ala., 1963); James
L. Richardson, *Germany and the Atlantic Alliance: The Interaction of Strategy and Politics*
(Cambridge, Mass., 1966); Roger Morgan, *The United States and West Germany, 1945–1973; A
Study in Alliance Politics* (London, 1974); Catherine McC. Kelleher, *Germany and the Politics of
Nuclear Weapons* (New York, 1975); Robert McGeehan, *The German Rearmament Question:
American Diplomacy and European Defense after World War II* (Urbana, 1971).

69. Primo Vannicelli, *Italy, NATO, and the European Community: The Interplay of Foreign Policy and Domestic Politics* (Cambridge,Mass., 1974); E. Timothy Smith, "The Fear of
Subversion: The United States and the Inclusion of Italy in the North Atlantic Treaty," *Diplomatic History* 7 (Spring 1983): 139–56.

70. Joe Wilkinson,"Denmark and NATO: The Power of a Small State in a Collective
Security System," *International Organization* 10 (Aug. 1956): 390–401; Nikolaj Petersen,
"Danish and Norwegian Alliance Policies, 1948–1949: A Comparative Analysis," *Cooperation
and Conflict* 14 (1979): 193–210; Geir Lundestad, *America, Scandinavia, and the Cold War,
1945–1949* (New York, 1980); see also Tim Greve, *Norway and NATO* (Oslo, 1949).

71. Alfred van Staden, "American-Dutch Relations since 1945" in J.W. Schulte Nordholt
and Robert P. Swierenga, eds., *A Bilateral Bicentennial: A History of Dutch-American Relations,
1782–1982* (New York, 1982).

72. Nikolaj Petersen, "The Alliance Policies of the Smaller NATO Countries," in Lawrence S. Kaplan and Robert W. Clawson," eds., *NATO after Thirty Years* (Wilmington, 1981);
Nils Ørvik, "NATO: The Role of the Small Members," *International Journal* 21 (Spring 1966):
173–85.

scholars under the direction of Omer de Raeymaeker at the University of Leuven have made a special study of smaller members in alignment.[73]

One member of the Leuven group, Luc Crollen, has written the major analysis of Portugal's role in NATO.[74] The most recent member of the organization, Spain, has a history of a shadow membership extending back at least to the Korean War, as is reflected in Lawrence Fernsworth's article in *Foreign Affairs* in 1953 and in Arthur Whitaker's survey of Spain's connection to NATO's security in 1961.[75]

Greece and Turkey entered NATO in 1952, but even as an original site of the Cold War, Turkey's potential connection with NATO was widely recognized among the original members of the alliance. It has been by scholars as well. Nuri Eren and Ihsan Gurkan have written on Turkey's military role in NATO, without special interest in the details of Turkey's joining the alliance. George McGhee specifically deals with Turkey's membership.[76]

There is more from the Greek side. Because the absorbing issue of the Greek civil war offered more excitement for the scholar as well as the journalist, the immediate postwar Greek problems dominate its historiography. The work of Stephen G. Xydis and John Iatrides concentrate on the civil war, while L.S. Stavrianos and William McNeill relate U.S. aid to Greece's accession to NATO. Hamilton Fish Armstrong identifies the meaning of both Greece and Turkey to SHAPE in the title of his article "Eisenhower's Right Flank." A more specialized monograph dealing with public attitudes is Theodore Couloumbis's analysis of Greek reactions to NATO's presence, particularly in the form of bases. A darker side of American intervention in Greece is presented by Lawrence Wittner. The missed opportunities of the Balkan alliance of Greece, Turkey, and Yugoslavia in associating with NATO in 1953 are the subject of John Iatrides's *Balkan Triangle.*[77]

There is an occasional piece on Iceland's connection with NATO, with the adjective "unique" properly placed in the title.[78] The role Iceland played in the fashioning of NATO deserves more study in part for some of the reasons that make Canada's

73. Omer de Raeymaeker et al., eds., *Small Powers in Alignment* (Leuven, 1974).

74. Luc Crollen, *Portugal, the United States and NATO* (Leuven, 1973).

75. Lawrence Fernsworth, "Spain in Western Defense," *Foreign Affairs* 31 (July 1953): 648–62; Arthur P. Whitaker, *Spain and the Defense of the West* (New York, 1961).

76. Nuri Eren, *Turkey, NATO and Europe: A Deteriorating Relationship* (Paris, 1977); Ihsan Gurkan, *NATO, Turkey, and the Southern Flank* (New Brunswick, 1980); George McGhee, "Turkey Joins the West," *Foreign Affairs* 32 (June 1954): 617–30.

77. Stephen G. Xydis, *Greece and the Great Powers: 1944–47* (Thessaloniki, 1963); John Iatrides, *Revolt in Athens: The Greek Communist "Second Round", 1944–1945* (Princeton, 1972); L.S. Stavrianos, *Greece: American Dilemma and Opportunity* (Chicago, 1952); William H. McNeill, *Greece: American Aid in Action, 1947–56* (New York, 1957); Hamilton Fish Armstrong, "Eisenhower's Right Flank," *Foreign Affairs* 29 (Oct. 1951): 651–63; Theodore A. Couloumbis, *Greek Political Reaction to American and NATO Influences* (New Haven, 1966); Lawrence S. Wittner, *American Intervention in Greece* (New York, 1982); John O. Iatrides, *Balkan Triangle: Birth and Decline of an Alliance across Ideological Boundaries* (The Hague, 1968).

78. Robert A. Fliegel, "Iceland: Unique in NATO," *Proceedings of United States Naval Institute* 16 (Aug. 1980): 32–37.

position so important. NATO among other things is a maritime alliance. E.H. Miller and James Eayrs deal with the early years of Canada's role, along with the statesmen Pearson and Reid.[79] For other kinds of NATO relationships the essays of Scott Bills and Thomas Campbell begin exploration of colonialism and the United Nations, respectively, and reveal other dimensions of the alliance.[80] On the one hand, the alliance's North Atlantic character from the beginning was challenged by the problems of colonial empires; it surfaced only in the case of Algeria in 1949 but it remained a problem. On the other hand, NATO was a regional organization of sorts, with the UN Charter cited frequently in its articles, but its ties to the UN or to regional arrangements generally were murky—and purposely so. These are significant areas for further research.

While the continued closure of diplomatic correspondence remains a serious obstacle to definitive studies, the growth of a European political community in which NATO was seen as a vital component has inspired considerable commentary on both sides of the Atlantic. The monumental work of Walter Lipgens, identifying and categorizing the many European groups that sprang from the chaos of World War II, is an indispensable reference for understanding the early stages of European integration.[81] There is a gap in the literature, however, between the Lipgens beginnings and the painful stages marking such steps as the Schuman Plan and the Council of Europe. More interest has been shown in the later European Economic Community than in its origins. The connection between NATO and the European movement in particular is worthy of study, as Lipgens himself has suggested in his essay on the subject.[82]

Examples of the literature inspired by the prospect of a European community are works by M. Margaret Ball, Ben T. Moore, Ernst Haas, and Karl Deutsch.[83] All of these studies were written in the late 1950s and were obviously written under the spell of the Treaty of Rome and the European Economic Community. They considered the early 1950s as the infrastructure for the community.

The American role in the building of a European community has been widely recognized by European as well as American scholars. In a multivolume doctoral dissertation Pierre Melandri has written the most thorough examination of the United States and the unification of Europe from 1948 to 1954. Two treatments of specific

79. E.H. Miller, "Canada's Role in the Origin of NATO," in Gerald N. Grob, ed., *Statesmen and Statecraft of the Modern West* (Barre, 1967); James Eayrs, *In Defence of Canada*, vol. 3, *Peacemaking and Deterrence* (Toronto, 1980); Lester B. Pearson, *Mike* (see note 8, above); Escott Reid, *Time of Fear and Hope* (see note 4, above).

80. Scott W. Bills, "The United States, NATO, and the Colonial World," in Kaplan and Clawson, *NATO after Thirty Years* (see note 72); Thomas M. Campbell, "NATO and the United Nations in American Foreign Policy: Building a Framework for Power," in ibid.

81. Walter Lipgens, *A History of European Integration, 1945–1947: The Formation of the European Unity Movement*, trans. P.S. Falla and A.J. J. Ryder (Oxford, 1982).

82. Walter Lipgens, "NATO and the European Community," in Kaplan and Clawson, *NATO after Thirty Years* (see note 72).

83. M. Margaret Ball, *NATO and the European Union Movement* (New York, 1959); Ben T. Moore, *NATO and the Future of Europe* (New York, 1958); Ernst B. Haas, *The Uniting of Europe: Political, Social, and Economic Forces, 1950–1957* (Stanford, 1958); Karl W. Deutsch, et al., *Political Community and the North Atlantic Area* (Princeton, 1968).

examples of United States involvement in European unification appeared in 1980 and 1981: Helmut Wagner's appreciation of American encouragement for a "united states of Europe," and Armin Rappaport's more detailed examination of differences between the executive and legislative branches in America's qualified support for European integration.[84] Less objective but valuable for its participant's perspective is Ernst van der Beugel's contribution, the work of a former official in OEEC and the Netherlands' foreign service. In 1955 Norman Padelford found the successful incorporation of Germany into NATO proof of the success of American efforts on Europe's behalf. A decade later Harold Van Buren Cleveland recognized a dichotomy between the Atlantic idea and the European idea, but believed that there was more harmony than conflict in the meeting of the two ideas. NATO could contain both.[85]

This long list of publications on NATO could be made even longer. As noted earlier the vast bulk of commentary in the past thirty years concerns the years after 1954, and many of the foregoing volumes, important as they are, devote only a small portion of their contents to the early years of NATO. In some cases the only reason for their concentration on the formative period of NATO's history is simply that they were published in the early 1950s.

What strikes this observer most forcefully is the disparity between the great array of primary materials, published and unpublished, and the scarcity of secondary studies. Inadequate and spotty as many of the archival resources are, there are nonetheless sufficient sources open for the interested scholar. I should like to make a prediction to accompany the one made thirty years ago in the first version of this essay: namely, that the early years of NATO will come alive as a subject of much more careful study. This too is a not particularly bold prediction. Its realization should be advanced by current interest on the part of the Western European Union and the political and military headquarters of NATO in declassifying records of the early years of the alliance's history.

84. Pierre Melandri, *Les Etats-Unis face a l'unification de l'Europe, 1945–1954* (Paris, 1980); in an unabridged form it was published in Paris in 1980. Helmut Wagner, "Der Amerikanische Beitrag zur Gründung der US von Europa," *Zeitschrift fur Politik* 17 (Sept. 1980): 261–76; Armin Rappaport, "The United States and European Integration: The First Phase," *Diplomatic History* 5 (Spring 1981): 121–49.

85. Ernst van der Beugel, *From Marshall Plan to European Integration to Atlantic Partnership: European Integration as a Concern of American Foreign Policy* (Amsterdam, 1966); Max Beloff, *The United States and the Unity of Europe* (Washington, D.C., 1963); Norman J. Padelford, "Political Cooperation in the North Atlantic Community," *International Organization* 9 (Aug. 1955): 353–65; Harold van Buren Cleveland, *The Atlantic Idea and Its European Rivals* (New York, 1966).

Appendix A. The Brussels Pact

Treaty of Economic, Social and Cultural Collaboration and Collective Self-Defense between the Governments of the United Kingdom and Northern Ireland, Belgium, France, Luxembourg, and the Netherlands, signed at Brussels, March 17, 1948.

ARTICLE I

Convinced of the close community of their interests and of the necessity of uniting in order to promote the economic recovery of Europe, the High Contracting Parties will so organize and coordinate their economic activities as to produce the best possible results, by the elimination of conflict in their economic policies, the coordination of production and the development of commercial exchanges.

The co-operation provided for in the preceding paragraph, which will be effected through the Consultative Council referred to in Article VII as well as through other bodies, shall not involve any duplication of, or prejudice to, the work of other economic organizations in which the High Contracting Parties are or may be represented but shall on the contrary assist the work of those organizations.

ARTICLE II

The High Contracting Parties will make every effort in common, both by direct consultation and in specialized agencies, to promote the attainment of a higher standard of living by their peoples and to develop on corresponding lines the social and other related services of their countries.

The High Contracting Parties will consult with the object of achieving the earliest possible application of recommendations of immediate practical interest, relating to social matters, adopted with their approval in the specialized agencies.

They will endeavor to conclude as soon as possible conventions with each other in the sphere of social security.

ARTICLE III

The High Contracting Parties will make every effort in common to lead their peoples towards a better understanding of the principles which form the basis of their

---

As printed in Department of State Publication 5669 (Nov.1954), pp. 59–62.

common civilization and to promote cultural exchanges by conventions between themselves or by other means.

ARTICLE IV

If any of the High Contracting Parties should be the object of an armed attack in Europe, the other High Contracting Parties will, in accordance with the provisions of Article 51 of the Charter of the United Nations, afford the party so attacked all the military and other aid and assistance in their power.

ARTICLE V

All measures taken as a result of the preceding Article shall be immediately reported to the Security Council. They shall be terminated as soon as the Security Council has taken the measures necessary to maintain or restore international peace and security.

The present Treaty does not prejudice in any way the obligations of the High Contracting Parties under the provisions of the Charter of the United Nations. It shall not be interpreted as affecting in any way the authority and responsibility of the Security Council under the Charter to take at any time such action as it deems necessary in order to maintain or restore international peace and security.

ARTICLE VI

The High Contracting Parties declare, each so far as he is concerned, that none of the international engagments now in force between him and any other of the High Contracting Parties or any third State is in conflict with the provisions of the present Treaty.

None of the High Contracting Parties will conclude any alliance or participate in any coalition directed against any other of the High Contracting Parties.

ARTICLE VII

For the purpose of consulting together on all the questions dealt with in the present Treaty, the High Contracting Parties will create a Consultative Council, which shall be so organized as to be able to exercise its functions continuously. The Council shall meet at such times as it shall deem fit.

At the request of any of the High Contracting Parties, the Council shall be immediately convened in order to permit the High Contracting Parties to consult with regard to any situation which may constitute a threat to peace, in whatever area this threat should arise; with regard to the attitude to be adopted and the steps to be taken in case of a renewal by Germany of an aggressive policy; or with regard to any situation constituting a danger to economic stability.

ARTICLE VIII

In pursuance of their determination to settle disputes only by peaceful means, the High Contracting Parties will apply to disputes between themselves the following provisions:

The High Contracting Parties will, while the present Treaty remains in force, settle all disputes falling within the scope of Article 36, paragraph 2, of the Statute of the International Court of Justice by referring them to the Court, subject only, in the case of each of them, to any reservation already made by that Party when accepting this clause for compulsory jurisdiction to the extent that that Party may maintain the reservation.

In addition, the High Contracting Parties will submit to conciliation all disputes outside the scope of Article 36, paragraph 2, of the Statute of the International Court of Justice.

In the case of a mixed dispute involving both questions for which conciliation is appropriate and other questions for which judicial settlement is appropriate, any Party to the dispute shall have the right to insist that the judicial settlement of the legal questions shall precede conciliation.

The preceding provisions of this Article in no way affect the application of relevant provisions or agreements prescribing some other method of pacific settlement.

ARTICLE IX

The High Contracting Parties may, by agreement, invite any other State to accede to the present Treaty on conditions to be agreed between them and the State so invited.

Any State so invited may become a Party to the Treaty by depositing an instrument of accession with the Belgian Government.

The Belgian Government will inform each of the High Contracting Parties of the deposit of each instrument of accession.

ARTICLE X

The present Treaty shall be ratified and the instruments of ratification shall be deposited as soon as possible with the Belgian Government.

It shall enter into force on the date of the deposit of the last instrument of ratification and shall thereafter remain in force for fifty years.

After the expiry of the period of fifty years, each of the High Contracting Parties shall have the right to cease to be a party thereto provided that he shall have previously given one year's notice of denunciation to the Belgian Government.

The Belgian Government shall inform the Governments of the other High Contracting Parties of the deposit of each instrument of ratification and of each notice of denunciation.

In witness whereof, the above-mentioned Plenipotentiaries have signed the present Treaty and have affixed thereto their seals.

Done at Brussels, this seventeenth day of March 1948, in English and French, each text being equally authentic, in a single copy which shall remain deposited in the archives of the Belgian Government and of which certified copies shall be transmitted by that Government to each of the other signatories.

Appendix B.
The Vandenberg Resolution

Whereas peace with justice and the defense of human rights and fundamental freedoms require international cooperation through more effective use of the United Nations: Therefore be it

Resolved, That the Senate reaffirm the policy of the United States to achieve international peace and security through the United Nations, so that armed force shall not be used except in the common interest, and that the President be advised of the sense of the Senate that this Government, by constitutional process, should particularly pursue the following objectives within the United Nations Charter:

(1) Voluntary agreement to remove the veto from all questions involving pacific settlements of international disputes and situations, and from the admission of new members.

(2) Progressive development of regional and other collective arrangements for individual and collective self-defense in accordance with the purposes, principles, and provisions of the Charter.

(3) Association of the United States, by constitutional process, with such regional and other collective arrangements as are based on continuous and effective self-help and mutual aid, and as affect its national security.

(4) Contributing to the maintenance of peace by making clear its determination to exercise the right of individual or collective self-defense under article 51 should any armed attack occur affecting its national security.

(5) Maximum efforts to obtain agreements to provide the United Nations with armed forces as provided by the Charter, and to obtain agreement among member nations upon universal regulation and reduction of armaments under adequate and dependable guaranty against violation.

(6) If necessary, after adequate effort toward strengthening the United Nations, review of the Charter at an appropriate time by a general conference called under article 109 or by the General Assembly.

S. 239, as printed in *Congressional Record*, 80 Cong. 2 sess., 11 June 1948, 94:7791.

Appendix C.
The North Atlantic Treaty

The Parties to this Treaty reaffirm their faith in the purposes and principles of the Charter of the United Nations and their desire to live in peace with all peoples and all governments.

They are determined to safeguard the freedom, common heritage and civilization of their peoples, founded on the principles of democracy, individual liberty and the rule of law.

They seek to promote stability and well-being in the North Atlantic area.

They are resolved to unite their efforts for collective defense and for the preservation of peace and security.

They therefore agree to this North Atlantic Treaty:

ARTICLE 1

The Parties undertake, as set forth in the Charter of the United Nations, to settle any international disputes in which they may be involved by peaceful means in such a manner that international peace and security, and justice, are not endangered, and to refrain in their international relations from the threat or use of force in any manner inconsistent with the purposes of the United Nations.

ARTICLE 2

The Parties will contribute toward the further development of peaceful and friendly international relations by strengthening their free institutions, by bringing about a better understanding of the principles upon which these institutions are founded, and by promoting conditions of stability and wellbeing. They will seek to eliminate conflict in their international economic policies and will encourage economic collaboration between any or all of them.

ARTICLE 3

In order more effectively to achieve the objectives of this Treaty, the Parties, separately and jointly, by means of continuous and effective self-help and mutual aid, will maintain and develop their individual and collective capacity to resist armed attack.

As printed in *North Atlantic Treaty Hearings*, Senate Committee on Foreign Relations,81 Cong. 1 sess., 3 pts. (Washington, D.C., 1949), 1:1–3.

ARTICLE 4

The Parties will consult together whenever, in the opinion of any of them, the territorial integrity, political independence or security of any of the Parties is threatened.

ARTICLE 5

The Parties agree that an armed attack against one or more of them in Europe or North America shall be considered an attack against them all; and consequently they agree that, if such an armed attack occurs, each of them, in exercise of the right of individual or collective self-defense recognized by Article 51 of the Charter of the United Nations, will assist the Party or Parties so attacked by taking forthwith, individually and in concert with the other Parties, such action as it deems necessary, including the use of armed force, to restore and maintain the security of the North Atlantic area.

Any such armed attack and all measures taken as a result thereof shall immediately be reported to the Security Council. Such measures shall be terminated when the Security Council has taken the measures necessary to restore and maintain international peace and security.

ARTICLE 6

For the purpose of Article 5 an armed attack on one or more of the Parties is deemed to include an armed attack on the territory of any of the Parties in Europe or North America, on the Algerian departments of France, on the occupation forces of any Party in Europe, on the islands under the jurisdiction of any Party in the North Atlantic area north of the Tropic of Cancer or on the vessels or aircrafts in this area of any of the Parties.

ARTICLE 7

This Treaty does not affect, and shall not be interpreted as affecting, in any way the rights and obligations under the Charter of the Parties which are members of the United Nations, or the primary responsibility of the Security Council for the maintenance of international peace and security.

ARTICLE 8

Each Party declares that none of the international engagements now in force between it and any other of the Parties or any third state is in conflict with the provisions of this Treaty, and undertakes not to enter into any international engagement in conflict with this Treaty.

ARTICLE 9

The Parties hereby establish a council, on which each of them shall be represented, to consider matters concerning the implementation of this Treaty. The council shall be so organized as to be able to meet promptly at anytime. The council shall set up such subsidiary bodies as may be necessary; in particular it shall establish immediately a defense committee which shall recommend measures for the implementation of Articles 3 and 5.

ARTICLE 10

The Parties may, by unanimous agreement, invite any other European state in a position to further the principles of this Treaty to contribute to the security of the North Atlantic area to accede to this Treaty. Any state so invited may become a party to the Treaty by depositing its instrument of accession with the Government of the United States of America. The Government of the United States of America will inform each of the Parties of the deposit of each such instrument of accession.

ARTICLE 11

This Treaty shall be ratified and its provisions carried out by the Parties in accordance with their respective constitutional processes. The instruments of ratification shall be deposited as soon as possible with the Government of the United States of America, which will notify all the other signatories of each deposit. The Treaty shall enter into force between the states which have ratified it as soon as the ratifications of the majority of the signatories, including the ratifications of Belgium, Canada, France, Luxembourg, the Netherlands, the United Kingdom and the United States, have been deposited and shall come into effect with respect to other states on the date of the deposit of their ratifications.

ARTICLE 12

After the Treaty has been in force for ten years, or at any time thereafter, the Parties shall, if any of them so requests, consult together for the purpose of reviewing the Treaty, having regard for the factors then affecting peace and security in the North Atlantic area, including the development of universal as well as regional arrangements under the Charter of the United Nations for the maintenance of international peace and security.

ARTICLE 13

After the Treaty has been in force for twenty years, any Party may cease to be a party one year after its notice of denunciation has been given to the Government of the

United States of America, which will inform the Governments of the other Parties of the deposit of each notice of denunciation.

ARTICLE 14

This Treaty, of which the English and French texts are equally authentic, shall be deposited in the archives of the government of the United States of America. Duly certified copies thereof will be transmitted by that Government to the Governments of the other signatories.

In witness whereof, the undersigned plenipotentiaries have signed this Treaty.

Done at Washington, the fourth day of April, 1949.

Abbreviations Used in the Text

ADA	Americans for Democratic Action
ANZUS	Australia, New Zealand, and the United States (Treaty)
CEEC	Committee of European Economic Cooperation
CENTO	Central Treaty Organization
DFEC	Defense Financial and Economic Committee
ECA	Economic Cooperation Administration
ECC	European Coordinating Committee
EDC	European Defense Community
ERP	European Recovery Program
FACC	Foreign Assistance Correlation Committee
JCS	Joint Chiefs of Staff
MAAG	Military Assistance Advisory Group
MAP	Military Assistance Program
MDAP	Mutual Defense Assistance Program
MPSB	Military Production and Supply Board
MTDP	Medium-Term Defense Plan
NAC	North Atlantic Council
NSC	National Security Council
OEEC	Organization of European Economic Cooperation
SACEUR	Supreme Allied Commander, Europe
SACLANT	Supreme Allied Commander, Atlantic
SEATO	Southeast Asia Treaty Organization
SHAPE	Supreme Headquarters Allied Powers Europe
UN	United Nations
W[E]U	Western [European] Union

Notes

Abbreviations Used in the Notes

AGPO   American Group on Pact Organization
DELWU   Delegate (U.S.) to the Western Union
FO   Foreign Office (Great Britain)
FRUS   *Foreign Relations of the United States* (Washington, D.C.)
JIC   Joint Intelligence Committee
NARS   National Archives and Records Service
PPS   Policy Planning Staff
PRO   Public Record Office (Great Britain)
RG   Record Group
S/D   Secretary of Defense
S/S   Secretary of State

For additional abbreviations, see list on page 231.

1. INTRODUCTION

1. Armin Rappaport, "The American Revolution of 1949," *NATO Letter* 12 (Feb. 1964): 3–8.

2. Thomas G. Paterson, "Presidential Foreign Policy, Public Opinion, and Congress: The Truman Years," *Diplomatic History* 3 (Winter 1979): 18.

3. Omar Bradley, speech to Jewish War Veterans, New York, 5 Apr. 1949, in *New York Times*, 6 Apr. 1949.

4. Great Britain, *Parliamentary Debates* (Commons), 2nd ser., 26 (1826): col. 397.

5. John Gimbel, *The Origins of the Marshall Plan* (Stanford, 1976); Timothy P. Ireland, *Creating the Atlantic Alliance: The Origins of the North Atlantic Treaty Organization* (Westport, Conn., 1981).

6. 3 Apr. 1949, memorandum of conversation, president, S/S, S/D, Atlantic Pact Foreign Ministers, in Department of State, Secretary's Memoranda, Lot 53 D 444.

7. Ibid.

8. Lord Ismay, the first secretary general of NATO, called it "the NATO method." Hastings, Lord Ismay, *NATO: The First Five Years, 1949–1954* (Paris, 1955), p.48.

9. George F. Kennan, *Memoirs, 1950–1963* (Boston, 1972), p. 253.

10. Harlan Cleveland uses this phrase in his *NATO: The Transatlantic Bargain* (New York, 1970), p. 189.

2. THE TREATIES OF PARIS AND WASHINGTON

1. *North Atlantic Treaty Hearings*, Senate Committee on Foreign Relations, 81 Cong. 1 sess., 3 parts (Washington, D.C., 1949), 3:1121.

2. James D. Richardson, ed., *A Compilation of the Messages and Papers of the Presidents, 1789–1897*, 10 vols. (Washington, D.C., 1889), 1:222.

3. George Liska, *Nations in Alliance: The Limits of Independence* (Baltimore, 1968), p. 13.

4. Lyman Butterfield et al., eds., *Diary and Autobiography of John Adams*, 1 Mar. 1776, 4 vols. (Cambridge, Mass., 1961), 2:235.

5. Samuel Flagg Bemis, *The Diplomacy of the American Revolution* (New York, 1935), pp. 70 ff.

6. Hector St. John de Crèvecoeur, *Letters from an American Farmer* (1782) (New York, 1957), p. 39.

7. Felix Gilbert, *To the Farewell Address: Ideas of Early American Foreign Policy* (Princeton, 1961), p. 66.

8. James H. Hutson, "Early American Diplomacy: A Reappraisal," in Lawrence S. Kaplan, ed., *The American Revolution and "A Candid World"* (Kent, Ohio, 1977), p. 45.

9. Thomas Paine, *Common Sense*, in Moncure D. Conway, ed., *The Writings of Thomas Paine*, 4 vols. (New York, 1967), 1:88–89.

10. Butterfield, *Adams Diary and Autobiography*, 3:337–38.

11. "Plan of a Treaty with France," *Secret Journals of the Congress of the Confederation*, 4 vols. (Boston, 1821), 2:7.

12. Ibid., p. 11.

13. Appendix IV (a) in Richard Henry Lee, *Life of Arthur Lee*, 2 vols. (Boston, 1829), 1:280.

14. B. Harrison et al., Committee of Secret Correspondence, to the Commissioners at Paris, 30 Dec. 1776, in Francis Wharton, ed., *Revolutionary Diplomatic Correspondence of the United States*, 6 vols. (Washington, D.C., 1889), 2:240.

15. Committee on Foreign Affairs to Commissioners in France, 30 May 1777, *Papers of the Continental Congress*, Reel 105, Library of Congress.

16. Franklin, Deane, and Lee to Vergennes, 5 Jan. 1777, Wharton, *Revolutionary Diplomatic Correspondence*, 2:246.

17. Deane to Dumas, 7 June 1777, ibid., 2:332–33.

18. Arthur Lee to Baron Schulenberg, 10 June 1777, ibid., 2:334.

19. Richard Henry Lee to Arthur Lee, 20 Apr. 1777, Lee Family Papers, Library of Congress, Reel 3.

20. 4 May 1778, Wharton, *Revolutionary Diplomatic Correspondence*, 2:569.

21. David Hunter Miller, *Treaties and Other International Acts of the United States of America*, 8 vols. (Washington, D.C., 1931), 2:568–69.

22. William C. Stinchcombe, *The American Revolution and the French Alliance* (Syracuse, N.Y., 1969), pp. 68–69, 122–23, 132, 157–62.

23. *North Atlantic Treaty Hearings*, 3:1024–25.

24. Ibid., p. 848.

25. Ibid., p. 853.

26. Washington, Farewell Address, in Richardson, *Messages and Papers of the Presidents*, 1:222.

27. *United States Foreign Aid Programs in Europe*, 23 Aug. 1951, Report of the Subcommittee of the Senate Committee on Foreign Relations on the United States Economic and Military Assistance to Free Europe (Green Subcommittee), 82 Cong. 1 sess., S. Doc. 56, p. 22.

28. Konrad Adenauer, *Memoirs, 1945–53*, trans. Beate Ruhm von Oppen (Chicago, 1965), p. 267; Dirk U. Stikker, *Men of Responsibility: A Memoir* (New York, 1966), p. 297.

29. Gordon A. Craig, "NATO and the New German Army," In William W. Kaufmann, ed., *Military Policy and National Security* (Princeton, 1956), pp. 221–23.

30. The intentions of Anglo-French diplomacy are clearly presented in *FRUS*, 1948, 3:1–16.

31. *North Atlantic Treaty Hearings*, 1:2.

32. F.T. Greene, memo for General Lyman L. Lemnitzer, "Initial Discussion with the French of Bilateral MDAP Agreement," 5 Dec. 1949, CD6-2-46, Military Archives, Modern Military Branch, RG 330, National Archives (hereafter cited as NARS); Ambassador in France to S/S 3 Dec. 1949, no. 5106, *FRUS*, 1949, 4:681.

33. See Laurence W. Martin, "The American Decision to Rearm Germany," in Harold Stein, ed., *American Civil-Military Decisions: A Book of Case Studies* (Birmingham, Ala., 1963), p. 646.

34. Notes on Debates in the Congress of the Confederation, 15 Mar. 1783, in William C. Hutchinson et al., eds., *The Papers of James Madison*, 12 vols. to date (Chicago and Charlottesville, Va., 1962), 6:329.

35. Niccolò Machiavelli, "Discourse on the First Decade of Titus Livius," in *Machiavelli: The Chief Works and Others*, trans. Allan Gilbert, 3 vols. (Durham, N.C., 1965), 1:409.

36. Charles Burton Marshall, "Alliances with Fledgling States," in Arnold Wolfers, ed., *Alliance Policy in the Cold War* (Baltimore, 1959), pp. 219–20.

37. "An Economic Theory of Alliances," *Review of Economics and Statistics* 48 (Aug. 1966): 266–79.

38. *North Atlantic Treaty Hearings*, 1:2.

39. See *Assignment of Ground Forces of the United States to Duty in the European Area Hearings*, Senate Committee on Foreign Relations and Committee on Armed Services, 82 Cong. 1 sess., on S. Con. Res. 8, Feb. 1951.

40. Dean Acheson, *Present at the Creation: My Years in the State Department* (New York, 1969), pp. 478–79.

41. See *New York Times*, 11 Jan. 1968, 14:4; 19 Oct. 1969, 25:1; 2 Dec. 1969, 2:4. The most powerful challenge was raised against the Nixon administration on 19 May 1971, when the Senate defeated an amendment to the Selective Service Act that would have reduced U.S. forces in Europe to 150,000; *Congressional Record*, 92 Cong. 1 sess., 1971, 117:15960.

42. Orville T. Murphy, "The Comte de Vergennes, the Newfoundland Fisheries, and the Peace Negotiation of 1783: A Reconsideration," *Canadian Historical Review* 46 (Mar. 1965): 41.

43. See in particular Arthur A. Richmond, "Napoleon and the Armed Neutrality of 1800: A Diplomatic Challenge to British Sea Power," *Royal Service Institution Journal* 104 (May 1959): 1–9.

3. ISOLATIONISM, THE UNITED NATIONS, AND THE COLD WAR

1. Quoted in Roland Stromberg, *Collective Security and American Foreign Policy: From the League of Nations to NATO* (New York, 1963), p. 180.

2. W.A. Scott and S.B. Withey, *The United States and the United Nations: The Public View* (New York, 1958), pp. 24–25.

3. George F. Kennan, *Memoirs, 1925–1950* (New York, 1969), pp. 330–31.

4. Ibid., p. 332.

5. Acheson, *Present at the Creation*, p. 219.

6. Speech to the Congress on Greece and Turkey: Truman Doctrine, 12 Mar. 1947, in *Public Papers of the Presidents of the United States: Harry S. Truman, 1947* (Washington, D.C.: 1963), p. 180.

7. Quoted in Joseph M. Jones, *The Fifteen Weeks* (New York, 1955), p. 91.

8. Truman Doctrine, in *Public Papers of the Presidents, Truman, 1947*, p. 177.

9. Jones, *Fifteen Weeks*, p. 160.

10. Vandenberg to John B. Bennett, 5 Mar. 1947, in Arthur H. Vandenberg, Jr., ed., *The Private Papers of Senator Vandenberg* (Boston, 1952), pp. 340–41.

11. Acheson, *Present at the Creation*, p. 223.

12. Scott and Withey, *United States*, p. 74.

13. Quoted in Jones, *Fifteen Weeks*, pp. 178–79.

14. Quoted in Henry W. Berger, "Senator Robert A. Taft Dissents from Military Escalation," in T.G. Paterson, ed., *Cold War Critics* (Chicago, 1971), p. 177.

15. Robert S. Allen and William V. Shannon, *The Truman Merry-go-Round* (New York, 1950), p. 253.

16. Jones, *Fifteen Weeks*, pp. 180–82.

17. Vandenberg, *Private Papers*, pp. 340–41, 345.

18. Jones, *Fifteen Weeks*, p. 180.

19. Acheson, *Present at the Creation*, p. 223.

20. Research and Policy Committee of the CED, *The American Program of European Economic Cooperation* (New York, 1947), pp. 10, 28.

21. *European Recovery Program Hearings*, Senate Committee on Foreign Relations, 80 Cong. 2 sess. (Washington, D.C., 1948), pp. 934, 1145.

22. Quoted in Gabriel A. Almond, *The American People and Foreign Policy* (New York, 1960), p. 204; *European Recovery Program Hearings*, p. 872.

23. *Christian Century*, 2, 7, 20 July 1947.

24. *The Nation*, 21 June 1947; Walter Lippmann, *The Cold War: A Study in U.S. Foreign Policy* (New York, 1947), p. 52.

25. *European Recovery Program Hearings*, pp. 936, 1429.

26. Quoted in Harry B. Price, *The Marshall Plan and Its Meaning* (Ithaca, N.Y., 1955), p. 60.

27. John Spanier, *American Foreign Policy since World War II* (New York: 1960), p. 60.

28. Vandenberg, *Private Papers*, p. 406.

29. *North Atlantic Treaty Hearings*, 1:242.

30. Truman, State of the Union Message, in *Public Papers of the Presidents, Truman, 1949*, p. 114.

31. *Department of State Bulletin* 20 (27 Mar. 1949): 386.

32. Acheson, *Present at the Creation*, p. 276.

33. *New York Times*, 22 Apr. 1949.

34. Vandenberg letter, 22 Feb. 1949, in Vandenberg, *Private Papers*, p. 478.

35. *North Atlantic Treaty Hearings*, 1:97.

36. Vandenberg letter 21 Feb. 1949, in Vandenberg, *Private Papers*, p. 480.

37. *North Atlantic Treaty Hearings*, 1:96.

38. Ibid., p. 117.

39. American Friends Service Committee, *The United States and the Soviet Union: Some Quaker Proposals for Peace* (New Haven, 1949), pp. 30–31.

40. *North Atlantic Treaty Hearings*, 3:836.

41. Ibid., 3:1128.

42. Ibid., 2:419.

43. Ibid., 3:950.

44. Ibid., 3:853–54, 1144–45.

45. Ibid., 3:941–42.

46. Ibid., 3:920.

47. Ibid., 2:399.

48. Quoted in Emmett Panzella, "The Atlantic Union Committee: A Study of a Pressure Group in Foreign Policy" (Ph.D. diss., Kent State Univ., 1969), pp. 33–34.

49. *Congressional Record*, 81 Cong. 1 sess., 1949, 95:9198.

50. Ibid., p. 9205.

51. Thomas M. Campbell, Jr., "NATO and the United Nations in American Foreign Policy: Building a Framework for Power," in Lawrence S. Kaplan and Robert W. Clawson, *NATO after Thirty Years* (Wilmington, Del., 1981), p. 148. Campbell claims that the Truman administration's tactics served the United Nations as well as NATO by removing the Soviet-American rivalry from the UN arena.

4. TOWARD THE BRUSSELS PACT

1. See Walter Lipgens, *Die Anfänge der Europäischen Einigungspolitik, 1945–1950* (Stuttgart, 1977), 1: 471.

2. Ibid., pp. 471–73; *Congressional Record*, 80 Cong. 1 sess., 1947, 93:2437. See also Tristram Coffin, *Senator Fulbright: Portrait of a Public Philosopher* (New York, 1966), pp. 101–2.

3. *Congressional Record*, 80 Cong. 1 sess., 1947, 93:3138.

4. Herbert Feis, *From Trust to Terror: The Onset of the Cold War, 1945–1950* (New York, 1970), p. 285.

5. Pierre Melandri, "Les Etats-Unis face a l'unification de l'Europe, 1945–1954," 3 vols. (Ph.D. diss., Univ. of Paris, 1977), 1:290–91; Georgette Elgey, *La république des illusions, 1945–1951, ou la vie secrète de la IVe république* (Paris, 1965), p. 380; Vincent Auriol, *Journal du septennat, 1947–1954*, 7 vols. (Paris, 1970–74), 1:638.

6. George C. Marshall, "Peace and Understanding—The Desire of all Mankind," address of S/S to Pilgrims Society, London, 12 Dec. 1947, *Department of State Bulletin* 17 (21 Dec. 1947): 1203.

7. Escott Reid, *Time of Fear and Hope: The Making of the North Atlantic Treaty* (Toronto, 1977), p. 36; Feis, *From Trust to Terror*, p. 286; Elgey, *République des illusions*, pp. 380–81; Melandri, "Les Etats-Unis face," 1:291.

8. Gallman to S/S, 22 Dec. 1947, *FRUS*, 1948, 3:1.

9. Elgey *République des illusions*, p. 381.

10. Lovett to U.S. Embassy in London, 24 Dec. 1947, 840.00/12-2247, General Records of the Department of State, 59, NARS.

11. Summary of a Memorandum Representing Mr. Bevin's Views on the Formation of a Western Union, *FRUS*, 1948, 3:5.

12. S/S to Inverchapel, 20 Jan. 1948, *FRUS*, 1948, 3:8.

13. Great Britain, *Parliamentary Debates* (Commons), 5th ser., 446 (1948): col. 383ff.

14. *European Recovery Program Hearings*, 2:771.

15. Ibid., 20 Jan. 1948, p. 588. Dulles was an important broker between American and European leaders during this period. He had attended the London Council of Foreign Ministers meeting as an advisor to Marshall and was, according to Kennan's memory, influential in impressing on the secretary of state the importance of a common Western defense in order to reassure the French and to make possible a frame for German economic revival. Kennan, *Memoirs, 1925–1950*, pp. 420–21. Theodore H. White, in *Fire in the Ashes: Europe in Mid-Century* (New York, 1953), p. 288, noted that Marshall discussed Bevin's ideas with Dulles on their voyage to New York. See Feis, *From Trust to Terror*, p. 286.

16. *European Recovery Program Hearings*, 2:384–85.

17. *New York Times*, 15 Jan. 1948.

18. Ibid., 24 Jan. 1948.

19. Ibid., 23 Feb. 1947. See Emmett E. Panzella, "The Atlantic Union Committee: Study of a Pressure Group in Foreign Policy" (Ph.D. diss., Kent State Univ., 1977), pp. 11–12.

20. See Ernest S. Lent, "The Development of United World Federalist Thought and Policy," *International Organization* 9 (Nov. 1955): 486, 490–91.

21. See Clarence K. Streit, *Union Now: A Proposal for a Federal Union of the Democracies of the North Atlantic* (New York, 1939); Panzella, "Atlantic Union Committee," p. 6; Lipgens, *Die Anfänge der Europäischen Einigungspolitik*, p. 63.

22. *European Recovery Program Hearings*, 21 Jan. 1948, p. 678; 5 Feb. 1948, pp. 1398–99.

23. Letter to the editor, *New York Times*, 8 Mar. 1948; Wheeler responded to Streit's attack in the *New York Times* of 17 Mar. 1948.

24. Even de Gaulle at this point sounded much like Bidault or Bevin as he called for U.S. military aid and for European political and economic measures in a speech at Compiègne on Mar. 7, 1948: "We must form the free states of Europe into an economic, diplomatic, and strategic group, combining their production and exchanges and their foreign policies and means of defense. . . . But it is clear that the United States support would be at the same time extended to the domain of defense and in a manner detailed and explicit on both sides as in the Marshall Plan regarding credits and exportations." "Discours prononcé à Compiègne," in Charles de Gaulle, *Discours et messages: Dans l'attente, 1946–1948* (Paris, 1970), pp. 169ff; *New York Times*, 8 Mar. 1948.

25. Quoted in Elliot R. Goodman, *The Fate of the Atlantic Community* (New York, 1975), pp. 9–10.

26. See Walter Hallstein, *United Europe: Challenge and Opportunity* (Cambridge, Mass., 1962), p. 8; Arnold J. Zurcher, *The Struggle to Unite Europe, 1940–58*, pp. 20–21; Lipgens, *Die Anfänge*, pp. 313–14.

27. Coudenhove-Kalergi made strenuous efforts to link the building of a European federation with resistance to communism. Note his flyer *How to Successfully Fight the Propaganda of the Cominform*, 2 Feb. 1948, in Office of European Affairs, 840.00/2-1648, RG 59, NARS.

28. Richard Coudenhove-Kalergi, *Kampf um Europa: Aus meinem Leben* (Zurich, 1940), p. 277; *New York Times*, 2 Jan. 1948. See also Zurcher, *Struggle to Unite Europe*, pp. 33ff. Melandri, "Les Etats-Unis face," 1:116–17.

29. Coudenhove-Kalergi, *Kampf um Europa*, pp. 278–79.

30. Ibid., p. 280. The committee was formally incorporated on April 23, 1948. *New York Times*, 24 Apr. 1948.

31. Jean Monnet, *Memoirs*, trans. Richard Mayne (Garden City, N.Y., 1978), pp. 271–72. See also Ernst H. van der Beugel, *From Marshall Aid to Atlantic Partnership: European Integration as a Concern of American Foreign Policy* (Amsterdam, 1966), p. 132.

32. Note Coudenhove-Kalergi's interpretation of the language of the Foreign Assistance Act, *Kampf um Europa*, p. 278.

33. Coudenhove-Kalergi to Bohlen, 16 Feb. 1948, 840.00/2-1648, RG 59, NARS.

34. Bohlen to Hickerson, 18 Feb. 1948, ibid.

35. An appointment was arranged for 11:30 a.m. on February 26. Hickerson to Bohlen, 20 Feb. 1948, ibid.; Bohlen to General Carter, 21 Feb. 1948; Hickerson's recommendation in regard to Coudenhove-Kalergi, ibid.; Bohlen to Hickerson, 24 Feb. 1948, ibid.

36. Bohlen to General Carter, 21 Feb. 1948, ibid. Coudenhove-Kalergi managed to meet Secretary Marshall long enough on March 3, 1948, to leave an autographed copy of one of his books. Marshall Carter, memorandum, George C. Marshall Research Library, Lexington, Va.

37. Marshall to Dorothy Thompson, 26 Mar. 1948, 840.00/3-248, RG 59, NARS.

38. Gladwyn Jebb, under secretary at the British Foreign Office, had been sent to Washington in February 1948 to sound out the United States on the extent of its commitment to the prospective Brussels pact. He was convinced that "the Secretary of State knew perfectly well what he was after, but he had to achieve his end by stages, gaining as many allies as he could in the process." *Memoirs of Lord Gladwyn* (London, 1972), p. 211.

39. Oral history interview, Theodore C. Achilles, Harry S. Truman Library, Independence, Mo.

40. Hickerson had thus been responsive to Bevin's imagery involving two circles, the inner one embracing the future Brussels Pact, the outer one including the United States and Canada. Interview, John D. Hickerson, Truman Library. See a similar reference in an interview conducted with Hickerson on July 19, 1977, by Steven P. Sapp and Lynne Dunn of Kent State University, in Kent State Univ. Library.

41. Memorandum, Hickerson to S/S, 19 Jan. 1948, *FRUS*, 1948, 3:6–7.

42. Memorandum, Kennan to S/S, 20 Jan. 1948, ibid., pp. 7–8.

43. Memorandum of conversation, by Hickerson, 21 Jan. 1948, ibid., pp. 9–12.

44. Memorandum of conversation, by Lovett, 27 Jan. 1948, ibid., pp. 12–14; Inverchapel to Lovett, 27 Jan. 1948, ibid., pp. 14–16; Lovett to Inverchapel, 2 Feb. 1948, ibid., pp. 17–18.

45. Millard to S/S, 9 Feb. 1948, 840.00/2-948, RG 59, NARS. Hickerson's memorandum of a conversation between Lovett and Inverchapel emphasized Lovett's statement that Marshall's approval of the Dunkirk model for the Dutch and the Belgians "is not correct." He said that Secretary Marshall's letter to the ambassador before Bevin's January 22 speech was a warm endorsement of the general idea of a Western union but did not go into the matter of specific measures suggested by Bevin for bringing this about. 7 Feb. 1948, *FRUS*, 1948, 3:22.

46. Caffery to S/S, 11 Feb. 1948, 840.00/2-1648, RG 59, NARS; Caffery to S/S, 19 Feb. 1948, *FRUS*, 1948, 3:27–29.

47. S/S to embassy in France, 27 Feb. 1948, *FRUS*, 1948, 3:34. It is worth noting that the unpublished version of the above telegram contains in parentheses the following: "we should not (repeat not) be asked." See 840.00/2-2248, RG 59, NARS.

48. *New York Times*, 17, 24 Feb. 1948.

49. *New York Herald-Tribune*, 18 Jan. 1948; Carl C. Van Doren, *The Great Rehearsal: The Story of the Making and Ratifying of the Constitution of the United States* (New York, 1948), p. 10.

50. *European Recovery Program Hearings*, 12 Jan. 1948, pp. 208, 209, 213.

51. *New York Times*, 27 Feb. 1948.

52. NSC 1/3, report to the National Security Council by the executive secretary on "The Position of the U.S. with Respect to Italy," 8 Mar. 1948, adopted 12 Mar. 1948, RG 59, NARS.

53. Quoted in Elgey, *République des illusions*, p. 382. See also Melandri, "Les Etats-Unis face," 1:293.

54. Douglas to S/S, 26 Feb. 1948, *FRUS*, 1948, 3:32–33.

55. Memorandum, Hickerson to S/S, 8 Mar. 1948, ibid., p. 40.

56. Ibid., pp. 41–42. In an aide-memoire, 11 Mar. 1948, Bevin responded to the idea of "an Atlantic security system" and to the threat to Norway by recommending that both countries "study without delay the establishment of such an Atlantic security system, so that, if the threat to Norway should develop, we could at once inspire the necessary confidence to consolidate the West against Soviet infiltration and at the same time inspire the Soviet Government with enough respect for the West to remove temptation from them and so ensure a long period of peace." Ibid., p. 47. See also Reid, *Time of Fear and Hope*, p. 42.

57. *New York Times*, 2 Mar. 1948.

58. Walter Millis, ed., *The Forrestal Diaries* (New York, 1951); p. 435. Millis refers to "the so-called Title VI part of the ERP bill." See also Reston's commentary, *New York Times*, 10 Mar. 1948. The NSC studies resulted ultimately in the NSC-9 series, "The Position of the United States with Respect to Support for Western Union and Other Related Free Countries," particularly NSC-9/1 of April 23, 1948. See *FRUS*, 1948, 3:100, note.

59. Revisionist historians have emphasized the manipulative potential in the crisis symbolized by Clay's telegram, claiming that the Truman administration exaggerated it to insure passage of the ERP and to inaugurate a new rearmament program. For some scholars, such as Joyce Kolko and Gabriel Kolko, *The Limits of Power: The World and United States Foreign Policy, 1945–1954* (New York, 1972), p. 490, the crisis itself was manufactured, since "the

Russians were also on a peace offensive that Washington ultimately feared as much as, if not more than, the events around Berlin itself." Richard M. Freeland, in *The Truman Doctrine and the Origins of McCarthyism: Foreign Policy, Domestic Politics, and Internal Security, 1946–1948* (New York, 1972), p. 286, states, "It seems impossible to avoid the conclusion that the war scare of 1948 was yet another exercise in crisis politics by the Truman administration." And Daniel Yergin, in *Shattered Peace: The Origins of the Cold War and the National Security State* (Boston, 1977), p. 351, asserts, "In truth, the telegram had much more to do with getting budgets through Congress than with anticipating Soviet behavior." Kennan shares the sense of "a real war scare" as a result of the combination of the Czech coup and Clay's telegram, which he regards as erroneous. Soviet behavior, he maintains, could be explained in their defensive reaction to the success of the Marshall Plan. *Memoirs, 1925–1950*, pp. 422–24. It is worth noting that Kennan was not as detached about Soviet objectives as his memoirs suggest. Just a few months before at the National War College he claimed, "Their immediate plans today probably envisage the consolidation of their power in Czechoslovakia as soon as possible and the actual seizure of power by violent means in Greece, and Italy and France." See Yergin, *Shattered Peace*, p. 480 n. 31.

60. Letter to editor, *New York Times*, 16 Feb. 1948; Paul-Henri Spaak, *The Continuing Battle: Memoirs of a European, 1936–1969* (Boston, 1971), p. 148.

61. The Canadian diplomat Escott Reid spoke for American and European leaders alike when he entitled his book on the origins of NATO *The Time of Fear and Hope*.

62. Gladwyn Jebb, memorandum of conversation with Sir Orme Sargent, Sir Ivone Kirkpatrick, and Bevin, 3 Mar. 1948, 73050, FO 371, PRO, Kew.

5. BRUSSELS PACT TO ATLANTIC ALLIANCE

1. Daniel Yergin, *Shattered Peace: The Origins of the Cold War and the National Security State* (Boston, 1977), p. 353.

2. Ibid.

3. See Truman message to Congress, 17 Mar. 1948, *Public Papers of the Presidents*, 1948, p. 184.

4. Harry S. Truman, *Memoirs*, 2 vols. (New York, 1965), 2:279.

5. Truman, *Public Papers*, p. 184.

6. Joint Message, Bidault and Bevin to S/S, 17 Mar. 1948, *FRUS*, 1948, 3:55–56; report prepared by Policy Planning Staff concerning Western Union and related problems, 23 Mar. 1948, PPS 27, ibid., 3:62.

7. Minutes, First Meeting, United States-United Kingdom-Canada Security Conversations, Washington, 22 Mar. 1948, ibid., 3:59–61.

8. Jean Chauvel, *Commentaire: D'Alger à Berne (1944–1952)* (Paris, 1962), p. 207.

9. See *FRUS*, 1948, 1:597n; *Mutual Defense Assistance Act of 1949, Hearings*, House Committee on Foreign Affairs, 81 Cong. 1 sess., 1 Aug. 1949, pp. 76–77.

10. Monnet, *Memoirs*, pp. 272–73.

11. *Congressional Record*, 80 Cong. 2 sess., 8 Mar. 1948, 94:2285.

12. Ibid., p. 2286.

13. Ibid., 29 Mar. 1948, pp. 3645–46.

14. Ibid., Van der Beugel, *From Marshall Aid to Atlantic Partnership* (Amsterdam, 1966), p. 166.

15. Bevin to Marshall, 3 Mar. 1948, Confidential File, 1945–1949, 840.20/3-1148, Box C-509, RG 59, NARS. See Cees Wiebes and Bert Zeeman, "The Pentagon Negotiations, March 1948: The Launching of the North Atlantic Treaty," *International Affairs* 59 (Summer 1983):351–63.

16. "Report by the NSC on the Position of the United States with Respect to Soviet-Directed World Communism," NSC-7, 30 Mar. 1948, *FRUS*, 1948, 1:546–50.

17. S. Shepard Jones to Bohlen, "American Public Opinion and Support for the Brussels Pact Allies," 13 Apr. 1948, points out that "by a ratio of 5–3 the public believes that the United States should promise to back up England, France, and other countries of Western Europe with our Armed Forces if they are attacked by some other country." If the action were "in line with the UN Charter" the majority would be even larger. Department of State Mss, 840.00/44138, Decimal File, 1945–49, Lot 57, D 271, Box 71, RG 59, NARS.

18. NSC-7, *FRUS*, 1948, 1:545–50.

19. Memorandum, Forrestal to NSC, Security Council, 17 Apr. 1948, ibid., 1:563.

20. Ibid.

21. Minutes, Fourth Meeting, United States-United Kingdom-Canada Security Conversations, Washington, 29 Mar. 1948, ibid., 3:69.

22. NSC-9, "The Position of the United States with Respect to Support for Western Union and Other Related Countries," 13 Apr. 1948, ibid., 3:85–88. Memorandum, JCS to S/D, "The Position of the United States with Respect to Support for Western Union and Other Related Free Countries," 23 Apr. 1948, Records of the Joint Chiefs of Staff, CCS 092 W. Europe, (3-12-48), RG 218, NARS.

23. Memorandum of conversation, by Lovett, 18 Apr. 1948 (participants: Vandenberg and Lovett), *FRUS*, 1948, 3:92–96.

24. Kennan to Souers, 23 Apr. 1948, with enclosures making up the substance of NSC 9/1, ibid., 100–103. This was followed by a meeting at Blair House on April 27, 1948, with Marshall and Dulles along with Vandenberg and Lovett, in which the idea of the Senate approving a resolution specifically endorsing a North Atlantic pact was not accepted. Instead, Vandenberg's single-page draft was unveiled. See Vandenberg, *Private Papers*, p. 406.

25. *Congressional Record*, 80 Cong. 2 sess., 11 June 1948, 94:7791.

26. Memorandum by George H. Butler, 19 Mar. 1948, *FRUS*, 1948, 3:59.

27. Memorandum, Kennan to S/S and Lovett, 29 Apr. 1948, ibid., 3:107; Reid, *Time of Fear and Hope*, p. 107.

28. *New York Times*, 9 Apr. 1948.

29. Ibid., 24 Apr. 1948.

30. Philip W. Bonsal to S/S, 17 Mar. 1948, no. 157, "European Unity Conference to be Held in the Hague," 840.00/3-1748, Box 5563, RG 59, NARS.

31. *New York Times*, 24 Apr., 6 May 1948.

32. Ibid., 24 May 1948.

33. Winston Churchill, "The Voice of Europe, 7 May 1948," in *Vital Speeches of the Day*, 14 (15 May 1948): 451.

34. Duncan Sandys to Marshall, 30 Apr. 1948, 840.00/4-1348, RG 59, NARS.

35. Dean Rusk, American Embassy to UN, to Hickerson, 3 May 1948, and Marshall to American Embassy, London, 4 May 1948, No. 1598, ibid.

36. Memorandum of conversation, by Achilles, 5 Apr. 1948, "U.S. Support for Brussels Treaty," meeting between Spaak and Lovett, Hickerson, and Achilles, *FRUS*, 1948, 3:76–78.

37. Sir George Rendel, Brussels, to FO, 23 Apr. 1948, no. 246, FO 371/73057/HN 08265, PRO.

38. Memorandum, Achilles to Hickerson, 19 May 1948, *FRUS*, 1948, 3:127–28.

39. Conversation between Bevin and Bidault at the latter's reception at the Quai d'Orsay on 16 Apr. 1948, FO 371/73057/HN 08265, PRO; President Vincent Auriol warned even more vigorously against entangling Western Europeans "dans le bloc américain. . . . Il faut organiser l'Europe occidentale puisque l'autre est faite. Mais Europe occidentale doit, tout en devenant économiquement, politiquement et militairement forte, offrir aux deux antagonistes des prop-

ositions de paix sur tous les problèmes." See Auriol, *Journal de Septennat, 1947–1954*, 9 Apr. 1948, 2:171–72.

40. James Reston, *New York Times*, 12 June 1948.

41. Memorandum of conversation with Spaak, 5 Apr. 1948, *FRUS*, 1948, 3:76; Reid, *Time of Fear and Hope*, pp. 107–9; Kennan, *Memoirs*, p. 429.

42. Reid, *Time of Fear and Hope*, p. 111.

43. Ibid., p. 80. W. Phillips Davison, *The Berlin Blockade* (Princeton, 1958), p. 106. The Polish newspaper *Zycie Warszavy* on April 4, 1958, published an article entitled "North Atlantic Alliance" describing Anglo-American plans, mentioning twice the name of British Parliamentary Under Secretary of State for Foreign Affairs Christopher Mayhew. One of Mayhew's assistants was Guy Burgess, a member of Maclean's spy network, according to Wiebes and Seeman, "Pentagon Negotiations." Theodore C. Achilles, head of the office of Western European Affairs, affirmed in response to a query from Senator Eastland that "Maclean had a thorough knowledge particularly of the Anglo-Canadian-US meetings in the Pentagon"; memorandum, 22 Dec. 1955. W.M. Chase to Loy W. Henderson, "The Department and the Former U.K. Diplomats, Donald Maclean and Guy Burgess, revealed as Soviet Spies," 741.13/12/2255, RG 59, NARS.

44. Theodore C. Achilles, "US Role in Negotiations That Led to Atlantic Alliance," *NATO Review* 27 (Aug. 1979): 13.

45. *Congressional Record*, 80 Cong. 2 sess., 11 June 1948, 94:7811–12, 7813.

46. Ibid., p. 7791. See chapter 3, above.

47. Kennan to Lovett, 7 May 1948, *FRUS*, 1948, 3:116–19.

48. NSC 9/3, 28 June 1948, ibid., 3:140–41.

49. "Note by the Executive Secretary of the Position of the United States with Respect to Providing Military Assistance to Nations of the Non-Soviet World," 1 July 1948, ibid., 1:585.

50. Ibid., 3:148ff.

51. Kenneth W. Condit, *The History of the Joint Chiefs of Staff: The JCS and National Policy, 1947–1949* (Wilmington, Del., 1979), p. 365. Memorandum, JCS to S/D, "The Position of the United States with Respect to Support for Western Union and Other Related Free Countries," 19 May 1948, CCS 092 W. Europe (3-12-48), Records of the JCS, RG 218, NARS.

52. *Memoirs of Lord Gladwyn*, p. 220.

53. Ibid.

54. George F. Kennan, *Memoirs, 1925–1950*, p. 429. Canadians had some reservations about their role as part of the North American "pillar." Escott Reid feared that "Canada would be odd-man-out in the alliance"; *Time of Fear and Hope*, p. 132.

55. The Democratic party platform of 1948 pledged "continued support of regional arrangements within the United Nations Charter, such as the Inter-American Regional Pact and the developing Western European Union." The Republicans in turn "welcome and encourage the sturdy progress toward unity in Western Europe"; K.H. Porter and Bruce Johnson, comps., *National Party Platforms, 1840–1956* (Urbana, 1956), pp. 432, 453.

56. In interviews conducted in 1976 Hickerson and Achilles of the United States confessed to giving only lip service to the idea of European unity, fearing that it might impede progress toward Atlantic unity. Jebb of the United Kingdom shared this concern. See Reid, *Time of Fear and Hope*, pp. 134–35. British Foreign Minister Bevin claimed in November 1948 that French Foreign Minister Schuman was relieved to find a way out of the Franco-Belgian Consultative Assembly that presumably would have not only alienated Britain but advanced a unified Europe at the expense of the more important Atlantic unity: 2 Nov. 1948, C.P. (48) 249, memorandum by S/S for Foreign Affairs, Cabinet Papers, PRO. The American presence in Europe was vital for Britain to reestablish its own former power through an overseas surrogate; for France the Atlantic connection provided not only a source of military weapons and supplies but also the counterweight to the German as well as the Soviet menace. See Alastair Buchan, "Mothers and Daugh-

ters (or Greeks and Romans)" in William P. Bundy, ed., *Two Hundred Years of American Foreign Policy* (New York, 1977), pp. 44–52; Chauvel, *Commentaire*, p. 207. Spaak, *Continuing Battle*, p. 150; Stikker, *Men of Responsibility* pp. 283–84.

57. See instructions for U.S. representatives attending Western Union Talks, an enclosure with 16 July 1948 memorandum by Gruenther to Hickerson, *FRUS*, 3:189. The First Meeting of the Washington Exploratory Talks on Security began on July 6, 1948; see minutes in ibid., 148ff. (Hereafter cited as Exploratory Talks.)

58. See Western Union progress report, London, by Ambassador Sir Oliver Franks, 7 July 1948, Minutes, Third Meeting, Exploratory Talks, ibid., 155–56.

59. Lovett's comments at Third Meeting, Exploratory Talks, 7 July 1948, ibid., 156.

60. See JCS 1844/13, "Short Range Emergency War Plan (HALFMOON), 21 July 1948," in Thomas H. Etzold and John L. Gaddis, eds., *Containment: Documents on American Policy and Strategy, 1945–1950* (New York, 1978), pp. 315, 318. It is worth noting, though, that at the Hague meeting of the WU's Defense Ministers Committee on April 7–8, 1949, an Outline Short Term Plan was approved which accepted the Rhine as a defense line. This was done despite the Netherlands defense minister's observation that three of his nation's provinces would be unprotected in the plan. "Fifth Periodic Informal Progress Report on the Accomplishments of DELWU, for the period 15 Mar.–15 Apr. 1949," prepared for the S/D, Records of the JCS, RG 218, NARS.

61. Condit, *History of the JCS*, pp. 366–68.

62. Ibid., 368–69.

63. Ibid., 372–73. To satisfy French concerns the JCS were willing to participate in the work of the Chiefs-of-Staff Committee; Lovett to S/S, 19 Oct. 1948. The JCS were sensitive to criticisms that "the brass hats were determining our foreign policy and that accordingly would like guidance from us"; Hickerson to Lovett, 18 Oct. 1948, 840.00/10-148, Box 507, RG 59, NARS.

64. Appendix B to Enclosure A to JCS 1868/58, 23 Nov. 1948, RG 330, NARS; appendix A to Enclosure A to JCS 1868/58, 13 Jan. 1949, ibid; Report JCS 1868/58, Feb. 11, 1949, "Military Assistance Program," p. 387., ibid.

65. Memorandum of conversation with Armand Bérard by Charles E. Bohlen, to S/S 6 Aug. 1948, *FRUS*, 1948, 3:207; memorandum of conversation, by Lovett, 20 Aug. 1948, ibid., 218.

66. Ibid., 219.

67. Memorandum, Bohlen to Lovett, 29 July 1948, 840.20/7-2948, RG 59, NARS.

68. U.S. special respresentative in Europe to S/S, 14 July 1948, *FRUS*, 1948, 3:183.

69. Lovett to Embassy in France, 20 Sept. 1948, ibid., 253; *Forrestal Diaries*, p. 521.

70. C.P. (48) 249, 2 Nov. 1948, "North Atlantic Treaty and Western Union," memorandum by Secretary of State for Foreign Affairs, p. 9, Cabinet Papers, FO 371/82/XY 07477, PRO.

71. Frederic Hoyer Millar to Ivone Kirkpatrick, 6 Nov. 1948, "Supply of U.S. Military Equipment to French Divisions," FO 371/73108/HN 08265, PRO.

72. Minutes, Fifth Meeting, Exploratory Talks, 9 July 1948, *FRUS*, 1948, 3:178.

73. Memorandum by Kennan to Lovett, 31 Aug. 1948, ibid., 225. Lovett appended a comment in Annex A to this memorandum in PPS files: "It can't be done." Unpublished paper, Larry I. Bland, "George Kennan and the Creation of NATO," meeting of Society for Historians of American Relations, Lawrence, Kansas, 10 Aug. 1979.

74. Kennan outlined his differences with Hickerson in his memo to Lovett, 31 Aug. 1948, *FRUS*, 1948, 3:225.

75. Information on meeting of the Consultative Council of the Western Union, July 19–20, at the Hague, from Lovink and Boon, in telegram of U.S. ambassador in the Netherlands to S/S, 21 July 1948, ibid., 3:194–95; memorandum, S/S to Lovett, 23 July 1948, ibid., 199.

76. Minutes, Fifth Meeting, Exploratory Talks, 9 July 1948, ibid., 171.

77. Ibid.

78. Quoted in Reid, *Time of Fear and Hope*, p. 195.

79. Minutes, Fourth Meeting, Exploratory Talks, 8 July 1948, *FRUS*, 1948, 3:165.

80. Lovett to Caffery, 24 Aug. 1948, quoted in Reid, *Time of Fear and Hope*, p. 196.

81. "To be fully satisfactory, a North Atlantic security system would have to provide also for that [security] of the North Atlantic territories of Denmark (especially Greenland), Norway, Iceland, Portugal (especially the Azores) and Ireland, which, should they fall into enemy hands, would jeopardize the security of both the European and North American members and seriously impede the flow of reciprocal assistance between them"; memorandum by participants in the Exploratory Talks, 6 July to 9 Sept., *FRUS*, 1948, 3:240.

82. This was the "London Paper," entitled "Notes on Paper of Washington Prepared in London by the Permanent Commission of the Brussels Powers," ibid., 310, 313. See also Reid, *Time of Fear and Hope*, p. 196.

83. Action Summary, International Working Group, Exploratory Talks, 15 Dec. 1948, Lot 53 D68, NATO Box 1, RG 353, NARS; "Procedure for Negotiations and Approaches to Other Governments," Annex D of Draft Treaty, 24 Dec. 1948, *FRUS*, 1948, 3:342–43.

84. Memorandum of conversation, by S/S with Foreign Minister Undén of Sweden, 14 Oct. 1948, *FRUS*, 1948, 3: 264; memorandum of conversation, S/S with Foreign Minister Lange of Norway, 20 Nov. 1948, ibid., p. 281. Some American anger was vented against Britain for supplying Sweden with aircraft just when the delay of military supplies was to have been a means of pressing the Swedes to give up the alternative Nordic Pact; memorandum, Hickerson to S/S, 21 Sept. 1948, ibid., pp. 253–54; Lovett to Embassy in Sweden, 2 Oct. 1948, ibid., p. 259.

85. Lovett to Embassy in Denmark, 17 Nov. 1948, ibid., p. 271; Ambassador in Portugal to S/S, 8 Oct. 1948, ibid., p. 263.

86. Memorandum by participants in Exploratory Talks, 6 July to 9 Sept. 1948, ibid., p. 241.

87. Memorandum by Hickerson to Lovett, 7 Oct. 1948, "Italy and the Western European Defense Pact," ibid., p. 261.

88. Memorandum, Fourteenth Meeting, Working Group Participating in Exploratory Talks, 7 Sept. 1948, ibid., p. 234; minutes, Tenth Meeting, Exploratory Talks, 22 Dec. 1948, ibid., pp. 325–30; memorandum, Thirteenth Meeting, Working Group Participating in Exploratory Talks, 2 Sept. 1948, ibid., pp. 227–28; Lovett to Embassy in Belguim, 22 Nov. 1958, ibid., pp. 282–83. Kennan had stressed Hickerson's strong support for Italian membership as early as August, even as he himself opposed Italian membership in the new alliance; memorandum, Kennan to Lovett, 31 Aug. 1948, ibid., p. 225.

89. Ibid., p. 242.

90. State Department paper prepared for Working Group, Exploratory Talks, 10 Aug. 1948, 840.20/8-1048, Lot 53, D68, NATO, Box 3, RG 353, NARS.

91. Article 3 of the Inter-American Treaty of Reciprocal Assistance notes that

(1) The High Contracting Parties agree that an armed attack by any State against an American State shall be considered as an attack against all the American States, and consequently, each one of the said Contracting Parties undertakes to assist in meeting the attack in the exercise of the inherent right of individual or collective self-defense recognized by Article 51 of the Charter of the United Nations.

(2) On the request of the State or States directly attacked and until the decision of the Organ of Consultation of the Inter-American System, each one of the Contracting Parties may determine the immediate measures which it may individually take in fulfillment of the obligation contained in the preceding paragraph and in accordance with the principle of continental solidarity. The Organ of Consultation shall meet without delay for the purpose of examining those measures and agreeing upon the measures of a collective character that should be taken.

In Charles I. Bevans, ed., *Treaties and Other International Agreements of the United States of America, 1776–1949*, Department of State Publication 8521 (June 1970), 4:560–61.

92. Minutes, Fifth Meeting, Exploratory Talks, 9 July 1948, on Item (4), "Nature of U.S. Association under Vandenberg Resolution with European Security Arrangements," *FRUS*, 1948, 3:176.

93. Lovett made the point that "the Rio Pact left assistance to the decision of the assisting country"; ibid., 180; memorandum, Tenth Meeting, Working Group Participating in Exploratory Talks, 12 Aug. 1948, ibid., p. 212.

94. Memorandum, Ninth Meeting, Working Group Participating in Exploratory Talks, 9 Aug. 1948, ibid., p. 211. Article IV of the Brussels Pact states: "If any of the High Contracting Parties should be the object of an armed attack in Europe, the other High Contracting Parties will, in accordance with the provisions of Article 51 of the Charter of the United Nations, afford the party so attacked all the military and other aid and assistance in their power." Margaret Carlyle, ed., *Documents in International Affairs, 1947–1948* (London, 1952), p. 227.

95. State Department paper prepared for Working Group, Exploratory Talks, 10 Aug. 1948, 840.20/8-1048, Lot 53 D 68, NATO Box 353, RG 59, NARS. See also memorandum, Tenth Meeting, Working Group Participating in Exploratory Talks, 12 Aug. 1948, *FRUS*, 1948, 3:212.

96. U.S. preference following closely the Rio text: "An armed attack by any State against a Party shall be considered as an attack against all the Parties and consequently, each Party undertakes to assist in meeting the attack in the exercise of the inherent right of individual or collective self-defense recognized by Article 51 of the Charter."

European preference conformed closely to the corresponding article in the Brussels Treaty: "If any Party should be the object of an armed attack in the area covered by the Treaty, the other Parties will, in accordance with the provisions of Article 51 of the Charter, afford the Party so attacked all the military and other aid and assistance in their power."

The following represented a compromise supported specifically by the Canadian representative: "Provision that each Party should agree that any act which, in its opinion, constituted an armed attack against any other Party in the area covered by the treaty be considered an attack against itself, and should consequently, in accordance with its constitutional processes, assist in repelling the attack by all military, economic and other means in its power in the exercise of the right of individual or collective self-defense recognized by Article 51 of the Charter." In an annex outlining provisions suitable for inclusion in a North Atlantic Security Pact, memorandum by Participants, Exploratory Talks, 9 Sept. 1948, "Washington Paper," *FRUS*, 1948, 3:247.

97. Annex A—Draft Treaty, 24 Dec. 1948, Article 5:

Paragraph 1 (Mutual Assistance)

The Parties agree that an armed attack against one or more of them occurring within the area defined below shall be considered an attack against them all; and consequently that, if such an attack occurs, each of them, in exercise of the right of individual or collective self-defense recognized by Article 51 of the Charter of the United Nations, will assist the party or parties so attacked by taking forthwith such military or other action, individually and in concert with other Parties, as may be necessary to restore and assure the security of the North Atlantic area. [Ibid., 335]

98. Brussels Pact communique, 27 Oct. 1948, in *Department of State Bulletin* 19 (7 Nov. 1948): 583; memorandum by ambassadors of Western Union countries to Department of State, 29 Oct. 1948, *FRUS*, 1948, 3:270; commentary on Washington Paper of 9 Sept., Department of External Affairs, Ottawa, 6 Dec. 1948, PA/HO Research Files, Lot 57-D271, RG 59, NARS.

99. Lovett made it clear that the European "governments were responsible for those conversations being held." See Minutes, Sixth Meeting, Washington Exploratory Talks on Security, 3 Sept. 1948, *FRUS*, 1948, 3:230; at the same time it was obvious to the British that the Americans identified the origins of the exploratory talks with the Vandenberg Resolution. "The conception of a North Atlantic Treaty has been widely canvassed in the United States, where it

has been regarded as an American initiative. The circumstance that the idea originated in this country is not known except to a very narrow circle of officials who have been careful not to reveal it." Memorandum by the Secretary of State for Foreign Affairs, 2 Nov. 1948, C.P. (48) 249, "North Atlantic Treaty and Western Union," PRO.

100. Reid, *Time of Fear and Hope*, pp. 55–56; memorandum of conversation by Lovett, 20 Aug. 1948, *FRUS*, 1948, 3:214–15. Theodore Achilles notes that Lovett and the ambassadors met only occasionally, and that the real work was done by the Working Group, which "met every working day from the beginning of July to the beginning of September. . . . the NATO spirit was born in that Working Group." Interview with Theodore C. Achilles, p. 28, Truman Library.

101. Memorandum of conversation by Hickerson with Daridan, Counselor of French Embassy, 29 Oct. 1948, 840.00/10/2948, RG 59, NARS; Lovett to Embassy in Belguim, 22 Nov. 1948, *FRUS*, 1948, 3:282–83; memorandum of conversation by Achilles with Hoyer Millar, 27 Nov. 1948, ibid., p. 287.

102. Memorandum by JCS to S/D, 24 Nov. 1948, NSC 9/6, "Developments with Respect to Western Union," ibid., p. 291.

103. Memorandum, FC (48), Appendix B to Enclosure A to JCS 1868/58, 23 Nov. 1948, "Western Union Defense Policy," DC 6-2-46, RG 330, NARS.

104. Montgomery's good faith is not in doubt. He was concerned about suspicions among British military circles that the Continent was indefensible, which gave rise in turn to European suspicions of Britain's intentions. "I became so alarmed at this attitude that I had a meeting with the British Chiefs of Staff on the 2nd of December 1948. I told them that French morale would not recover unless that nation could be convinced that Britain would contribute a fair quota of land forces to the defence of Western Europe." *The Memoirs of Field-Marshal the Viscount Montgomery* (Cleveland, 1958), pp. 458–59.

105. Memorandum by Kennan, 24 Nov. 1948, *FRUS*, 1948, 3:285, 286, 288. The official comments of the Canadian government support some of Kennan's arguments, particularly his emphasis on the economic and social functions of the alliance: "The Treaty should be something more than a defense treaty or a defensive military alliance. The idea of a treaty was based on a community of principles and ideas, and the Canadian Government wished this to be recognized in the body of the treaty rather than only by a phrase in the preamble." In keeping with this spirit Ambassador Hume Wrong urged the removal of such a term as "High Contracting Parties" from the text. Minutes, Ninth Meeting, Exploratory Talks, Dec. 13, 1948, ibid., pp. 316–17; minutes, Tenth Meeting, Exploratory Talks, 22 Dec. 1948, ibid., p. 325.

106. Altiero Spinelli, *The Eurocrats: Conflict and Crisis in the European Community* (Baltimore, 1966), pp. 10–11, identifies three approaches to European unification: federalist, functionalist, and confederalist.

107. Note the useful charting of the relationships among the various groups involved in European unification on the inside back cover of Lipgens, *Die Anfänge*.

108. Spinelli placed Churchill with de Gaulle among the "confederates" rather than the "functionalists"; *Eurocrats*, pp. 16–17.

109. C.P. (48) 162, response of Foreign Minister Bevin to deputation from the British section of the International Committee of the Movements for European Unity, 12 June 1948, p. 4, FO 271/82/XY D7477, PRO; President Vincent Auriol, responding to William Bullitt's importunities, observed on August 25: "En tout cas, je crois qu'il faut en effet organiser l'Europe, sinon dans un sens federatif, en tout cas dans le sens d'une confederation ou d'une union d'etats. Car il ne faut pas aller trop vite." *Journal du Septennat*, 2:370; This was much the same sentiment Chauvel was said to ascribe to Schuman; C.P. (48) 249, memorandum by S/S for Foreign Affairs, 2 Nov. 1948, p. 8, FO 371/82, PRO.

110. Kennan's views are in Minutes, Fifth Meeting, Exploratory Talks, 9 July 1948, *FRUS*, 1948, 3:177.

111. Achilles confessed to Reid a generation later that he and Hickerson gave only lip

service to the idea of European unity, and felt at the time that emphasis on European unity delayed Atlantic unity; Reid, *Time of Fear and Hope*, pp. 134–35.

112. See M. Margaret Ball, *NATO and the European Union Movement* (New York, 1959), p. 19; Chauvel, *Commentaire*, p. 210.

113. Gladwyn Jebb to Ivone Kirkpatrick and Oliver Sargent, 24 Aug. 1948, FO 371/73097/HM D8238, PRO; Ivone Kirkpatrick to Oliver Sargent, 28 Aug. 1948, FO 371/73097HM 08238, PRO.

114. State Department statement in S/S to Caffery, 27 Aug. 1948, *FRUS*, 1948, 3:222–23.

115. Ibid., p. 223.

116. *New York Times*, 19 Aug. 1948. Ambassador Douglas reported to Secretary Marshall Britain's recognition that "the French action has put us on the spot." 19 Aug. 1948, no. 3772, 840.00/8-1948, RG 59, NARS.

117. C.P. (48) 162, 17 June 1948, FO 371/82/XY D7477, PRO; Churchill reversed himself two months later after France had proposed "a practical form of action." He wanted the British government "to place themselves more in line with Western European opinion upon an issue which they themselves have already done much to promote." Churchill to Attlee, 21 Aug. 1948, FO 371/73097/HM D8238, PRO.

118. Oliver Sargent to British Embassy, Paris, Moley, 20 Aug. 1948, FO 371/73097/GN 08238, PRO; T.R. Snow, British Legation, Berne, to Bevin, 21 Sept. 1948, no. 218, FO 371/73098/8238, PRO.

119. Snow to Bevin, 21 Sept. 1948, ibid.

120. "There is nothing surprising in the American reaction. . . . As long as the State Department confine themselves to endorsing 'practical measures' or 'steps which promote the idea of European Unity,' we have no reason to complain." This was the response of Franks from Washington on the U.S. attitude to the United Europe movements, 29 Aug. 1948, FO 371/73097/HM 08238, PRO. The sense of the Foreign Office was that the American attitude showed "rather an odd state of mind." P.M. Crosthwaite postscript in memorandum by A.A.D. Montague Browne, 31 Aug. 1948, ibid.

121. This was reported by Franks to FO, 27 Aug. 1948, no. 4104, FO 371/73097/HM 08238, PRO. On September 1 he reported that even the *New York Herald-Tribune* called the U.S. statement as having "officially backed" the French initiative; Franks to Foreign Office, ibid.

122. Dewey in a major speech at Salt Lake City on September 30, 1948, spoke more specifically and with greater emphasis on European federation than did the Republican party platform: "European unity, that's no new idea and that's no wild-eyed dream, it has been the dream and realistic vision of far sighted statesmen for thirty years. A federation of western Europe's 270,000,000 people with one strong, economic, and political unit would be the greatest triumph of statesmanship in history. It would be the foremost guarantee of peace in the world. And to achieve it will be a major objective of our foreign policy." *Vital Speeches of the Day* 15 (15 Oct. 1948): 15.

123. Franks observed in detail the charges of Sumner Welles that Bevin was "strangely addicted to politics of utter sterility," and of Walter Lippmann, who found the source of British obstructionism in British socialism. Franks to FO, 1 Sept. 1948, no. 371, FO 371/73097/HM 08238, PRO; Roger Makins related a conversation with William Bullitt of the Committee for a Free and United Europe, in which Bullitt "was running the usual contemporary American line that the U.K. were hanging back over European cooperation & that we ought to go for a closer political union—in spite of the political & financial instability of France & Italy." Makins to Bevin, 14 Oct. 1948, ibid.

124. On Coudenhove, T.M. Snow of the British delegation at Berne claimed that "the Count played a valuable and important part as pioneer in sponsoring the idea of Western Federation, but since then time has gone on, and he has been eclipsed by other figures." Snow to Bevin, 21 Sept. 1948, no. 218, ibid. "Anybody who joins forces with Bill Bullitt has some hideous

surprises in store for him" and "He is a viper of the first order" were two Whitehall comments on the significance of Bullitt's posture at Interlaken. FO Minutes, on "Formation in the U.S.A. of a 'Committee on a Free and United Europe,' by Mr. Bullitt who represented the Committee at the Interlaken Conference," FO 371/73097/HM 08238, PRO; Franks to Bevin, 26 Oct. 1948, no. 1304, PRO. Fulbright had been in Europe in the summer of 1948 and let it be known that "the British government seems to be at the moment undecided about the matter and reluctant to take any positive step on the political level. . . . I do not feel that they are doing enough and I believe that we should do our best to persuade them to take more positive leadership in this movement." Fulbright to Dr. Reginald Lang, 2 Oct. 1948, J. William Fulbright Papers, Univ. of Arkansas Library, Fayetteville.

125. C.P. (48) 249, "North Atlantic Treaty and Western Union," 2 Nov. 1948, pp. 6–8, FO 371/82/XY D7477, PRO; A.H. Robertson, *The Council of Europe: Its Strength, Functions and Achievements* (New York, 1956), p. 6. The compromise was smoothed by the willingness of the Executive Committee of the European Movement to offer a European consultative assembly alongside the council of ministers. The assembly would have no legislative powers. Frances E. Willis, first secretary of the American embassy to the United Kingdom, to S/S, 2 Dec. 1948, "Memorandum submitted by the Executive Committee of the European Movement to the Five Power Committee on European Unity," no. 2376, 840.00/12-248, RG 59, NARS. On December 21, 1948, Ambassador Caffery sent to the secretary of state "European Union," no. 1487, a draft of the future Council of Europe that combined British and French positions. It contained a consultative assembly along with ministers representing national governments. 840.00/12-2148, RG 5, NARS.

126. Memorandum, S/S for Foreign Affairs on North Atlantic Treaty and Western Union, 2 Nov. 1948, C.P. (48) 29, p. 8, FO 371/82/XY D477, PRO.

127. Ibid., p. 7.

6. COMPLETING THE TREATY

1. Adam B. Ulam, *Expansion and Coexistence: Soviet Foreign Policy, 1917–1973*, 2nd ed. (New York, 1974), pp. 486–87, 490–92.

2. Walter LaFeber, *America, Russia, and the Cold War, 1945–1980*, 4th ed. (New York, 1980), p. 83.

3. Robert Cecil, "Legends Spies Tell: A Reappraisal of the Absconding Diplomats," *Encounter* 50 (Apr. 1978): 11; for the role of Maclean see also Andrew Boyle, *The Fourth Man* (New York, 1979), p. 333. See chapter 5, n. 43, above.

4. LaFeber, *America, Russia, and the Cold War*, p. 83. *North Atlantic Treaty Hearings*, 1:203.

5. Acheson, *Present at the Creation*, p. 267.

6. See W. Phillips Davison, *The Berlin Blockade* (Princeton, 1958), pp. 270–80; Hans Herzfeld, *Berlin in der Weltpolitik, 1945–1970* (Berlin, 1973), pp. 269ff; note memorandum of conversation by Jessup, 5 Apr. 1949, *FRUS*, 1949, 3:714.

7. "With regard to the question of the establishment of a goverment in Western Germany, it is a well-known fact that the three Governments are proceeding with preparations for the establishment of such a Government. These preparations will continue." From Jessup's statement of 27 Apr. 1949, *FRUS*, 1949, 3:736. See also Philip C. Jessup, "Park Avenue Diplomacy— Ending the Berlin Blockade," *Political Science Quarterly* 87 (Sept. 1972): 377–400.

8. Acheson, *Present at the Creation*, pp. 272–73.

9. Kennan, *Memoirs, 1925–1950*, pp. 443ff.

10. Robert D. Murphy, *Diplomat among Warriors* (Garden City, N.Y., 1968), pp. 317, 321. Acheson ridiculed Murphy's view of the airlift as a surrender of American rights. This was "silly" to Acheson; *Present at the Creation*, p. 263.

11. Lucius Clay for Voorhees, 1 May 1949, in Jean Edward Smith, ed., *The Papers of General Lucius D. Clay*, 2 vols. (Bloomington, 1974), 2:1137–38.

12. Ulam, *Expansion and Coexistence*, p. 504.

13. Russian declaration delivered to Foreign Ministry, proposing a nonaggression pact, 5 Feb. 1949, in *Aftenposten*, 7 Feb. 1949, enclosed in telegram no. 51 of U.S. Ambassador C. Ulrick Bay to S/S, 10 Feb. 1949, *FRUS*, 1949, 4:92–93. See Grethe Vaernø, "Norway and the Atlantic Alliance, 1948–1949," *NATO Review* 29 (June 1981): 16–20.

14. See Harald Wigforss, "Sweden and the Atlantic Pact," *International Organization* 3 (Aug. 1949): 439. U.K. Ambassador Franks noted in March that Norway's objections to an early draft of Article 1 of the Treaty were based on its similarity to the language of the nonagression pact offered a month before by the Soviet Union.

15. Memorandum of the Soviet government on the North Atlantic Treaty, 31 Mar. 1949, in Alvin Z. Rubinstein, ed., *The Foreign Policy of the Soviet Union* (New York, 1960), pp. 268–69. Text also in *Pravda* and *Izvestia*, 1 and 2 Apr. 1949; in *Current Digest of the Soviet Press* 1, no. 11 (3 May 1949): 31–33. French reaction, denying any intention to repudiate the Franco-Soviet pact, was particularly strong. Auriol, *Journal du Septennat*, 14 Mar. 1949 3:155, and commentary in *Le Monde*, 3 and 4 Apr. 1949, which devoted almost as much space to responding to the Soviet charges as to the pact itself.

16. It is noteworthy that the Soviet press made a point of reproducing American comments depicting the alliance as bellicose and dangerous: "A union created for the purpose of war" from the *Chicago Tribune*, and a Society of Friends resolution deploring "division of the world into two rival camps." *Current Digest of the Soviet Press* 1, no. 14 (3 May 1949): 35, 39.

17. Lawrence S. Kaplan, "The United States, the NATO Treaty and the UN Charter," *NATO Letter* 17 (May 1969): 24–25; Plenary Meeting of UN General Assembly, 192nd Meeting, 13 Apr. 1949, *Official Records of the Third Session of the General Assembly*, pp. 62ff.

18. Kaplan, "United States, the NATO Treaty, and the UN Charter," p. 25. Plenary Meeting of UN General Assembly, 195th Meeting, 14 Apr. 1949, *Official Records of the Third Session of the General Assembly*, p. 129.

19. William Taubman found more optimism than pessimism in the Soviet self-image of 1949; *Stalin's American Policy: From Entente to Detente to Cold War* (New York, 1982), pp. 208–9.

20. Sir V. Mallet, Rome, to FO, 19 Mar. 1949, no. 343, FO 71, PRO.

21. Marshall D. Shulman, *Stalin's Foreign Policy Reappraised* (Cambridge, Mass., 1963), pp. 92–97.

22. Sir O. Harvey, Paris, to FO, 22 Jan. 1949, no. 96, FO 371/74214, PRO; Caffery, Paris, to S/S, 5 Jan. 1949, NARS 840.00/1-549. "From the time that the subject first became a live issue, there has been a suspicion at the back of many Frenchmen's minds that His Majesty's Government were opposed to the idea of European unity and that though for face-saving purposes, we would not refuse outright to discuss or even to participate in some scheme, our contribution would tend to be negative and our support lukewarm."

23. Kirk to Acting S/S, 20 Jan. 1949, *FRUS*, 1949, 4:40–41; Ambassador in France to S/S, 21 Jan. 1949, ibid., pp. 42–43.

24. Harvey to FO, 22 Jan. 1949, no. 96, FO 371/74214, PRO. Auriol observed that Schuman was going to London to point out to the British the importance of union to American public opinion; *Journal du Septennat*, 12 Jan. 1949, 3:9.

25. Frances E. Willis, U.S. Embassy in London, to S/S, 7 Mar. 1949, "Draft Proposal for a Council of Europe," no. 377, 840.00/3-749, RG 59, NARS.

26. For details of functions the cabinet discussion of 24 February 1949 made it clear that the key to British acceptance of the Council of Europe was that the "minister to the Assembly"

would not be constitutionally answerable to his colleagues in the assembly. 24 Feb. 1949, Cabinet 15 (49), CAB 128, vol. 5, PRO.

27. Jebb claimed, though, that he had suggested Strasbourg to Bevin not simply because he had been happy as a student there but because of its symbolic value; ibid., p. 225; Auriol, *Journal du Septennat*, 8 Feb. 1949, 2:97.

28. Hoyer Millar to Kirkpatrick, FO, 7 Jan. 1949, FO 371/79213, 1071/72, PRO; Kirkpatrick to Hoyer Millar, 24 Jan. 1949, FO 371/79213, 1071/72, PRO. Hoyer Millar claimed that the idea came from a remark of Thomas Finletter, head of the ECA in London.

29. *Extension of European Recovery Program Hearings*, Senate Committee on Foreign Relations, 81 Cong. 1 sess., 11 Feb. 1949, pp. 195–97.

30. Ibid., pp. 200–201.

31. "Signs of real progress by Western Europe towards closer political unity, the State Department think, would tend to have a beneficial effect upon the attitude of Congress both on E.R.P. and on the Atlantic Pact. Mr. Acheson is therefore anxious to be able to refer to as much information as possible on what has been accomplished." Franks to FO, 31 Jan. 1949, no. 611, FO 371/79243, PRO; FO to Franks, 2 Feb. 1949, no. 1320, FO 371/79243, PRO; Hoyer Millar to Jebb, 10 Feb. 1949, FO 371/10719/72, PRO.

32. Coudenhove-Kalergi to Duncan Sandys, executive president of the European Movement, 18 Jan. 1949; and Coudenhove-Kalergi to Fulbright, 2 Feb. 1949, Fulbright Papers. Allen Dulles of the American Committee on United Europe later informed Fulbright that the committee which Coudenhove-Kalergi had helped to establish had never met. The court's problem, Dulles believed, confirmed his own concerns about Americans becoming tied to any specific European group. Allen W. Dulles to Fulbright, 17 Feb. 1949, Fulbright Papers.

33. "It has become quite evident, of course, that the British are opposed to a federation and there is no question but that they have great influence with our Department of State." Fulbright to Coudenhove-Kalergi, 12 Feb. 1949; and Fulbright to Allen W. Dulles, 12 Feb. 1949, Fulbright Papers.

34. *Extension of European Recovery Program Hearings*, pp. 198–99.

35. Fulbright never ceased to regret that his amendments to the ECA in 1948 and 1949 supporting political unification of Europe were rejected. The Foreign Relations Committee, he believed, "rejected the cement" which was "indispensable to the salvation of the West and the prevention of another world war." *Congressional Record*, 81 Cong. 1 sess., 30 Mar. 1949, p. 3457.

36. Clay to ACSUSA, Washington, D.C., 16 Mar. 1949, no. FMPC 582, 840.00/3-1649, RG 59, NARS; Murphy to Riddlesberger, Berlin, 19 Mar. 1949, 840.00/3-1649, ibid.

37. Ambassador Franks recognized this situation in January. The issue of "Europe's inadequate progress towards federation is . . . not one to which I would attach much importance in connection with the Pact. I have repeatedly reported the desire of American opinion and Congress to see further steps taken in Western Europe towards political integration, and this will undoubtedly be a major talking point in discussions on Capitol Hill on the Pact but I do not think that Congress's acceptance of the Atlantic Pact is really likely to turn on this issue." Franks to FO, 31 Jan. 1949, no. 611, FO 371/79243, PRO.

38. *Extension of European Recovery Program Hearings*, p. 199.

39. *North Atlantic Treaty Hearings*, 2:368–69.

40. P.N. Crosthwaite, memo on Field Marshall Montgomery's task as chairman of the WU Commanders in Chief Committee, 24 Dec. 1948, FO 371/79247, PRO; Sir George Rendel to FO, 20 Jan. 1949, no. 18, FO 371/79248, ibid.; Auriol, *Journal du Septennat*, 21 Jan. 1949, 3:42.

41. Sir Oliver Harvey to Kirkpatrick, 26 Jan. 1949, FO 371, PRO. The British ambassador in Paris reported his embarrassment at Montgomery's stand.

42. A.A.D. Montague Browne, memo on French attitude to Brussels Treaty Defence Organization, 12 Jan. 1949, FO 371/79248, PRO. The memorandum of December 24, 1948, on Montgomery's tasks as chairman emphasized the view of de Lattre, that the commanders in chief were not to be subordinate to Montgomery, and Ramadier's position that the Chiefs of Staff Committee had exceeded their powers in allowing this; P.N. Crosthwaite, FO 371/79247, PRO. F.K. Roberts in a memo of January 29, 1949, on Montgomery's functions, observed that the French would prefer to consider the Chiefs of Staff Committee a "study group"; FO 371/79249, PRO.

43. In a "Note for the Record" of January 11, 1949, de Lattre professed to the British Defense Minister "the highest appreciation of Field Marshal Montgomery's ability and particularly of the efforts that the Field Marshal had made to understand his character"; FO 371/79248, PRO.

44. William R. Tyler, Memo of conversation between de Lattre and Public Affairs Officer of U.S. Embassy in Paris, 11 Feb. 1949, no. 165, 840.00/2-1440, RG 59, NARS. De Lattre made much the same statement to Auriol: "Les Anglais ne croient pas à la sécurité de l'Europe occidentale; ils jouent à la défaite et essaient d'avoir la défense des îles." *Journal du Septennat*, 21 Jan. 1949 3:42.

45. Kirkpatrick to General Hollis, 25 Jan. 1949, expressing also the feeling that Ramadier was "very narrow and obstinate" as well as subversive. This is a draft of a letter that was suspended, FO 371/79248, PRO. A few days before, Sir George Rendel, British Ambassador in Brussels, expressed his "fear that the French have been lobbying the Belgian military authorities and may even have got at the Minister of Defence himself." Rendel to FO, 20 Jan. 1949, no. 18, FO 371/79248, PRO.

46. Harvey to Kirkpatrick, 10 Jan. 1949, FO 371/79248, PRO.

47. A.A.D. Montague Browne, comments on Schuman statement in Council of the Republic on 1 Mar. 1949, 3 Mar. 1949, no. 240, FO 371/79230, PRO.

48. A.V. Alexander to Bevin, 2 Feb. 1949, FO 371/79250, PRO.

49. Schuman's statement to Council of the Republic, 1 Mar. 1949: "Nous sommes ainsi ramenés à l'objectif essentiel de la diplomatie française depuis 1918: obtenir, en faveur, d'une politique d'assistance mutuelle, l'adhésion des Etats-Unis qui diposent d'un potential industriel écrasant et dont la présence a nos côtes redrait certaine l'issue d'une eventuelle troisième guerre mondiale et soufirait donc toute vraisemblance a prévenir cette guerre." *Journal Officiel, Debats Parliamentaires*, 16th, séance du 1 mars 1949, p. 476.

50. René Courtain, "French Views on European Union," *International Affairs* 25 (Jan. 1949): 10.

51. Appendix B to Enclosure A of JCS 1868/58, 23 Nov. 1958, CD6-2-46 RG 330, NARS; Appendix A to Enclosure A of JCS 1868/58, 13 Jan. 1949, ibid. See also L.S. Kaplan, *A Community of Interests: NATO and the Military Assistance Program, 1948–1951* (Washington, D.C., 1980), p. 23.

52. Kaplan, *Community of Interests*, pp. 23–25.

53. "Military Assistance Program," JCS Report 1868/58, 11 Feb. 1949, p. 387, CD6-2-46, RG 330, NARS.

54. Kaplan, *Community of Interests*, p. 29.

55. Douglas to S/S, 2 Mar. 1949, no. 750, *FRUS*, 1949, 3:138; Caffery to S/S, 10 Mar. 1949, no. 1004, 840.20/3-1049, RG 59, NARS.

56. Kaplan, *Community of Interests*, pp. 30–31.

57. S/S to embassy in U.K., 4 Mar. 1949, no. 736, *FRUS*, 1949, 4:163; Douglas to S/S, 7 Mar. 1949, no. 821, ibid., p. 166; Verbatim Report, MAP, North Atlantic Pact Discussions, Washington, 2 Apr. 1949, RG 353, NARS; Douglas to S/S, 27 Mar. 1949, no. 1220, *FRUS*, 1949, 4:251–52; S/S to Embassy in Netherlands, 21 July 1949, N7-1(3)-A.3, RG 330, NARS.

58. Contrast FACC D-3, Draft No. 8, "Basic Policies of the Military Assistance Program," 7 Feb. 1949, *FRUS*, 1949, 1:256, with the more conciliatory spirit in S/S to Embassy in U.K., 12 Mar. 1949, *FRUS*, 1949, 4:196–97.

59. Douglas to S/S, 27 Mar. 1949, ibid., p. 251.

60. Douglas to S/S, 26 Mar. 1949, ibid., p. 251.

61. Douglas to S/S, 16 Mar. 1949, ibid., p. 231. Acting Secretary of State Lovett acknowledged even as he tried to mitigate the weight of the JCS concerns for allied bases, as expressed in a JCS memorandum, "Base Rights for the United States in Return for Military Aid to Foreign Nations," 31 Dec. 1948, ibid., 1948, 3:347; Lovett to S/D Forrestal, 17 Jan. 1949, ibid., 1949, 4:37–39.

62. Douglas to S/S, 16 Mar. 1949, ibid., p. 231. The ambassador's speculations about Bevin's attitude ranged from the foreign minister's "genuine concern that the WU countries approach to US should be completely on their own" to an attempt to "protect British leadership in the WU"; Douglas to S/S, 16 Mar. 1949, no. 1007, 840.00/13-1649, RG 59, NARS.

63. Douglas to S/S, 22 Mar. 1949, no. 1105, 840.20/3-2249, RG 59, NARS; Douglas to S/S, 23 Mar. 1949, no. 1124, ibid., Minutes, First Meeting, ECC, 25 Mar. 1949, *FRUS*, 1949, 4:245.

64. Reply of the U.S. government to the "Request from the Brussels Treaty Powers to the U.S. Government for Military Assistance," 6 Apr. 1949, *FRUS*, 1949, 4:287–88; see also Kaplan, *Community of Interests*, p. 32.

65. Kaplan, *Community of Interests*, p. 33. Ambassador Franks illustrated this spirit of equality when he claimed that the United States had "jumped the gun" in inviting the stepping-stone countries to be original signatories. The action "is not in accordance with the recommendation of the Permanent Commission which hoped that these countries would accede after the signature." Franks to FO, 8 Mar. 1949, no. 1371, FO 371/79231, PRO.

66. FACC to Douglas, 4 Apr. 1949, no. 1157, 840.00/4-449, RG 59, NARS.

67. See discussion in chapter 5, pp. 82-84, above.

68. Minutes, Fifth Meeting, Exploratory Talks, 9 July 1948, *FRUS*, 1948, 3:171. (See p. 83, above.)

69. Lovett used the term "arms pie" in a letter to Caffery, 24 Aug. 1948, cited in Reid, *Time of Fear and Hope*, p. 196.

70. See Memorandum by Participants, Exploratory Talks, 9 Sept. 1948, *FRUS*, 1948, 3:244; Forrestal to S/S, 10 Feb. 1949, JCS Memorandum, "Anticipated Position of Scandinavia in Strategic Considerations," ibid., 1949, 4:95ff.

71. See discussion in chapter 5, p. 83, above, for 1948 events. Harald Wigforss, "Sweden and the Atlantic Pact," *International Organization* 3 (Aug. 1949): 443.

72. Geir Lundestad, *America, Scandinavia, and the Cold War, 1945–1949* (New York, 1980), pp. 291–93, notes the vagueness of the Karlstad Formula; U.S. ambassador in Denmark to acting S/S, 10 Jan. 1949, *FRUS*, 1949, 4:17.

73. Ambassador in Sweden to acting S/S, 14 Jan. 1949, *FRUS*, 1949, 25–26; Memorandum of Conversation by the S/S with Swedish ambassador, 9 Feb. 1949, ibid., pp. 89–90; S/S to embassy in Norway, 13 Feb. 1949, on conversations between S/S and Norwegian Foreign Minister Halvord Lange, ibid., 102–6.

74. In an aide-memoire on February 9, 1949, the Irish government informed the State Department that "any military alliance with . . . the state that is responsible for the unnatural division of Ireland . . . would be entirely repugnant to the Irish people"; in file 283(s), part 7, "North Atlantic Security Pact," Canadian Department of External Affairs, Ottawa, cited in Reid, *Time of Fear and Hope*, p. 196.

75. There were no objections heard at an executive session of the Senate Foreign Relations Committee on February 18, 1949, when Acheson noted that "the Irish have made it quite clear that they will not want to participate in any arrangement unless this group will get the British to do

away with the division of Ireland, which is obviously a matter far beyond the scope of anything of this sort, so if the Irish take that view, they are out as far as participants in this proposed treaty are concerned." *The Vandenberg Resolution and North Atlantic Treaty, Hearings in Executive Session*, Senate Foreign Relations Committee, Historical Series, 18 Feb. 1949, p. 89.

76. Extract of letter from N. Pritchard, Office of U.K. Representative to Eire, to N.E. Archer, Commonwealth Relations Office, 7 Mar. 1949, FO 371/79235 8710, 1074/72, PRO.

77. Hoyer Millar to Hickerson, 6 Jan. 1949, FO 371/79222 8619, PRO; Memorandum of conversation by S/S with Irish Minister for External Affairs Sean MacBride, 11 Apr. 1949, *FRUS*, 1949, 4:293.

78. Ambassador in Portugal to S/S, 9 Mar. 1949, *FRUS*, 1949, 4:179ff; Ambassador in Portugal to S/S, ibid., 22 Mar. 1949, ibid., 243.

79. *Vandenberg Resolution and North Atlantic Treaty*, 18 Feb. 1949, p. 89; S/S to the embassy in Portugal, 14 Mar. 1949, *FRUS*, 1949, 4:201–2.

80. *Vandenberg Resolution and North Atlantic Treaty*, 6 June 1949, pp. 297–98.

81. Harvey to Bevin, 2 Mar. 1949, FO 371/79231 8710, 1074/72G, PRO.

82. Crosthwaite to Mallet and Shuckburgh, 1 Mar. 1949, FO 371/79229 8710, 1074/726, PRO.

83. A.A.D. Montague Browne to Oliver Harvey, 1 Mar. 1949, "North Atlantic Pact: French attitude regarding inclusion of Italy and Algeria," FO 371/79229 8710, 1074/726, PRO.

84. The term is Escott Reid's (*Time of Fear and Hope*, p. 120), and its validity is confirmed in E. Timothy Smith, "The Fear of Subversion: The United States and the Inclusion of Italy in the North Atlantic Treaty," *Diplomatic History* 7 (Spring 1983): 151–53.

85. See memorandum by the JCS for S/D, "North Atlantic Pact," 5 Jan. 1949, *FRUS*, 1949, 4:13.

86. Bradley observed to his British counterpart that if the Italians were not in NATO, they would "probably be ripe to accede to Soviet demands on outbreak of war, and even go communist"; T. Hollis to G. Jebb, 20 Jan. 1949, FO 371/79222 8619, PRO; Hickerson to McWilliams, 24 Nov. 1948, 840.20/11-2448, RG 59, Box C-510, NARS. Interview with John D. Hickerson by E. Timothy Smith, 18 June 1980.

87. Interview with Hickerson by E. Timothy Smith, 18 June 1980.

88. Acheson memorandum of conversation with Truman, 28 Feb. 1949, *FRUS*, 1949, 4:125.

89. Acheson memorandum of conversation with Senators Connally, George, and Vandenberg, 28 Feb. 1949, 840.20/2-2849, RG 59, NARS.

90. Memorandum by S/S of discussion with Truman, 2 Mar. 1949, *FRUS*, 1949, 4:141.

91. V. Mallet, Rome, to FO, 1 Mar. 1949, no. 280, FO 371/79229 8710, PRO.

92. Memorandum by S/S of discussion with Truman, 2 Mar. 1949, *FRUS*, 1949, 4:141.

93. Acheson, *Present at the Creation*, pp. 223–24.

94. Kennan, *Memoirs*, pp. 427–28.

95. Vandenberg, *Private Papers*, p. 500. Italics included.

96. Vandenberg could not resist commenting on an article by Joseph Alsop claiming that Connally "openly resented" Vandenberg's preeminence. As he wrote his wife on July 31, 1949, "I was . . . amused today at Alsop's column. This will make old Tawm [Connally] fairly burn in his boots." Ibid., pp. 505–6. Franks saw less humor in this situation: Connally "is of course a man of lesser calibre and may not fully understand the issues involved. But I suspect that he is jealous of Vandenberg and disposed to be difficult about the North Atlantic Pact on the grounds that it derives largely from the Vandenberg Resolution." Franks to FO, 15 Feb. 1949, no. 939, FO 371/79225 8630, 1074/72, PRO.

97. Quoted in Ronald Steel, *Walter Lippmann and the American Century* (Boston, 1980), pp. 458–59.

98. Condit, *History of the JCS*, 2:291.

99. Memo (Top Secret), DJS to Generals Wedemeyer and Norstad and Admiral Struble, 25 Feb. 1949, in ibid., 2:296. From this advice the plan OFFTACKLE was made with final approval on December 8, 1949.

100. See Claude Delmas, "France and the Creation of the Atlantic Alliance," *NATO Review* 28 (Aug. 1980): 3–24. The particular citation was noted by the U.K. Ambassador to France in a cable to FO, 26 Feb. 1949, no. 49, FO 371/79251 8710, PRO.

101. Minutes, Twelfth Meeting, Exploratory Talks, 8 Feb. 1949, *FRUS*, 1949, 4:73–75. *Le Monde*, 19 Feb. 1949, found the Senate's discussion to have taken "un tour quelque byzantin."

102. Minutes, Twelfth Meeting, Exploratory Talks, 8 Feb. 1949, *FRUS*, 1949, 4:74, 85.

103. Reid, *Time of Fear and Hope*, p. 150.

104. Minutes, Twelfth Meeting, Exploratory Talks, 8 Feb. 1949, *FRUS*, 1949, 4:76. Chauvel in Paris noted in particular that since "the text preferred by the Western European Powers had been publicised together with the modification proposed by the Senators, any subsequent adjustment of our position would appear to the public opinion as a surrender to Soviet pressure." Harvey to FO, 17 Feb. 1949, no. 173, FO 371/79226/8647, PRO.

105. Acheson, *Present at the Creation*, p. 281. Acheson observed that Donnell "was not my favorite Senator. He combined the courtliness of Mr. Pickwick and suavity of an experienced waiter with the manner of a prosecuting attorney in the movies—the gimlet eye, the piercing question. In administering the *coup de grace* he would do it with a napkin over his arm and his ears sticking out perpendicularly like an alert elephant's." Hoyer Millar's description is a little less colorful: "A constitutional lawyer in private life with a rather precise, not to say fussy mind," to Gladwyn, 17 Feb. 1949, FO 371/79230, PRO; *Congressional Record*, 81 Cong. 1 sess., 14 Feb. 1949, 95:1163.

106. Franks observed that "Connally's intervention was lamentable and served only to make matters infinitely worse. Senator Borah himself could hardly have done better with his remarks cautioning the United States against playing the role of Sir Galahad and plunging into war every time a gun was fired and similar inanities such as letting European nations declare war and letting us fight." Franks to FO, 15 Feb. 1949, no. 938, FO 371/79225 8630, PRO.

107. Franks felt that Vandenberg's role was somewhat different: "He undoubtedly wants a strong pact and I am not too worried about what he said yesterday in the Senate. It is part of his technique, if he wants something badly, to avoid showing his feelings too obviously in the early stage. He may have felt yesterday that he would only have stultified his position had he disclosed his full support for the pact." Franks to FO, 15 Feb. 1949, no. 939, FO 371/79925 8630, PRO. Acheson did note that immediately after the explosion on the floor Vandenberg emphasized that action under Article 5 "should be a matter for individual determination and also that the word 'military' should be omitted." Memorandum of conversation by the S/S with Connally and Vandenberg, 14 Feb. 1949, *FRUS*, 1949, 4:109.

108. Connally recommended "as it may deem necessary" to make plain that "military" may not be deemed necessary; *FRUS*, 1949, 4:109. Bevin expressed his anxiety also when he claimed that by removing "the crucial sentence to the effect that an attack against one or more of the signatories is an attack against them all," it does damage. "The sentence does not bind the United States to any action, but it has great psychological value for the European countries"; FO to Washington, 17 Feb. 1949, no. 1932 FO 371/79226 8647, 1074/726, PRO; FO to Paris, Brussels, the Hague, 16 Feb. 1949, no. 447, FO 371/79226 8647, PRO.

109. Memorandum by the S/S for Foreign Affairs, 19 Feb. 1949, "North Atlantic Pact," C.P. (49)34, pp. 1–2, CAB 129/32 8605, PRO. See also Alexander M. Rendel, "Uncertainty Continues as Atlantic Treaty Nears Completion," *NATO Review* 28 (Apr. 1980): 15–18.

110. Franks to FO, 15 Feb. 1949, no. 939, FO 371/79225 8630, PRO.

111. Memorandum, Bohlen to S/S, 16 Feb. 1949, *FRUS*, 1949, 4: 113–16; memorandum of conversation by Acheson with the president on North Atlantic Pact, 17 Feb. 1949, ibid., p. 117; oral history interview with Theodore Achilles by Richard D. McKinzie, 13 Nov. and 18 Dec. 1972, p. 42, Harry S. Truman Library, Independence, Mo.

112. Vandenberg to Dulles, 19 Mar. 1949; and Dulles to Vandenberg, 21 Mar. 1949, John Foster Dulles Collection, Seeley G. Mudd Library, Princeton University.

113. For a time there was some thought of postponing signing until April 9 since Churchill had been scheduled for a dinner with Truman on March 24 and was not to return until April 8. Instead, Churchill postponed his trip, to the relief of the Foreign Office, which feared a Soviet peace offensive at the UN on April 5, 1949. FO to embassy in Washington, 11 Mar. 1949 no. 2883, PRO.

114. *New York Times*, 2 Apr. 1949. See also Trygve Lie, *In the Cause of Peace: Seven Years with the United Nations* (New York, 1954), pp. 439–40.

115. To a Michigan correspondent he wrote on February 21, 1949, that "we can achieve every essential result for the North Atlantic Pact by staying strictly within the Constitution of the United States and within the Charter of the United Nations." Vandenberg, *Private Papers*, p. 478; see also 43, above.

116. Acheson's observations in minutes, Sixteenth Meeting, Exploratory Talks, 7 Mar. 1949, *FRUS*, 1949, 4:170–71.

117. Franks to FO, 8 Mar. 1949, no. 1365; E.M. Rose memorandum, 11 Mar. 1949: "I certainly think it undesirable to state that the Pact is a regional arrangement. There never has been such a thing yet under the Charter (the pan-American Union is the nearest), at least no one has specifically claimed that their organization was a regional arrangement. . . . Nor do we know what precedents we may be creating for the future"; in 14 Mar. 1949 commentary by Roger Allen. The foregoing represent views of the Foreign Office's UN Department, FO 371/79233, 1074/72G, PRO.

118. Jessup speech in *New York Times*, 9 Feb. 1949; Hoyer Millar to Jebb, FO 371/79229 8710, PRO. E. Beckett commentary on U.S. State Department's views on the Charter, 9 Mar. 1949, FO 371/79233, PRO.

119. Minutes, Twelfth Meeting, Exploratory Talks, 8 Feb. 1949, *FRUS*, 1949, 4:86.

120. See Reid, *Time of Fear and Hope*, p. 170. Reid speculated that Acheson regarded the article as "an unnecessary and complicating factor with Congress as well as a possible duplication of existing bilateral agreements between the United States and its European allies under the ECA." Reid to chargé d'affairs in Stockholm, 22 Feb. 1949, Reid Papers, vol. 7, 283(s), Public Archives of Canada, Ottawa.

121. Lovett's comments in minutes, Ninth Meeting, Exploratory Talks, 13 Dec. 1948, *FRUS*, 1948, 3:318. Connally's analogy was expressed in a memorandum from Achilles to Reid in 1976, quoted in *Time of Fear and Hope*, p. 173. Acheson, according to Hickerson, said that he "didn't like [Article 2] worth a damn"; ibid., p. 178.

122. Reid, *Time of Fear and Hope*, p. 177; Franks to FO, 26 Feb. 1949, FO 371/79229 8710, PRO.

123. Ambassador Bonnet's statement included Italy and Norway in France's consideration; minutes, Fourteenth Meeting, Exploratory Talks, 1 Mar. 1949, *FRUS*, 1949, 9:129.

124. Lovett pointed out that "US military advisers doubted seriously the wisdom of including Algeria and it was necessary to find some way of meeting the views of all the various parties." Minutes, Eleventh Meeting, Exploratory Talks, 14 Jan. 1949, ibid., p. 32. Bonnet mentioned that "the omission of Algeria would be as difficult to justify in France as the exclusion of some of the northern territories in Canada and the United States." Minutes, Twelfth Meeting, Exploratory Talks, 8 Feb. 1949, ibid., p. 87.

125. Ibid., p. 87. Reid speculated that if a Franco-American deal on Algeria had been made in January, Italy might not have entered NATO in April; *Time of Fear and Hope*, p. 217.

126. Achilles interview, Truman Library, pp. 63–64.

127. Memorandum, Hickerson to S/S, 17 Feb. 1949, *FRUS*, 1949, 4:120–21; minutes, conference of foreign ministers at Washington, 2 Apr. 1949, ibid., pp. 272–73.

128. Condit, *History of the JCS*, 2:383–84.

129. Reid, *Time of Fear and Hope*, p. 187.

130. Minutes, Eleventh Meeting, Exploratory Talks, 14 Jan. 1949, *FRUS*, 1949, 4:33.

131. Jebb to Bevin, 26 Jan. 1949, FO 371/79224, PRO.

132. Franks to FO, 4 Mar. 1949, no. 1285, FO 371/79231, PRO; Shuckburgh memorandum to Jebb, 9 Mar. 1949, FO 371/79231, PRO.

133. FO to embassy in Washington, 7 Mar. 1949, no 2589, FO 371/79231, PRO; Franks to FO, 8 Mar. 1949, no. 1371, FO 371/79231, PRO.

134. Franks to FO, 14 Mar. 1949, no 1487, FO 371/79232, PRO; FO Minutes, 14 Mar. 1949, FO 371/79232, PRO.

135. *New York Times*, 5 Apr. 1949; Acheson, *Present at the Creation*, p. 274.

136. Achilles interview, Truman Library, pp. 71–72; Dalton Diary, 20 Mar. 1949, Hugh Dalton Papers, I 37 (5), London School of Economics.

7. TREATY TO ORGANIZATION

1. Ismay, *NATO*, p. 23; requests from "Brussels Treaty Powers to the U.S. Government for Military Assistance," 5 Apr. 1949, *FRUS*, 1949, 4:285–87.

2. U.S. reply, 6 Apr. 1949, *FRUS*, 1949, 4:287–88.

3. Memorandum, Kennan for Rusk, 7 Sept. 1949, ibid., 1:382; minutes, 171st Meeting, Policy Planning Staff, 16 Dec. 1949, ibid., p. 414.

4. Memorandum, Kennan to acting S/S, 1 June 1949, ibid., 4:301.

5. *Vandenberg Resolution and North Atlantic Treaty*, 8 Mar. 1949, pp. 158–59; memorandum of conversation, 24 June 1949, Acheson Papers.

6. Memorandum of conversation, 24 June 1949, Acheson Papers.

7. *Vandenberg Resolution and North Atlantic Treaty*, pp. 180–81.

8. Ibid., p. 174.

9. Record of discussions at meeting of Senate Committee on Foreign Relations, *FRUS*, 1949, 1:288–91; memorandum of conversation with Truman, 12 May 1949, 840.20/5-1249, RG 59, NARS.

10. Central Intelligence Agency, "Review of the World Situation," 15 June 1949, p. 6, President's Secretary File, Harry S. Truman Library, Independence, Mo.; Caffery to S/S, 7 Apr. 1949, *FRUS*, 1949, 4:288–89.

11. S/S to embassy in France, 10 Aug. 1949, *FRUS*, 1949, 4:318; Bonbright to S/S, 15 Aug. 1949, ibid., p. 320. See also Ireland, *Creating the Entangling Alliance*, pp. 160–61.

12. Minutes, 6th session, Consultative Council of Western Union, Luxembourg, 17–18 June 1949, 2nd Plenary Meeting, 18 June 1949, Metric Document no. 277, DG 1/1/2, Western European Union Archives, London.

13. *North Atlantic Treaty Hearings*, 19 May 1949, 3:1153; 17 May 1949, 3:1097.

14. See for example the exchange between Acheson and Senators Donnell and Watkins, ibid., 1:62–87.

15. *Congressional Record*, 81 Cong. 1 sess., 11 July 1949, p. 9206; S. Res. 134, ibid., 14 July 1949, p. 9422.

16. See L.S. Kaplan, "NATO and the Language of Isolationism," *South Atlantic Quarterly* 57 (Spring 1958): 214–15.

17. *North Atlantic Treaty Hearings*, 16 May 1949, 3:1007.

18. *Department of State Bulletin* 20 (27 Mar. 1949): 386.

19. See Warren Austin testimony, *North Atlantic Treaty Hearings*, 28 Apr. 1949, 1:117.

20. Vandenberg telegram to Dulles, 2 May 1949, Vandenberg Papers, Bentley Historical Library, University of Michigan, Ann Arbor.

21. Memorandum of conversation, 24 June 1949, Official Conversations of Acheson, RG 59, NARS.

22. Kaplan, *Community of Interests*, p. 44.

23. Vandenberg to Walter Lippmann, 9 Aug. 1949, Vandenberg Papers.

24. *Military Assistance Program Hearings*, Committee on International Relations, Selected Executive Session, 29 July 1949, U.S. House of Representatives, Historical Series, 1:30–31.

25. Ibid., p. 33.

26. Ibid., p. 30.

27. *Military Assistance Program Hearings*, Senate, Committees on Foreign Relations and Armed Services, 81 Cong. 1 sess., 9 Aug. 1949, p. 49.

28. "Seventh Periodic Informal Progress Report on the Accomplishments of DELWU, for the period 15 May–15 June 1949," prepared for S/D, Records of the JCS, RG 218, NARS.

29. "Eighth Periodic Informal Progress Report on the Accomplishments of DELWU for the period 15 June–15 July 1949," prepared for S/D Records of the JSC, RG 218, NARS.

30. Minutes, 71st meeting, WU Permanent Commission, London, 26 May 1949, D 1/2/4, Western European Union Archives, London.

31. The sum originally recommended by the JCS had been $1.786 billion. The president fixed the amount at $1.45 billion to be requested of Congress on April 20, 1949. See Condit, *History of the JCS*, 2:429–30.

32. Memorandum, Gross to S/S, 6 Aug. 1949, *FRUS*, 1949, 1: 379; *Military Assistance Program Hearings*, Senate, Committees on Foreign Relations and Armed Services, 9 Aug. 1949, p. 49.

33. *Military Assistance Program Hearings*, 9 Aug. 1949, p. 78.

34. See Kaplan, *Community of Interests*, pp. 33–34.

35. Summary minutes, Second Meeting at American embassy, European Coordinating Committee, London, 2 June 1949, ECC/M/39/2, RG 330, NARS; Holmes to S/S, 10 June 1949, *FRUS*, 1949, 4:304.

36. PL 329, Mutual Defense Assistance Act of 1949, Title I, secs. 101, 102, 103, 81 Cong. 1 sess., *U.S. Statutes at Large*, 1949, 63, pt. 1:715–16.

37. Acheson, *Present at the Creation*, p. 313. Statement by the president on announcing the first atomic explosion in the U.S.S.R., 23 Sept. 1949, *Public Papers of the Presidents, Harry S. Truman*, 1949:485.

38. *New York Times*, 29 Sept. 1949; undated, 1949, Box 229, Papers of Tom Connally, Library of Congress.

39. See particularly memorandum, Twitchell for Duff, et al., 7 Oct. 1949, with Harriman's telegram attached, N7-1(1)-F3, RG 330, NARS.

40. Kaplan, *Community of Interests*, pp. 61–62.

41. Minutes, 90th meeting, WU Permanent Commission London, 15 Nov. 1949, DG1/2/5, Western European Union Archives, London.

42. Kaplan, *Community of Interests*, pp. 62–64.

43. R.L. Hall to Sir Leslie Rowan, "'Integration': Personal Impressions of the Implications of Economic Integration," 3 Jan. 1950, FO 371/87136/B9048, UR 3211/2, PRO.

44. Frances E. Willis, first secretary, American embassy, to S/S, "Official British Attitude toward the Council of Europe," 12 May 1949, no. 813, 840.00/5-1249, RG 59, NARS; Armin Rappaport, "The United States and European Integration: The First Phase," *Diplomatic History* 5 (Spring 1981): 137.

45. Douglas to S/S, "The Council of Europe," 12 Apr. 1949, no. 2690, 840.00/4-849,

RG 59, NARS; Dalferes to S/S, 19 Aug. 1949, no. 29, 840.00/8-1049, RG 59, NARS.

46. *Department of State Bulletin* 21 (22 Aug. 1949): 269. See also *FRUS*, 1949, 4:317–18.

47. Kennan, *Memoirs*, p. 476.

48. 78th meeting, 17 May 1949, Policy Planning Staff Records, RG 59, NARS.

49. Ibid.

50. 92nd meeting, 3 June 1949, ibid.

51. 93rd meeting, 6 June 1949, ibid.

52. Ibid.; 101st meeting, 14 June 1949, ibid.

53. Kennan, *Memoirs*, pp. 483, 489.

54. Clayton Roberts and Patterson, exchanges with Fulbright, *North Atlantic Treaty Hearings*, 2:390–91, 565, 613.

55. *New York Times*, 28 Oct. 1949.

56. Frederick T. Roper, USUN, to Howard Johnson, UNA/P, 9 Dec. 1949, 840.00/12-2249, RG 59, NARS; Johnson to Hickerson, 16 Dec. 1949, commenting on a draft position paper on the Atlantic Union Resolution, ibid; Hickerson's response to Johnson, 22 Dec. 1949, ibid.

57. Streit to Bevin, 12 Sept. 1949, AN 3196/10210/45, PRO; Aubrey Neil Morgan to Bevin, 14 Sept. 1949, ibid.; Bevin's regrets to Streit, 15 Sept. 1949, ibid.

58. 101st meeting, Policy Planning Staff Records, RG 59, NARS.

59. Personal message of Bevin to S/S, 25 Oct. 1949, enclosed in communication from Hoyer Millar to S/S, 26 Oct. 1949, *FRUS*, 1949, 4:348.

60. Rappaport, "United States and European Integration," p. 139.

61. Millard to S/S, 27 Oct. 1949, *FRUS*, 1949, 4:438.

62. Paul G. Hoffman, "An Expanding Economy through Economic Integration: The Major Task of Western Europe," *Vital Speeches* 16 (15 Nov. 1949): 68–70; memorandum of conversation, James E. Webb, "ECA Adminstrator Hoffman's forthcoming trip to Europe," 3 Nov. 1949, NARS. Rappaport notes that "although not as sanguine as Hoffman," there was substantial agreement between State and the ECA over the approach to European integration. State's caveats, however, seem to suggest that the harmony was more apparent than real. Rappaport, "United States and European Integration," p. 140. See also Ireland, *Creating the Entangling Alliance*, pp. 164–65.

63. Kennan, *Memoirs*, p. 478.

64. Sir Leslie Rowan, British embassy, Washington, to R.L. Hall, 20 Mar. 1950, 3211/13, FO 371/87137 9059, PRO. Italics included.

65. Acheson memorandum for Truman on documents on negotiations on Germany, 8 Apr. 1949, *FRUS*, 1949, 3: 176. See also Ireland, *Creating the Entangling Alliance*, p. 138.

66. *North Atlantic Treaty Hearings*, 2 May 1949, 1:282.

67. Ibid., 2:341; *Vandenberg Resolution and North Atlantic Treaty*, 2 June 1949, pp. 271–72. See Ireland, *Creating the Entangling Alliance*, p. 139.

68. On slender evidence Ireland concluded that the Senate report had supported the inclusion of Germany in the partnership. See *Creating the Entangling Alliance*, p. 140.

69. *North Atlantic Treaty Hearings*, 29 Apr. 1949, 1:201; 2 May 1949, 1:281; 27 Apr. 1949, 1:61.

70. See report in *New York Times*, 22 Nov. 1949.

71. 93rd meeting, 6 June 1949, Policy Planning Staff Records, RG 59, NARS.

72. Minutes, 89th meeting, WU Permanent Commission, London, 28 Oct. 1949, DG 1/2/5, WEU Archives.

73. Robert Murphy, acting director of the Office of German and Austrian Affairs, recognized the problem in his memorandum of 23 Mar. 1949, *FRUS*, 1949, 3:133–34.

74. Bruce to S/S, 22 Oct. 1949, ibid., 4:343. Bohlen was particularly emphatic on the need of Britain to offset Germany in his communications with Kennan. He felt that Kennan's visit to

Britain had been used by the British to weaken this relationship. See in particular his letter to Kennan, 29 Oct. 1949, Kennan Papers, Seeley G. Mudd Library, Princeton Univ.

75. Kennan to Bohlen, 7 Nov. 1949, ibid.; 81st meeting, Policy Planning Staff, 20 May 1949, RG 59, NARS; Kennan, *Memoirs*, pp. 480–81.

76. Kennan to Bohlen, 12 Oct. 1949, Kennan Papers, Seeley G. Mudd Library, Princeton University.

77. Acheson's memorandum of conversation with the president disavowing talk of rearming Germany, 17 Nov. 1949, Acheson Papers; memorandum of conversation with Henri Bonnet, French ambassador, 1 Dec. 1949, ibid.

78. Minutes, 95th meeting, WU Permanent Commission, London, 22 Dec. 1949, DG 1/2/4, WEU Archives, London.

79. These are Acheson's words but Bonnet's thoughts, as expressed in the secretary's conversation with French Foreign Minister Schuman; S.S. to acting S/S, 26 Sept. 1949, *FRUS*, 1949, 4:338–39. The same term, "historic policy decision" appeared in a letter from Kennan to Bohlen, 12 Oct. 1949, Kennan Papers.

80. Both of the above communications referred to an article published by the Alsop brothers on September 2 and one by Walter Lippmann on September 26 hinting that Kennan was the inspiration for this decision to separate the U.S., Britain, and Canada from the rest of Europe in NATO. Kennan claimed that Stewart Alsop was willing to say that none of this information came from him.

81. Auriol, *Journal du Septennat*, 30 Dec. 1949, 3:240–41.

82. R.M. Cheseldine to Byroade, 14 Dec. 1949 (a personal note), *FRUS*, 1949, 3:355–59.

83. See Kaplan, *Community of Interests*, p. 54.

84. The first three sessions, on September 17 and November 18, 1949, and January 6, 1950, were all held in Washington. See Ismay, *NATO*, pp. 24–27.

85. See minutes, American Group on Pact Organization, AGPO M-1, 15 Aug. 1949, CD 6-4-18, RG 330, NARS: AGPO M-3, 17 Aug. 1949, ibid.

86. S/S to embassy in Italy, 12 Aug. 1949, *FRUS*, 1949, 4:219–20; Condit, *History of the JCS*, pp. 383ff.; report by Joint Strategic Plans Committee to JCS on "The JCS Position on British-U.S. Cooperation for Planning within the NAT," Records of the JCS, 1946–53, part 2, reel 4, RG 218, NARS; Ismay, *NATO*, p. 25.

87. JCS 1868/100, 19 Aug. 1949, pp. 730–31, 092, Western Europe (3-12-48), RG 218, NARS.

88. See minutes, American Group on Pact Organization (AGPO)M-1, 15 Aug. 1949; S/S to embassy in U.K., 13 Aug. 1949, *FRUS*, 1949, 4:321–22; JCS 1868/114, 21 Sept. 1949, Enclosure D on proposed military organization under NATO, Records of the JCS, RG 218, NARS.

89. Commentary on status of North Atlantic Pact Organization, AGPO, 15 Aug. 1949; Halaby, memo for S/D, 18 Nov. 1949, on second meeting, North Atlantic Council (NAC), enclosing report to NAC on Defense Financial and Economic Committee (DFEC), 17 Nov. 1949, CD 125-2-1, RG 330, NARS.

90. Kaplan, *Community of Interests*, p. 54.

91. Portuguese Foreign Minister Caeiro da Matta made his country's position clear in a meeting with Acheson two days before the Treaty was signed. See minutes, conference of foreign ministers, 2 Apr. 1949, Washington, *FRUS*, 1949, 4:274–77; conversations on North Atlantic Pact with countries other than Canada and Brussels Pact countries, 21 Apr. 1949, PACT D-6/2, RG 59, NARS.

92. S/S to embassy in Italy, 3 Sept. 1949, *FRUS*, 1949, 4:323–24; Dunn to S/S, 17 Sept. 1949, ibid., p. 329. Memorandum for Mr. MacKay by D.C. Crean, 23 Aug. 1949, on conversation in Ottawa concerning Italian ambassador's interest in Canada's joining the Steering Group; Department of External Affairs Records, Ottawa.

93. Cyrus L. Sulzberger in *New York Times*, 1 May 1949.

94. Acheson, *Present at the Creation*, p. 329.

95. N.E. Halaby, chairman, report by the Military Production and Supply Board to the North Atlantic Defense Committee on "A Concept for Providing Production and Supply of Munitions under the North Atlantic Treaty," D.C. 4, pp. 1–4, White House Central Files, Harry S. Truman Library, Independence, Mo.

96. Proceedings, second meeting, North Atlantic Defense Committee, Paris, 1 Dec. 1949, pp. 22ff, White House Central Files, Harry S. Truman Library; memorandum of conversation, S/S with S/D, 16 Dec. 1949, *FRUS*, 1949, 4:362–64.

97. Memorandum, Twitchell for Duff et al., 7 Oct. 1949, with Harriman's telegram attached, N7-1(1)-F3, RG 330, NARS: N.E. Halaby, memorandum for S/D, 4 Oct. 1949, CD6-4-18, ibid.

98. N.E. Halaby, memorandum for S/D, 4 Oct. 1949, CD6-4-18, ibid.

99. Condit, *History of the JCS*, 2:294–302.

100. Roger Hilsman, "NATO: The Developing Strategic Context," in Klaus Knorr, ed., *NATO and American Security* (Princeton, 1959), p. 14.

101. The Standing Group issued a directive on January 4, 1950, setting July 1, 1954, as the target date for completion of build-up; S.G. 13/16, 4 Jan. 1950, CCS 092 W. Europe (3-12-48), sec. 40, RG 218, NARS.

102. The JCS found this plan too expensive and asked their representative on the Standing Group, General Bradley, to seek a more "realistic" estimation of NATO's needs. JCS, memorandum for NATO Standing Group, 22 Mar. 1950, on NATO Medium Term Defense Plan, RG 218, NARS.

103. The strategic concept of the integrated defense of the North Atlantic area was approved by the Defense Committee on December 1. The text is in *FRUS*, 1949, 4:353–56; Truman, memorandum for S/S, 27 Jan. 1950, "NATO Strategic Concept," Central Files, Box 25, Truman Library.

8. THE IMPACT OF THE KOREAN WAR

1. Harry S. Truman, *Memoirs*, vol. 2, *Years of Trial and Hope* (Garden City, N.Y., 1956), p. 333.

2. Merle Miller, *Plain Speaking: An Oral Biography of Harry S. Truman* (Berkley, 1973), p. 274.

3. Charles E. Bohlen, *Witness to History, 1929–1969* (New York), p. 304.

4. See discussion in *International Security* 4 (Fall 1979): 116–58, by Samuel F. Wells, Jr., "Sounding the Tocsin: NSC 68 and the Soviet Threat"; and responses by John L. Gaddis and Paul Nitze, "NSC 68 and the Soviet Threat Reconsidered," ibid., 4 (Spring 1980): 164–76.

5. See Paul Y. Hammond, "NSC-68: Prologue to Rearmament," in Warner R. Schilling, Paul Y. Hammond, and Glenn H. Snyder, *Strategy, Politics and Defense Budgets* (New York, 1962), p. 306; see also NSC-68, Apr. 14, 1950, *FRUS*, 1950, 1:235–92.

6. Hammond, "NSC-68," p. 319.

7. Acheson, *Present at the Creation*, p. 425; Gaddis Smith, *Dean Acheson* (New York, 1972), p. 161; Ronald J. Stupak, *The Shaping of Foreign Policy: The Role of Secretary of State as Seen by Dean Acheson* (Indianapolis, 1969), p. 36.

8. Ronald Steel, *Imperialists and Other Heroes: A Chronicle of the American Empire* (New York, 1971), p. 17; Kolko and Kolko, *Limits of Power*, pp. 508–9.

9. Richard J. Barnet, *Roots of War* (New York, 1972), p. 273.

10. David S. McLellan and John M. Reuss, "Foreign and Military Policies," in Richard S. Kirkendall, ed., *The Truman Period as a Research Field* (Columbia, Mo., 1967), p. 34.

11. Lloyd C. Gardner, "Truman Era Foreign Policy: Recent Historical Trends," in Kirkendall, *Truman Period*, p. 63.

12. "Domino" was first applied to Indochina in a press conference of President Eisenhower on April 7, 1954; see *Public Papers of the Presidents of the United States, 1947–1955* (Washington, D.C., 1964), 1954, p. 383.

13. Stephen E. Ambrose, "The Failure of a Policy Rooted in Fear," *Progressive* 34, no. 11 (Nov. 1970): 18.

14. Norman Graebner offered a different view of the Korean War's effect on the election of 1952: "The tragedy of the campaign was that Eisenhower, who had been nominated to quell the neo-isolationist tendencies in the Republican party, had actually tightened the grip of such views on the party." *The New Isolationism: A Study in Politics and Foreign Policy since 1950* (New York, 1956), p. 109.

15. See William Adams Brown, Jr., and Redvers Opie, *American Foreign Assistance* (Washington, D.C., 1953), p. 482.

16. See Roger Hilsman, "NATO: The Developing Strategic Concept," in *NATO and American Security*, ed. Klaus Knorr (Princton, 1959), p. 14.

17. *Mutual Defense Assistance Program Hearings*, U.S. Congress, Senate Committees on Foreign Relations and Armed Services, 81 Cong. 2 sess., 2 June 1950, p. 15.

18. Reports of Communist plans to stop shipments at French docks, *New York Times*, 28 Jan. 1950; at British docks, ibid., 26 Apr. 1950.

19. *Le Monde*, 5 Apr. 1950.

20. *MDAP Hearings*, 2 June 1950, p. 12.

21. *North Atlantic Treaty Hearings*, 1 sess., 27 Apr. 1949, pp. 57–61; cited in Laurence W. Martin, "The American Decision to Rearm Germany," in *American Civil-Military Decision: A Book of Case Studies*, ed. Harold Stein (Birmingham, Ala., 1963), p. 646.

22. *To Amend the Mutual Defense Assistance Act of 1949, Hearings*, U.S. Congress, House Committee on Foreign Affairs, 81 Cong. 2 sess., June 1950, p. 22; cited in Martin, "American Decision to Rearm Germany," p. 645.

23. Adenauer, *Memoirs*, p. 267.

24. Stikker, *Men of Responsibility*, p. 297.

25. Peter Calvocoressi, ed., *Survey of International Affairs: 1949–50* (London, 1953), p. 155.

26. "United States Interests, Positions, and Tactics at Paris," *FRUS*, 1949, 3:295.

27. Ibid., pp. 295–96.

28. Quoted in Martin, "American Decision to Rearm Germany," p. 650.

29. *New York Times*, 5 July 1950.

30. Adenauer, *Memoirs*, p. 273.

31. "Final Communique," Fourth Session, North Atlantic Council, London, 19 May 1950, in Ismay, *NATO*, p. 183.

32. *Reviews of the World Situation, 1949–50, Hearings*, U.S. Congress, Senate Committee on Foreign Relations, 81 Cong. 2 sess., 24 July 1950, p. 320.

33. *Supplemental Appropriations for 1951, Hearings*, U.S. Congress, Senate Committee on Appropriations, 81 Cong. 2 sess., 30 Aug. 1950, p. 285.

34. Ibid., p. 286.

35. Ibid., p. 287.

36. Adenauer, *Memoirs*, p. 273.

37. Quoted in Calvocoressi, *Survey of International Affairs*, pp. 159–60.

38. Adenauer, *Memoirs*, pp. 278ff.

39. *New York Times*, 2 Aug. 1950.

40. Harold Callender in *New York Times*, 1 Aug. 1950.

41. *New York Times Magazine*, 13 Aug. 1950.

42. *Spectator*, 11 Aug. 1950, p. 169.

43. Note Acheson's satisfaction with the Schuman Plan, in Princeton Seminars, 9 Sept. 1953, Reel 2, Harry S. Truman Library. Schuman's qualified statement on German units in a European army before the North Atlantic Council is recorded in Verbatim Record 3, C-5-VR/3, 16 Sept. 1950, M-88, Box 152 (2206), Foreign Affairs Documents and Reference Center, Department of State, Washington, D.C.

44. A description attributed to a member of the French delegations; see Martin, "Decision to Rearm Germany," p. 650.

45. Acheson, *Present at the Creation*, p. 437.

46. Summary minutes, NACO M-2, staff meeting of U.S. delegation to NAC, 5th session, 16 Sept. 1950, M-88, box 152 (2206), Foreign Affairs Documents and Reference Center, Department of State; Jules Moch, *Histoire du réarmement allemand dupuis 1950* (Paris, 1965), pp. 46–47.

47. 16 Sept. 1950, Verbatim Record 3, C-5-VR/3, p. 6, Foreign Affairs Documents and Reference Center, Department of State.

48. Dean Acheson, *Sketches from Life of Men I Have Known* (New York, 1961), p. 29.

49. Summary record, C5-R/2, 2nd meeting, 5th session, NAC, 15 Sept. 1950, M-88, box 152 (2206), Foreign Affairs Documents and Reference Center, Department of State.

50. Summary record, C5-R/3, 3rd meeting, 5th session, NAC, 16 Sept. 1950, ibid.

51. Stikker, *Men of Responsibility*, pp. 298–99.

52. "Final Communique," 5th session, NAC, New York, 2 Sept. 1950, in Ismay, *NATO*, p. 186.

53. Acheson, *Sketches from Life*, p. 42.

54. Acheson, *Present at the Creation*, p. 441.

55. Ibid., p. 444.

56. Ibid., p. 459.

57. Spofford to S/S, 16 Nov. 1950, *FRUS*, 1950, 3:458–59; Report by North Atlantic Military Committee, 12 Dec. 1950, ibid., 3:542–44.

58. Adenauer, *Memoirs*, pp. 307–9. See also Robert McGeehan, *The German Rearmament Question: American Diplomacy and European Defense after World War II* (Urbana, 1971), pp. 67–74.

59. Raymond Poidevin pronounced the EDC doomed by the summer of 1953 as the safeguards against German revanchism inside a European army were balanced unfavorably against the absence of Britain from the Community and the dissolution of the French forces inside a unified European force. "La France devant le problème de la CED: Incidences nationales et internationales (été 1951 à été 1953)," *Revue d'histoire de la deuxième guerre mondiale et des conflits contemporains* 33 (Jan. 1983): 35–57.

60. Acheson, *Present at the Creation*, pp. 362–66.

61. Herbert Hoover, "We Should Revise Our Foreign Policies" 20 Dec. 1955, in *Addresses upon the American Road, 1950–55* (Stanford, 1955), pp. 11–22.

62. Joseph P. Kennedy speech, 12 Dec. 1950, quoted in *American Foreign Relations in the Twentieth Century*, ed. Manfred Jonas (New York, 1967), pp. 170–73.

63. Acheson, *Present at the Creation*, p. 488.

64. *Congressional Record*, 82 Cong. 1 sess., 1951, 97:54–61. See Acheson, *Present at the Creation*, pp. 492–93, for commentary on Taft's speech of January 5, 1951; and Taft, on the same theme, in *Assignment of Ground Forces of the United States to Duty in the European Area, Hearings*, U.S. Congress, Senate Committees on Foreign Relations and on Armed Services, 82 Cong. 1 sess., 1951, pp. 609–11.

65. S. Con. Res. 8, cited in *Assignment of Ground Forces, Hearings*, p. 555.

66. Statement by General Eisenhower, 1 Feb. 1951, ibid., pp. 1–8; statement by Secretary of State Marshall, ibid., pp. 39–40.

67. Ibid., p. 67.

68. Ibid., p. 69. Henry A. Kissinger, in *Nuclear Weapons and Foreign Policy* (New York, 1969), p. 135, concluded that "the importance of forces ready to intervene rapidly was surely one of the lessons of the Korean War."

69. *Assignment of Ground Forces, Hearings*, p. 79.

70. Ibid., p. 93.

71. Ibid., pp. 109–11.

72. Ibid., pp. 555–56.

73. Taft claimed that "the Senate resolution and the concurrent resolution adopted by the Senate on 4 April 1951 was a clear statement by the Senate that it has the right to pass on any question of sending troops to Europe to implement the Atlantic Pact." See Robert A. Taft, *A Foreign Policy for Americans* (New York, 1951), p. 36; S. Res. 99, S. Con. Res. 18, *Congressional Record*, 82 Cong. 1 sess., 4 Apr. 1951, 97:3282-83, 3293.

74. Smith, *Dean Acheson*, p. 252.

75. Elsey to Bell, 7 Feb. 1951, Elsey Files, Papers of Harry S. Truman, Truman Library.

76. Kaplan, *Community of Interests*, p. 167.

77. A resolution of the Consultative Council noted that "the continued existence of the Western Union defense organization is no longer necessary." At the same time the council asserted that "The reorganization of the military machinery shall not affect the right of the Western Union Defense Minister and Chief of Staff to meet as they please to consider matters of mutual concern to the Brussels Treaty Powers." Records, 10th session, Consultative Council, Brussels, 20 Dec. 1950, DG1/1/2, Western European Union Archives, London.

78. "Tour of North Atlantic Treaty Organization Capitals and Germany by the Supreme Allied Commander, Europe," *FRUS*, 1951, 3:392ff; see particularly notes on a meeting at the White House, 31 Jan. 1951, ibid., pp. 449–51.

79. 9 Dec. 1954, "Report by the Secretary General of Progress during the Period, 3 December 1953 to 7 December 1954," C-M(54) 115, Ismay Papers, University of London, King's College Centre for Military Archives; Ismay, *NATO*, pp. ix, x; Robert S. Jordan, *The NATO International Staff / Secretariat, 1952–1957* (London, 1967), pp. 293–94.

80. Upon the announcement of Admiral Fechteler's appointment as SACLANT, Eisenhower observed that "I have a very deep suspicion that none of us has really learned the lessons from World War II that he should have learned. Among other things, the super-sensitiveness of the British public to anything and everything Naval is one of the factors that apparently we have not thought through carefully, particularly as it may have an effect on the success of NATO, in which we are investing so much." Eisenhower to Harriman, 2 Mar. 1951, Harriman folder, Box 55, 16–52 file, Dwight D. Eisenhower Library, Abilene, Kansas.

81. Bruce to William C. Foster, 5 Dec. 1952, CD 091.7 (Europe), RG 330, NARS.

82. Dillon to Dulles, 29 June 1953, Paris, Dulles File, General Correspondence Series, Box 2, Eisenhower Library.

83. Ismay to Montgomery, 6 July 1953, Ismay Papers, III/12/7.

84. Legislative Leadership Meeting, Supplementary Notes, 18 Dec. 1983, Legislative Meeting Series, Box 3, Eisenhower Library.

85. Dulles to president, 27 Oct. 1954, Dulles/Herter series, Anne Whitman files, Box 3, Eisenhower Library. It is worth noting that as early as September 2, 1954, Premier Mendes-France appeared open to a new security arrangement that would include Great Britain and Germany under NATO auspices. Dillon to Department of State, *FRUS*, 1952–54, 5, pt. 2:1132-35.

86. In an interview on March 24, 1972, Gen. Alfred M. Gruenther claimed that "the actual size of our force in Europe was not that important in our planning as long as it was large enough to

show the Russians that we were serious in our commitment there through NATO." Quoted in Richard F. Grimmett, "The Politics of Containment: The President, the Senate and American Foreign Policy, 1947–1956" (Ph.D. diss., Kent State Univ., 1973), p. 138; See also David R. Kepley, "The Senate and the Great Debate of 1951," *Prologue* 14 (Winter 1982): 213–226.

87. See Robert E. Osgood, *NATO: The Entangling Alliance* (Chicago, 1962), pp. 83–87.

88. Acheson, *Present at the Creation*, p. 626. Ismay, *NATO*, p. 115; report by NAC Deputies, Lisbon, 20 Feb. 1952, "Relations between EDC and NATO," *FRUS*, 1952–54, 5, pt. 1:247–51.

89. Hilsman's claim is a modest one. According to Ismay, "At the end of 1953, we had 18 M-Day facing 30 Russian M-Day divisions," Ismay to Churchill, 12 Feb. 1954, Ismay Papers, III/12/23a.

90. U.S. Department of State, *Building a Mutual Defense: Mutual Defense Assistance Program, 1 April 1951–9 October 1951*, pub. no. 4473 (Feb. 1952), p. 12.

91. See in particular a briefing memorandum prepared for S/S, 7 Dec. 1951, "Summary of Temporary Council Committee Report," *FRUS*, 1951, 3:389–92; Osgood, *NATO*, pp. 82–83.

92. See Brown and Opie, *American Foreign Assistance*, p. 554.

93. "Final Communique," 9th session, North Atlantic Council, Lisbon, 20–25 Feb. 1952, in Ismay, *NATO*, p. 191.

94. Ibid., p. 122.

95. George F. Kennan, *Russia, the Atom, and the West* (New York, 1958), p. 87. For other views see Lawrence S. Kaplan, "NATO and the Warsaw Pact: The Past," in Robert W. Clawson and Lawrence S. Kaplan, eds., *The Warsaw Pact: Political Purpose and Military Means* (Wilmington, 1982), pp. 67–84.

96. Raymond Aron, *The Imperial Republic: The United States and the World, 1945–1973*, trans. Frank Jellinek (Englewood Cliffs, N.J., 1974), pp. 50–51. Emphasis in original.

9. WESTERN EUROPE IN THE "AMERICAN CENTURY"

1. *Der Spiegel*, 24 Aug. 1981; Walter Laqueur, "America's Fissuring Alliance," *New York Times*, 25 Oct. 1981.

2. Henry Luce, "The American Century," *Life* 10 (17 Feb. 1941): 65.

3. U.S. Congress, Senate, *Congressional Record*, 80 Cong. 2 sess., 1948, 94:2285.

4. Carl Van Doren, *The Great Rehearsal: The Story of the Making and Ratification of the Constitution of the United States* (New York, 1948), p. viii. See pp. 60–61, above.

5. Luce, "American Century," p. 65.

6. Blanche Wiesen Cook, *The Declassified Eisenhower: A Divided Legacy* (New York, 1981), pp. xv–xvii. Cook finds a sinister meaning in the pretensions implied in the term "American Century," as well as an all-embracing authority: "All political decisions made during the course of World War II carried its decree."

7. William Strang to Ambassador Oliver Franks, 20 Dec. 1949, AN3854/1053/456, PRO.

8. David Calleo, *Atlantic Fantasy: The United States, NATO, and Europe* (Baltimore, 1970), pp. 27–28.

9. René Etiemble's *Parlez-vous franglais* (Paris, 1964) created a stir and led to the appointment of a High Commission of Twelve in the following year, chaired by President Georges Pompidou, to take steps in defense of the purity of the French language. See also *New York Times*, 2 Dec. 1965.

10. Theodore Draper notes that the dates for its demise range from 1945 to the mid-1970s but shares the view of Alastair Buchan that the American Century lasted until the mid-1960s. "The Western Misalliance," *Washington Quarterly* 4 (Winter 1981): 34–45. See also Donald W. White, " 'The American Century': The History of an Idea, 1941–1971" (Ph.D. diss., New York Univ., 1979), pp. 282ff.

11. Sir Geoffrey de Freitas, former vice-president of the European parliament, suggests that "the low profile" of British investment abroad resulted from Britain's long tradition of international trading. Professor Howard Temperley attributes American visibility to the association of "American investment with Americanization and this in turn with modernization." In Second Colloquium, 12–14 Sept. 1950, J.R. Greenaway, ed., *The American-European Balance since 1939* (University of East Anglia, Seminar in Atlantic Studies), pp. 44–45, The pamphlet also has a different version of this address under the title "The Political Perspective," pp. 13–20.

12. According to the Committee on Foreign Investment in the United States, an interagency monitoring group established in 1975, the United States held $192.65 billion in direct investment overseas, compared with $54.43 billion of foreign direct investment in the United States. Foreign investment in the U.S. recently is growing more rapidly than U.S. investment abroad. Between 1975 and 1979, U.S. direct holdings overseas rose by 55 percent, while foreign direct investment in America grew by 97 percent. *Wall Street Journal*, 3 Aug. 1981.

13. For Bricker's comments on "cruel and unusual punishment," see U.S. Congress, Senate Foreign Relations Committee, *Supplemental Hearings on Agreement Regarding Status of Forces of Parties of the North Atlantic Treaty*, 83 Cong. 1 sess., 24 June 1953, pp. 81–82.

14. *New York Times*, 29 Mar. 1956; 24 June 1956; 24 Nov. 1956. See also *NATO Letter* (Apr. 1956), pp. 9–10. In its consideration of "Military Implications of Communist Penetration of the Icelandic Cabinet, JCS, 1950/91," pp. 527–28, the most serious recommendation made by a report of the Joint Intelligence Committee (JIC) to the Joint Chiefs of Staff on September 26, 1956, was that access to nonsensitive classified information be limited to friends in the government. By suspending Iceland from participating in NATO organs dealing with sensitive matters, the JIC hoped to force the Icelandic government to reconsider its position. *The Declassified Documents Quarterly Catalog* 6 (Arlington, 1980): 261.

15. Telegram 818, Henry S. Villard to S/S, 25 Nov. 1949, N7-1(3)-B.7, RG 330, NARS; Kaplan, *Community of Interests*, pp. 60–64.

16. LaFeber, *America, Russia, and the Cold War*, pp. 75ff.

17. Ronald Steel entitled one of his chapters "Accidental Empire," in *Pax Americana* (New York, 1967).

18. See chapter 3, above.

19. See in particular Ernest Bevin's view as expressed in Douglas to Acheson, 26 Feb. 1948, *FRUS*, 1948, 3:32-33.

20. Theodore C. Achilles recalls being advised by John D. Hickerson as early as New Year's eve of 1947 that there was no alternative to a military alliance. Oral history interview, T.C. Achilles, Truman Library.

21. Armin Rappaport, "The United States and European Integration: The First Phase," *Diplomatic History* 5 (Spring 1981): 121.

22. Note the exchange between Secretary of State Acheson and Chairman of the Senate Foreign Relations Committee Tom Connally. *Extension of the European Recovery Program, Hearings*, U.S. Senate, Committee on Foreign Relations, 81 Cong. 1 sess., 1949, pp. 195–97.

23. This confession was made to Canadian diplomat Escott Reid in a personal communication from Achilles in 1976. Achilles recalled that he and Hickerson believed that an emphasis on European unity would retard progress toward Atlantic unity. Reid, *Time of Fear and Hope*, p. 134. (See p. 79, above.)

24. Sir Edmund Hall-Patch to E.A. Berthoud, "Views of the State Department on Integration," 14 Feb. 1950, UR3211/28, PRO.

25. George Kennan and the Policy Planning Staff of the State Department, along with outside consultants, examined at great length the directions a European unification might take in the spring and summer of 1949, particularly Gladwyn Jebb's postulation of a "third world power of approximately equal strength to the United States and the Soviet Union." The question was

never fully addressed. See minutes, 78th meeting, Policy Planning Staff, 17 May 1949, PPS Records, 1947–53, RG 59, NARS; and George F. Kennan, *Memoirs, 1925–1950*, pp. 480ff. (See p. 132, above.)

26. Rappaport, in "United States and European Integration," p. 148, notes not only that some skepticism existed in the early years in the State Department concerning the compatibility of the community with American objectives, but also that State shared the national consensus that a united Europe was better for America than a divided Europe.

27. *North Atlantic Treaty Hearings*, 2:368-69. (See p. 102, above.)

Index